S0-AYC-565

A SUBJECT BIBLIOGRAPHY OF THE SECOND WORLD WAR

Also by A. G. S. Enser

FILMED BOOKS AND PLAYS 1928–1974

A SUBJECT BIBLIOGRAPHY OF THE SECOND WORLD WAR: BOOKS IN ENGLISH 1939–1974

A. G. S. Enser
FLA FRSA

A Grafton Book

ANDRE DEUTSCH

First published 1977 by
André Deutsch Limited
105 Great Russell Street London WC1

Photoset and printed photolitho in Great Britain by
Ebenezer Baylis and Son Ltd,
The Trinity Press, Worcester, and London

ISBN 0 233 96742 7

To the memory of
L/C Leonard A. Baker,
South Lancashire Regiment
(The Prince of Wales's Volunteers),
who gave his life on D-Day at
Hermanville (Sword Beach), Normandy,
6 June 1944

CONTENTS

PREFACE

The Second World War was truly world wide, involving men, women and children on a scale that no previous war had ever done. Consequently, the number of books written about it, in various languages, is not only vast but continues to grow. So great is this number that neither the researcher nor the general reader has very many published aids to help him. Separate collections and select bibliographies are maintained in most countries, in their respective national libraries. Special sources—for example, in the United Kingdom, the Imperial War Museum and the War Office Library—not only cover the printed word but also manuscripts, diaries, photographs and other related material.

To date, the only general bibliography on books in English on the Second World War is that compiled by Janet Ziegler (Hoover Institution Press, Stanford University 1971), covering the years 1945–65. Unfortunately it does not cover the vital period 1939–44, nor, obviously, the post-1965 publications, and it would appear to be intended mainly for use in an academic library.

The present compilation is intended as a guide, useful and time-saving, to both the general reader and the researcher, in any type of library - public, special, polytechnic or university. It is hoped that the bibliography will be kept up to date by supplements at periodic intervals.

SCOPE

This subject index covers the years 1939 to 1974, omitting, in general, works of less than thirty pages, poetry, fiction, juvenile literature, humour, cartoons and the publications of the War Graves Commission.

In the main the entries have been taken from the

Cumulative Book Index, the *British National Bibliography* and *Whitaker*. Place and date of first publication is given where known, as is any change of title in the United Kingdom, United States, or in subsequent editions.

ARRANGEMENT

The subject headings are arranged in alphabetical order. Within each subject heading, generally, the entries are also arranged alphabetically by author or title. Exceptions to this are BRITISH ARMY; MEMOIRS; and UNITED STATES ARMY. For these the arrangement is as follows:

BRITISH ARMY (general); Eighth Army; Fourteenth Army; Twenty-first Army Group; Divisions (in numerical order); Corps (in alphabetical order); Regiments (in alphabetical order).

MEMOIRS are arranged alphabetically under the name of the subject, except for major personalities such as Churchill, Roosevelt or Stalin, who have separate subject headings with *see also* references.

UNITED STATES ARMY (general); Third Army; Sixth Army; Ninth Army; Corps; Divisions (in numerical order); Regiments (in numerical order); Cavalry; Combat Teams; Corps of Engineers; Ordnance; Quartermaster Corps; Railways; Signals; Tank Destroyers; Transportation Corps; Miscellaneous.

Major events are given separate subject headings (Arnhem; Anzio; Bataan) with *see also* references to related or wider subject material.

Bibliographical information is minimal but sufficient for identification. Of course, general agreement in the placing of every entry under a subject cannot be expected in a compilation of this nature on such a complex event as the Second World War; but I have aimed to place each entry where the majority of users would expect to find it, bearing in mind the subject arrangement. It must be emphasised that no claim is made to the entries being exhaustive, and I shall be pleased to be informed of omissions and errors.

ACKNOWLEDGMENTS

I wish to pay especial thanks to Janet Ziegler, though I did not discover her book until I had researched all the years included in her bibliography. My thanks are due also for the help given by the professional staff of the former County Borough of Eastbourne public libraries, who served under me before my retirement; to Peter Lewis, University Librarian of Sussex University, for facilities so readily granted; to W. S. Hudson, Deputy Chief Librarian of Kensington and Chelsea, both as a colleague and fellow member of the same corps in the Second World War; and particularly to my wife for her encouragement and practical help.

A. G. S. Enser
Eastbourne, April 1975

ABBREVIATIONS

Ala	Alabama
anon	anonymous
Ariz	Arizona
Aus	Austria
Aust	Australia
Berks	Berkshire
bib	bibliography
Bucks	Buckinghamshire
Calif	California
Chesh	Cheshire
comp	compiler
Conn	Connecticut
ed(s)	editor(s)
Fla	Florida
Flints	Flintshire
Fr	France
Ga	Georgia
Ger	Germany
Hants	Hampshire
Herts	Hertfordshire
HMS	His Majesty's Ship
HMSO	His/Her Majesty's Stationery Office
Holl	Holland
Ill	Illinois
Ind	Indiana
IoM	Isle of Man
Is	Israel
jun	junior
Kan	Kansas
Kty	Kentucky
La	Louisiana
Lancs	Lancashire
Leics	Leicestershire
Lincs	Lincolnshire
Mass	Massachusetts
Md	Maryland
Mich	Michigan
Middx	Middlesex

Minn	Minnesota
Miss	Missouri
NB	New Brunswick
NC	North Carolina
NH	New Hampshire
NJ	New Jersey
NM	New Mexico
NS	Nova Scotia
NY	New York State
NZ	New Zealand
Neb	Nebraska
Neths	Netherlands
North	Northumberland
Northants	Northamptonshire
Okl	Oklahoma
Ore	Oregon
p	pages
Pa	Pennsylvania
Pem	Pembrokeshire
pl	plates
pseud	pseudonym
RAF	Royal Air Force
rev ed	revised edition
SA	South Africa
SC	South Carolina
Switz	Switzerland
Tas	Tasmania
Tenn	Tennessee
Tex	Texas
UK	United Kingdom
UP	University Press
US	United States of America
USMC	United States Marine Corps
USS	United States Ship
und	undated
unp	unpaged
Va	Virginia
vol	volume
Vt	Vermont
WA	Western Australia
Washington DC	Washington District of Columbia
Wilts	Wiltshire
Wis	Wisconsin
Worcs	Worcestershire
Wyo	Wyoming
Yorks	Yorkshire

SUBJECT BIBLIOGRAPHY

ABYSSINIA

DOWER, Kenneth C G (comp)
Abyssinian patchwork: an anthology *(London: Muller 1949), 289p.*

MACDONALD, John F
Abyssinian adventure *(London: Cassell 1957), ix, 213p.*

PANKHURST, Estelle S *and* PANKHURST, R K P
Ethiopia and Eritrea: the last phase of the re-union struggle, 1941–1952 *(Woodford Green, Essex: Lalikela 1954), 360p.*

STEER, George L
Sealed and delivered: a book on the Abyssinian campaign *(London: Hodder & Stoughton 1942), 256p.*

ADDRESSES AND SPEECHES

BEVERIDGE, *Sir* William H
Pillars of security and other war-time essays and addresses *(London: Allen & Unwin 1943), 216p.*

CONANT, James B
Our fighting faith *(Cambridge, Mass: Harvard UP 1944), 121p.*

MACLEISH, Archibald
Time to act: selected addresses *(Boston, Mass: Houghton Mifflin 1943), 198p.*

MASSEY, Vincent
The sword of lionheart and other wartime speeches *(Boston, Mass: Humphries 1942), 117p.*

WILSON, Theodore Allen
WW2: readings on critical issues *(New York: Scribner 1974), 515p.*
[*see also* outstanding personalities directly under their names, e.g. *CHURCHILL, ROOSEVELT, STALIN*].

ADMINISTRATION

BENDA, Harry J *and others* (eds)
Japanese military administration in Indonesia *(New Haven, Conn: Yale UP 1965), 279p.*

CONNOR, Sydney *and* FRIEDRICH, Carl J (eds)
Military government *(Philadelphia, Pa: American Academy of Political and Social Science 1950), 261p.*

DONNISON, Frank S V
British military administration in the Far East, 1943–46 *(London: HMSO 1956), 483p.*
Civil affairs and military government, North-West Europe, 1944–1946 *(London: HMSO 1961), 436p.*

FRIEDRICH, Carl J *and others*
American experiences in military government in World War II *(New York: Rinehart 1948), 436p.*

FURER, Julius A
Administration of the Navy Departments in World War II *(Washington DC: US Government Printing Office 1959), 1,042p.*

GULICK, Luther H
Administrative reflections from World War II *(Alabama: Alabama UP 1948), xii, 139p.*

HARRIS, Charles R S
Allied military administration of Italy, 1943–1945 *(London: HMSO 1958), xv, 479p.*

HOLBORN, Hajo
American military government: its organization and policies *(Washington DC: Infantry Journal Press 1947), 243p.*

KAMMERER, Gladys M
Impact of war on Federal personnel administration, 1939–1945 *(Lexington, Kty: Kentucky UP 1951), 372p.*

MAGINNIS, John J
Military government journal: Normandy to Berlin *(Amherst, Mass: Massachusetts UP 1971), 351p.*

RENNEL, Francis J, *1st baron Rennel Rodd*
British military administration of occupied territories in Africa during the years 1941–1947 *(London: HMSO 1948), 637p.*

ROSEN, S McKee
The combined boards of the 2nd World War: an experiment in international administration *(New York: Columbia UP 1951), 288p.*

TAYLOR, Philip H *and* BRAIBANTI, Ralph
Administration of occupied area: a study guide *(Syracuse, NY: Syracuse UP 1948), 111p.*

AFGHANISTAN

FOX, John
Afghan adventure *(London: Hale 1958), 190p.*

AFRICAN FORCES

BARBER, D H
Africans in khaki *(London: Edinburgh House 1948), viii, 120p.*

BENT, Rowland A R
Ten thousand men of Africa: the story of the Bechuanaland Pioneers and Gunners, 1941-1946 *(London: HMSO 1952), xii, 128p.*

BRELSFORD, William V (ed)
The story of the Northern Rhodesia Regiment *(Lusaka: Government Printer 1954), 134p.*

BURMAN, Ben L
The generals wear cork hats: an amazing adventure in war-time diplomacy *(New York: Taplinger 1963), 203p.*

GRAY, Brian
Basuto soldiers in Hitler's war *(Maseru: Basutoland Government 1953), 97p.*

JACKSON, Henry C
The fighting Sudanese *(London: Macmillan 1954), 84p.*

SALMON, E Marling
Beyond the call of duty: African deeds of bravery in wartime *(London: Macmillan 1952), xiii, 99p.*

[*see also* SOUTH AFRICA]

AFRIKA KORPS

CHAMBERLAIN, Peter *and* ELLIS, Chris
Afrika Korps: German military operations in the Western Desert, 1941-42 *(Edgware, Middx: Almark 1971), 32p.*

MACKSEY, Kenneth J
Africa Korps *(New York: Ballantine 1968), 161p, bib.*

[*see also* MIDDLE EAST, NORTH AFRICA]

AGRICULTURE

BRITNELL, George *and* FOWKE, Vernon C
Canadian agriculture in war and peace *(Stanford, Calif: Stanford UP 1962), 502p.*

CRAWFORD, John G *and others*
Wartime agriculture in Australia and New Zealand, 1939-50 *(Stanford, Calif: Stanford UP 1954), 354p.*

GOLD, Bela
Wartime economic planning in agriculture: a study in the relocation of resources *(New York: Columbia UP 1949), 594p.*

HARKNESS, *Sir* Douglas

A tract on agricultural policy *(London: King & Staples 1945), 82p.*

The war and British agriculture *(London: King & Staples, 1942), 109p.*

MURRAY, Keith A H

Agriculture *(London: HMSO 1955), 422p.*

SMITH, Arthur

Agriculture's challenge to the nation *(London: Heinemann 1941), 236p.*

TINLEY, James M

South African food and agriculture in World War II *(Stanford, Calif: Stanford UP 1954), 138p.*

WILCOX, Walter W

The farmer in the Second World War *(Ames: Iowa State College Press 1947), 410p.*

ZAGOROV, Slavcho D *and others*

The agricultural economy of the Danubian countries, 1935-1945 *(Stanford, Calif: Stanford UP 1955), 478p.*

[*see also* FOOD]

AIRBORNE FORCES

AYLING, Keith

They fly to fight: the story of the Airborne Divisions *(New York: Appleton 1944), 191p.*

BRAMMALL, Ronald

The Tenth: a record of service of the 10th Battalion, the Parachute Regiment, 1942-1945, and the 10th Battalion, the Parachute Regiment (T.A.) (county of London), 1947-1965 *(Ipswich: Eastgate 1965), xxxi, 486p, bib.*

BUCKERIDGE, Justin P

550 Infantry Airborne Battalion *(Birmingham, Mich: Boots, The Airborne Quarterly 1945), 94p.*

BURGETT, Donald

Currahee! 'We stand alone!': a paratrooper's account of the Normandy invasion *(London: Hutchinson 1967), 192p.*

BURWELL, Lewis C

Scrapbook: a pictorial and historical record of the deeds, exploits, adventures, travels and life of the 27th Troop Carrier Squadron for the year 1944 *(Charlotte, NC 1947), 130p.*

CARTER, Ross S

Those devils in baggy pants *(New York: Appleton 1951), 191p.*

CHAMBERS, George W

Keith Argraves, paratrooper: an account of the service of a Christian medical corpsman in the U.S. Army Paratroops during World War II *(Nashville, Tenn: Southern 1946), 157p.*

COVINGTON, Henry L

A fighting heart: an unofficial story of the 82nd Airborne Division *(Fayetteville, NC: Davis 1949), 75p.*

EDWARDS, Roger

German airborne troops, 1936–45 *(London: Macdonald & Janes 1974), 160p.*

FLANAGAN, Edward M

The Angels: a history of the 11th Airborne Division 1943–1946 *(Washington DC: Infantry Journal Press 1948), 176p.*

GAVIN, James M

Airborne warfare *(Washington DC: Infantry Journal Press 1947), 186p.*

GREAT BRITAIN. Ministry of Information

By air to battle: official account of the British Airborne Division *(London: HMSO 1945), 144p.*

GREGORY, Barry

British airborne troops *(London: Macdonald & Janes 1974), 160p.*

GUILD, Frank H

Action of the tiger: the saga of the 437th Troop Carrier Group *(Tyler, Tex: City 1950), 177p.*

HUSTON, James A

Out of the blue: U.S. Army airborne operations in World War II *(Lafayette, Ind: Purdue University Studies 1972), 327p.*

LORD, William G

History of the 508th Parachute Infantry *(Washington DC: Infantry Journal Press 1948), 120p.*

MACDONALD, Charles B

Airborne *(New York: Ballantine 1970), 159p.*

By air to battle *(New York: Ballantine 1969), 160p, bib.*

NEWNHAM, Maurice

Prelude to glory: the story of the creation of Britain's parachute army *(London: Low 1947), xviii, 350p.*

NORTON, Geoffrey G

The Red Devils: the story of the British airborne forces *(London: Cooper 1971),* [9], 260p.

PACKE, M

First Airborne *(London: Secker & Warburg 1948), viii, 252p.*

PAY, Don R
Thunder from heaven: story of the 17th Airborne Division, 1943-1945 *(Birmingham, Mich: Boots, The Airborne Quarterly 1947), 179p.*

PEGASUS (pseud)
More thrills with the paratroops *(London: Hutchinson 1944), 152p.*
Parachutist *(London: Jarrolds 1944), 127p.*
Thrills with the paratroops *(London: Hutchinson 1943), 160p.*

RAPPORT, Leonard *and* NORTHWOOD, Arthur
Rendezvous with destiny: a history of the 101st Airborne Division *(Washington DC: Infantry Journal Press 1948), 810p.*

SAMPSON, Francis L
Look out below! *(Washington DC: Catholic University of America 1958), 234p.*

SAUNDERS, Hilary St G
The red beret: the story of the Parachute Regiment at war, 1940-1945 *(London: Joseph 1950), 336p.*

SOSABOWSKI, Stanislaw
Freely I served *(London: Kimber 1960), 203p, later edition published as:* Parachute general.

STAINFORTH, Peter
Wings of the wind [1st Airborne Division] *(London: Faber 1952), 253p.*

TUGWELL, Maurice
Airborne to battle: a history of airborne warfare, 1918-1971 *(London: Kimber 1971), 367p.*

WARREN, John C
Airborne missions in the Mediterranean, 1942-1945 *(Washington DC: USAF Historical Division 1955), 137p.*
Airborne operations in World War II, European theatre *(Washington DC: USAF Historical Division 1956), 239p.*

WELLER, George
The story of the paratroops *(New York: Random House 1958), 184p.*

WHITING, Charles
Hunters from the sky: the German Parachute Corps, 1941-1945 *(New York: Stein & Day 1974), 231p.*

WILLIANS, Terence W
Panic takes time: the nine lives of a parachutist *(London: Parrish 1956), 249p.*

[*see also* MEDITERRANEAN, NORMANDY, WESTERN EUROPE 1944-45]

AIRCRAFT CARRIERS

BENTON, Brantford B (ed)
Battle baby: a pictorial history of the escort carrier U.S.S. Savo Island (CVE 78) *(Baton Rouge, La: Army & Navy 1946), 132p.*

BROWN, David
Carrier operations in World War II: *vol 1* The Royal Navy *(London: Allan rev ed 1974), 160p. vol 2* The Pacific Navies, Dec. 1941–Feb. 1943 *(London: Allan 1974), 152p.*

BRYAN, Joseph
Aircraft carrier *(New York: Ballantine 1954), 205p.*

BURNS, Eugene
Then there was one! the U.S.S. Enterprise and the first year of War *(New York: Harcourt 1944), x, 179p.*

CARRIER war in the Pacific *(New York: American Heritage 1966), 153p.*

CLARK, Joseph J *and* REYNOLDS, C G
Carrier admiral *(New York: McKay 1967), 333p.*

FERRIS, James S (ed)
The aircraft carrier, U.S.S. Wasp, CV 18 *(Boston, Mass: Crosby 1946), 105p.*

FLIGHT quarters: the war story of the U.S.S. Belleau Wood, aircraft carrier *(Los Angeles: Cole-Holmquist 1946), 192p.*

'FORMIDABLE commission': H.M.S. Formidable *(London: Seeley 1948), 158p.*

GILBERT, Price
The escort carriers in action: the story in pictures of the escort carrier force, U.S. Pacific Fleet, 1945, with a supplement for the Flagship U.S.S. Makin Island *(Atlanta, Ga: Ruralist 1946), 228p.*

GRIFFIN, Alexander R
A ship to remember: the saga of the Hornet *(New York: Howell, Soskin 1943), xi, 13–288p.*

HEALISS, Ronald
Adventure 'Glorious' *(London: Muller 1955), 144p.*

HOEHLING, Adolph A
The Franklin comes home *(New York: Hawthorn 1974), 132p.*

JAMESON, *Sir* William
Ark Royal, 1939–1941 *(London: Hart-Davis 1957), 371p.*

JENSEN, Oliver O
Carrier war *(New York: Simon & Schuster 1945), 172p.*

JOHNSTON, Stanley
Queen of the flat tops: the U.S.S. Lexington and the Coral Sea Battle *(New York: Dutton 1942), 7–280p.*

McCraken, Kenneth D
Baby flat-top *(New York: 1944), 180p.*

Macintyre, Donald
Aircraft carriers *(New York: Ballantine 1968), 160p, bib.*

Markey, Morris
Well done! an aircraft carrier in battle action *(New York: Appleton 1945), 223p.*

Mears, Frederick
Carrier combat *(New York: Doubleday 1944), xvi, 156p.*

Miller, Max
Daybreak for our carrier *(New York: McGraw-Hill 1944), 7-184p.*

Moore, John C
Escort carrier *(London: Hutchinson 1944), 48p.*

Olds, Robert
Helldiver squadron: the story of carrier bombing squadron 17 with Task Force 58 *(Toronto: Dodd 1944), xi, 225p.*

Ommanney, Francis D
Flat-top: the story of an escort carrier *(London: Longmans Green 1945), 63p.*

Poolman, Kenneth
Ark Royal *(London: Kimber 1956), x, 11-202p.*
Escort carrier, 1941-1945: an account of British escort carriers in trade protection *(London: Allan 1972), 160p.*
The catafighters and merchant aircraft carriers *(London: Kimber 1970), 128p.*
Illustrious *(London: Kimber 1955), 246p.*

Prep Charlie: a history of the peregrinations of our fighting lady U.S.S. Wasp while mothering air group Eighty-one *(New York: Personnel of the USS Wasp and Air Group 81 1945), 206p.*

Reynolds, Clark G
The fast carriers: the forging of an air navy *(New York: McGraw-Hill 1968), 498p.*

Russell, *Sir* Herbert *and* Pursey, Harry
Ark Royal: the story of a famous ship *(London: Lane 1942), 92p.*

Sherman, Frederick C
Combat command: the American aircraft carriers in the Pacific war *(New York: Dutton 1950), 427p.*

Stafford, Edwin P
The big E: the story of U.S.S. Enterprise *(New York: Random House 1962), 499p.*

STEICHEN, Edward
The blue ghost: a photographic log and personal narrative of the aircraft carrier U.S.S. Lexington in combat operation *(New York: Harcourt 1947), 149p.*
USS CHENANGO
The Chenanigan, victory edition, 1942-1945 *(Los Angeles, Calif: Kater 1945), 64p.*
USS ESSEX
Saga of the Essex *(Baton Rouge, La: Army & Navy Pictorial 1946), 141p.*
WINSTON, Robert A
Aircraft carrier *(New York: Harper 1942), 88p.*
Fighting squadron: a sequel to dive bomber; a veteran squadron leader's first-hand account of carrier combat with Task Force 58 *(New York: Holiday 1946), 182p.*
[*see also* CORAL SEA, MEDITERRANEAN, PACIFIC, NAVAL WARFARE, ROYAL NAVY, UNITED STATES NAVY]

AIRCRAFT PRODUCTION

TAYLOR, Frank J *and* WRIGHT, Lawson
Democracy's air arsenal *(New York: Duell 1947), 208p.*
USAAF
Source book of World War II basic data, airframe industry *(Dayton, Ohio: Wright Field 1947-48), 2 vols.*

AIR OBSERVATION POST

PARHAM, Hetman J *and* BELFIELD, E M G
Unarmed into battle: the story of the air observation post *(Winchester, Hants: Warren 1956), 168p.*

AIR RAID PRECAUTIONS

GREAT BRITAIN. Air Raid Precaution Department
Air raid precautions *(New York: Chemical 1942), 282p.*
LUCAS, Edgar
Practical air raid protection *(London: Jordan 1939), 153p.*

AIR SEA RESCUE

BARKER, Ralph
Down in the drink: true stories of the Goldfish Club *(London: Chatto & Windus 1955), 253p.*

AIRSHIPS

US Naval Air Station, Lakehurst, NJ

They were expendable: airship operation, World War II, 7 December 1941 to September 1945 *(London: Trenton 1946), 56p.*

AIR TRANSPORT COMMAND

Cave, Hugh B

Wings across the world: the story of Air Transport Command *(New York: Dodd 1945), 175p.*

Cleveland, Reginald M

Air transport at war *(New York: Harper 1946), 324p.*

Lee, James

Operation lifeline: the history and development of the naval air transport service *(Chicago, Ill: Ziff-Davis 1946), 171p.*

AIR WARFARE (general)

Allen, Bruce

Air offensive against Germany *(New York: Holt 1943), xi, 152p.*

Keep the peace through air power *(London: Allen & Unwin 1944), 172p.*

Andrews, Allen

The air marshals *(London: Macdonald 1970), 299p.*

Belot, Raymond de

The struggle for the Mediterranean, 1939-1945 *(Princeton, NJ: Princeton UP 1951), xix, 287p.*

Block, Geoffrey

The wings of warfare: an introduction to the military aircraft engaged in the Western theatre of war *(London: Hutchinson 1945), 133p.*

Bowman, Gerald

War in the air: by arrangement with the B.B.C. *(London: Evans 1956), 224p.*

Boyce, Joseph C (ed)

New weapons for air warfare: fire control equipment, proximity fuzes, and guided missiles *(Boston, Mass: Little, Brown 1947), 292p.*

Brittain, Vera

Seed of chaos: what mass bombing really means *(London: New Vision 1944), 118p.*

Caidin, Martin

Black Thursday *(New York: Dutton 1960), 320p.*

CALDWELL, Cyril C
Air power and total war *(New York: Coward-McCann 1943), xi, 244p.*

CHARLTON, Lionel E O
The Royal Air Force and the U.S.A.A.F.: a complete record in text and pictures, Sept. 1939/Dec. 1940 - Oct. 1944/Sept. 1945 *(London: Hutchinson 1941-7), 5 vols.*

CHISHOLM, Roderick
Cover of darkness *(London: Chatto & Windus 1953), 222p.*

CLOSTERMANN, Pierre
Flames in the sky *(London: Chatto & Windus 1952), 200p.*

COOK, Graeme
Wings of glory: stories of air adventure *(London: Hart-Davis 1971), 151p.*

DE SEVERSKY, Alexander P
Victory through air power *(London: Hutchinson 1942), viii, 9-160p.*

DICKENS, *Sir* Gerald C
Bombing and strategy: the fallacy of total war *(London: Sampson Low 1947), xiii, 90p.*

DUPUY, Trevor N
The air war in the West, September 1939-May 1941 *(New York: Watts 1963), [8], 76p.*
The air war in the West, June 1941-April 1945 *(New York: Watts 1963), [6], 66p.*

FITZSIMONS, Bernard (ed)
War planes and air battles of World War II *(London: Phoebus 1973), 160p.*

FORD, Corey *and* MCBAIN, Alastair
The last time I saw them *(New York: Scribner 1946), 244p.*

FULLER, John F C
Thunderbolts *(London: Skeffington 1946), 139p.*

GIBBS, R P M
Not peace but a sword *(London: Cassell 1943), 255p.*

GLENNY, Arthur W F
Attack from the air *(London: Todd 1943), 63p.*
Mediterranean air power and the Second Front *(London: Conrad 1944), 62p.*

GOYAL, S N
Air power in modern warfare *(Bombay: Thackery 1952), 131p.*

GURNEY, Gene
The war in the air [a pictorial history of World War II air forces in combat] *(New York: Crown 1962), 352p.*

HARMON, Thomas D
Pilots also pray *(New York: Crowell 1944), vii, 181p.*

HENRY, Mike
Air gunner *(London: Foulis 1964), 240p.*

HOWARD-WILLIAMS, Ernest L
Now or never: back from the Mediterranean, an airman speaks his mind *(London: Alliance 1943), 84p.*

HURREN, Bernard J
Eastern Med: a personal narrative *(London: Muller 1943), 160p.*
No specific gravity *(London: Temple 1944), 140p.*

INFIELD, Glenn B
The Poltava affair: a Russian warning; an American tragedy *(New York: Macmillan 1973), 265p.*

JABLONSKI, Edward
Double strike: the epic air raids on Regensburg-Schweinfurt, Aug 17, 1943 *(New York: Doubleday 1974), 271p.*
Terror from the sky *(New York: Doubleday 1971), 175p.*
Tragic victories *(New York: Doubleday 1971), 207p.*

JACKSON, Robert
Storm from the skies: the strategic bombing offensive, 1943–1945 *(London: Barker 1974), [7], 174p.*

JOHNSON, James E
Full circle: the story of air fighting *(London: Chatto & Windus 1964), xi, 290p.*

LAWSON, Don (ed)
Great air battles: World War I and II *(New York: Lothrop 1968), 223p.*

LEE, Asher
Air power *(London: Duckworth 1955), 200p.*

MACCLOSKEY, Monro
Secret air missions *(New York: Rosen 1966), 159p.*

MICHIE, Allan A
Air offensive against Germany *(New York: Holt 1943), xi, 152p.*

MILLER, Norman M
I took the sky road *(New York: Dodd 1945), xii, 212p.*

MINGOS, Howard L
American heroes of the war in the air *(New York: Lanciar 1943), vol I, 557p.*

MUNSON, Kenneth G
Aircraft of World War II *(London: Allan 1962), 256p.*
ABC enemy aircraft, German and Italian of World War II *(London: Allan 1961), 64p.*

NARRACOTT, Arthur H
Air power in war *(London: Muller 1945), 168p.*
Unsung heroes of the air *(London: Muller 1943), 168p.*
OLSEN, Jack
Aphrodite: desperate mission *(New York: Putnam 1970), 328p.*
PILE, *Sir* Frederick
Ack-ack: Britain's defence against air attack during the Second World War *(London: Harrap 1949), 352p.*
PRICE, Alfred
Battle over the Reich *(New York: Scribner 1973), 207p.*
RICKSON, P A *and* HOLLIDAY, A
Mission accomplished *(London: Kimber 1974), x, 224p.*
SAINT EXUPÉRY, Antoine de
Airman's odyssey *(New York: Reynal 1943), 3 vols in I, 437p.*
SAUNDBY, *Sir* Robert
Air bombardment: the story of its development *(London: Chatto & Windus 1961), xii, 276p.*
SCHUYLER, Keith C
Elusive horizons *(Cranbury, NJ: Barnes 1969), 176p.*
SCOTT, Robert L
Damned to glory *(New York: Scribner 1944), 13-228p.*
God is my co-pilot *(New York: Scribner 1943), xi, 277p.*
SHORES, Christopher F
Pictorial history of the Mediterranean air war *(London: Allan 1972), 2 vols.*
SOUTHALL, Ivan
Seventeen seconds *(New York: Macmillan 1974), 139p; previously published as* Softly tread the brave.
SPAIGHT, James M
Bombing vindicated *(London: Bles 1944), 159p.*
Volcano island *(London: Bles 1943), 144p.*
SUNDERMAN, James F
World War II in the air *(New York: Watts 1962-63), 2 vols.*
TEDDER, Arthur W, *1st baron Tedder*
Air power in war *(London: Hodder & Stoughton 1948), 124p.*
TURNER, John F
Famous air battles *(London: Barker 1963), 215p.*
US AEROSPACE STUDIES INSTITUTE
The role of airpower in guerilla warfare, World War II *(Maxwell Air Force Base, Ala 1962), 264p.*
VEALE, Sydney E
American war planes in action *(London: Pilot 1944), 47p.*

VERRIER, Anthony
The bomber offensive *(London: Batsford 1968), x, 373p, bib.*
WALTERS, *Mrs* Maude (ed)
Combat in the air *(New York: Appleton 1944), xii, 275p.*
WEBSTER, *Sir* Charles *and* FRANKLAND, Noble
The strategic air offensive against Germany, 1939-1945 *(London: HMSO 1961), 4 vols.*
WHITE, Edwin L
Ten thousand tons by Christmas *(New York: Vantage 1970), 187p.*
WHITE, William L
Queens die proudly *(London: Hamilton 1943), 227p.*
WHITEHOUSE, Arthur G J
The years of the war birds *(New York: Doubleday 1960), 384p.*
WHITNEY, Cornelius V
Lone and level sands *(New York: Farrar 1951), 314p.*
WILLIAMS, Alford J
Airpower *(New York: Coward-McCann 1940), x, 433p.*
WILLIAMS, Eric
Great air battles: an outline of war in the air with fourteen first-hand accounts by airmen who took part *(London: Pan 1971), viii, 116p.*
WIMPERIS, Harry E
Defeating the bomber *(London: Dent 1941), 60p.*
[*see also* BOMBERS, FIGHTERS, ROYAL AIR FORCE, USAAF, US NAVY]

ALASKA

DRISCOLL, Frank
War discovers Alaska *(Philadephia, Pa: Lippincott 1943), 7-352p.*
FORD, Corey
Short cut to Tokyo: the battle for the Aleutians *(New York: Scribner 1943), 141p.*
GARFIELD, Brian W
The thousand-mile war: World War II in Alaska and the Aleutians *(New York: Doubleday 1969), 351p.*
GILMAN, William
Our hidden front *(New York: Reynal 1944), 266p.*
HANDLEMAN, Howard
Bridge to victory: the story of the reconquest of the Aleutians *(New York: Random House 1943), 275p.*
MARSTON, Marvin R
Men of the tundra: Eskimos at war *(New York: October House 1969), 227p.*

MILLS, Stephen E
Arctic war birds: Alaska aviation of World War II: a pictorial history *(Seattle, Wash: Superior 1971), 191p.*
MORGAN, Murray C
Bridge to Russia: those amazing Aleutians *(New York: Dutton 1947), 222p.*
PANETH, Philip
Alaskan backdoor to Japan *(London: Alliance 1943), 108p.*
POTTER, Jean C
Alaska under arms *(New York: Macmillan 1942), x, 200p.*
US WAR DEPARTMENT
The capture of Attu *(Washington DC: Infantry Journal Press 1944), viii, 144p.*

ALBANIA

AMERY, Julian
Sons of the eagle: a study in guerilla war *(London: Macmillan 1948), xii, 354p.*
DAVIES, Edmund F
Illyrian venture: the story of the British military mission to enemy-occupied Albania, 1943–44 *(London: Lane 1952), 247p.*
[*see also* BALKANS, GREECE, YUGOSLAVIA]

ALEXANDER (1st earl Alexander of Tunis)

ALEXANDER, Harold R L G, *1st earl Alexander of Tunis*
The Alexander memoirs, 1940–1945 *(London: Cassell 1962), xiii, 210p.*
HILLSON, Norman
Alexander of Tunis: a biographical portrait *(London: W. H. Allen 1952), [ii], 252p.*
JACKSON, William G F
Alexander of Tunis as military commander *(London: Batsford 1971), viii, 344p, bib.*
NICOLSON, Nigel
Alex: the life of Field Marshal Earl Alexander of Tunis *(London: Weidenfeld & Nicolson 1973), xiii, 346p, bib.*

ALTMARK

FRISCHAUER, Willi *and* JACKSON, Robert
'The Navy's here!': the Altmark affair *(London: Gollancz 1955), 255p; US title:* The Altmark affair.

GREAT BRITAIN. Foreign Office *and* NORWAY Legation
Correspondence between H.M.'s Government in the U.K. and the Norwegian Government respecting the German steamer 'Altmark' *(London: HMSO 1950), 16p.*
[*see also* SURFACE RAIDERS]

AMBULANCES

CARTWRIGHT, Reginald
Mercy and murder: an American ambulance driver's experiences in Finland, Norway and France *(London: Iliffe 1941), viii, 86p.*

DAVIES, A T
Friend's ambulance unit: the story of the F.A.J. in the Second World War, 1939–1946 *(London: Allen & Unwin 1948), 494p.*

GEER, Andrew
Mercy in hell: an American ambulance driver with the Eighth Army *(New York: McGraw-Hill 1943), xi, 264p.*

LESLIE, Anita
A train to nowhere: an ambulance driver's adventures on four fronts *(London: Hutchinson 1948), 192p.*

MYERS, Betty
Captured: my experiences as an ambulance driver and as a prisoner of the Nazis *(London: Harrap 1941), 256p.*

THOMAS, Evan W
An ambulance in Africa *(New York: Appleton 1943), x, 175p.*

AMPHIBIOUS WARFARE

BARBEY, Daniel E
MacArthur's amphibious navy: 7th Amphibious Force operations, 1943–1945 *(Annapolis, Md: US Naval Institute 1969), 375p.*

BROWN, John M
To all hands: an amphibious adventure *(New York: McGraw-Hill 1943), xii, 236p.*

BURTON, Earl
By sea and by land: the story of our amphibious forces *(New York: McGraw-Hill 1944), 7–218p.*

CRESWELL, John
Generals and admirals: the story of amphibious command *(Toronto: Longmans 1952), viii, 192p.*

HEAVEY, William T
Down ramp!: the story of the Army Amphibian Engineers *(Washington DC: Infantry Journal Press 1947), 272p.*

HOLMAN, Gordon
Stand by to beach *(London: Hodder & Stoughton 1944), 223p.*
ISELY, Jeter *and* CROWL, P A
U.S. Marines and amphibious war: its theory and its practice in the Pacific *(Princeton, NJ: Princeton UP 1951), vii, 636p.*
KERWIN, Pashal E
Big men in the little navy: the amphibious force in the Mediterranean, 1943–1944 *(Paterson, NJ: St Anthony Guild 1946), 129p.*
MAUND, Loben E H
Assault from the sea *(London: Methuen 1949), xiv, 311p.*
NEVILLE, Ralph
Survey by starlight: a true story of reconnaissance work in the Mediterranean *(London: Hodder & Stoughton 1949), 206p.*
SWAN, William N
Spearheads of invasion: an account of the seven major invasions carried out by the Allies in the South-West Pacific area during the 2nd World War *(London: Angus & Robertson 1953), 307p.*
[*see also* COMMANDOS, MEDITERRANEAN, PACIFIC, US MARINES]

ANIMALS

BOURNE, Dorothea St H
They also serve *(London: Winchester 1947), 240p.*
DEMPEWOLFF, Richard F
Animal reveille *(New York: Doubleday 1943), xiii, 240p.*
DOWNEY, Fairfax D
Dogs for defense: American dogs in the 2nd World War *(New York: McDonald 1955), 159p.*
GILROY, James
Furred and feathered heroes of World War II *(New York: Viking 1947), 64p.*
GOING, Clayton G
Dogs at war *(New York: Macmillan 1944), vii, 179p.*
IDRIESS, Ion L
Horrie, the wog-dog with the A.I.F. in Egypt, Greece, Crete and Palestine *(Sydney: Angus & Robertson 1945), 232p.*
RIDDELL, James
Dog in the snow *(London: Joseph 1957), 143p.*
VARLEY, Edwin
The Judy story: the dog with six lives *(London: Souvenir 1973), 163p.*

ANZIO

ANZIO beachhead, 22 January-25 May 1944 *(Washington DC: Government Printing Office 1948), 122p.*

BLUMENSON, Martin
Anzio: the gamble that failed *(London: Weidenfeld & Nicolson 1963), xii, 204p, bib.*

FEHRENBACH, T R
The battle of Anzio: the dramatic story of one of the major engagements of World War II *(Derby, Conn: Monarch Books 1962), 160p.*

HARR, Bill
Combat boots: tales of fighting men including the Anzio derby *(New York: Exposition 1952), 17-232p.*

HIBBERT, Christopher
Anzio: bid for Rome *(New York: Ballantine 1970), 116p, bib.*

SHEEHAN, Fred
Anzio, epic of bravery *(Norman, Okla: Oklahoma UP 1964), 239p.*

TREVELYAN, Raleigh
The fortress: a diary of Anzio and after *(London: Collins 1956), 222p.*

VAUGHAN THOMAS, Wynford
Anzio *(London: Longmans Green 1961), xii, 243p, bib.*
[*see also* ITALIAN CAMPAIGN]

ARCTIC

BROOKES, Ewart
The gates of hell *(London: Jarrolds 1960), 144p.*

CARR, William G
Checkmate in the North: the Axis planned to invade America *(New York: Macmillan 1944), 304p.*

LIVERSIDGE, Douglas
The Third Front: the strange story of the secret war in the Arctic *(London: Souvenir 1960), 219p.*

OGDEN, Michael
The battle of North Cape *(London: Kimber 1962), 207p.*

POPE, Dudley
73 North: the battle of the Barents Sea *(London: Weidenfeld & Nicolson 1958), 320p.*
[*see also* GREENLAND, ICELAND, ROYAL NAVY]

ARDENNES

COLE, Hugh M

The Ardennes: battle of the bulge *(Washington DC: Department of Army 1965), 720p.*

DAVIS, Franklin M

Breakthrough: the epic story of the battle of the bulge *(Derby, Conn: Monarch 1961), 159p.*

DRAPER, Theodore

The 84th Infantry Division in the battle of the Ardennes, December 1944–January 1945 *(New York: Viking 1946), 260p.*

EISENHOWER, John S D

The bitter woods: the dramatic story of Hitler's surprise Ardennes offensive *(New York: Putnam 1969), 506p, bib.*

ELSTOB, Peter

Bastogne: the road block *(New York: Ballantine 1968), 160p, bib.*

Hitler's last offensive *(London: Secker & Warburg 1971), xvi, 413p, bib.*

GALLAGHER, Richard

The Malmedy massacre *(New York: Paperback Library 1964), 158p.*

MARSHALL, Samuel L A *and others*

Bastogne: the story of the first eight days in which the 101st Airborne Division was closed within the ring of German forces *(Washington DC: Infantry Journal 1946), 261p.*

MERRIAM, Robert E

Dark December: the full account of the battle of the bulge *(Chicago, Ill: Ziff-Davis 1947), 234p; later published as* The battle of the Ardennes.

NOBECOURT, Jacques

Hitler's last gamble: the battle of the Ardennes *(London: Chatto & Windus 1967), 302p, bib.*

STRAWSON, John

The battle of the Ardennes *(London: Batsford 1972), xi, 212p, bib.*

TOLAND, John

Battle: the story of the bulge *(London: Muller 1960), ii, 335p.*

WHITING, Charles

Massacre at Malmedy: the story of Jochen Peiper's battle group, Ardennes, December 1944 *(London: Cooper 1971), xii, 247p, bib.*

ARMOURED CORPS

CARTER, Joseph
The history of the 14th Armoured Division *(Atlanta, Ga: Love 1945), 294p.*

COMBAT history of the 6th Armoured Division in the European Theater of operations 18 July 1944–8 May 1945 *(Yadkinville, NC: Ripple 194–), 176p.*

CROW, Duncan
British and Commonwealth armoured formations (1919–46) *(Windsor, Berks: Profile 1972), [4], 104p.*

DUNCAN, Nigel W
79th Armoured Division (Hobo's Funnies) *(Windsor, Berks: Profile 1972), [4], 70p.*

FOLEY, John
Mailed fist *(London: Hamilton 1957), 172p.*

FORBES, Patrick
6th Guards Tank Brigade: the story of Guardsmen in Churchill tanks *(London: Sampson Low 1946), 244p.*

A HISTORY of the 44th Royal Tank Regiment in the war of 1939–45 *(Brighton, Sussex: 44th Royal Tank Regimental Association 1965), xi, 214p.*

HOWE, George F
The battle history of the 1st Armoured Division, 'Old Ironsides' *(Washington DC: Combat Forces 1954), 471p.*

JOLLY, Alan
Blue flash: the story of an armoured regiment *(London: Solicitors' Law Society 1952), xii, 168p.*

JONES, William E
Buzzings of Company B; 23rd Armored Infantry Battalion of the 7th Armored (Lucky Seventh) Division *(Winston-Salem, NC: Clay 1951), 59p.*

KOYEN, Kenneth A
The Fourth Armored Division: from the beach to Bavaria *(Munich: Herder 1946), 295p.*

LEACH, Charles R
In tornado's wake: a history of the 8th Armored Division *(Chicago, Ill: Eighth Armored Division 1956), 232p.*

MARTEL, Giffard Le Q
Our armoured forces *(London: Faber 1945), 406p.*

MASTERS, David
With pennants flying: the immortal deeds of the Royal Armoured Corps *(London: Eyre & Spottiswoode 1943), 159p.*

MILSOM, John *and* CHAMBERLAIN, Peter
German armoured cars of two world wars *(London: Arms & Armour 1974), 128p.*

MURLAND, J R W
The Royal Armoured Corps *(London: Methuen 1943), viii, 106p.*

NICHOLS, Lester M
Impact: the battle story of the Tenth Armoured Division *(New York: Bradbury, Sayles, O'Neill 1954), 325p.*

ROBINETT, Paul M
Armor command: the personal story of a commander of the 13th Armored Regiment of CCB, 1st Armored Division and of the Armored School during World War II *(Washington DC: 1958), 252p.*

ROSSE, Laurence, *6th earl and* HILL, E R
The story of the Guards Armoured Division *(London: Bles 1956), 320p.*

SPIELBERGER, Walter J *and* FEIST, Uwe
Armor in the Western Desert *(Fallbrook, Calif: Aero 1968), unp.*

THE STORY of the 79th Armoured Division, October 1942-June 1945 *(Hamburg 1945), 314p.*

TRAHAN, E A (ed)
A history of the Second U.S. Armored Division, 1940 to 1946 *(Atlanta, Ga: Love 1947), 1 vol.*

US ARMY
History 67th Armored Regiment *(Brunswick, Ger.: Westermann 1945), 407, 39p.*
Spearhead in the West, 1941–45: the Third Armored Division *(Frankfurt-am-Main-Schwanheim, Henrich 1945), 260p.*
The Thirteenth Armoured Division: a history of the Black Cats from Texas to France, Germany and Austria, and back to California *(Baton Rouge, La: Army & Navy 1945), 145p.*

VERNEY, G L
The Desert Rats: the history of the 7th Armoured Division, 1938–1945 *(London: Hutchinson 1954), 312p, bib.*
The Guards Armoured Division: a short history *(London: Hutchinson 1955), 184p, bib.*

WILSON, Andrew
Flame thrower *(London: Kimber 1956), 202p.*
[*see also* BRITISH ARMY, ITALIAN CAMPAIGN, NORTH AFRICA, TANKS, US ARMY]

ARNHEM

BAUER, Cornelis
The battle of Arnhem: the betrayal myth refuted *(London: Hodder & Stoughton 1966), 254p, bib.*

FARRAR-HOCKLEY, Anthony
Airborne carpet: Operation Market Garden *(London: Macdonald 1970), 160p, bib.*

GIBSON, Ronald
Nine days (17th-25th September, 1944) *(Ilfracombe, Devon: Stockwell 1956), 96p; later published as* Cloud over Arnhem.

HAGEN, Louis
Arnhem lift: the diary of a glider pilot *(London: Pilot 1945), 120p.*

HEAPS, Leo
Escape from Arnhem: a Canadian among the lost Paratroops *(Toronto: Macmillan 1945), 159p.*

HIBBERT, Christopher
The battle of Arnhem *(London: Batsford 1962), 224p, bib.*

HORST, Kate A ten
Cloud over Arnhem: September 17th-26th, 1944 *(London: Wingate 1959), 63p.*

MACKENZIE, Charles B
It was like this!: a short factual account of the battle of Arnhem and Oosterbeck *(London: Bailey & Swinfen, 2nd amplified ed. 1956), 37p.*

SWIECICKI, Marek
With the Red Devils at Arnhem *(London: Max Love 1945), 92p.*

URQUHART, Robert E
Arnhem *(London: Cassell 1958), xvi, 239p.*

WHITING, Charles
A bridge at Arnhem *(London: Futura 1974), 264p, bib.*

[*see also* AIRBORNE FORCES, GLIDER PILOTS]

ART AND ARTISTS

AIR raids: war pictures by British artists *(London: Oxford UP 1943), 50 illus.*

ARDIZZONE, Edward
Baggage to the enemy *(London: Murray 1941), 121p.*

BALDWIN, Hanson W
The Navy at war: paintings and drawings by combat artists *(New York: Morrow 1943), 5–159p.*

BANKSON, Budd
I should live so long *(Philadelphia, Pa: Lippincott 1952), 287p.*

BRODIE, Howard
War drawings: World War II, Korea *(Melbourne, Aust: National Press 1963), unp.*

COALE, Griffith B
North Atlantic patrol: the log of a sea going artist *(New York: Farrar 1942), xii, 48p.*

COMFORT, Charles F
Artist at war *(Toronto: Ryerson 1956), 187p.*

CRANE, Aimee (ed)
Art in the armed forces: pictured by men in action *(New York: Scribner 1944), 8-232p.*
G.I. sketch book *(Washington DC: Infantry Journal Press 1944), 136p.*
Marines at war *(New York: Scribner 1943), 7-128p.*

FASOLA, Cesare
The Florence galleries and the war: history and records with a list of missing works of art *(Florence: Casa Editrice Monsalvato 1945), 112p.*

FLANNER, Janet
Men and monuments *(Freeport, Long Island, NY: Books for Libraries 1970), xxi, 297p.*

HARTT, Frederick
Florentine art under fire *(Princeton, NJ: Princeton UP 1949), 147p.*

HOWE, Thomas C
Salt mines and castles: the discovery and restitution of looted European art *(Indianapolis, Ind: Bobbs-Merrill 1946), 334p.*

JENKINSON, Hilary *and* BELL, H E (comps)
Italian archives during the war and at its close *(London: HMSO 1947), 55p.*

LAVAGNINO, Emilio
Fifty war-damaged monuments of Italy *(Rome: Instituto Poligrafico dello Stato 1946), 132p.*

MAGRIEL, Paul D (ed)
Art and the soldier *(Biloxi, Miss: Special Service, Kesterfield 1943), 68p.*

METHUEN, Paul A
Normandy diary: being a record of survivals and losses of historical monuments in Northwest France, together with those in the Island of Walcheren and in that part of Belgium traversed by 21st Army Group in 1944–45 *(London: Hale 1952), 263p.*

NEWTON, Eric (ed)
War through artists' eyes: paintings and drawings by British war artists *(London: Murray 1945), 96p.*

RICHARDS, James M (ed)
The bombed buildings of Britain: a record of the architectural casualties *(London: Architectural Press 1947), 202p.*

RORIMER, James J
Survival: the salvage and protection of art in war *(New York: Abelard 1950), 291p.*

ROXAN, David *and* WANSTALL, Ken
The jackdaw of Linz: the story of Hitler's art thefts *(London: Cassell 1964), 196p; US title:* The rape of art.

SABER, Clifford
Desert rat sketch book *(New York: Sketchbook 1959), 187p.*

SEAGO, Edward
With the Allied Armies in Italy *(London: Collins 1945), 103 pl.*

SEDDON, Richard
A hand uplifted *(London: Muller 1963), 208p.*

TOPOLSKI, Feliks
Britain in peace and war *(London: Methuen 1941), 128p.*
Russia in war *(London: Methuen 1942), 128p.*
Three continents, 1944–45 *(London: Methuen 1946), 224p.*

WAR pictures by British artists *(Toronto: Oxford UP 1942), 4 vols.*

WOOLLEY, *Sir* Charles L
A record of the work done by the military authorities for the protection of the treasures of art and history in war areas *(London: HMSO 1947), 71p.*

WORKS of art in Austria (British zone of occupation): losses and survivals in the war *(London: HMSO 1946), 60p.*

WORKS of art in Germany (British zone of occupation): losses and survivals in the war *(London: HMSO 1946), 65p.*

WORKS of art in Greece, the Greek Islands and the Dodecanese: losses and survivals in the war *(London: HMSO 1946), 63p.*

WORKS of art in Italy: losses and survivals in the war *(London: HMSO 1945–46), 2 vols.*

ARTILLERY

BIDWELL, Shelford
Gunners at war: a tactical study of the Royal Artillery in the twentieth century *(London: Arms & Armour 1970), 248p.*

BRAZILLER, George (ed)
The 133rd AAA Gun Battalion *(Munich: Oldenburg 1945), 109p.*

BULLARD, Oral
The hot loop: a history of the 383rd Anti-Aircraft Artillery Battalion; U.S. January 1943–November 1945; overseas November 1943–December 1945 *(Waterloo, Iowa: 1950), 111p.*

CAPLETON, Eric W
Shadash-149: the war story of the 149th Regiment RA., 1939–1945 *(Wallasey, Ches: Old Comrades 1963), xix, 268p, bib.*

COOPER, John P
The history of the 110th Field Artillery *(Baltimore, Md: War Records Division, Maryland Historical 1953), 318p.*

DUNCAN, William E *and others* (eds)
The Royal Artillery commemoration book, 1939–1945 *(London: Bell 1950), xi, 790p.*

EELES, Henry S
The history of the 17th Light Anti-Aircraft Regiment R.A., 1938–1945 *(Tunbridge Wells, Kent: Courier 1945), 251p.*

FARNUM, Sayward H
The five by five: a history of the 555th Anti-Aircraft Artillery Automatic Weapons Battalion (mobile) *(Boston, Mass: Athenaeum 1946), 136p.*

GISE, Benjamin *and* RICHARDS, Van N (eds)
On target: a history of the 862nd AAA-AW-BN in the Second World War *(New York: Marbridge 194–), 168p.*

THE HISTORY of the 7th Medium Regiment, Royal Artillery during World War 2, 1939–1945 *(London: Langrishe 1951), ix, 222p.*

HOGG, Ian V
German artillery of World War Two *(London: Arms & Armour 1974), 350p.*
The guns: 1939/45 *(New York: Ballantine 1970), 159p.*

KLEMOW, Sid (ed)
The tracer: a record of the 195th AAA AW BN(SP) Mojave to Berlin *(Halle, Ger 1945), I vol.*

LAMB, David A
View from the bridge: the story of the 191st Field Regiment of the Royal Artillery, the Herts & Essex Yeomanry, 1942–1944 *(Watford, Herts: Lamb 1971), 114p.*

LOWERY, Tom (ed)
778 AAA AW BN(SP) from activation to victory *(Munich 1945), 121p.*

MCLEAN, Donald B (ed)
Japanese artillery: weapons and tactics *(Wickenburg, Ariz: Normount Technical 1973), 204p.*

SCOTT, Peter T (comp)
Shoot, move and communicate: 194th Field Artillery Battalion *(Munich 1946), 152p.*
SMITH, Frank E
Battle diary: the story of the 243rd Field Artillery Battalion in combat *(New York: Hobson 1946), 214p.*
US ARMY
XII Corps Artillery in combat, 13 Aug 1944 to 8 May 1945 *(Regensburg, Ger 1945), 1 vol.*
From Texas to Teisnach with the 457 AAA AW Battalion *(Nancy, Fr: Humblot 1945), 223p.*
The history of 375 Field Artillery BN *(Stuttgart 1945), 174p.*
184th AAA Gun Battalion, Iceland, England, France, Belgium, Holland, Germany *(Fulda, Ger 1945), 66p.*
The 119th Field Artillery Group, World War II, European theater of operations *(Offenbach, Ger: Gross-Steinheim 1945), 213p.*
On the way: combat experience of the 693rd Field Artillery BN in the European theater of operations, Normandy, Northern France, Rhineland, Central Europe *(Salzburg, Aus 1945), 89p.*
Our story: 387th AAA AW BN(SP) *(Göttingen, Ger 1945), 199p.*
Thunderbolt Battalion, 1941–1945: 65th Armoured Field Artillery Battalion *(Philadelphia, Pa: Jardine 1947), 215p.*
Thundering thunderbolt: the story of the 790th Field Artillery Battalion *(Laon, Fr 1945), 72p.*
305th Field Artillery Battalion, 27th Infantry Division *(Hakodate, Jap: Yuji Itagaki 1946), 72p.*
345th Field Artillery Battalion, 90th Infantry Division Third U.S. Army *(Munich: Bruckmann 1945), 77p.*
War history of the 536th AAA AW BN(M) 1942–1944 *(Baton Rouge, La: Army & Navy Pictorial 1947), 107p.*
WATKINS, J H *and* LESLIE, Donald
On target: a souvenir of 'Ack-Ack' *(London: Territorial 1955), 65p.*
[*see also* BRITISH ARMY, US ARMY]

ATHENIA

CAULFIELD, Max
A night of terror: the story of the Athenia affair *(London: Muller 1958), 222p; US title:* Tomorrow never came.

ATLANTIC CHARTER

JOHNSEN, Julia E (comp)
The eight points of post-war world reorganization *(New York: Wilson 1942), 126p.*

MORTON, Henry C V
Atlantic meeting: an account of Mr. Churchill's voyage in H.M.S. Prince of Wales in August 1941 and the conference with President Roosevelt which resulted in the Atlantic Charter *(London: Methuen 1943), 160p.*

ROOSEVELT–CHURCHILL declaration, the Atlantic Charter *(New York: Universal 1941), 16p.*

WILSON, Theodore A
The first summit: Roosevelt and Churchill at Placentia Bay, 1941 *(Boston, Mass: Houghton Mifflin 1969), xvii, 344p, bib.*

ATLAS

BROWN, Ernest F
The war in maps: an atlas of the New York Times *(London: Oxford UP 1946), 197p.*

HORRABIN, James F
An atlas-history of the Second World War *(London: Nelson 1942–46), 10 vols.*

STEMBRIDGE, Jasper H
The Oxford war atlas *(New York: Oxford UP 1941–46), 4 vols.*

ATOM BOMB

AMRINE, Michael
The great decision: the secret history of the atomic bomb *(London: Heinemann 1960), 215p.*

BAKER, Paul R
The atomic bomb: the great decision *(New York: Holt, Rinehart & Winston 1968), vi, 122p, bib.*

BATHCHELDER, Robert C
The irreversible decision *(Boston: Houghton Mifflin 1962) 306p.*

CHINNOCK, Frank W
Nagasaki: the forgotten bomb *(Cleveland, Ohio: World 1969), xiv, 304p, bib.*

CLARK, Ronald W
The birth of the bomb: the untold story of Britain's part in the weapon that changed the world *(London: Phoenix House 1961), 209p.*

FEIS, Herbert
Japan subdued: the atomic bomb and the end of the war in the Pacific *(Princeton, NJ: Princeton UP 1961), vi, 199p; later published as:* The atomic bomb and the end of World War II.

GIGON, Fernand
Formula for death: $E=MC^2$ (the atom bombs and after) *(London: Wingate 1958), 223p.*

GIOVANNITTI, Len *and* FREED, Fred
The decision to drop the bomb *(New York: Coward-McCann 1965), 348p, bib.*

GROUEFF, Stéphane
Manhattan project: the untold story of the making of the atomic bomb *(London: Collins 1967) 416p.*

GROVES, Leslie R
Now it can be told: the story of the Manhattan project *(New York: Harper 1962), 464p.*

HACHIYA, Michihiko
Hiroshima diary: the journal of a Japanese physician, August 6–September 30, 1945 *(London: Gollancz 1955), 256p.*

HERSEY, John
Hiroshima *(London: Dakers 1946), 127p.*

HEWLETT, Richard G *and* ANDERSON, Oscar E
A history of the United States Atomic Energy Commission: vol I, the new world, 1939–1946 *(Philadelphia: Pa State UP 1962), 766p.*

HUIE, William B
The Hiroshima pilot *(New York: Putnam 1964), 318p.*

IRVING, David
The German atomic bomb: the history of nuclear research in Nazi Germany *(New York: Simon & Schuster 1967), 329p.*

JUNGK, Robert
Brighter than a thousand suns: a personal history of the atomic scientists *(London: Gollancz 1958), 350p.*

KNEBEL, Fletcher *and* BAILEY, Charles
No high ground!; the inside story of the men who planned and dropped the first atomic bomb *(London: Weidenfeld & Nicolson 1960), xii, 272p, bib.*

LAMONT, Lansing
Day of trinity *(New York: Atheneum 1965), 333p.*

LAWRENCE, William I
Dawn over zero: the story of the atomic bomb *(London: Museum 1947), 251p.*

LIFTON, Robert J
Death in life: the survivors of Hiroshima *(New York: Random House 1968),* [7], *594p, bib.*

MARX, Joseph L
Nagasaki: the necessary bomb? *(New York: Macmillan 1971), 239p.*

MERTON, Thomas
The original child bomb: points for meditation to be scratched on the walls of a cave *(New York: New Directions 1962), limited autographed edition.*

MILLER, Merle *and* SPITZER, Abe
We dropped the A-bomb *(New York: Crowell 1946), 152p.*

NAGAI, Takashi
We of Nagasaki: the story of survivors in an atomic wasteland *(London: Gollancz 1951), 207p.*

OSADA, Arata (comp)
Children of the A-bomb: the testament of boys and girls of Hiroshima *(New York: International 1959), 256p.*

OUGHTERSON, Ashley W *and* WARREN, Shields (eds)
Medical effects of the atomic bomb in Japan *(New York: McGraw-Hill 1956), 477p.*

PHYSICAL and medical effects of the atomic bomb in Hiroshima *(Tokyo: Maruzen 1958), 117p.*

SMYTH, Henry De W
Atomic energy for military purposes: the official report on the development of the atomic bomb under the auspices of the U.S. Government, 1940–1945 *(Princeton, NJ: Princeton UP 1945), 264p.*

TRUMBULL, Robert
Nine who survived Hiroshima and Nagasaki: personal experiences of nine men who lived through the atomic bombings *(New York: Dutton 1957), 148p.*

US STRATEGIC BOMBING SURVEY
The effects of the atomic bombs on Hiroshima and Nagasaki *(San Francisco, Calif: Gannon 1973), 46p.*

YASS, Marion
Hiroshima *(London: Wayland 1971), 128p.*
[*see also* AIR WARFARE HEAVY WATER SCIENCE]

AUSTRALIA

BATESON, Charles
The war with Japan *(London: Barrie & Rockliff 1968), 417p.*

BEAN, Charles E W
War aims of a plain Australian *(Sydney: Angus & Robertson 1943), vii, 174p.*

BENNETT BREMNER, E
Front-line airway: the war story of Qantas Empire Airways Ltd *(Sydney: Angus & Robertson 1944), 11-193p.*

BINNING, John
Target area *(Sydney: Australasian 1943), 179p.*

BUGGY, Hugh
Pacific victory: a short history of Australia's part in the war against Japan *(North Melbourne: Victorian Railway 1945), 301p.*

BULCOCK, Roy
Of death but once *(Melbourne: Cheshire 1947), 213p.*

BUTLIN, Sydney J
War economy *(Canberra: Australian War Memorial 1955), 1 vol.*

CHAPMAN, Ivan
Details enclosed *(Sydney: Angus & Robertson 1958), 233p.*

CLARK, Russell S
An end to tears *(Sydney: Huston 1946), 180p.*

DEVANNY, Jean
Bird of paradise *(Sydney: Johnson 1945), 284p.*

EVATT, Herbert V
Foreign policy of Australia *(Sydney: Angus & Robertson 1945), 266p.*

FOENANDER, Orwell de R
Wartime labour developments in Australia *(Melbourne: Melbourne UP 1943), xxx, 177p.*

HOLE, Tahu
Anzacs into battle *(London: Hodder & Stoughton 1942), xvi, 17–471p.*

JACKSON, C O B
Proud story: the official history of Australian Comforts Fund *(Sydney: Johnston 1949), 336p.*

JOHNSTON, George H
Australia at war *(Sydney: Angus & Robertson 1942), xviii, 265p.*
Pacific partner *(New York: Duell 1944), ix, 227p.*

MANN, Molly *and* FOOTT, Bethia
We drove the Americans *(London: Angus & Robertson 1944), 185p.*

MEADOWS, Maureen C
I loved those Yanks *(Sydney: Dash 1948), 336p.*

MEEKING, Charles *and* BARTLETT, N (eds)
Pictorial history of Australia at war, 1939–45 *(Canberra: Australian War Memorial 1958), 5 vols.*

MELLOR, David P
The role of science and industry *(Canberra: Australian War Memorial 1958), 738p.*

OFFENBURG, Kurt
Japan at our gates *(Sydney: Gayle 1942), 96p.*
War in the Pacific? *(Sydney: Gayle 1941), 96p.*

PAGET, *Mrs* K M
Out of the hand of the terrible *(Melbourne: Bacon 1945), 111p.*

REINHOLD, William J
The bulldog Wau road *(Brisbane: Queensland UP 1946), 53p.*

ROWELL, *Sir* Sydney Fairbairn
Full circle *(Melbourne: Melbourne UP 1974), 206p.*

STUART, Gilbert
Kind-hearted tiger *(Boston, Mass: Little, Brown 1964), 375p.*

WALKER, Allan S
Clinical problems of war *(Canberra: Australian War Memorial 1952), 720p.*
The island campaigns *(Canberra: Australian War Memorial 1957), 426p.*
Middle East and Far East *(Canberra: Australian War Memorial 1961), 701p.*

WALKER, Allan S *and others*
Medical services of the R.A.N. and R.A.A.F., with section on women in the Army Medical Services *(Canberra: Australian War Memorial 1961), 574p.*

WALKER, Edward R
The Australian economy in war and reconstruction *(London: Oxford UP 1947), 427p.*

WIGMORE, Lionel
The Japanese thrust *(Canberra: Australian War Memorial 1957), xvii, 715p.*

AUSTRALIAN AIR FORCE

BEEDE, John
They hosed them out: a story of Australian gunners in the R.A.F. *(Sydney: Horwitz 1968), 224p.*

FIRKINS, Peter C
Strike and return: the story of the exploits of No. 460 R.A.A.F. Bomber Command in the World War *(Perth: Paterson Brokensha 1964), 200p. 200p.*

GILLISON, Douglas
Royal Australian Air Force, 1939–1942 *(Canberra: Australian War Memorial 1962), 786p.*

GRAHAM, Burton *and* SMYTH, Frank
A nation grew wings: the graphic story of the Australian-built Beauforts of the R.A.A.F. in New Guinea *(Melbourne: Winterset House 1947), 277p.*

GREEN, Alex
We were the (RIFF) R.A.A.F. *(Perth: Petersons 194-), 87p.*

HERINGTON, John
Air war against Germany and Italy, 1939–1943 *(Canberra: Australian War Memorial 1954), 731p.*

JOHNSTON, Frank (ed)
R.A.A.F. over Europe *(London: Eyre & Spottiswoode 1946), 189p.*

LAWSON, J H W
Four five five: the story of 455 (R.A.A.F.) Squadron *(Melbourne: Wilke 1951), 207p.*

ODGERS, George
Air war against Japan, 1943–1945 *(Canberra: Australian War Memorial 1957), xiii, 533p.*

POWELL, Gordon G
Two steps to Tokyo: a story of the R.A.A.F. in the Trobriand and Admiralty Islands *(Melbourne: Oxford UP 1945), xii, 222p.*
R.A.A.F. log *(Canberra: Australian War Memorial 1943), 200p.*

RUSSELL, J (pseud)
Sand rising *(Sydney: Johnson 1945), 139p.*

SOUTHALL, Ivan
Bluey Truscott: Squadron Leader Keith William Truscott, R.A.A.F., D.F.C. and Bar *(London: Angus & Robertson 1958), x, 203p.*

These eagles: story of the R.A.A.F. at war *(Canberra: Australian War Memorial 1942), 200p.*
They shall not pass unseen *(Sydney: Angus & Robertson 1956), [9], 214p.*

VICTORY roll: The Royal Australian Air Force in its sixth year of war *(Canberra: Australian War Memorial 1945), 200p.*

WATERS, John C A
Valiant youth: the men of the R.A.A.F. *(Sydney: Johnston 1945), 103p.*

AUSTRALIAN ARMY

ACKLAND, John *and* ACKLAND, Richard (eds)
Word from John: an Australian soldier's letters to his friends *(Melbourne: Cassell 1944), xii, 228p.*

ACTIVE service *(Canberra: Australian War Memorial 1941), 129p.*

AITKEN, Edward F
The story of the 2/2nd Australian Pioneer Battalion *(Melbourne: 2/2nd APB Association 1953), 288p.*

ALLCHIN, Frank
Purple and blue: the history of the 2/10th Battalion, A.I.F. (The Adelaide Rifles), 1939-1945 *(Adelaide: Griffin 1958), 454p.*

ARGENT, Jack N L ('Silver John')
Target tank: the history of the 2/3rd Australian Anti-Tank Regiment, 9th Division, A.I.F. *(Paramatta, Cumberland, Aust: 1957), 350p.*

THE ARMY Christmas books *(Canberra: Australian War Memorial 1941-45), 5 vols.*

BENSON, S E
The story of the 42 Australia Infantry Battalion *(Sydney: Dymock's Book Arcade 1952), 220p.*

BOSS-WALKER, Geoffrey
Desert sand and jungle green: a pictorial history of the 2/43rd Australian Infantry Battalion (Ninth Division) in the Second World War, 1939-1945 *(Hobart, Tas: Oldham 1948), 164p.*

BURCHETT, Wilfred G
Democracy with a tommygun *(Melbourne: Cheshire 1946), 291p.*

BURNS, John
The brown and the blue diamond at war: the story of the 2/27th Battalion A.I.F. *(Adelaide: Griffin 1960), 259p.*

CALLINAN, Bernard J
Independent Company: the 2/2 and 2/4 Australian Independent Companies in Portuguese Timor, 1941-1943 *(London: Heinemann 1954), xxxiii, 235p.*

CHARLOTT, Rupert
The unofficial history of the 29/46th Australian Infantry Battalion A.I.F. Sept. 1939-Sept. 1945 *(Sydney: Halstead 1952), 147p.*

THE CORPS of Royal Australian Engineers in the Second World War *(Melbourne: Speciality 1947), 54p.*

CREMOR, W E
Action front: the history of the 2/2nd Australian Field Regiment, Royal Australian Artillery, A.I.F. *(Melbourne: 2/2nd Field Regiment Association 1961), 234p.*

FAIRCLOUGH, H
Equal to the task; par oneri: the history of the Royal Australian Army Service Corps *(Melbourne: Cheshire 1962), 310p.*

FEARNSIDE, Geoffrey
Bayonets abroad: a history of the 2/13th Battalion A.I.F. in the Second World War *(Sydney: Waite & Bull 1953), 434p.*

GLENN, John G
From Tobruk to Tarakan: the story of a fighting unit *(Adelaide: Rigby 1960), 269p.*

GOODHART, David
We of the turning tide *(London: Preece 1947), xiv, 260p.*
The history of the 2/7th Australian Field Regiment *(Adelaide: Rigby 1952), 380p.*

HARTLEY, Frank J
Sananandra interlude: the 7th Australian Division Cavalry Regiment *(Melbourne: Victoria Book Depot 1949), 101p.*

HAYWOOD, E V
Six years in support: official history of the 2/1st Australian Field Regiment *(Sydney: Angus & Robertson 1959), 211p.*

HENRY, R L
The story of the 2/4th Field Regiment: a history of a Royal Australian Artillery Regiment during the Second World War *(Melbourne: Merrion 1950), 410p.*

HETHERINGTON, John A
Australian soldier *(Sydney: Johnston 1943), 102p.*

JACOBS, James W *and* BRIDGLAND, R J (eds)
Through: the story of Signals 8 Australian Division and Signals A.I.F., Malaya *(Sydney: 8 Division Signals Association 1949), 270p.*

KEOGH, Eustace G
Middle East, 1939–1943 *(Melbourne: Wilkie 1959), 302p.*
South West Pacific, 1941–45 *(Melbourne: Grayflower 1965), 479p.*

KERR, Colin G
Tanks in the East: the story of an Australian Cavalry Regiment *(Melbourne: Oxford UP 1945), 200p.*

KHAKI and green: with the Australian Army at home and overseas *(Canberra: Australian War Memorial 1943), 204p.*

LAFFIN, John
Anzacs at war: the story of Australian and New Zealand battles *(London: Abelard-Schuman 1965), 224p.*
Middle East journey *(Sydney: Angus & Robertson 1958), 193p.*

THE LOGBOOK: collected records of 2/7th Australian Service Battery, R.A.A., A.I.F., 1940–1945 *(Sydney: Patersons 1946), 76p.*

LONG, Gavin M

Greece, Crete and Syria *(Canberra: Australian War Memorial 1953), 587p.*

The final campaigns *(Canberra: Australian War Memorial 1963), xx, 667p.*

To Benghazi *(Canberra: Australian War Memorial 1952), ix, 336p.*

McFARLAN, Graeme

Etched in green: the history of the 22nd Australian Infantry Battalion, 1939–1946 *(Adelaide: Griffin 1961), 262p.*

McKIE, Ronald

The heroes *(Sydney: Angus & Robertson 1960), 3-285p; US title:* The survivors.

MARSHALL, Alan J

Nulli secundus log: [2/2nd Australian Infantry Battalion, A.I.F.] *(Sydney: Consolidated 1946), 130p.*

MASEL, Philip

The second 28th: the story of a famous battalion of the 9th Australian Division *(Perth: 2/28th Battalion and 24th Anti-Tank Comrades Association 1961), 196p.*

MATTHEWS, Russell

Militia Battalion at war: the history of the 58/59th Australian Infantry Battalion in the Second World War *(Melbourne: 58/59th Battalion Association 1961), 236p.*

NEASRY, P C

Blokes I knew: Libya-Syria, 1941 *(Sydney: Johnson, 1944), 9-191p.*

O'BRIEN, John W

Guns and gunners: the story of the 2/5th Australian Field Regiment in World War II *(Sydney: Angus & Robertson 1950), xviii, 267p.*

PENFOLD, A W *and others*

Galleghan's greyhounds: the story of the 2/30th Australian Infantry Battalion, 22nd November, 1940–10th October, 1945 *(Sydney: Angus & Robertson 1950), 267p.*

RUSSELL, William B

The Second Fourteenth Battalion: a history of an Australian Infantry Battalion in the Second World War *(Sydney: Angus & Robertson 1948), 336p.*

SELBY, David
Hell and high fever *(London: Angus & Robertson 1957)*, [*8*], *198p*.

SERLE, R P (ed)
The Second Twentyfourth Australian Infantry Battalion of the 9th Australian Division: a history *(Brisbane: Jacarawa 1963), 378p*.

SOLDIERING on: the Australian Army at home and overseas *(Canberra: Australian War Memorial 1942), 200p*.

STAND easy *(Canberra: Australian War Memorial 1945), 208p*.

UREN MALCOLM, John L
A thousand men at war: the story of the 2/16th Battalion, A.I.F. *(London: Heinemann 1959), 259p*.

WHITE, Osmar E D
Green armour *(Sydney: Angus & Robertson 1945), 246p*.

WIENEKE, James
6th Division sketches, Aitape to Wewak, 1944–1945 (Sydney: 1946), 60p.

WOOD, Thomas
Cobbers campaigning *(London: Cape 1940), 159p*.

YEATES, James D *and* LOH, W G
Red Platypus: a record of the achievement of the 24th Australian Infantry Brigade, Ninth Australian Division, 1940–45 *(Perth: Imperial 1945), 83p*.

AUSTRALIAN NAVY

FEAKES, Henry J
White ensign – Southern Cross: a story of the King's ships of Australia's Navy *(Sydney: Smith 1952), 246p*.

GILL, George H
Royal Australian Navy *(Canberra: Australian War Memorial 1957), vol. I: 1939–1942, xviii, 686p*.

H.M.A.S. *(Canberra: Australian War Memorial 1943), 2 vols*.

JOHNSTON, George H
Lioness of the seas: story of H.M.S. Sydney *(London: Gollancz 1941), 248p; US title:* Action at sea.

JONES, Thomas M *and* IDRIESS, I L
The silent service: action stories of the Anzac Navy *(London: Angus & Robertson 1952), 2nd ed. rev. and enl. 372p*.

McDONNELL, James E
Fleet destroyer *(Melbourne: The Book Department 1945), 102p*.

McKie, Ronald
Proud echo [H.M.A.S. Perth] *(Sydney: Angus & Robertson 1953), xvii, 158p.*
Moyes, John F
Scrap-iron flotilla *(Sydney: NSW Bookstall 1943), 218p.*
Pacini, John
With the RAN to Tokio: Navy souvenir number *(Melbourne: United 1945), 52p.*
Parkin, Ray
Out of the smoke [H.M.A.S. Perth] *(London: Hogarth 1960), 311p.*
Parry, A F
H.M.A.S. Yarra: the story of a gallant ship *(London: Angus & Robertson 1944), 224p.*
Porthole: being the chronicle of the operations, experiences and peregrinations of H.M.A.S. Shropshire in the Second World War, 1939–1945 *(Sydney: Sands 1946), 95p.*
Rhys, Lloyd
My ship is so small *(Melbourne: Georgian 1946), 127p.*
Ross, W H
Stormy petrel: the life story of H.M.A.S. Sydney *(Perth: Patersons 1946), 296p.*
[*see also* DARWIN, FAR EAST, JAPAN *and* PRISONERS, MEDITERRANEAN, MIDDLE EAST, NEW GUINEA, PACIFIC]

AUSTRIA

Burmetz, Paul
Our share of morning *(New York: Doubleday 1961), 360p.*
Buttinger, Joseph
In the twilight of socialism: a history of the revolutionary socialists of Austria *(New York: Praeger 1953), 577p.*
Lania, Leo (pseud)
Darkest hour: adventures and escapes *(Boston, Mass: Houghton Mifflin 1941), ix, 235p.*
Pauli, Hertha E
Break of time *(New York: Hawthorn 1972), 239p.*
Tilt, Notburga
The strongest weapon *(Ilfracombe, Devon: Stockwell 1972), 227p.*
Watson, Ann
They came in peace *(Palos Verdes Estate, Calif: TW 1972), 382p.*
[*see also* TREATIES]

AUXILIARY TERRITORIAL SERVICE (ATS)

CAVADINI, Ada
This was the A.T.S. *(London: Crisp 1946), 108p.*

COTTERELL, Anthony
She walks in battle dress: the day's work in the A.T.S. *(London: Christophers 1942), vi, 7-96p.*

GWYNNE-VAUGHAN, *Dame* Helen C I
Service with the Army *(London: Hutchinson 1942), 163p.*

HOLDSWORTH, Irene
Yes, ma'am *(London: Hutchinson 1943), 80p.*

NEILL-FRASER, R M
We serve (an account of life in the Auxiliary Territorial Service) *(London: Hodder & Stoughton 1942), 160p.*

SHERMAN, Margaret
No time for tears in the A.T.S. *(London: Harrap 1944), 168p.*

AXIS POWERS

DEAKIN, Frederick W
The brutal friendship: Mussolini, Hitler and the fall of Italian Fascism *(London: Weidenfeld & Nicolson 1962), 806p.*

IKLE, Frank W
German-Japanese relations, 1936-1946 *(New York: Bookman 1956), 243p.*

LEMKIN, Raphael
Axis rule in occupied Europe: laws of occupation, analysis of government proposals for redress *(New York: Columbia UP 1944), xxxviii, 674p.*

MESKILL, Johanna M M
Hitler and Japan: the hollow alliance *(New York: Atherton 1966), 245p.*

MUSMAN, Richard
Hitler and Mussolini *(London: Chatto & Windus 1968), 112p, bib.*

PADMANABHAN, C E
Hitler-Stalin Axis war *(Madras, India: Short, Bewes 1962), 657p.*

PLEHWE, Friedrich-Karl von
The end of an alliance: Rome's defection from the Axis in 1943 *(London: Oxford UP 1971), xiv, 161p.*

PRESSEISEN, Ernst L
Germany and Japan: a study in totalitarian diplomacy *(The Hague: Nijhoff 1958), 368p.*

SCHROEDER, Paul W
Axis Alliance and Japanese-American relation, 1941 *(Ithaca NY: Cornell UP 1958), 246p.*

WISKEMANN, Elizabeth
The Rome-Berlin Axis: a study of the relations between Hitler and Mussolini *(London: Oxford UP 1949), 446p, bib.*

AZORES

VINTRAS, Roland E
The Portuguese connection: the secret history of the Azores base *(London: Bachman & Turner 1974), 183p, bib.*

BADGES

BADGES and emblems of the services *(London: NAG Press 1940), 64p.*

COLE, Howard N
Heraldry in war: formation badges, 1939-1945 *(Aldershot, Hants: Gale & Polden 1946), 143p.*

KERRIGAN, Evans E
American badges and insignia *(New York: Viking 1967), xvii, 286p, bib.*

ROSIGNOLI, Guido
Army badges and insignia of World War 2: Great Britain, Poland, Belgium, Italy, U.S.S.R., U.S.A., Germany *(London: Blandford 1972), 228p.*

WILKINSON, Frederick
Badges of the British Army, 1820-1960 *(London: Arms & Armour 1969), 59p.*

BALKANS

ANSEL, Walter
Hitler and the middle sea *(Durham, NC: Duke UP 1972), 514p.*

ESDAILLE, David (pseud)
Death at my heels *(London: Chapman & Hall 1942), xi, 13-*256p.

GERMAN antiguerilla operations in the Balkans, 1941-1944: a historical study *(Washington DC: Department of Army 1954), 82p.*

THE GERMAN campaigns in the Balkans, Spring 1941: a historical study *(Washington DC: Department of Army 1953), 161p.*

HOLLINGWORTH, Clare
There's a German just behind me *(London: Secker & Warburg 1942), 300p.*

JAMIESON, Edward
The Balkans fight for freedom *(London: Lawrence & Wishart 1942), 5-70p.*

KINGSCOTE, Flavia
Balkan exit *(London: Bles 1942), 11-180p.*

MAITLAND, Patrick
European dateline *(London: Quality 1946), 211p.*

PADEV, Michael
Escape from the Balkans *(London: Cassell 1943), 256p.*

PARIS, Edmond
Genocide in satellite Croatia, 1941-1945: a record of racial and religious persecutions and massacres *(Chicago, Ill: American Institute for Balkan Affairs 1962), 306p.*

PATMORE, Derek
Balkan correspondent *(New York: Harper 1941), xii, 319p.*

ST. JOHN, Robert
Foreign correspondent *(London: Hutchinson 1960), 240p.*
From the land of silent people *(London: Harrap 1942) 264p.*

WHITE, Leigh
The long Balkan night *(New York: Scribner 1944), x, 473p.*
[*see also* ALBANIA, GREECE, RUMANIA, YUGOSLAVIA]

BALTIC

MEIKSINS, Gregory
Baltic riddle: Finland, Estonia, Latvia, Lithuania - key points of European peace *(New York: Fischer 1943), x, 271p.*

ORAS, Arts
Baltic eclipse *(London: Gollancz 1948), 307p.*

SVABE, Arveds
Genocide in the Baltic States *(Stockholm: Latvian National Fund in the Scandinavian Countries 1952), 50p.*
[*see also* FINLAND, LATVIA, LITHUANIA]

BATAAN

ABRAHAM, Abie
Ghost of Bataan speaks *(New York: Vantage 1971), 244p.*

CONROY, Robert
The battle of Bataan: America's greatest defeat *(New York: Macmillan 1969), [9], 85p, bib.*

DYESS, William E
Dyess story: the eye-witness account of the death march from Bataan *(New York: Putnam 1944), 7-182p; UK title:* Death march from Bataan.

FALK, Stanley L
Bataan: the march of death *(New York: Norton 1962), 192p, bib; UK title:* The march of death.

HERSEY, John R
Men on Bataan *(New York: Knopf 1942), 313p.*

IND, Allison
Bataan; the judgment seat: the saga of the Philippine command of the U.S. Army Air Force, May 1941 to May 1942 *(New York: Macmillan 1944), 395p.*

LEVERING, Robert W
Horror trek: a true story of Bataan, the death march and three years in Japanese prison camps *(Mt Vernon, Ohio: Levering 1948), ix, 233p.*

MILLER, Ernest B
Bataan uncensored *(Long Praire, Minn: Hart 1949), 403p.*

REDMOND, Juanita
I served on Bataan *(Philadelphia, Pa: Lippincott 1943), 11-167p.*

UNDERBRINK, Robert L
Destination Corregidor *(Annapolis, Md: US Naval Institute 1971), 240p.*

WAINWRIGHT, Jonathan M
General Wainwright's story: the account of four years of humiliating defeat, surrender, and captivity *(Westport, Conn: Greenwood 1970), 314p.*

[*see also* CORREGIDOR, PHILIPPINES]

BATTLE NAMES

GREAT BRITAIN. War Office Battles Nomenclature Committee. The official names of battles, actions and engagements fought by the land forces of the Commonwealth during the Second World War, 1939-1945 *(London: HMSO 1956), 48p.*

JOSLEN, H F
Orders of battle: U.K., and Colonial Formations and Units in the 2nd World War, 1939-1945 *(London: HMSO 1960), 2 vols.*

BATTLE OF BRITAIN

ALLEN, Hubert R
Battle for Britain: the recollections of H. R. 'Dizzy' Allen, DFC *(London: Barker 1973), 175p.*
Who won the battle of Britain? *(London: Barker 1974), xi, 196p, bib.*

BICKERS, Richard
Ginger Lacey, fighter pilot: Battle of Britain top scorer *(London: Hale 1962), xii, 13-189p.*

BISHOP, Edward
The Battle of Britain *(London: Allen & Unwin 1960), 3-236p, bib.*
Their finest hour: the story of the Battle of Britain, 1940 *(New York: Ballantine 1968), 160p, bib.*

BOORMAN, Henry *and* LONG, Howard
Recalling the Battle of Britain: a photographic essay based upon the records of the 'Kent Messenger' and other contemporary sources of World War 2 *(Maidstone, Kent: Kent Messenger [1965]), [4], 71p.*

CLARK, Ronald W
Battle for Britain: sixteen weeks that changed the course of history *(London: Harrap 1965), 175p.*

CLARK, R W *and others*
The hundred days that shook the world *(Hemel Hempstead, Herts: Christopher Marlowe 1969), 128p.*

COLLIER, Basil
The Battle of Britain *(London: Batsford 1962), 3-183p.*

COLLIER, Richard
Eagle Day: the Battle of Britain, August 6-September 14, 1940 *(London: Hodder & Stoughton [1966]), 316p, bib.*

HOBBS, Anthony
The Battle of Britain *(London: Wayland 1973), 96p, bib.*

HOUGH, Richard
The Battle of Britain: the triumph of R.A.F. fighter pilots *(New York: Macmillan 1971), [8], 88p, bib.*

HOWARD-WILLIAMS, Ernest L
Immortal memory: drafted during the Battle of Britain from the combat reports of those who took part *(London: Bamber 1947), 62p.*

HUTCHINSON, Tom
'Battle of Britain': a true story of those dramatic four months in 1940 *(London: Purnell 1969), 4-93p, bib.*

JULLIAN, Marcel
The Battle of Britain, July-September, 1940 *(London: Cape 1967), 295p.*

McKEE, Alexander
Strike from the sky: the story of the Battle of Britain *(London: Souvenir [1960]), 288p.*

MASTERS, David
So few: the immortal record of the Royal Air Force *(London: Eyre & Spottiswoode 1941), 340p.*

MIDDLETON, Drew
The sky suspended: the Battle of Britain *(London: Secker & Warburg 1960), 255p.*

NARRACOTT, Arthur H
In praise of the Few: a Battle of Britain anthology *(London: Muller 1947), 64p.*

OFFENBURG, Jean H M
Lonely warrior: the journal of a Battle of Britain fighter pilot *(London: Souvenir 1956), 239p.*

REID, John P M
Some of the Few *(London: Macdonald 1960), 60p.*

REYNOLDS, Quentin J
All about the Battle of Britain *(New York: Random House 1953), [9], 118p.*

SAUNDERS, Hilary St G
The Battle of Britain, August-October, 1940 *(London: HMSO 1941), 56p; US title:* First great air battle in history.

SMITH, Norman D
The Battle of Britain *(London: Faber 1962), 3-127p.*

SPAIGHT, James M
Battle of Britain, 1940 *(London: Bles 1941), 231p.*

TAYLOR, Telford
The breaking wave: the German defeat in the Summer of 1940 *(New York: Simon & Schuster 1967), xi, 13-381p, bib.*

TOWNSEND, Peter
Duel of eagles *(London: Weidenfeld & Nicolson 1970), xvii, 455p.*

WOOD, Derek *and* DEMPSTER, Derek
The narrow margin: the Battle of Britain and the rise of air power, 1930-40 *(London: Hutchinson 1961), 536p, bib.*

WRIGHT, Robert
Dowding and the Battle of Britain *(London: Macdonald 1969), 285p.*

[*see also* GERMAN AIR FORCE, ROYAL AIR FORCE]

BATTLESHIPS

ASH, Bernard
Someone had blundered: the story of the 'Repulse' and the 'Prince of Wales' *(London: Joseph 1960), 267p.*

BAKER, R W (ed)
History of the U.S.S. Washington, 1941-1946 *(New York: Kelly 1946), 116p.*

BENNETT, Geoffrey
The loss of the 'Prince of Wales' and 'Repulse' *(London: Allan 1973), 95p, bib.*

BERTHOLD, Will
The sinking of the 'Bismarck' *(London: Longmans Green 1958), vii, 191p.*

BRADFORD, Ernle
The mighty 'Hood' *(London: Hodder & Stoughton 1959), 223p, bib.*

BRENNAND, Frank
Sink the 'Bismarck'! *(London: Landsborough 1960), 160p, bib.*

BRENNECKE, Hans J
The 'Tirpitz': the drama of the 'Lone Queen of the North' *(London: Hale 1963), 187p.*

BUSCH, Fritz O
The drama of the Scharnhorst: a factual account from the German viewpoint *(London: Hale 1956), 186p; US title:* Holocaust at sea.

FORESTER, Cecil S
Hunting the 'Bismarck' *(London: Joseph 1959), 110p; US title:* The last nine days of the Bismarck.

FRANKLIN, Alan G C *and* FRANKLIN, Gordon
One year of life: the story of H.M.S. Prince of Wales *(London: Blackwood 1944), 93p.*

GRENFELL, Russell
The 'Bismarck' episode *(London: Faber 1948), 176p.*

HELM, Thomas
Ordeal by sea: the tragedy of the U.S.S. Indianapolis *(New York: Dodd 1963), 243p.*

HOUGH, Richard
The hunting of Force Z: the brief controversial life of the modern battleship, and its tragic close with the destruction of the 'Prince of Wales' and 'Repulse' *(London: Collins 1963), 255p; bib; US title:* Death of the battleship.

KENNEDY, Ludovic H C
Pursuit: the chase and the sinking of the Bismarck *(New York: Viking 1974), 254p.*

KRANCKE, Theodor *and* BRENNECKE, Hans J
The battleship 'Scheer' *(London: Kimber 1956), 200p; US title:* Pocket battleship.

LUEY, Allen T *and* BRUVOLD, H P
Minnie: the war cruise of the U.S.S. Minniapolis *(Kalamazoo, Mich: Luey 1946), 126p.*

McKEE, Alexander
Black Saturday: the tragedy of the 'Royal Oak' *(London: Souvenir 1959), 220p.*

McMURTRIE, Francis E
The cruise of the Bismarck *(London: Hutchinson 1941), 70p.*

NEWCOMB, Richard F
Abandon ship! [U.S.S. Indianapolis] *(London: Constable 1960), 215p.*

PEILLARD, Leonce
Sink the Tirpitz! *(London: Cape 1968), 360p, bib.*

PRIEN, Gunther
I sank the 'Royal Oak' *(London: Gray's Inn 1954), 196p.*

RAVEN, Alan
King George the Fifth class battleships *(London: Bivouac 1972), [417p].*

SCHOFIELD, Brian B
The loss of the Bismarck *(London: Allan 1972), 96p, bib.*

SHIRER, William L
The sinking of the 'Bismarck' *(New York: Random House 1962), 136p; UK title:* All about the sinking of the Bismarck.

SOPOCKO, Eryk K S
Gentlemen, the Bismarck has been sunk *(London: Methuen 1942), 93p.*

THOMPSON, Kenneth *and others*
H.M.S. Rodney at war: being an account of the part [she] played in the war from 1939 to 1945 *(London: Hollis & Carter 1946), 180p.*

THE U.S. SHIP Texas in World War II: a pictorial review of the accomplishments of the thirty-one year old battleship *(New York: Publishers 1947), 111p.*

VULLIEZ, Albert *and* MORDAL, Jacques
Battleship 'Scharnhorst' *(London: Hutchinson 1958), 256p.*

WATERS, John M
Bloody winter. [Tirpitz] *(Princeton, NJ: Van Nostrand [1968], xv, 279p, bib.*

WATTS, Anthony J
The loss of the 'Scharnhorst' *(London: Allan 1970), 84p, bib.*

WOODWARD, David
The 'Tirpitz': the story including the destruction of the 'Scharnhorst', of the campaign against the German battleship *(London: Kimber 1953), xii, 13-223p, bib.*

[*see also* GERMAN NAVY, ROYAL NAVY, US NAVY]

BBC (BRITISH BROADCASTING CORPORATION)

CUMBERLEDGE, G (ed)
BBC War Report, 6th June 1944–5th May 1945 *(London: Oxford UP 1946), 542p.*

NEWSOME, Noel F
Man in the street (of the B.B.C.) talks to Europe *(London: Staples 1945), vii, 260p.*

[*see also* PROPAGANDA, RADIO]

BELGIUM

BELGIAN AMERICAN EDUCATIONAL FOUNDATION
The Belgian campaign and the surrender of the Belgian Army, May 10–28, 1940 *(New York: The Foundation 1940), 85p.*

BELGIUM: the official account of what happened, 1939–1940 *(London: Evans 1941), 120p.*

BRUSSELMANS, Anne
Rendez-vous 127: the diary of Madame Brusselmans, M.B.E., September 1940–September 1944 *(London: Benn 1954), 173p.*

CAMMAERTS, Emile
Prisoner at Laeken: King Leopold *(London: Cresset 1941), xxxvi, 268p.*

DE VOS, Jean
I was Hitler's slave *(London: Quality 1942), 122p.*

DUNCAN, Sylvia *and* DUNCAN, Peter
Anne Brusselmans, M.B.E. *(London: Benn 1959), 207p.*

DUNER, Paul
A year and a day *(London: Drummond 1942), 219p.*

GOFFIN, Robert
Was Leopold a traitor?: the story of Belgium's eighteen tragic days *(London: Hamilton 1941), 210p.*

GORIS, Johannes A (ed)
Belgium in bondage *(New York: Fischer 1943), 259p.*
Belgium under occupation *(New York: Moutus 1947), 240p.*

MOTZ, Roger
Belgium unvanquished *(London: Drummond 1942), 135p.*

NEAVE, Airey
The little cyclone *(London: Hodder & Stoughton 1954), 189p.*

RAVEN, Hélène J
Without frontiers *(London: Hutchinson 1960), 222p.*

RIGBY, Françoise
In defiance *(London: Elek 1960), 224p.*

SOMERHAUSEN, Anne S
Written in darkness: a Belgian woman's record of the occupation, 1940–1945 *(New York: Knopf 1946), 339p.*

TREVELYAN, Mary
I'll walk beside you; letters from Belgium, September 1944–May 1945 *(London: Longmans Green 1946), 111p.*

YDEWALLE, Charles d'
Interlude in Spain *(London: Macmillan 1944), viii, 213p.*

[*see also* ARDENNES, WESTERN EUROPE 1939–40, WESTERN EUROPE 1944–5]

BERLIN

ANDERSON, Hartvig
The dark city: a true account of adventure of a secret agent in Berlin *(London: Cresset 1954), 314p.*

ANDREAS-FRIEDRICH, Ruth
Berlin underground, 1939–1945 *(New York: Holt 1945), 312p.*

BYFORD-JONES, W
Berlin twilight *(London: Hutchinson 1947), 192p.*

FREDBORG, Arvid
Behind the steel wall: a Swedish journalist in Berlin, 1941–43 *(New York: Viking 1944), ix, 305p.*

HORSTMANN, Lali
Nothing for tears *(London: Weidenfeld & Nicolson [1953]), xiii, 207p.*

KARDORFF, Ursula von
Diary of a nightmare: Berlin, 1942–1945 *(London: Hart-Davis 1965), 224p.*

KLEIN, Catherine
Escape from Berlin *(London: Gollancz 1944), 149p.*
KUBY, Erich
The Russians and Berlin, 1945 *(London: Heinemann 1968), xii, 372p, bib.*
RYAN, Cornelius
The last battle *(London: Collins 1966); 3–463p, bib.*
SHIRER, William L
Berlin diary: the journal of a foreign correspondent, 1934–1941 *(London: Hamilton 1941), 491p.*
SMITH, Jean E
The defence of Berlin *(Baltimore: Johns Hopkins 1963), 431p.*
STRAWSON, John
The battle for Berlin *(London: Batsford 1974), viii, 182p, bib.*
STUDNITZ, Hans G von
While Berlin burns: the diary of Hans-Georg von Studnitz, 1943–1945 *(London: Weidenfeld & Nicolson [1964]), 290p.*
TULLY, Andrew
Berlin: story of a battle *(New York: Simon & Schuster 1963), 304p.*
A WOMAN in Berlin, anon *(New York: Harcourt 1954), 319p.*
ZIEMKE, Earl F
The battle for Berlin: end of the Third Reich *(New York: Ballantine 1968), 160p, bib.*
[*see also* GERMANY]

BISMARCK SEA BATTLE

GRAHAM, Burton
None shall survive: the graphic story of the annihilation of the Japanese armada in the Bismarck Sea Battle *(Sydney: Johnston 1944), 144p.*

BLITZ ON UNITED KINGDOM (APART FROM LONDON)

BEAUJON, Paul (pseud)
Bombed but unbeaten *(New York: Typhophiles 1941), xvi, 100p.*
LEE, Asher
Blitz on Britain *(London: Four Square 1960), 160p, bib.*
MARCHANT, Hilde
Women and children last: a woman reporter's account of the battle of Britain *(London: Gollancz 1941), 190p.*

MASON, Francis K
Battle over Britain: a history of the German air assaults on Great Britain, 1917-18 and July-December 1940, and of the development of Britain's air defences between the World Wars *(London: McWhirter Twins 1969), 636p, bib.*
NIXON, Barbara M
Raiders overhead *(London: Drummond 1943), 166p.*
RICHARDS, William L
Pembrokeshire under fire: the story of the air-raids of 1940–41 *(Haverfordwest, Pem: Hammond 1965), 80p.*
STRANGE, William
Into the Blitz: a British journey *(Toronto: Macmillan 1941), xvi, 318p.*

BLOCKADE

HAUGHE, Eilid O *and* HARTMANN, Vera
Flight from Dakar *(London: Allen & Unwin 1954), 200p.*
McKEE, Alexander
The coal scuttle brigade *(London: Souvenir 1958), 223p.*
SELIGMAN, Adrian
No stars to guide *(London: Hodder & Stoughton 1947), 255p.*
SPAIGHT, James M
Blockade by air: the campaign against Axis shipping *(London: Bles 1942), 159p.*
[*see also* CONVOYS]

BOMB DISPOSAL

HAARER, Alec E
A cold-blooded business *(London: Staples 1958), ix, 10–208p.*
HARTLEY, Arthur B
Unexploded bomb: a history of bomb disposal *(London: Cassell 1958), xv, 272p.*
TURNER, John F
Highly explosive: the exploits of Major 'Bill' Hartley, M.B.E., G.M., of Bomb Disposal *(London: Harrap 1961), x, 208p.*

BOMBERS

AYLING, Keith
Bombardment aviation *(Harrisburg, Pa: Military Service 1944), 234p.*
Bombers *(New York: Crowell 1944), 194p.*

BARKER, Ralph
The ship busters: the story of the R.A.F. torpedo bombers *(London: Chatto & Windus 1957), 272p.*
Strike hard - strike sure: epics of the bombers *(London: Chatto & Windus 1963), x, 210p.*
The thousand plan: the story of the first thousand bomber raid on Cologne *(London: Chatto & Windus 1965), ix, 260p.*

BERGER, Carl
B.29: the Superfortress *(New York: Ballantine 1970), 160p, bib.*

BLUE, Allan G
The fortunes of war: the 492nd Bomb Group on daylight operations *(Fallbrook, Calif: Aero 1967), 96p.*

BOWYER, Michael J F
Bombing colours - RAF bombers, their marking and operations, 1937-1973 *(Cambridge: Patrick Stephens 1973), 284p.*

BRADDON, Russell
Cheshire, V.C.: a study of war and peace *(London: Evans 1954), 217p; US title:* New wings for a warrior.

BRICKHILL, Paul
The dam busters *(London: Evans 1951), 269p.*

BURKE, Edmund
Guy Gibson, V.C. *(London: Arco 1961), 128p.*

BUSHBY, John
Gunner's moon: a memoir of the RAF night assault on Germany *(London: Allan 1972), 189p.*

CALMEL, Jean
Night pilot *(London: Kimber 1955), xii, 13-200p.*

CASPER, Jack A
History and personnel, 489th, 340th Bomb Group: combat campaign participated in by the 489th Bomb Squadron (M) *(Middletown, Ohio 1947), 247p.*

CHARLWOOD, Donald E
No moon tonight *(London: Angus & Robertson 1956), 221p.*

CHESHIRE, Leonard
Bomber pilot *(London: Hutchinson 1943), 136p.*

FRANKLAND, Noble
Bomber offensive: the devastation of Europe *(New York: Ballantine 1969), 160p, bib.*
The bombing offensive against Germany: outlines and perspectives *(London: Faber & Faber 1965), 3-128p.*

FREEMAN, Roger A
American bombers of World War Two *(Windsor, Berks: Hylton Lacey 1973), vol I.*

GARBETT, Mike *and* GOULDRING, Brian
The Lancaster at war *(London: Allan 1971), 144p.*

GIBSON, Guy
Enemy coast ahead *(London: Joseph 1946), 288p.*

GREEN, William
Famous bombers of the Second World War *(London: Macdonald 1959–60), 2 vols.*

GREY, Charles G
Bombers *(London: Faber 1941), xx, 252p.*

HARRIS, *Sir* Arthur
Bomber offensive *(London: Collins 1947), 288p.*

HENRY, Mike (pseud)
Air gunner *(London: Foulis 1964), 240p.*

HERBERT, Flight Lieutenant (pseud)
L for Lucy *(Edinburgh: Skladneca Ksugarska 1945), 140p.*

HESS, William
P-51 bomber escort *(New York: Ballantine 1971), 160p, bib.*

JABLONSKI, Edward
Flying Fortress: the illustrated biography of the B-17s and the men who flew them *(London: Sidgwick & Jackson 1974), 362p.*

LAMBERMONT, Paul M
Lorraine Squadron *(London: Cassell 1956), xi, 196p.*

LAWRENCE, W J
No. 5 Bomber Group RAF (1939–1945) *(London: Faber 1951), 253p.*

LAY, Beirne
I've had it: the survival of a bomb group commander *(New York: Harper 1945), 141p.*

LIVY-LEVEL, Phillippe *and* REMY (pseud)
The gates burst open *(London: Arco 1955), 192p; later published as:* Bombs away.

LORD, D R
Germany quivers *(London: A VH 1943), 79p.*

McCLENDON, Dennis C
The Lady Be Good: mystery bomber of World War II *(New York: Day 1962), 192p.*

MORRISON, Wilbur H
The incredible 305th: the 'Can do' bombers of World War II *(New York: Duell 1962), 181p.*

POLLARD, Alfred O
Bombers over the Reich *(London: Hutchinson 1942), viii, 9–208p.*

REILLY, Robin
The sixth floor *(London: Frewin 1969), 224p, bib.*

RIVAZ, Richard C
Tail gunner *(London: Jarrolds 1943), 96p.*
Tail gunner takes over *(London: Jarrolds 1945), 112p.*

ROBERTSON, Bruce
Lancaster: the story of a famous bomber *(Los Angeles, Calif: Publications 1964), 216p.*

SANDERS, Bruce
Bombers fly east *(London: Jenkins 1943), 186p.*

SCHUYLER, Keith C
Elusive horizons *(Cranbury, NJ: Barnes 1969), 176p.*

SEAVEN, Michael
Hell and high altitude!: the thoughts, letters and diary notes of a pilot in the Bomber Command, R.A.F. *(London: Methuen 1943), 184p.*

SINCLAIR, William B
The big brothers: the story of the B-29s *(San Antonio, Tex: Naylor 1972), 132p.*

SPOONER, Anthony
In full flight *(London: Macdonald 1965), 272p.*

STEINBECK, John
Bombs away!: the story of a bomber team *(New York: Viking 1942), 5-185p.*

TRIPP, Miles
The eighth passenger: a flight recollection and discovery *(London: Heinemann 1969), xi, 188p.*

TUBBS, Douglas B
Lancaster bomber *(New York: Ballantine 1971), 159p.*

WOOLDRIDGE, John de L
Low attack: the story of two Royal Air Force Squadrons from May 1940 until May 1943 *(London: Sampson Low 1946), 176p.*

[*see also* AIR WARFARE, GERMANY, GERMAN AIR FORCE, RADAR, ROYAL AIR FORCE, US ARMY AIR FORCE]

BORMANN

BORMANN, Martin *and* BORMANN, Gerda
The Bormann letters: the private correspondence between Martin Bormann and his wife from January 1943 to April 1945 *(London: Weidenfeld & Nicolson 1954), xxiii, 200p.*

McGOVERN, James
Martin Bormann *(London: Barker 1968), [9],237p, bib.*

STEVENSON, William
The Bormann brotherhood *(London: Barker 1973), 334p.*

WHITING, Charles
The hunt for Martin Bormann *(New York: Ballantine 1973), 160p.*

BORNEO

COAST, John
Recruit to revolution: adventure and politics in Indonesia *(London: Christophers 1952), 308p.*

DROSTE, Chris B
Till better days *(London: Hurst & Blackett 1946), 104p.*

HARRISSON, Tom
World within: a Borneo story *(London: Cresset 1959), xii, 349p.*

KEITH, Agnes N
Three came home *(London: Joseph 1948), 253p.*

RYAN, Peter
Fear drive my feet *(Sydney: Angus & Robertson 1959), 251p.*

US ARMY. Japan HQ
Borneo operations, 1941-1945 *(Tokyo: Office of Chief of Military History, Department of Army 1957), 101p.*

WALLACE, Walter
Escape from hell: the Sandakan story *(London: Hale 1958), 175p.*

BOY SCOUTS

SAUNDERS, Hilary St G
The left handshake: the Boy Scout movement during the war, 1939-1945 *(London: Collins 1949), 256p.*

BRISTOL

M, V A
The diary of a Bristol woman, 1938-1945 *(Ilfracombe, Devon: Stockwell 1951), 248p.*

MACINNES, Charles M
Bristol at war *(London: Museum 1962), xi, 202p.*

SHIPLEY, Paul (comp)
Bristol siren nights: diaries and stories of the blitzes *(Bristol: Rankin 1943), 72p.*

SHIPLEY, Paul *and* RANKIN, Howard (comps)
Bristol's bombed churches: a descriptive and pictorial record of their histories and destruction *(Bristol: Rankin 1945), 68p.*

UNDERDOWN, Thomas H J
Bristol under blitz: the record of an ancient city and people during the battle of Britain, 1940-1 *(Bristol: Arrowsmith 1942), 48p.*

BRITAIN

AGAR, Herbert
Britain alone, June 1940–June 1941 *(London: Bodley Head 1972), 227p, bib.*

ALLEN, Bruce (pseud) *and* GRAEBNER, Walter (eds)
Their finest hour: the way in the first person *(London: Allen & Unwin 1940), 9–182p.*

ALLINGHAM, Margery
Oaken heart *(London: Joseph 1941), 272p.*

ANDERSON, Verily
Spam tomorrow *(London: Hart-Davis 1956), 264p.*

ANGELL, *Sir* Norman
For what do we fight? *(London: Hamilton 1939), viii, 275p.*

ARBIB, Robert S
Here we are together: the notebook of an American soldier in Britain *(New York: Longmans Green 1946), 211p.*

THE ARCHER (pseud)
England expects . . . clear-thinking and plain-speaking in war *(London: Dakers 1942), 259p.*

ATTLEE, Clement R
War comes to Britain *(London: Gollancz 1940), 256p.*

BALLANTINE, W M
Scotland's record *(Edinburgh: Albyn 1946), 184p.*

BANNING, *Mrs* Margaret
Letters from England, Summer 1942 *(New York: Harper 1943), 315p.*

BILLINGHAM, Elizabeth
America's first two years: the story of American volunteers in Britain, 1939–1941 *(London: Murray 1942), 63p.*

BLACKWOOD, Frances
Mrs. England goes on living *(Toronto: McClelland 1943), 321p.*

BLOOM, Ursula H
War isn't wonderful *(London: Hutchinson 1961), 222p.*

BONNELL, John S
Britons under fire *(New York: Harper 1941), vii, 178p.*

BOTTOME, Phyllis
Formidable to tyrants *(London: Faber 1941), 275p; US title:* Mansion House of liberty.

BRITAIN under fire *(London: Country Life 1941), 96p.*

BRITISH people at war *(London: Odhams 1944), 255p.*

BRITTAIN, *Sir* Harry E
Come the three corners: achievements of the Empire overseas since war began *(London: Hutchinson 1940), 9-222p.*

BRITTAIN, Vera
England's hour *(London: Macmillan 1941), xvi, 301p.*

CALDER, Angus
The people's war: Britain 1939-45 *(London: Cape 1969), 656p, bib.*

CARTER, Ernestine (ed)
Grim glory: pictures of Britain under fire *(London: Lund 1941), 68p; US title:* Bloody but unbowed.

CASSANDRA (pseud)
The English at war *(London: Secker & Warburg 1941), 127p.*

CATO (pseud)
Guilty men *(New York: Stokes 194-), xvi, 144p.*

COBB, Ivor G
Journal of the war years . . . and one year later, including the unavoidable subject, by George Bernard Shaw *(Worcester: Littlebury 1948), 2 vols.*

COLE, George D H *and others*
Victory or vested interest? *(London: Routledge 1942), vii, 97p.*

COLLIER, Basil
The defence of the United Kingdom *(London: HMSO 1957), xix, 557p.*

CRISP, Dorothy
The dominance of England *(London: Holborn 1960), 299p.*
England's purpose *(London: Rich & Cowan 1941), vii, 9-191p.*

CUNNINGHAM-REID, Alec S
Besides Churchill - who? *(London: W. H. Allen 1941), 128p.*

DAVIES, David D
Foundations of victory *(London: Collins 1941), 192p.*

DIMBLEBY, Richard
The waiting year *(London: Hodder & Stoughton 1945), 186p.*

DOVIE, Vera
The daughters of Britain *(Oxford: Ronald 1950), 159p.*

DRAWBELL, James W
All change here *(London: Hutchinson 1943), 239p.*
Night and day *(London: Hutchinson 1945), 272p.*
Dorothy Thompson's England journey: the record of an Anglo-American partnership *(London: Collins 1942), 256p.*

DRUMMOND, *Mrs* Ruth
A woman faces war *(New York: Kinsey 1940), 183p.*

DUTT, Rajani P
Britain in the world front *(London: Lawrence & Wishart 1942), 218p.*

ELLIOT, Walter C
Long distance *(London: Constable 1943), xiii, 216p.*

ELLIOTT, William Y *and* HALL, H D (eds)
The British Commonwealth at war *(New York: Knopf 1943), xiv, 516p.*

ELTON, Godfrey E, *1st baron Elton*
A notebook in wartime *(London: Collins 1941), 239p.*
Saint George or the dragon: towards a Christian democracy *(London: Collins 1942), 254p.*

THE ENGLISHMAN (pseud)
War letters to America *(London: Jarrolds 1940), 285p.*

EVANS, Trevor
Strange fighters, we British! *(London: Hale 1941), ix, 190p.*

EYLES, Margaret L
For my enemy daughter *(London: Gollancz 1941), 246p.*

FAIRFAX, Ernest
Calling all arms: the story of how a loyal company of British men and women lived through six historic years *(London: Hutchinson 1945), 159p.*

FORBES-ROBERTSON, Diana *and* STRAUS, R W (eds)
War letters from Britain *(New York: Putnam 1941), ix, 240p.*

FOREVER England: the battle for Britain and the men who fight it *(London: Collins 1941), 256p.*

FREEMAN, Robert M
Pepys and wife go to it *(London: Hale 1941), 302p.*

FYFE, Henry H
Britain's war-time revolution *(London: Gollancz 1944), 248p.*
But for Britain: the story of an unforgettable year *(London: Macdonald 1943), v, 7-158p.*

GEE, Herbert L
Wartime pilgrimage: some account of a hopeful journey *(London: Epworth 1943), 144p.*

GRANT, Douglas
The fuel of the fire *(London: Cresset 1950), 236p.*

GRAVES, Charles
Drive for freedom: how Britain equipped her fighting services, speedily made good her losses after Dunkirk, and achieved astonishing new records in production for victory *(London: Hodder & Stoughton 1945), 135p.*

GREAT BRITAIN. British Information Services
Britain against Germany: a record in pictures *(New York: British Information Services 1945), 127p.*

GREENWOOD, Arthur
Why we fight: labour's case *(London: Routledge 1940), 9-221p.*

GRETTON, George H
Victory begins at home: a programme of minimum war aims *(London: Allen & Unwin 1941), xxvi, 29-183p.*

HARRISSON, Tom *and* MADGE, Charles (eds)
War begins at home by Mass Observation *(London: Chatto & Windus 1940), 434p.*

HODSON, James L
Home front [1942-1943] *(London: Gollancz 1944), 320p.*

HOLLIS, Christopher
Our case [what we are fighting for - and why] *(London: Longmans Green 1939), 63p.*

INGERSOLL, Ralph
Report on England, November 1940 *(London: Lane 1941), 247p.*

JOSEPH, Michael
The sword in the scabbard *(London: Joseph 1942), 224p.*

KENDALL, Alan
Their finest hour: an evocative memoir of the British people in wartime, 1939-1945 *(London: Wayland 1972), 192p, bib.*

KENNEDY, John F
Why England slept *(London: Hutchinson 1940), 256p.*

KLEMMER, Harvey
They'll never quit: an American tribute to the people of Britain *(London: Davies 1941), xii, 224p.*

KNOX, Collie
Heroes all *(London: Hodder & Stoughton 1941), 319p.*

KRABBE, Henning (ed)
Britain at war: great descriptions and speeches from the Second World War *(Copenhagen: Gyldenal 1946), 288p.*

LAIRD, Stephen *and* GRAEBNER, Walter
Hitler's Reich and Churchill's Britain: a conversation *(London: Batsford 1942), viii, 116p; US title:* Conversation in London.

LEE, Jennie
This great journey *(New York: Farrar 1942), xxii, 298p; UK title:* Tomorrow is a new day.

LEVY, Arnold
This I recall, 1939-1945 *(London: St Catherine 1946), 311p.*

LONGMATE, Norman
How we lived then: a history of everyday life during the Second World War *(London: Hutchinson 1971), xv, 568p.*

MACALPIN, Michael
Mr. Churchill's socialists: the evidence and some conclusions *(London: Lawrence & Wishart 1941), xi, 13-185p.*

MCDONALD, Walter R
By bomber to Britain *(Brisbane: Telegraph News 1944), 190p.*

MACQUARRIE, Hector
Front to back *(London: Cape 1941), 7-286p.*

MACRAE, Robert S
Winston Churchill's toyshop *(Kineton, Warwicks: Roundwood 1971), 228p.*

MEE, Arthur
Nineteen-forty, our finest hour *(London: Hodder & Stoughton 1941), viii, 9-218p.*

MENZIES, Robert G
To the people of Britain at war *(London: Longmans Green 1941), 95p; US title:* People's war.

MICHIE, Allan A *and* GRAEBNER, Walter (eds)
Their finest hour: the war in the first person *(London: Allen & Unwin 1940), 9-182p.*

MOREHOUSE, Clifford P
Wartime pilgrimage: an American churchman's view of Britain in 1942 *(New York: Morehouse 1942), 7-237p.*

MORRISON, Herbert S
Looking ahead *(London: Hodder & Stoughton 1943), 247p.*

MORTON, Henry C V
I saw two Englands: the record of a journey before the war and after the outbreak of war, in the year 1939 *(London: Methuen 1942), vii, 296p.*

NEVINS, Allan
This is England today *(New York: Scribner 1941), x, 164p.*

NEWMAN, Bernard
British journey *(London: Hale 1945), 336p.*

NEWNES, George, Ltd
Our finest years: a 25th anniversary pictorial presentation of the Second World War (1939-1945), *(London: Newnes 1964), 100p.*

OLIVIER, Edith
Night thoughts of a country landlady: being the pacific experiences of Emma Nightingale in time of war *(London: Batsford 1944), ix, 86p.*

OURSELVES in wartime: an illustrated survey of the Home Front in the Second World War *(London: Odhams 1944), 256p.*

PANTER-DOWNES, Mollie
A letter from England *(Boston, Mass: Little, Brown 1940), 259p.*

PELLING, Henry
Britain and the Second World War *(London: Collins 1970), 352p, bib.*

POPE-HENNESSEY, Ladislaus H R
Can Britain attack? *(London: Collins 1941), 96p.*

PRIESTLEY, John B
Britain at war *(New York: Harper 1942), 15–118p.*
Britain speaks *(New York: Harper 1940), vii, 263p.*
Out of the people *(London: Collins & Heinemann 1941), 127p.*

PUDNEY, John
Who only England know: log of a war-time journey of unintentional discovery of fellow-countrymen *(London: Lane 1943), 160p.*

REED, Douglas
All our tomorrows *(London: Cape 1942), 336p.*
Lest we regret *(London: Cape 1943), 7–337p.*
Prophet at home *(London: Cape 1941), 414p.*

REYNOLDS, Quentin J
The wounded don't cry *(London: Cassell 1941), 7–253p.*

ROBERTSON, Ben
I saw England *(London: Jarrolds 1941), 213p.*

THE ROYAL family in wartime *(London: Odhams 1945), 128p.*

ROYDE-SMITH, Naomi G
Outside information: being a diary of rumours, together with letters from others and some account of events in the life of an unofficial person in London and Winchester during the months of Sept. and Oct. 1940 *(London: Macmillan 1941), vii, 190p.*

SAVA, George (pseud)
A link of two hearts *(London: Faber 1946), 229p.*

SCHOENFELD, Maxwell P
The war ministry of Winston Churchill *(Ames, Iowa: Iowa State UP 1972), 283p.*

SPENDER, Stephen
Citizens in war, and after *(London: Harrap 1945), 112p.*

STEDRY, Vladimir
Until our summer comes *(London: Allen & Unwin 1945), 98p.*

STRACHEY, Amy
These two strange years: letters from England, Oct. 1939–Sept. 1941 *(London: Oxford UP 1942), 54p.*

STREET, Arthur G
Hitler's whistle *(London: Eyre & Spottiswoode 1943), 296p.*

STRUTHER, Jan (pseud)
Women of Britain: letters from England *(New York: Harcourt 1941), 334p.*

TANGYE, Derek (ed)
Went the day well . . . *(London: Harrap 1942), 240p.*

THANE, Elswyth
England was an island once *(New York: Harcourt 1940), 324p.*

TITMUSS, Richard M
Problems of social policy *(London: HMSO 1950), 596p.*

TOMLINSON, Henry M
The turn of the tide *(London: Hodder & Stoughton 1945), 179p.*

TURNER, Ernest S
The phoney war on the home front *(London: Joseph 1961), 311p.*

VARNEY, Joyce J
A Welsh story *(Indianapolis, Ind: Bobbs-Merrill 1965), 313p.*

WADGE, D Collett
Women in uniform *(London: Sampson Low 1946), 386p.*

WAKEHURST, John de V L, *2nd baron Wakehurst*
Our second chance *(London: Angus & Robertson 1944), 115p.*

WANLESS, Alexander (comp)
British people at war, 1939–1945; compiled from the daily press *(Cupar, Fife: Innes 1956),* [5], *466p.*

WARD, Alfred C
A literary journey through wartime Britain *(Toronto: Oxford UP 1943), 95p.*

WERNER, Jack
We laughed at Boney (or We've been through it all before) *(London: W H Allen 1943), viii, 133p.*

WESTERBY, Robert
A voice from England *(New York: Duell 1940), 156p.*

WILSON, Norman S
A united people goes to war *(London: Hodder & Stoughton 1939), 120p; US title:* Britain goes to war.

WYLIE, Ida A R
Flight to England *(New York: Random House 1943), 9–192p.*
[*see also* ADDRESSES AND SPEECHES]

BRITISH ARMY (general)

BARCLAY, Cyril N
On their shoulders: British generalship in the lean years, 1939-1942 *(London: Faber 1964), 184p.*

BRIANT, Keith
Fighting with the Guards *(London: Evans [1958]), xii, 13-224p, bib.*

CASPER, Bernard M
With the Jewish brigade *(London: Goldston 1947), 128p.*

CHARTERIS, John
The British Army today *(New York: British Information Service 1945), 61p.*

DE GUINGAND, *Sir* Francis
Generals at war *(London: Hodder & Stoughton [1964]), 256p.*

FIRBANK, Thomas
I bought a star *(London: Harrap 1951), 240p.*

GOLDING, Claud
Footslogging it to Berlin: being a record of the valour of British Infantrymen in the present war *(London: Blandford 1944), 128p.*

GUN BUSTER (pseud)
Zero hours *(London: Hodder & Stoughton 1942), 177p.*

GWYNNE-BROWNE, Arthur
F.S.P.: an N.C.O.'s description of his and others' first six months of war, Jan. 1st-June 1st, 1940 *(London: Chatto & Windus 1942), 159p.*

HAY, Ian (pseud)
Arms and the men *(London: HMSO 1950), 330p.*

HISLOP, John
Anything but a soldier *(London: Joseph 1965), 189p.*

HUSTON, James A
Biography of a battalion: being the life and times of an Infantry Battalion in Europe in World War II *(Gering, Neb: Courier 1950), xiii, 306p.*

INFANTRY Officer: a personal record *(London: Batsford 1943), 80p.*

KERSH, Gerald
Clean, bright and slightly oiled *(London: Heinemann 1946), 140p.*

MELLOR, Anthony H S
Machine gunner *(London: Hutchinson 1944), 127p.*

REID, Miles
Last on the list *(London: Cooper 1974), xii, 228p.*

SELLWOOD, A V
The Saturday night soldiers *(London: Wolf 1966), 207p.*
SHEPPARD, Eric W *and* YEATS-BROWN, Francis C C
The Army: a complete record in text and pictures *(London: Hutchinson 1941–7), 5 vols.*
TOLLEMACHE, Edward D H (comp)
The British Army at war *(London: Murray 1941), 72p; later published as:* The turning tide.
WATNEY, John
He also served *(London: Hamilton 1971), 165p.*
WATTS, Stephen
Moonlight on a lake in Bond Street *(London: Bodley Head 1961), 207p.*
YEATS-BROWN, Francis C C
The Army from September 1939 to December 1940 *(London: Hutchinson 1941), 312p.*

(Eighth Army)
CRAWFORD, Robert J
I was an Eighth Army soldier *(London: Gollancz 1944), 86p.*
RAINIER, Peter W
Pipeline to battle: an engineer's adventures with the Eighth Army *(London: Heinemann 1944), vi, 238p.*
SAMWELL, H P
An infantry officer with the Eighth Army *(Edinburgh: Blackwood 1945), 208p.*
TUCKER, *Sir* Francis I S
Approach to battle: a commentary; Eighth Army, November 1941 to May 1943 *(London: Cassell 1963), 410p.*
[*see also* EL ALAMEIN, ITALIAN CAMPAIGN, NORTH AFRICA]

(14th Army)
KARAKA, Dosoo F
With the 14th Army *(London: Crisp 1945), 85p.*
[*see also* BURMA]

(21st Army Group)
DARBY, Hugh *and* CUNLIFFE, Marcus
A short story of 21st Army Group *(Aldershot, Hants: Gale & Polden 1949), xi, 144p.*
NORTH, John
North-West Europe 1944–5: the achievement of the 21st Army Group *(London: HMSO 1953), [10], 270p.*

(Divisions)

4th Division WILLIAMSON, Hugh
The Fourth Division, 1939 to 1945 *(London: Newman Neame 1951), xxxi, 348p.*

15th Division MARTIN, Hugh C
The history of the Fifteenth Scottish Division, 1939–1945 *(Edinburgh: Blackwood 1948), 383p.*
WOOLLCOMBE, Robert
Lion rampant *(London: Chatto & Windus 1955), 223p.*

43rd Division ESSAME, Hubert (comp)
The 43rd Wessex Division at war, 1944–1945 *(London: Clowes 1952), xi, 292p.*

50th Division CLAY, Ewart W
The path of the 50th: the story of the 50th (Northumbrian) Division in the Second World War, 1939–1945 *(Aldershot, Hants: Gale & Polden 1950), xiii, 327p.*

51st Division BORTHWICK, James
51st Highland Division in North Africa and Sicily *(Glasgow: Mackenzie 1945), 63p.*
SALMOND, James B
The history of the 51st Highland Division, 1939–1945 *(Edinburgh: Blackwood 1953), xiv, 287p.*

52nd Division BLAKE, George
Mountain and flood: the history of the 52nd (Lowland) Division, 1939–1946 *(Glasgow: Jackson 1950), xx, 265p.*

53rd Division BARCLAY, Cyril N
The history of the 53rd (Welsh) Division in the Second World War *(London: Clowes 1956), xvii, 223p.*

59th Division KNIGHT, Peter
The 59th Division: its history *(London: Muller 1954),* [*13*], *110p.*

78th Division RAY, Cyril
Algiers to Austria: a history of the 78 Division in the Second World War *(London: Eyre & Spottiswoode 1952), xxi, 253p.*
[*see also* ARMOURED FORCES]

(Corps)

Royal Armoured Corps [*see* ARMOURED FORCES]

Royal Army Medical Corps COTTERELL, Anthony
R.A.M.C. *(London: Hutchinson 1943), 116p.*

Royal Army Ordnance Corps FERNYHOUGH, Alan H
History of the Royal Army Ordnance Corps, 1920–1945 *(London: Director of Ordnance Services* [*1967*]*), xvi, 492p.*

Royal Army Service Corps LANGSTAFF, C K
Diary of a driver with the R.A.S.C., in Britain and France, 1939–1940 *(London: Epworth 1943), 59p.*
NELSON, Michael
Captain Blossom: recollections of his struggle against the Third Reich and the British Army *(London: Cooper, 1973),* [7], *174p.*
THE STORY of the Royal Army Service Corps, 1939–1945 *(London: Bell 1955), 720p.*
Royal Army Veterinary Corps CLABBY, J
The history of the Royal Army Veterinary Corps, 1919–1961 *(London: J. A. Allen 1963), 244p.*
Royal Artillery [*see* ARTILLERY]
Royal Corps of Electrical and Mechanical Engineers KENNETT, Brian B *and* TATMAN, J A (comps)
Craftsman of the Army: the story of the Royal Electrical and Mechanical Engineers *(London: Cooper 1970), xiii, 425p.*
Royal Corps of Military Police CROZIER, Stephen F
The history of the Corps of Royal Military Police *(Aldershot, Hants: Gale & Polden 1951), xvi, 224p.*
HEARN, Cyril V
Desert assignment *(London: Hale 1963), 192p.*
Royal Corps of Signals HARRIS, Lionel H
Signal venture *(Aldershot, Hants: Gale & Polden 1951), 278p.*
NALDER, Reginald F H
The history of the British Army Signals in the Second World War *(Aldershot, Hants: Royal Signals Institution 1953), xii, 377p.*
Royal Engineers ARMSTRONG, Anthony (pseud)
Sappers at war *(Aldershot, Hants: Gale & Polden 1949), 98p.*
MORRIS, Arthur H M (ed)
The 'Four-Two': scraps from the history of the 42nd Field Company, R.E. *(Aldershot, Hants: Gale & Polden 1952), xii, 62p.*
PACKENHAM-WALSH, R P
History of the Corps of Royal Engineers: *(Chatham, Kent: Institution of Royal Engineers 1958), vol. 8:* 1938–1948; campaigns in France and Belgium, 1939–40; Norway; Middle East; East Africa; Western Desert; North West Africa; and activities in U.K. *xv, 488p.*
Vol. 9: 1938–1948; campaigns in Sicily and Italy; the war against Japan; North West Europe, 1944–45 *xviii, 644p.*
Royal Pioneer Corps PERLES, Alfred
Alien corn *(London: Allen & Unwin 1944), 9–243p.*

RHODES-WOOD, E H
A war history of the Royal Pioneer Corps, 1939–1945 *(Aldershot, Hants: Gale & Polden 1960), xvi, 368p.*

(Regiments)

Argyll and Sutherland Highlanders ANDERSON, Robert C B
History of the Argyll and Sutherland Highlanders, Ist Battalion *(Stirling: Hughes 1956), vol. 2: 1939–54, xv, 304p.*

BARKER, Frank R P
History of the Argyll and Sutherland Highlanders, 9th Battalion, 54th Light AA Regiment, 1939–45 *(London: Nelson 1950), 131p.*

CAMERON, Ian C
History of the Argyll and Sutherland Highlanders, 7th Battalion from El Alamein to Germany *(London: Nelson 1946), 242p.*

FLOWER, Desmond
History of the Argyll and Sutherland Highlanders, 5th Battalion, 91st Anti-Tank Regiment, 1939–45 *(London: Nelson 1950), xii, 395p.*

GRAHAM, Frederick C C
History of the Argyll and Sutherland Highlanders, 1st Battalion (Princess Louise's), 1939–1945 *(London: Nelson 1948), 247p.*

MCELWEE, William L
History of the Argyll and Sutherland Highlanders, 2nd Battalion, reconstituted, European Campaign, 1944–45 *(London: Nelson 1949), 212p.*

MALCOLM, Alec D
History of the Argyll and Sutherland Highlanders, 8th Battalion, 1939–47 *(London: Nelson 1949), 284p.*

PAUL, William P
History of the Argyll and Sutherland Highlanders, 6th Battalion, 93rd Anti-Tank Regiment, R.A. *(London: Nelson 1949), 134p.*

SUTHERLAND, Douglas
The Argyll and Sutherland Highlanders (the 91st and 93rd Highlanders) *(London: Cooper 1969), xi, 127p.*

The Bedfordshire and Hertfordshire Regiment PETERS, G W N
The Bedfordshire and Hertfordshire Regiment (the 16th Regiment of Foot) *(London: Cooper 1970), 120p.*

The Black Watch FERGUSSON, Bernard
The Black Watch and the King's enemies *(London: Collins 1950), 384p.*

MADDEN, B J G
The history of the 6th Battalion, the Black Watch (Royal Highland Regiment) 1939–1945 *(Perth, Scot: Leslie 1948), xvi, 143p.*

The Border Regiment SHEARS, Philip J
The story of the Border Regiment, 1939–1945 *(London: Nisbet 1948), xv, 184p.*

The Cameronians BARCLAY, Cyril N
The history of the Cameronians (Scottish Rifles) *(London: Sifton 1948), vol. iii: 1933–46, 280p.*

The Coldstream Guards HOWARD, Michael *and* SPARROW, John
The Coldstream Guards, 1920–1946 *(London: Oxford UP 1951), xvii, 593p.*

PEREIRA, Jocelyn
A distant drum: war memories of the Intelligence Officer of the 5th Battalion Coldstream Guards, 1944–45 *(Aldershot, Hants: Gale & Polden 1948), xiii, 213p.*

QUILTER, David C (comp)
No dishonourable name: the 2nd and 3rd Battalions, Coldstream Guards, 1939–1946 *(London: Clowes 1947), [4], 334p.*

The County of London Yeomanry GRAHAM, Andrew
Sharpshooters at war: the 3rd, 4th and the 3rd/4th County of London Yeomanry, 1939–1945 *(London: Sharpshooters Regimental Association 1964), xvii, 252p.*

The Derbyshire Yeomanry JONES, Arthur J
The Second Derbyshire Yeomanry: an account of the Regiment during World War, 1939–45 *(Bristol: White Swan 1949), 134p.*

The Dorsetshire Regiment BREDIN, A E C
Three assault landings: the story of the 1st Battalion, The Dorsetshire Regiment in Sicily, Italy and North West Europe *(Aldershot, Hants: Gale & Polden 1946), 172p.*

WATKINS, G J B
From Normandy to the Weser: the war history of the Fourth Battalion, The Dorset Regiment *(Dorchester: Dorset 1956). unp.*

WHITE, Oliver G W
Straight on for Tokyo: the war history of the 2nd Battalion the Dorsetshire Regiment, 54th Foot, 1939–1948 *(Aldershot, Hants: Gale & Polden 1948), 425p.*

The Durham Light Infantry LEWIS, Peter J (comp)
8th Battalion; the Durham Light Infantry, 1939–1945 *(Newcastle-upon-Tyne: Bealls 1949), 319p.*

RISSIK, David
The D.L.I. at war: the history of the Durham Light Infantry, 1939–1945 *(Brancepeth Castle, Durham: Durham Light Infantry [1953]), xvi, 352p.*

The Duke of Cornwall's Light Infantry GODFREY, Ernest G
The history of the Duke of Cornwall's Light Infantry, 1939–45 *(Aldershot, Hants: Wellington 1966), xiii, 437p.*

The Duke of Wellington's Regiment BARCLAY, Cyril N (ed)
The history of the Duke of Wellington's Regiment, 1919–1952 *(London: Clowes 1953), xxi, 387p.*

East Lancashire Regiment
History of the East Lancashire Regiment in the war, 1939–1945 *(Manchester: Rawson 1953), xv, 331p.*

East Surrey Regiment DANIELL, David S
History of the East Surrey Regiment *(London: Benn 1957), vol. 4: 1920–52, 283p.*

The Essex Regiment MARTIN, Thomas A
The Essex Regiment, 1929–1950 *(Warley Barracks, Brentwood: Essex Reg Association 1952), xx, 668p.*

The Fife and Forfar Yeomanry SELLAR, Robert J B
The Fife and Forfar Yeomanry, 1919–1956 *(Edinburgh: Blackwood [1961]), xiii, 288p.*

GHQ Liaison Regiment HILLS, Reginald J T
Phantom was there *(London: Arnold 1951), 344p.*

The Gordon Highlanders LINDSAY, *Sir* Martin
So few got through: the Gordon Highlanders in the 51st Highland Division from the Normandy beachhead to the Baltic *(London: Collins 1946), 256p.*

MILES, Wilfrid
The life of a Regiment: the Gordon Highlanders *(Aberdeen: Aberdeen UP 1961), vol. 5: 1919–45, xv, 422p.*

The Green Howards SYNGE, William A T
The story of the Green Howards, 1939–1945 *(Richmond, Yorks: Green Howards 1952), xxviii, 428p.*

The Grenadier Guards
The Grenadier Guards, 1939–1945 *(Aldershot, Hants: Gale & Polden 1946), 79p.*

FORBES, Patrick *and* NICOLSON, Nigel
The Grenadier Guards in the war of 1939–45 *(Aldershot, Hants: Gale & Polden 1949), 2 vols.*

The Household Cavalry ORDE, Roden P G
The Household Cavalry at war: Second Household Cavalry Regiment *(Aldershot, Hants: Gale & Polden 1953), xxi, 624p.*

WYNDHAM, Humphrey
The Household Cavalry at war: First Household Cavalry Regiment *(Aldershot, Hants: Gale & Polden 1952), xiii, 189p.*

The Honourable Artillery Company JOHNSON, Roy F
Regimental fire: the Honourable Artillery Company in World War 2, 1939–1945 *(London: HAC [1958]), xx, 440p.*

XIth Hussars CLARKE, Dudley
The Eleventh at war: being the story of the XIth Hussars (Prince Albert's Own) through the years 1934–1945 *(London: Joseph 1952), 504p.*

The Irish Guards FITZGERALD, D J L
History of the Irish Guards in the Second World War *(Aldershot, Hants: Gale & Polden 1949), 624p.*

King Edward VII's Own Goorkha Rifles STEVENS, George R
History of the 2nd King Edward VII's Own Goorkha Rifles (The Sirmoor Rifles) *(Aldershot, Hants: Gale & Polden 1952), vol. 3: 1921–48, xv, 322p.*

King George V's Own Lancers POCOCK, John G
The spirit of a regiment: being the history of the 19th King George's Own Lancers, 1921–1947 *(Aldershot, Hants: Gale & Polden 1962), xvi, 114p.*

The King's Dragoon Guards MCCORQUODALE, D *and others*
History of the King's Dragoon Guards, 1938–1945 *(Glasgow: McCorquodale [1950]), xv, 403p.*

The King's Own Scottish Borderers GUNNING, Hugh
Borderers in battle: the war story of the King's Own Scottish Borderers, 1939–1945 *(Berwick-on-Tweed, North: Martin 1948), 287p.*

The King's Own Yorkshire Light Infantry ELLENBERGER, G F
History of the King's Own Yorkshire Light Infantry, 1939–1948 *(Aldershot, Hants: Gale & Polden 1961), xvi, 184p.*

HINGSTON, Walter G
Never give up: the history of the King's Own Yorkshire Light Infantry, 1919–1942 *(London 1950), 243p.*

King's Royal Irish Hussars FITZROY, Olivia
Men of valour: the third volume of the history of the VIII King's Royal Irish Hussars, 1927–1958 *(Gyrn Castle, Llanasa, Lldywell, Flints: Sir Geoffrey V. Bates 1961), xix, 375p.*

The King's Royal Rifle Corps WAKE, *Sir* Hereward *and* DEEDES, W F (eds)
Swift and bold: the story of the King's Royal Rifle Corps in the Second World War, 1939–1945 *(Aldershot, Hants: Gale & Polden 1949), 416p.*

17/21st Lancers FFRENCH BLAKE, R L V
A history of the 17/21st Lancers, 1922–1959 *(London: Macmillan 1962), 283p.*

The Leicestershire Yeomanry BOUSKELL-WADE, George C
There is honour likewise . . .: the story of 154 (Leicestershire Yeomanry) Field Regiment *(Leicester: Backus 1948), 138p.*

The London Rifle Brigade DURAND, Algernon T M *and* HASTINGS, Robert H W
The London Rifle Brigade, 1919–1950 *(Aldershot, Hants: Gale & Polden 1952), xi, 320p.*

The London Scottish BARCLAY, Cyril N (ed)
The London Scottish in the Second World War, 1939–1945 *(London: Clowes 1952), xix, 459p.*

The Loyal Regiment DEAN, Charles G T
The Loyal Regiment (North Lancashire), 1919–1953 *(Fulwood Barracks, Preston, Lancs: Loyal Regiment 1955), 329p.*

The Manchester Regiment BELL, Archibald C
History of the Manchester Regiment: First and Second Battalions, 1922–1948 *(Altrincham, Chesh: Sherratt 1954), vol. 3, xx, 554p.*

The Northamptonshire Regiment JERVOIS, Wilfrid J
The history of the Northamptonshire Regiment, 1934–1948 *(Northampton: Northamptonshire Regiment 1953), xxiii, 448p.*

The Northumberland Hussars Yeomanry BRIGHT, Joan
History of the Northumberland Hussars Yeomanry, 1924–1949 *(Newcastle-upon-Tyne: Mawson, Swan & Morgan 1949), 406p.*

The Oxfordshire & Buckinghamshire Light Infantry NEVILLE, *Sir* James E H (ed)
The Oxfordshire & Buckinghamshire Light Infantry Chronicle: the record of the 43rd, 52nd, 4th, 5th, 6th, 7th, 70th, 1st and 2nd Buckinghamshire Battalions, the Regimental Depot and Regimental Training Centre in the Second German War *(Aldershot, Hants: Gale & Polden 1950–4), vol. 2: June 1940–June 1942; vol. 3: July 1942–May 1944; vol. 4: June 1944–December 1945.*

Princess Louise's Kensington Regiment
'The Kensingtons': Princess Louise's Kensington Regiment, Second World War *(London: Kensington Old Comrades Association [1952]), 392p.*

Queen Alexandra's Own Gurkha Rifles BARCLAY, Cyril N (ed)
The Regimental history of the 3rd Queen Alexandra's Own Gurkha Rifles *(London: Clowes 1953), vol. 2: 1927–47, xx, 316p.*

The Queen's Bays BEDDINGTON, William R
A history of the Queen's Bays (the 2nd Dragoon Guards), 1929–1945 *(Winchester, Hants: Warren 1954), [16], 271p.*

The Queen's Own Cameron Highlanders
Historical records of the Queen's Own Cameron Highlanders *(Edinburgh: Blackwood [1953]), vols 5 and 6: 1932–48.*

The Queen's Own Hussars DAVY, George M O
The Seventh and three enemies: the story of World War II and the 7th Queen's Own Hussars *(Cambridge: Heffer 1953), xiv, 468p.*

The Queen's Own Royal West Kent Regiment CHAPLIN, Howard D
The Queen's Own Royal West Kent Regiment, 1920–1950 *(London: Joseph 1954), 510p*
CLARKE, Edward B *and* TILLOTT, Alan T
From Kent to Kohima: being the history of the 4th Battalion The Queen's Own Royal West Kent Regiment (T.A.), 1939–1947 *(Aldershot, Hants: Gale & Polden 1951), xii, 259p.*

The Queen's Own Worcester Hussars GUTTERY, David R
The Queen's Own Worcester Hussars, 1922–1956 *(Stourbridge, Worcs: Mark & Moody 1958), [9], 159p.*

The Queen's Royal Lancers BARCLAY, Cyril N
History of the 16/5th The Queen's Royal Lancers, 1925–1961 *(Aldershot, Hants: Gale & Polden 1963), [15], 235p.*
BRIGHT, Joan (ed)
The Ninth Queen's Royal Lancers, 1936–1945: the story of an Armoured Regiment in battle *(Aldershot, Hants: Gale & Polden 1951), xxxi, 359p.*

The Queen's Royal Regiment BULLEN, Roy E
History of the 2/7th Battalion, The Queen's Royal Regiment, 1939–1946 *(London: Neale [1958]), xi, 161p.*
FOSTER, R C G (comp)
History of the Queen's Royal Regiment *(Aldershot, Hants: Gale & Polden 1953), vol. 8: 1924–48, xix, 595p.*

Reconnaissance Regiment TAYLOR, Jeremy L
This band of brothers: a history of the Reconnaissance Corps of the British Army *(Bristol: White Swan 1947), 271p.*
Record of a reconnaissance regiment: a history of the 43rd Reconnaissance Regiment (The Gloucester Regiment), 1939–1945 *(Bristol: White Swan 1950), 252p.*

The Rifle Brigade HASTINGS, Robin H W
The Rifle Brigade in the Second World War, 1939–1945 *(Aldershot, Hants: Gale & Polden 1950), xx, 475p.*

The Royal Berkshire Regiment BLIGHT, Gordon
The history of the Royal Berkshire Regiment (Princess Charlotte of Wales's), 1920–1947 *(London: Staples 1953), xx, 499p.*

The Royal Dragoons PITT-RIVERS, Julian A
The story of the Royal Dragoons, 1938-1945: being the history of the Royal Dragoons in the campaigns of North Africa, the Middle East, Italy and North West Europe *(London: Clowes [1956]), xv, 160p.*

The Royal Fusiliers PARKINSON, Cyril N
Always a Fusilier: the war history of the Royal Fusiliers (City of London Regiment), 1939-1945 *(London: Sampson Low 1950), xvi, 320p.*

The Royal Gloucestershire Hussars PITMAN, Stuart
Second Royal Gloucestershire Hussars: Libya-Egypt, 1941-1942 *(London: St Catherine 1950), 96p.*

The Royal Hampshire Regiment DANIELL, David S
Regimental history of the Royal Hampshire Regiment *(Aldershot, Hants: Gale & Polden 1955), vol. 3: 1918-54, xiii, 294p.*

The Royal Inniskilling Fusiliers FOX, *Sir* Frank
The Royal Inniskilling Fusiliers in the Second World War: a record of the war as seen by the Royal Inniskilling Fusiliers, three battalions of which served *(Aldershot, Hants: Gale & Polden 1951), xv, 204p.*

The Royal Leicestershire Regiment UNDERHILL, William G (ed)
The Royal Leicestershire Regiment, 17th Foot: a history of the years, 1928-1956 *(South Wigston, Leics: Royal Leicestershire Regiment [1958]), ix, 277p.*

The Royal Lincolnshire Regiment GATES, Lionel C (comp)
The history of the Tenth Foot, 1919-1950; compiled from war diaries, officers narratives and other sources *(Aldershot, Hants: Gale & Polden 1953), xii, 355p.*

The Royal Norfolk Regiment CAREW, Tim
The history of the Royal Norfolk Regiment *(London: Hamilton 1967), 157p.*

KEMP, Peter K
History of the Royal Norfolk Regiment, 1919-1951 *(Norwich: Regimental Association of the Royal Norfolk Regiment 1953), vol. 3, [2], 192p.*

The Royal Northumberland Fusiliers BARCLAY, Cyril N
The history of the Royal Northumberland Fusiliers in the Second World War *(London: Clowes 1952), xxii, 241p.*

The Royal Parachute Regiment [*see* AIRBORNE FORCES]

The Royal Scots (The Royal Regiment) MUIR, Augustus
The First of Foot: the history of the Royal Scots (The Royal Regiment) *(Edinburgh: Royal Scots History Committee 1961), xvi, 504p.*

The Royal Scots Fusiliers KEMP, James C
The history of the Royal Scots Fusiliers, 1919–1959 *(Glasgow: House of Grant [1963]), xvi, 423p.*

The Royal Scots Greys CARVER, Richard M P
Second to none: the Royal Scots Greys, 1919–1945 *(Glasgow: McCorquodale [1954]), xvi, 210p.*

The Royal Warwickshire Regiment CUNLIFFE, Marcus
History of the Royal Warwickshire Regiment, 1919–1955 *(London: Clowes [1957]), xi, 200p.*

The Royal Welch Fusiliers KEMP, Peter K *and* GRAVES, John
The red dragon: the story of the Royal Welch Fusiliers, 1919–1945 *(Aldershot, Hants: Gale & Polden 1960), xvi, 414p.*

The Royal Wiltshire Yeomanry PITT, P W
Royal Wilts: the history of the Royal Wiltshire Yeomanry, 1920–1945 *(London: Burrop, Mathieson 1946), 234p.*

The Scots Guards ERSKINE, David H (comp)
The Scots Guards, 1919–1955 *(London: Clowes [1957]), xx, 624p.*

The Scottish Reconnaissance Regiment KEMSLEY, Walter *and* RIESCO, Michael R
The Scottish lion on patrol: being the story of the 15th Scottish Reconnaissance Regiment, 1943–1946 *(Bristol: White Swan 1950), 232p.*

The Sherwood Foresters BARCLAY, Cyril N
The history of the Sherwood Foresters (Nottinghamshire and Derbyshire Regiment), 1919–1957 *(London: Clowes 1959), xvi, 182p.*

The Sherwood Rangers LINDSAY, Thomas M
Sherwood Rangers *(London: Mathieson 1952), [II], 182p.*

The South Lancashire Regiment MULLALY, Brian R
The South Lancashire Regiment; the Prince of Wales's Volunteers *(Bristol: White Swan 1955), 520p.*

The Staffordshire Yeomanry KEMP, Peter K
The Staffordshire Yeomanry (Q.O.R.R.) in the First and Second World Wars, 1914–1918, and 1939–1945 *(Aldershot, Hants: Gale & Polden 1950), xii, 168p.*

The Suffolk Regiment NICHOLSON, Walter N
The Suffolk Regiment, 1928–1946 *(Ipswich: East Anglian Magazine 1948), 374p.*

The Welch Regiment DECOURCY, John
The history of the Welch Regiment, 1919–1951; amplified and enlarged by Major-General C. E. N. Lomax *(Cardiff: Western Mail 1952), 337p.*

The Welsh Guards ELLIS, L F
The Welsh Guards at war *(Aldershot, Hants: Gale & Polden 1946), 386p.*

The West Yorkshire Regiment SANDES, Edward W C
From pyramid to pagoda: the story of the West Yorkshire Regiment (The Prince of Wales's Own) in the war, 1939–45, and afterwards *(York: West Yorkshire Regiment [1952]), xv, 306p.*

The Wiltshire Regiment PARSONS, Anthony D *and others*
The maroon square: a history of the 4th Battalion the Wiltshire Regiment (Duke of Edinburgh's) in North West Europe, 1939–46 *(London: Franey 1955), 231p.*

The Worcestershire Regiment BIRDWOOD, Christopher B B
The Worcestershire Regiment, 1922–1950 *(Aldershot, Hants: Gale & Polden 1952), 302p.*

The York and Lancaster Regiment SHEFFIELD, O F
The York and Lancaster Regiment *(Aldershot, Hants: Gale & Polden 1956), vol 3: 1919–53, [15], 297p.*
[*see also* ARMOURED CORPS]

BRITISH FREE CORPS

SETH, Ronald
Jackals of the Reich: the story of the British Free Corps *(London: New English Library 1972), 170p.*

BURMA

ALLEN, Louis
Sittang; the last battle: the end of the Japanese in Burma, July–August, 1945 *(London: Macdonald 1973), xx, 267p, bib.*

ALLIED FORCES
The campaign in Burma *(London: HMSO 1946), 175p.*
The Wasbies: the story of the Women's Auxiliary Service (Burma) *(London: War Facts [1946]), 79p.*

ANDERS, Leslie
The Ledo road: General Joseph W. Stilwell's highway to China *(Norman, Okl: Oklahoma UP 1965), 255p.*

AYLING, Keith
Old Leatherface of the Flying Tigers: the story of General Chennault *(Indianapolis, Ind: Bobbs-Merrill 1945), 7–274p.*

BAKER, Alan
Merrill's marauders *(New York: Ballantine 1972), 159p.*

BARKER, A J
The march on Delhi *(London: Faber 1963), 3–302p, bib.*

BARNARD, Jack
The Hump!: the greatest untold story of the war *(London: Souvenir 1960), 192p.*
BARRETT, Neil H
Chingpaw *(New York: Vantage 1962), 173p.*
BEAMISH, John
Burma drop *(London: Elek 1958), 223p.*
BELDEN, Jack
Retreat with Stilwell *(London: Cassell 1943), vi, 368p.*
Still time to die *(New York: Harper 1944), 322p.*
BRODRICK, Alan H
Beyond the Burma Road *(London: Hutchinson 1945), 112p.*
BURCHETT, Wilfred G
Bombs over Burma *(London: Wadley & Ginn 1945), 12-260p.*
Trek back from Burma *(Allahabad, India: Kitabistan 1945), 330p.*
Wingate adventure *(Melbourne: Cheshire 1944), 8-185p.*
Wingate's phantom army *(Bombay: Thacker 1944), 233p.*
CALVERT, Michael
Fighting mad *(London: Jarrolds 1964), 224p.*
Prisoners of hope *(London: Cape 1952), 303p.*
CAMPBELL, Arthur
The siege: a story from Kohima *(London: Allen & Unwin 1956), xiv, 15-213p.*
CAREW, Tim
The longest retreat: the Burma campaign, 1942 *(London: Hamilton 1969), xii, 276p, bib.*
CHAPHEKAR, Shankarrao G
A brief study of the Burma campaign, 1943-45 *(Poona, India: Maharashta Militarisation Board 1955), 100p.*
CHRISTIAN, John L
Burma *(London: Paradena, Perkins 1945), 12-176p.*
Burma and the Japanese invader *(Bombay: Thacker 1945), 418p.*
COLLIS, Maurice
Last and first in Burma (1941-1948) *(London: Faber 1956), 303p.*
COOPER, Kenneth W
The little men *(London: Hale 1973), 186p.*
CORPE, Hilda R
Prisoner beyond the Chindwin *(London: Barker 1955), 158p.*
DAVIS, Patrick
A child at arms *(London: Hutchinson 1970), [13], 258p.*
DORN, Frank
Walkout: with Stilwell in Burma *(New York: Crowell 1971), 258p.*

DUPUY, Trevor N
Asiatic land battles: Allied victories in China and Burma *(London: Edmund Ward [1965]), 66p.*

ELDRIDGE, Fred
Wrath in Burma: the uncensored story of General Stilwell and international manoeuvres in the Far East *(New York: Doubleday 1946), 320p.*

EVANS, *Sir* Geoffrey
The Johnnies *(London: Cassell 1964), xiii, 231p.*

EVANS, *Sir* Geoffrey *and* BRETT-JAMES, Antony
Imphal: a flower on lofty heights *(London: Macmillan 1962), xiv, 348p, bib.*

FELLOWES-GORDON, Ian
Amiable assassins: the story of the Kachin guerillas of North Burma *(London: Hale 1957), 159p.*
The battle for Naw Seng's kingdom: General Stilwell's North Burma campaign and its aftermath *(London: Cooper 1971), x, 176p; US title:* The magic war.

FERGUSSON, Bernard
Return to Burma *(London: Collins 1962), 256p.*
The wild green earth *(London: Collins 1946), 254p.*

FRIEND, John
The long trek *(London: Muller [1957]), [3], 187p.*

GEREN, Paul
Burma diary *(New York: Harper 1943), 57p.*

GODDEN, Rumer
Bengal journey: a story of the part played by women in the province, 1939–1945 *(London: Longmans Green 1945), 132p.*

GREAT BRITAIN. Air Ministry
Wings of the Phoenix: the official story of the air war in Burma *(London: HMSO 1949), 143p.*

HALLEY, David
With Wingate in Burma: being the story of the adventures of Sgt. Tony Aubrey of the King's Liverpool Regiment during the 1943 Wingate Expedition into Burma *(London: Hodge 1945), 189p.*

HANLEY, Gerald
Monsoon victory *(London: Collins 1946), 189p.*

HEMINGWAY, Kenneth
Wings over Burma *(London: Quality 1944), 192p.*

HO YUNG-CHI
The big circle *(New York: Exposition 1948), 152p.*

HUNT, Gordon
One more river *(London: Collins 1945), 255p.*

HUNTER, Charles N
Galahad *(San Antonio, Tex: Naylor 1963), 233p.*

INDIA. War Department
On to Rangoon *(Bombay: Claridge 1945), 64p.*

IRVIN, Anthony S
Burmese outpost *(London: Collins 1945), 160p.*

LOWRY, M A
An infantry company in Arakan and Kohima *(Aldershot, Hants: Gale & Polden 1950), xiv, 132p.*

MACHORTON, Ian
Safer than a known way: one man's epic struggle against Japanese and jungle *(London: Odhams 1958), 224p; US title:* The hundred days of Lt. McHorton.

MCKELVIE, Roy
The war in Burma *(London: Methuen 1948), 306p.*

MACKENZIE, K P
Operation Rangoon jail *(London: Johnson 1954), 201p.*

MCLINTOCK, James D
Manipur Road: story of the Mandalay campaign *(Westport, Conn: Associated Booksellers 1959), 158p; UK title:* Road to hell.

MADAN, N N
The Arakan operations, 1942–1945 *(Delhi: Combined Inter-Services Historical Section 1954), 371p.*

MAINS, Tony
The retreat from Burma: an intelligence officer's personal story *(London: Foulsham 1973), 151p.*

MASTERS, John
The road past Mandalay: a personal narrative *(London: Joseph 1961), 344p.*

MATTHEWS, Geoffrey
The re-conquest of Burma, 1943–1945 *(Aldershot, Hants: Gale & Polden 1966), xi, 104p.*

MORRISON, Ian
Grandfather Longlegs: the life and gallant death of Major H. P. Seagrim *(London: Faber 1947), 239p.*

MOUNTBATTEN, Louis, *1st earl Mountbatten of Burma*
Report to the Combined Chiefs of Staff by the Supreme Allied Commander, South-East Asia, 1943–1945 *(London: HMSO 1951), 280p.*

NU, U
Burma under the Japanese *(London: Macmillan 1954), xxviii, 132p.*

OATTS, Lewis B
The jungle in arms *(London: Kimber 1962), 207p.*

OGBURN, Charlton
The marauders *(New York: Harper 1959), 319p, bib.*

OWEN, Frank
The campaign in Burma *(London: HMSO 1946), 175p.*

PAGE, Robert C
Air commander Doc *(New York: Ackerman 1945), 186p.*

PEACOCK, Geraldine
The life of a jungle walla: reminiscences in the life of Lt. Col. E. H. Peacock, D.S.O., M.C. *(Ilfracombe, Devon: Stockwell 1958), 134p.*

PHILLIPS, Cecil E L
The raiders of Arakan *(London: Heinemann 1971), x, 198p, bib.*
Springboard to victory *(London: Heinemann 1966), xiv, 242p.*

RANDOLPH, John H
Marsmen in Burma *(Houston, Tex: Randolph 1946), 229p.*

ROMANUS, Charles F *and* SUNDERLAND, Riley
Time runs out in CBI *(Washington DC: Department of Army 1959), 428p.*

RUSSELL, Stanley F
Muddy exodus: a story of the evacuation of Burma, May 1942 *(London: Epworth 1943), 64p.*

RUSSELL, Wilfrid W
Forgotten skies: the story of the air forces in India and Burma *(London: Hutchinson 1946), 128p.*

SEAGRAVE, Gordon S
Burma surgeon *(New York: Norton 1943), 189p.*
Burma surgeon returns *(New York: Norton 1946), 268p.*

SEARLE, Ronald
Forty drawings *(Cambridge: Cambridge UP 1946), II, 40pl.*

SHORT, Stanley W
On Burma's eastern frontier *(London: Marshall, Morgan & Scott 1945), 144p.*

SINGH, Bishan
Burma retreat *(Kanpur, India: Vasuder Sing 1949), 100p.*

SLIM, William, *1st viscount Slim*
Defeat into victory *(London: Cassell, unabridged ed. 1972), 576p.*

SMYTH, *Sir* John
Before the dawn: a story of two historic retreats. Burma and Dunkirk *(London: Cassell 1957), xv, 220p.*

STIBBE, Philip
Return via Rangoon *(London: Wolsey 1947), 224p.*

SUTTON, Barry
Jungle pilot *(London: Macmillan 1946), 127p.*

SWINSON, Arthur
Kohima *(London: Cassell 1966), xix, 275p, bib.*

TAINSH, A R
. . . And some fell by the wayside: an account of the North Burma evacuation *(Bombay: Orient Longmans 1948),* [7], *175p.*

TAYLOR, Joe G
Air supply in the Burma campaigns *(Maxwell Air Force Base, Ala: USAF History Division, Air University 1957), 163p.*

THOMAS, Lowell
Back to Mandalay *(London: Muller 1952), 255p.*

TUNG PE, U
Sun over Burma *(Rangoon: Rasika Ranjani 1949), 114p.*

TYSON, Geoffrey
Forgotten frontier *(Calcutta: Target 1945), 146p.*

WILSON, Richard C
The Imphal shrimps, from 'High Appreciation: recollections of a captain' *(Chester: Tug 1962), 53p.*
[*see also* CHINA, CHINDITS, INDIA]

CALAIS

LEVER, Clifford
On my heart too!: the epic of Calais, 1940 *(London: Epworth 1943), 64p.*

NEAVE, Airey
The flames of Calais: a soldier's battle, 1940 *(London: Hodder & Stoughton 1972), 224p, bib.*

CAMOUFLAGE

BARKAS, Geoffrey
Camouflage story (from Aintree to Alamein) *(London: Cassell 1952), 216p.*

BRADFORD, George
Armour camouflage and markings, North Africa 1940–1943 *(London: Arms & Armour 1974), 96p.*

DAVIES, William J K
Wehrmacht camouflage and markings, 1939–1945 *(London: Almark 1972), 56p.*

GOULDING, James
Camouflage and markings: R.A.F. Fighter Command, Northern Europe, 1936–1945 *(London: Ducimus 1971), 294p.*

HODGES, Peter
Royal Navy warships camouflage, 1939–1945 *(London: Almark 1973), 80p.*

MUNDAY, E A
USAAF heavy bomb group markings and camouflage, 1941–1945 Consolidated B-24 Liberator *(Reading, Berks: Osprey 1972), 48p.*

WARD, Richard
Focke-Wulf Fw 190A, F, G- Luftwaffe *(Reading, Berks: Osprey 1974), 50p.*
Luftwaffe bomber and fighter camouflage and markings, 1940: Heinkel HE III, Junkers Ju 88, Dornier Do17 *(Reading, Berks: Osprey 1972), vol. I: 52p; vol. 2:* Bf 110 - Ju 87 - Fw 200 - He 59 - He 115 - Do 215 - Do 18 - Do 24 - Av 196 *(1973),* [*50p*].
USAAF Heavy Bomb Group markings and camouflage, 1941–1945: Boeing B-17 Flying Fortress *(Reading, Berks: Osprey 1973),* [*50p*].

WISE, Terence
American military camouflage and markings, 1939–1945 *(London: Almark 1973), 96p.*

CANADA

ARMSTRONG, Elizabeth H
French Canadian opinion on the war, January, 1940–June, 1941 *(Toronto: Hyerson 1942), vii, 44p.*

BECKLES, Gordon
Canada comes to England *(London: Hodder & Stoughton 1941), 166p.*

DAFOE, John W (ed)
Canada fights: an American democracy at war *(New York: Farrar 1941), vi, 280p.*

DAWSON, Robert M
The conscription crisis of 1944 *(Toronto: Toronto UP 1961), 136p.*

DZIUBAN, Stanley W
Military relations between the United States and Canada, 1939–1945 *(Washington DC: Department of Army 1959), 432p.*

FEASBY, W R (ed)
Official history of the Canadian Medical Services, 1939–1945 *(Ottawa: Queen's Printer 1953–6), 2 vols.*

GOOD, Mabel T
Men of valour *(London: Macmillan 1948), xii, 137p.*
GRANATSTEIN, Jack L
Conscription in the Second World War, 1939–1945: a study in political management *(Toronto: Ryerson 1969), 85p.*
HALTON, Matthew H
Ten years to Alamein *(Forest Hills, NY: Transatlantic Arts 1945), 220p.*
HILL, B Kirkbride (ed)
The price for freedom: a written and photographic record of over 500 of those who lost their lives in the Second World War while serving in the Armed Forces of Canada, Sept. 1939 to June 1942 *(Toronto: Ryerson 1943), 189p.*
KENNEDY, John de N
History of the Department of Munitions and Supply: Canada in the Second World War *(Ottawa: King's Printer 1950), 2 vols.*
KING, William L M
Canada at Britain's side *(London: Macmillan 1941), xii, 332p.*
LAVOILETTE, Forrest E
Canadian Japanese and World War II: a sociological and psychological account *(Toronto: Toronto UP 1948), x, 332p.*
MALONE, Richard S
Missing from the record *(Toronto: Collins 1946), 227p.*
PICKERSGILL, J W
The Mackenzie King record *(Toronto: Toronto UP 1960), vol I: 1939–44.*
PLUMPTRE, Arthur F W
Mobilizing Canada's resources for war *(New York: Macmillan 1942), xxiii, 306p.*
SIMONDS, Peter
Maple leaf up, maple leaf down: the story of the Canadians in the Second World War *(New York: Island 1947), 356p.*

CANADIAN AIR FORCE

COSGROVE, Edmund
Canada's fighting pilots *(Toronto: Clarke, Irwin 1965), 190p.*
COUGHLIN, Tom
The dangerous sky: Canadian airmen in World War II *(London: Kimber 1968), x, 214p.*
GRIFFIN, D F
First steps to Tokyo: the Royal Canadian Air Force in the Aleutians *(New York: Dent 1944), vi, 50p.*

McMillan, Don A
Only the stars know *(London: Dent 1944), cxxxviiip.*

The R.C.A.F. overseas: the fifth year *(London: Oxford UP 1949), 537p.*

CANADIAN ARMY

Burns, Eedson L M
General Mud *(Toronto: Clarke, Irwin 1970), 254p.*
Manpower in the Canadian Army, 1939-1945 *(Toronto: Clarke, Irwin 1956), 184p.*

Canada. Department of National Defence
The Canadian Army at war *(Ottawa: King's Printer 1945-6), 3 vols.*

Cassidy, George L
Warpath: the story of the Algonquin Regiment, 1939-1945 *(Toronto: Ryerson 1948), 372p.*

Clegg, Howard
A Canuck in England: journal of a Canadian soldier *(London: Harrap 1942), 160p.*

Cosgrove, Edmund C
The evaders *(Toronto: Clarke, Irwin 1970), 301p.*

5th Canadian Light Anti-Aircraft Regiment: Regimental history, World War II (March 1, 1941-May 8, 1945) *(Groningen: De Waal 1945), 64p.*

The Governor General's Horse Guards, 1939-1945 *(Toronto: Canadian Military Journal 1945), 243p.*

Johnson, Charles M
Action with the Seaforths *(New York: Vantage 1954), 342p.*

King, William L M
Canada and the fight for freedom *(New York: Duell 1945), xxiv, 326p.*

Londerville, J D
The pay services of the Canadian Army overseas in the war of 1939-45 *(Ottawa: Runge 1950), 315p.*

McAvity, J M
Lord Strathcona's Horse (Royal Canadians): a record of achievement *(Toronto: Ryerson 1947), 280p*

Mowat, Farley
The Regiment *(Toronto: McClelland 1973), 2nd ed. 317p.*

Munro, Ross
Gauntlet to Overlord: the story of the Canadian Army *(Toronto: Macmillan 1945), 477p.*

PAVEY, Walter G
An historical account of the 7th Canadian Reconnaissance Regiment (17th Duke of York's Royal Canadian Hussars) in the World War of 1939–1945 *(Montreal 1948), 139p.*

QUEEN-HUGHES, R W
Whatever men dare: a history of the Queen's Own Cameron Highlanders of Canada, 1935–1960 *(Winnipeg 1960), 247p.*

SPENCER, Robert A
History of the Fifteenth Canadian Field Regiment, Royal Canadian Artillery, 1941 to 1945 *(New York: Elsevier 1945), 302p.*

STACEY, Charles P
Canada's battle in Normandy *(Ottawa: King's Printer 1946), 159p.*
Official history of the Canadian Army in the Second World War *(Ottawa: King's Printer 1957–60) 3 vols.*

WHITCOMBE, Fred (ed)
The pictorial history of Canada's Army overseas, 1939–1945 *(Toronto: McClelland 1947), 300p.*
[*see also* DIEPPE, NORMANDY, WESTERN EUROPE *1944–5*]

CANADIAN NAVY

CANADA'S war at sea *(Montreal: Beatty 1944), 2 vols in 1.*

MILNE, Gilbert A
H.M.C.S. *(Toronto: T. Allen 1960), 141p.*

SCHULL, Joseph
The far distant ships: an official account of Canadian Naval operations in the Second World War *(Ottawa: Cloutier 1952), 527p.*
Ships of the great days: Canada's Navy in World War II *(London: Macmillan 1963), 156p.*

CANARIS

ABSHAGEN, Karl H
Canaris *(London: Hutchinson 1956), 264p.*

AMORT, Cestmir *and* JEDLICKA, I M
The Canaris file *(London: Allan Wingate 1970), 158p.*

COLVIN, Ian
Chief of Intelligence *(London: Gollancz 1951), 224p, bib.*
[*see also* SECRET SERVICES]

CANTERBURY

GARNET, Clew
Our V sign *(Canterbury: Jennings 1942), 5–43p.*

WILLIAMSON, *Mrs* Catherine E
Though the streets burn *(Ashford, Kent: Headley 1949), xvi, 321p.*

CAPE MATAPAN

PACK, Stanley W C
The battle of Matapan *(London: Batsford 1961), 183p.*
Night action off Cape Matapan *(London: Allan 1972), 146p.*

SETH, Ronald
Two fleets surprised: the story of the battle of Cape Matapan, Mediterranean, March, 1941 *(London: Bles 1960), xxi, 201p.*
[*see also* MEDITERRANEAN, ROYAL NAVY]

CASABLANCA

ARMSTRONG, Anne
Unconditional surrender: the impact of the Casablanca policy upon World War II *(New Brunswick, NJ: Rutgers UP 1961), 304p.*

CASSINO

BOHMLER, Rudolf
Monte Cassino *(London: Cassell 1964), [10], 314p, bib.*

BOND, Harold L
Return to Cassino: a memoir of the fight for Rome *(London: Dent 1964), [6], 208p, bib.*

CONNELL, Charles
Monte Cassino: the historic battle *(London: Elek [1963],) 207p.*

GRAHAM, Dominick
Cassino *(New York: Ballantine 1971), 161p, bib.*

MAJDALANY, Fred
Cassino: portrait of a battle *(London: Longmans Green 1957), xii, 270p, bib.*
The monastery *(London: Lane 1945), 176p.*

SENGER UND ETTERLIN, Fridd M von
Neither fear nor hope: the wartime career of General Fridd von Senger und Etterlin, defender of Cassino *(London: Macdonald 1963), 368p.*
[*see also* ITALIAN CAMPAIGN]

CATHOLICISM

CIANFARRA, Camille M
The Vatican and the war *(New York: Dutton 1944), 7-344p; UK title:* The war and the Vatican

FALCONI, Carlo
The silence of Pius XII *(Boston, Mass: Little, Brown 1970), 3-430p.*

FRIEDLANDER, Saul
Pius XII and the Third Reich: a documentation *(London: Chatto & Windus 1966),* [1], *xxv, 238, viip.*

GWYNN, Denis R
The Vatican and the war in Europe *(London: Burns Oates 1940), xxv, 217p.*

LEHMANN, Leo H
Vatican policy in the Second World War *(New York: Agora 1946), 51p.*

LEWY, Guenter
The Catholic Church and Nazi Germany *(London: Weidenfeld & Nicolson [1964]), xv, 416p.*

LYNN, Rita Le B
The national Catholic community service in World War II *(Washington, DC: Catholic University of America Press 1952), 290p.*

MOORE, Edith
No friend of democracy: a study of Roman Catholic policies, their influence on the course of the war and growth of Fascism *(London: International 1945), 5th ed., 52p.*

RHODES, Anthony R E
The Vatican in the age of the dictators, 1922-1945 *(London: Hodder & Stoughton 1973), 383p.*

ROMAN CATHOLIC CHURCH
Records and documents of the Holy See relating to the Second World War *(London: Herder 1968), xxx, 495p, bib.*

SHEEN, Fulton J
Declaration of dependence *(Milwaukee, Wis: Bruce 1941), vii, 140p.*

WAAGENAAR, Sam
The Pope's Jews *(London: Alcove 1974), 487p.*

WALKER, Reginald F
Pius of peace: a study of the pacific work of his holiness Pope Pius XII in the World War, 1939-1945 *(Dublin: Gill 1946), 182p.*

ZAHN, Gordon
German Catholics and Hitler's war *(London: Sheed & Ward 1963), 232p.*
[*see also* JEWS]

CENSORSHIP

BROME, Vincent
Europe's free press: the underground newspapers of occupied lands described as far as the censor permits *(London: Feature 1943), 127p.*

KOOP, Theodore F
Weapon of silence *(Chicago, Ill: Chicago UP 1946), 304p.*

MOORAD, George
Behind the iron curtain *(Philadelphia, Pa: Fireside 1946), xiv, 309p.*

RILEY, Norman
999 and all that *(London: Gollancz 1940), 223p.*

SUMMERS, Robert E (comp)
Wartime censorship of press and radio *(New York: Wilson 1942), 297p.*

THOMSON, George P
Blue pencil admiral: the inside story of press censorship *(London: Sampson Low 1947), 216p.*

[*see also* PRESS, RADIO]

CEYLON

CEYLON. Ministry of Agriculture and Lands
How Lanka fed herself during the war, 1939–1945 *(Colombo, Ceylon 1947), 106p.*

CHANNEL DASH

POTTER, John D
Fiasco: the break-out of the German battleships *(London: Heinemann 1970), [10], 235p, bib.*

ROBERTSON, Terence
Channel dash: the drama of twenty-four hours of war *(London: Evans 1958), 208p.*

CHANNEL ISLANDS

ARROL, Anthony M (pseud)
The best of it *(Guernsey: Williams & Wardley 1956), [5], 67p.*

CORTURIEND, V V
Isolated island: a history and personal reminiscences of the German occupation of the Island of Guernsey, June 1940–May 1945 *(Guernsey: Guernsey Star 1948), 334p.*

COYSH, Victor
Swastika over Guernsey: an outline of the German occupation and the liberation of the Island *(Guernsey: Guernsey Press [1955]), 32p, bib.*

DALMAV, John
Slave worker in the Channel Islands *(Guernsey: Guernsey Press 1956), 24p.*

DURAND, Ralph A
Guernsey under German rule *(London: Guernsey Society 1946), 183p.*

FALLA, Frank W
The silent war *(London: Frewin 1967), 172p.*

FOLEY, Edwin
Appointment with Mars *(London: Fellowship of Reconciliation 1956), 16p.*

HATHAWAY, *Dame* Sybil M C B
Dame of Sark: an autobiography *(New York: Coward-McCann 1962), 211p.*

HIGGS, Dorothy P
Guernsey diary, 1940–1945: a human record of the occupation years *(London: Linden, Lewis 1947), 64p.*

MAUGHAM, Reginald C F
Jersey under the jackboot *(London: W H Allen 1946), 158p.*

MAYNE, Richard
Jersey occupied: unique pictures of Nazi rule, 1940–1945 *(Norwich: Jarrold 1970), 65p.*

MOLLET, Ralph
Jersey under the swastika: an account of the occupation of the island by the German Forces, 1st July 1940 to 12th May 1945 *(London: Hyperion 1945), 110p.*

SINEL, Leslie P
The German occupation of Jersey: a diary of events from June 1940 to June 1945 *(St Helier: Jersey Evening Post 1946), 318p.*

TOMS, Carel
Hitler's fortress islands *(London: New English Library 1967), 160p.*

WOOD, Alan *and* WOOD, Mary
Islands in danger: the story of the German occupation of the Channel Islands, 1940–1945 *(London: Evans 1955), 255p, bib.*

WYATT, Horace M
Jersey in jail, 1940–45 *(Jersey: Huelin 1945), 92p.*

CHAPLAINS

CHAPMAN, Robert B
Tell it to the chaplain *(New York: Exposition 1952), 10–151p.*

CONNELLY, Kenneth A
Chaplain's assistant: from the correspondence of Corporal Kenneth A. Connelly, Jr *(Seattle, Wash: Craftsman 1945), 103p.*

CUTTER, James B
Captivity captive *(London: Cape 1954), 222p.*

GARRENTON, John S
Flying chaplain *(New York: Vantage 1957), 107p.*

GLASSER, Arthur F
And some believed: a chaplain's experiences with the Marines in the South Pacific *(Chicago, Ohio: Moody 1946), 208p.*

HAGGERTY, James E
Guerrilla padre in Mindanao *(New York: Longmans Green 1946), 257p.*

McLUSKEY, James F
Parachute padre *(London: SCM 1951), 175p.*

METCALF, George R
With Cross and shovel: a chaplain's letters from England, France and Germany, 1942–1945 *(Duxbury, Mass: 1960), 263p.*

O'CALLAGHAN, William
I was chaplain on the Franklin *(New York: Macmillan 1956), 153p.*

PADRE(pseud)
They told it to the chaplain *(New York: Vantage 1953), 138p.*

POLLOCK, P Hamilton
Wings on the Cross: a padre with the R.A.F. *(Dublin: Clonmore 1954), 199p.*

THE PRIEST goes to war: a pictorial outline of the work of the Catholic chaplains in the Second World War *(New York: Society for the Propagation of the Faith 1946), 128p.*

RAY, Samuel H
A chaplain afloat and ashore *(Salado, Tex: Jones 1962), 122p.*

READ, Frances W
G.I. parson *(New York: Morehouse & Gorham 1945), 117p.*

ROGERS, Edward K
Doughboy chaplain *(Boston, Mass: Meador 1946), 230p.*

SAMPSON, Francis L
Paratrooper padre *(Washington DC: Catholic University of America 1948), ix, 137p.*

SMITH, Waldo E L
What time the tempest: an Army chaplain's story *(Toronto: Ryerson 1953), 306p.*
TAGGART, William C *and* CROSS, Christopher
My fighting congregation *(New York: Doubleday 1943), xii, 176p.*
THOMPSON, Douglas W
Captives to freedom *(London: Epworth 1955), 188p.*
UNDERHILL, M L *and others*
New Zealand's chaplains in the Second World War *(Wellington, NZ: War Historical Branch, Internal Affairs Department 1950), 188p.*
US ARMY CHAPLAIN CORPS
American chaplains of the Fifth Army *(Milan: Chaplain Corps 1945), 86p.*

CHIANG KAI-SHEK

CHIANG KAI-SHEK
All we are and all we have: speeches and messages since Pearl Harbour, Dec. 9 1941–Nov. 17, 1942 *(New York: Day 1943), 61p.*
Resistance and reconstruction: messages during China's six years of war *(New York: Harper 1943), xxiv, 322p.*
Voice of China: speeches of Generalissimo and Madame Chiang Kai-Shek between Dec. 7 1941 and Oct. 10, 1943 *(London: Hutchinson 1944), 112p.*
The collected wartime messages, 1937–1945 *(New York: Day 1946), 2 vols in 1.*
PANETH, Philip
Chiang Kai-Shek carries on *(London: Alliance 1944), 160p.*
Generalissimo Chiang Kai-Shek *(London: Staples 1943), 7–79p.*
[*see also* CHINA]

CHILDREN

BRADY, Alice
Children under fire *(Los Angeles, Calif: Columbia 1942), 182p.*
BRINDZE, Ruth
You can help your country win *(New York: Vanguard 1943), x, 226p.*
CARROLL-ABBING, John P
A chance to live: the story of the lost children of the war *(New York: Longmans Green 1952), 216p.*
CHILDREN in bondage: a survey of child life in the occupied countries of Europe and Finland *(London: Longmans Green 1943), 136p.*

GOLLOMB, Joseph *and* TAYLOR, Alice
Young heroes of the war *(New York: Vanguard 1943), 11–239p.*
LOWRIE, Donald A
The hunted children *(New York: Norton 1963), 256p.*
MACARDLE, Dorothy
Children of Europe: a study of the children of liberated countries; their war-time experiences; their reactions, and their needs, with a note on Germany *(London: Gollancz 1949), 349p.*
PATRI, Angelo
Your children in wartime *(New York: Doubleday 1943), ix, 115p.*
WOLF, *Mrs* Anna W M
Our children face war *(Boston, Mass: Houghton, Mifflin, 1942), vii, 214p.*
ZOFF, Otto
They shall inherit the earth *(New York: Day 1943), xii, 258p.*
[*see also* EVACUEES]

CHINA

ADAMSON, Iain
The forgotten men *(London: Bell 1965), 195p.*
ADOLPH, Paul E
Surgery speaks to China: the experiences of a medical missionary to China in peace and war *(Germantown, Pa: China Inland Mission 1945), 195p.*
BAKER, Gilbert
The changing scene in China *(London: SCM 1946), 139p.*
BAND, Claire *and* BAND, William
Two years with the Chinese communists *(New Haven, Conn: Yale UP 1948), xii, 347p; UK title:* Dragon fangs.
BOOKER, Edna *and* POTTER, J S
Flight from China *(New York: Macmillan 1945), x, 236p.*
BRICE, Martin H
The Royal Navy and the Sino-Japanese incident 1937–41 *(London: Allan 1973), 167p.*
BRIGGS, Margaret
Daughter of the Khans *(New York: Norton 1955), 285p.*
CAIDIN, Martin
The ragged, rugged warriors *(New York: Dutton 1966), 384p.*
CALDWELL, Oliver J
A secret war: Americans in China 1944–1945 *(Southern Illinois UP 1973), xx, 218p.*
CHINA. Ministry of Information
China after five years of war *(London: Gollancz 1943), 236p.*

FEIS, Herbert
The China tangle: the American effort in China from Pearl Harbor to the Marshall mission *(Princeton, NJ: Princeton UP 1953), 445p.*

FENG, I (pseud)
Give me back my rivers and hills! *(New York: Macmillan 1945), xviii, 136p.*

FLOWERS, Wilfred S
A surgeon in China: vivid personal experiences with a British Red Cross unit *(London: Carey 1946), 52p.*

GAYN, Mark *and* CALDWELL, John C
American agent *(New York: Holt 1947), 220p.*

GILKEY, Langdon
Shanking compound: the story of men and women under pressure *(New York: Harper 1966), xiii, 242p.*

GLINES, Carroll V
Four came home *(Princeton, NJ: Van Nostrand 1966), xiv, 227p.*

HAGER, Alice
Wings for the dragon: the air war in Asia *(New York: Dodd 1945), 307p.*

HEIFERMAN, Ron
Flying tigers: Chennault in China *(New York: Ballantine 1971), 160p, bib.*

KOENIG, William J
Over the Hump: airlift to China *(New York: Ballantine 1972), 160p, bib.*

KOPP, Hans
Himalaya shuttlecock *(London: Hutchinson 1957), 191p.*

LIANG, Chin-tung
General Stilwell in China 1942–1944: the full story *(Jamaica NY: St Johns UP 1972), 321p.*

LIN YUTANG
Between tears and laughter *(London: Crisp 1945), 234p.*
The vigil of a nation *(Toronto: Longmans Green 1945), 262p.*

LLEWELLYN, Bernard
I left my boots in China *(London: Allen & Unwin 1953), 175p.*

LOO, PIN-FEI
It is dark underground *(London: Putnam 1946), 200p.*

MCROBERTS, Duncan
Pleading China *(Grand Rapids, Mich: Zondervan 1946), 141p.*
While China bleeds *(Grand Rapids, Mich: Zondervan 1943), 162p.*

MILES, Milton E
A different kind of war: the little-known story of the combined guerilla forces created in China by the U.S. Navy and the Chinese during World War II *(New York: Doubleday 1967), 629p.*

MORRIS, David
China changed my mind *(London: Cassell 1948), 202p.*

NELSON, Daniel
Journey to Chungking *(Minneapolis, Minn: Augsburg 1945), 154p.*

NOONAN, William
The surprising battalion: Australian commandos in China *(Sydney: Bookstall Company 1945), 194p.*

P' AN CHAO-YING
China fights on, an inside story of China's long struggle against our common enemies *(London: Revell 1945), 188p.*

PAYNE, Pierre S R
Chungking diary *(London: Heinemann 1945), 526p; US title:* Forever China

POWELL, Lyle S
A surgeon in wartime China *(Lawrence, Kan: Kansas UP 1946), 233p.*

REES, Ronald
China can take it *(London: Edinburgh House 1942), 64p.*

REYNOLDS, Quentin J
Officially dead *(London: Cassell 1946), 190p.*

ROMANUS, Charles F *and* SUNDERLAND, Riley
Stilwell's mission to China *(Washington DC: Department of Army 1953), 441p.*

ROONEY, Douglas D
Stilwell *(New York: Ballantine 1971), 160p, bib.*

ROSINGER, Lawrence K
China's crisis *(New York: Knopf 1945), 259p.*
China's wartime policies, 1937-1944 *(Princeton, Pa: Princeton UP 1945), 133p.*

SAMSON, Gerald
The Far East ablaze *(London: Joseph 1945), 183p.*

SCOTT, Robert L
Flying tiger: Chennault of China *(New York: Doubleday 1959), 285p.*

SELLWOOD, Arthur V
Stand by to die [H.M.S.Li Wo] *(London: New English Library 1961), 128p.*

SUES, Ilona R
Shark's fins and millet *(Boston, Mass: Little, Brown 1944), x, 331p.*
TENNIEN, Mark A
Chungking listening post *(New York: Creative Age 1945), 201p.*
THORNE, Bliss K
The Hump: the great militariy airlift of World War II *(Philadelphia, Pa: Lippincott 1965), 188p.*
TIPTON, Laurance
Chinese escapade *(New York: Macmillan 1949), vii, 247p.*
TOLAND, John
The flying tigers *(New York: Random House 1963), 170p.*
TUCHMAN, Barbara W
Stilwell and the American experience in China, 1911–45 *(New York: Macmillan 1970), xvii, 621p, bib; UK title:* Sand against the wind.
WHITE, John Alexander
The United States Marines in North China *(Millbrae, Calif: White 1974), 217p.*
WHITE, Theodore H (ed)
The Stilwell papers *(New York: Schocken 1972), 357p.*
WHITE, Theodore H *and* JACOBY, A W
Thunder out of China *(New York: Sloane 1946), xvi, 331p.*
YOUNG, Arthur N
China and the helping hand, 1937–1945 *(Cambridge, Mass: Harvard UP 1963), xx, 502p.*
[*see also* BURMA, CHINDITS]

CHINDITS

BAGGALEY, James
A Chindit story *(London: Souvenir 1954), 163p.*
BOYLE, Patrick R
Jungle, jungle, little Chindit *(London: Hollis & Carter 1946), 97p.*
CALVERT, Michael
Chindits—long range penetration *(New York: Ballantine 1973), 159p.*
DENNY, John H
Chindit indiscretion *(London: Johnson 1956), 256p.*
FERGUSSON, Bernard
Beyond the Chindwin: being an account of the adventures of number Five Column of the Wingate expedition into Burma, 1943 *(London: Collins 1945), 256p.*

JEFFREY, William F
Sunbeams like swords *(London: Hodder & Stoughton 1951), 176p.*

ROLO, Charles J
Wingate's raiders: an account of the incredible adventures that raised the curtain on the battle of Burma *(London: Harrap 1944), 129p.*

SHAW, James
The march out: the end of the Chindit adventure *(London: Hart-Davis 1953), 206p.*

WILCOX, W A
Chindit Column 76 *(London: Longmans Green 1945), 137p.*
[*see also* BURMA, CHINA, WINGATE]

CHRISTIAN SCIENCE

THE STORY of Christian Science wartime activities, 1939–1946 *(Boston, Mass: Christian Science 1947), 434p.*

CHURCHILL

BERLIN, *Sir* Isaiah
Mr. Churchill in 1940 *(London: Murray 1964), 39p.*

BROAD, Lewis
The war that Churchill waged *(London: Hutchinson 1960), 472p, bib.*

CHURCHILL, Winston L S
The dawn of liberation: war speeches *(London: Cassell 1945), 327p.*
End of the beginning: war speeches *(London: Cassell 1943), xiv, 258p.*
Great war speeches *(London: Transworld 1957), 384p.*
Onwards to victory: war speeches 1943 *(London: Cassell 1944), x, 278p.*
Secret session speeches *(London: Cassell 1946), 96p.*
The unrelenting struggle: war speeches *(London: Cassell 1942), x, 371p.*
Victory speeches *(London: Cassell 1945), 307p.*
War speeches, 1940–45: the 52 most important speeches delivered during the war, with a list of the principal events from the invasion of Norway to the surrender of Japan *(London: Cassell 1946), 282p.*
War speeches *(London: Cassell 1951–52), 3 vols.*

COSGROVE, Patrick
Churchill at war *(London: Collins 1944), vol. I:* Alone, 1939–40 *3-379p, bib.*
GARDNER, Brian
Churchill in his time: a study in a reputation, 1939–1945 *(London: Methuen 1968), xvi, 349p, bib.*
GRETTON, *Sir* Peter
Former naval person: Winston Churchill and the Royal Navy *(London: Cassell 1968), [14], 338p, bib.*
HIGGINS, Trumbull
Winston Churchill and the Second Front, 1940–1943 *(Toronto: Oxford UP 1957), 281p.*
MASON, David
Churchill *(New York: Ballantine Books 1972), 160p, bib.*
MORAN, Charles M, *1st baron Moran*
Winston Churchill: the struggle for survival, 1940–1965 *(London: Constable 1966), xviii, 824p.*
PAWLE, Gerald
The war and Colonel Warden: based on the recollections of Commander C. R. Thompson, personal assistant to the Prime Minister, 1940–45 *(London: Harrap 1963), [4], 427p.*
THOMPSON, Reginald W
Generalissimo Churchill *(London: Hodder & Stoughton 1973), 252p, bib.*
THOMPSON, Walter H
I was Churchill's shadow *(London: Johnson 1951), 200p.*
TICKELL, Jerrard
Ascalon: the story of Sir Winston Churchill's wartime flights from 1943–1945 *(London: Hodder & Stoughton 1964), 128p.*
WHEELER-BENNETT, *Sir* John
Action this day: working with Churchill *(London: Macmillan 1968), 272p.*
[*see also* HISTORY]

CICERO

BAZNA, Elyesa
I was Cicero *(London: Deutsch 1962), 192p.*
MOYZISCH, Ludwig C
Operation Cicero *(London: Wingate 1950), 208p.*

CIVIL DEFENCE

BILLINGHAM, Elizabeth
Civil Defence in war *(London: Murray 1941), 72p.*

DANIELL, Raymond
Civilians must fight *(New York: Doubleday 1941), xiv, 322p.*
DUPUY, Richard E *and* CARTER, Hodding
The civilian defence of the United States *(New York: Farrar 1942), 296p.*
GREAT BRITAIN. Ministry of Information
Front line [the official story of the Civil Defence of Great Britain] *(London: HMSO 1942), 7-157p.*
IMPACT of air attack in World War II: selected data for civil defence planning *(Washington DC: Government Printing Office 1953), 3 vols.*
O'BRIEN, Terence H
Civil Defence *(London: HMSO 1955), xvii, 729p.*
SHIRLAW, Gerald B
Casualty: training, organization and administration of civil defence casualty services *(London: Secker & Warburg 1940), xix, 283p.*
STRACHEY, Evelyn J St L
Post D: some experiences of an air raid warden *(London: Gollancz 1941), 135p; US title:* Digging for Mrs. Miller.
SWANWICK, Francis W
A.R.P. (Civil Defence) in the Borough of Heston & Isleworth, 1938–1945 *(Hounslow: Swanwick 1961), 65p.*

CLYDE RIVER

DRUMMOND, John D
A river runs to war *(London: W H Allen 1960), 208p.*

COASTAL COMMAND

BOLITHO, Hector
Command performance: the authentic story of the last battle of the Coastal Command R.A.F. *(New York: Howell & Soskin 1946), 261p.*
Task for Coastal Command: the story of the battle of the South-West Approaches *(London: Hutchinson 1946), 141p.*
DUDLEY-GORDON, Tom
Coastal Command at war *(London: Jarrolds 1943), x, 11-191p; US title:* I seek my prey in the waters.
GREAT BRITAIN. Air Ministry
Coastal Command: the Air Ministry's account of the part played by Coastal Command in the battle of the seas *(New York: Macmillan 1943), 143p.*

GREY, Charles G
Sea flyers *(London: Faber 1942), 256p.*
JOUBERT de la FERTE, Philip B
Birds and fishes: the story of Coastal Command *(London: Hutchinson 1960), 224p.*
WILSON, Michael C D *and* ROBINSON, A S L
Coastal Command leads the invasion *(London: Jarrolds 1945), 160p.*
[*see also* ROYAL AIR FORCE, ROYAL NAVY]

COASTGUARDS

INGRAHAM, Reg
First fleet: the story of the U.S. Coast Guard at war *(Indianapolis, Ind: Bobbs-Merrill 1944), 7-310p.*
MERCEY, Arch A *and* GROVE, Lee (eds)
Sea, surf and hell: the U.S. Coast Guard in World War II *(New York: Prentice-Hall 1945), 352p.*
WILLOUGHBY, Malcolm F
The Coast Guards, TRS, First Naval District *(Boston, Mass: Lauriat 1945), 247p.*
The U.S. Coast Guard in World War II *(Annapolis, Md: US Naval Institute 1957), 347p.*

COLLABORATORS

LITTLEJOHN, David
The patriotic traitors: a history of collaboration in German-occupied Europe, 1940–45 *(London: Heinemann 1972), xv, 391p, bib.*
[*see also* BRITISH FREE CORPS, LORD HAW-HAW]

COMMANDOS

ARNOLD, Richard
The true book about Commandos *(London: Muller [1954]), 144p.*
COOK, Graeme
Commandos in action *(London: Hart-Davis, MacGibbon 1973), 176p, bib.*
DURNFORD-SLATER, John
Commando *(London: Kimber 1953), x, 11-222p.*
FERGUSSON, Bernard
The watery maze: the story of Combined Operations *(London: Collins 1961), 445p, bib.*

GILCHRIST, Donald
Castle Commando *(Edinburgh: Oliver & Boyd 1960),* [7], *146p.*
HOLMAN, Gordon
Commando attack *(London: Hodder & Stoughton 1942), 160p.*
KEYES, Elizabeth M
Geoffrey Keyes, V.C., M.C. *(London: Newnes 1956), 278p.*
LEPOTIER, [Adolphe]
Raiders from the sea *(London: Kimber 1954), 200p.*
McDOUGALL, Murdoch C
Swiftly they struck: the story of No. 4 Commando *(London: Odhams 1954), 208p.*
MIKES, H George
The epic of Lofoten *(London: Hutchinson 1941), 79p.*
MILLAR, George
The Bruneval raid: flashpoint of the radar war *(London: Bodley Head 1974), 208p, bib.*
MILLS-ROBERTS, Derek
Clash by night: a Commando chronicle *(London: Kimber 1956), 204p.*
MOULTON, James L
Haste to the battle: a Marine Commando at war *(London: Cassell 1963), xvi, 210p.*
PHILLIPS, Cecil E L
Cockleshell heroes *(London: Heinemann 1956), xii, 252p.*
SAMAIN, Bryan
Commando men: the story of a Royal Marine Commando in North-West Europe *(London: Stevens 1948), 188p.*
SAUNDERS, Hilary St G
Combined operations: the official story of the Commandos *(New York: Macmillan 1943), xiii, 155p.*
The green beret: the story of the Commandos *(London: Joseph 1949), 320p.*
SCHOFIELD, Stephen
Musketoon: a Commando raid, Glomfjord, 1942 *(London: Cape 1964), 156p.*
STRUTTON, Bill *and* PEARSON, Michael
The secret invaders *(London: Hodder & Stoughton 1958), 287p.*
VACULIK, Serge
Air Commando *(London: Jarrolds 1954), 303p.*
YOUNG, Peter
Commando *(London: Macdonald 1970), 160p, bib.*
Storm from the sea *(London: Kimber 1958), 221p.*

CONCENTRATION CAMPS

BAILEY, K G
Dachau *(London: Brown-Watson 1961), 156p.*

BERNARD, Jean-Jacques
The camp of slow death *(London: Gollancz 1945), 132p.*

BOOM, Corrie ten
A prisoner and yet - [Ravensbruck] *(London: Christian Literature Crusade 1954), 160p.*

BOR, Josef
The Terezin 'Requiem' *(London: Heinemann 1963), 83p.*

BOSWORTH, Allan R
America's concentration camps *(New York: Norton 1967), 283p.*

BUBER, Margarete
Under two dictators *(London: Gollancz 1949), 331p.*

CATALOGUE of camps and prisons in Germany and German occupied territories, September 1, 1939–May 8, 1945 *(Arolsen, Ger: International Tracing Service 1949–50), 2 vols.*

COHEN, Elie A
The abyss: a confession *(New York: Norton 1973), 111p.*
Human behaviour in the concentration camp *(New York: Norton 1953), 295p.*

COLLIS, W Robert *and* HOGERZEIL, Han
Straight on *(London: Methuen 1947), 178p.*

DAILY MAIL (newspaper)
Lest we forget: the horrors of Nazi concentration camps revealed for all time in the most terrible photographs ever published *(London: Associated Newspapers 1945), 79p.*

DEATH marches. Marches de la mort. Routes and distances *(Washington DC: United Nations Central Tracing Bureau 1946), 3 vols.*

DONAT, Alexander
The holocaust kingdom: a memoir *(New York: Holt 1965),* [5], *361p.*

DUFOURNIER, Denise
Ravensbruck: the women's camp *(London: Allen & Unwin 1948), 150p.*

FARAMUS, Anthony C
The Faramus story: being the experiences of Anthony Charles Faramus *(London: Wingate* [*1954*]*), 178p.*

FRANKL, Viktor E
From death-camp to existentialism: a psychiatrist's path to a new therapy *(Boston, Mass: Beacon 1959), 111p.*

FRIEDMAN, Filip
This was Oswiecim: the story of a murder camp *(London: United Jewish Appeal 1946), 84p.*

GEVE, Thomas
Youth in chains *(Jerusalem: Mass 1958), 262p.*

GWIAZDOWSKI, Alexander P
I survived Hitler's hell *(Boston, Mass: Meador 1954), 182p.*

HAJSMAN, Jan
The brown heart: the concentration camp, Europe under the rule of Hitler *(Prague: Orbis 1948), 212p.*

HARCOURT, Pierre d'
The real enemy *(London: Longmans Green 1967),* [5], *186p.*

HARDMAN, Leslie H
The survivors: the story of the Belsen remnant *(London: Vallentine, Mitchell* [*1958*]*), x, 113p.*

HART, Kitty
I am alive [Auschwitz] *(London: Abelard-Schuman 1961), 160p.*

HEIMLER, Eugene
Night of the mist *(London: Bodley Head 1959), 192p.*

HOESS, Rudolf
Commandant of Auschwitz: the autobiography of Rudolf Hoess *(London: Weidenfeld & Nicolson 1959), 252p.*

IZBICKI, John
The naked heroine: the story of Lydia Lova [Ravensbruck] *(London: Spearman* [*1963*]*), xi, 189p.*

JURETZKO, Werner I
Years without hope *(Mamaroneck, NY: Kraus 1971), 127p.*

KESSEL, Sim
Hanged at Auschwitz *(London: Talmy Franklin 1973), 192p.*

KLEIN, Gerda W
All but my life *(New York: Hill & Wang 1957), 224p; UK title:* My tortured years.

KOESTLER, Arthur
Scum of the earth *(London: Cape 1941), 255p.*

KOGON, Eugen
The theory and practice of hell: the German concentration camps and the system behind them *(London: Secker & Warburg 1950), 307p.*

KRAUS, Ota *and* KULKA, Erich
The death factory: document on Auschwitz *(London: Pergamon 1966), vii, 284p, bib.*

KRAUSS, Maria A
Courage her passport: the story of Maria Augusta Krauss *(London: Muller 1963), 204p.*

LAZAR, Albert O (pseud)
Innocents condemned to death: chronicles of survival *(New York: William-Frederick 1961), 97p.*

LECHENE, Evelyn
Mauthausen: the history of a death camp *(London: Methuen 1971), 296p, bib.*

LEDERER, Zdenek
Ghetto Theresienstadt *(London: Goldston 1953), viii, 275p, bib.*

LEGENDRE, Gertrude S
The sands ceased to run *(New York: William-Frederick 1947), 245p.*

LENGYEL, Olga
Five chimneys: the story of Auschwitz *(New York: Ziff-Davis 1947), 220p; later published as:* I survived Hitler's ovens.

LEVI, Primo
If this is a man *(London: Deutsch 1960),* [2], *206p; US title:* Survival in Auschwitz.
The truce: a survivor's journey home from Auschwitz *(London: Bodley Head 1965), 222p; US title:* The reawakening.

MAUREL, Micheline
An ordinary camp *(New York: Simon & Schuster 1958), 141p; UK title:* Ravensbruck.

MECHANICUS, Philip
Waiting for death: a diary *(London: Calder & Boyars 1968), 267p; US title:* Year of fear.

MINNEY, Rubeigh J
I shall fear no evil: the story of Dr. Alina Brenda [Auschwitz] *(London: Kimber 1966), xiv, 15-223p.*

MOIR, Guthrie
Beyond hatred *(Philadelphia, Pa: Fortress 1970), 183p.*

NEWMAN, Judith
In the hell of Auschwitz: the wartime memories *(New York: Exposition 1964), 136p.*

NYISZLI, Miklos
Auschwitz: a doctor's eye-witness account *(New York: Fell 1960), 158p.*

PAT, Jacob
Ashes and fire *(New York: International Universities Press 1948), 254p.*

PAWLOWICZ, Sala K
I will survive *(New York: Norton 1962), 253p.*

PERL, Gisella
I was a doctor in Auschwitz *(New York: International Universities Press 1948), 189p.*

POLLER, Walter
Medical Block, Buchenwald: the personal testimony of Inmate 966, Block 36 *(London: Souvenir 1961), 277p.*

PURY, Roland de
Journal from my cell *(New York: Harper 1946), 140p.*

RAVEN, Hélène J
Without frontiers *(London: Hutchinson 1960), 221p.*

RAVENSBRUCK, *(Berlin: Kongress [1961]), 4–152p.*

RAWICZ, Slavomir
The long walk: a gamble for life *(London: Constable 1956), 239p.*

ROSENFELD, Else R B
The four lives of Elsbeth Rosenfeld, as told by her to the B.B.C. *(London: Gollancz 1964), 158p.*

ROUSSET, David
The other kingdom *(New York: Reynal & Hitchcock 1947), 173p; UK title:* A world apart.

RUSSELL, Edward F L, *2nd baron Russell of Liverpool*
The scourge of the Swastika: a short history of Nazi war crimes *(London: Cassell 1954), xii, 260p.*

SALVESEN, Sylvia
Forgive-but do not forget *(London: Hutchinson 1958), 234p.*

SALWEY, Ruth
Twenty-seven steps of humiliation *(London, Wimbledon, Surrey: Ridgway Courcy 1946), 101p.*

SERENY, Gitta
Into that darkness: from mercy killing to mass murder. [Story of Franz Stangl, Kommandant of Treblinka] *(London: Deutsch 1974), 380p.*

SIMON, Ulrich
A theology of Auschwitz *(London: Gollancz 1967), 160p.*

SINGTON, Derrick
Belsen uncovered *(London: Duckworth 1946), 208p.*

SMITH, Marcus J
Dachau: the harrowing of hell *(Albuquerque, NM: New Mexico UP 1972), 291p.*

SOUPAULT, Philippe
Age of assassins: the story of Prisoner N.1234 *(New York: Knopf 1946), 315p.*

STEINER, Jean F
Treblinka *(New York: Simon & Schuster 1967), xiii, 336p.*
STURTON, Stephen D
From mission hospital to concentration camp *(London: Marshall, Morgan & Scott 1948), 128p.*
SZALET, Leon
Experiment 'E': a report from an extermination laboratory *(New York: Didier 1945), 284p.*
SZMAGLEWSKA, Seweryne
Smoke over Birkenau *(New York: Holt 1947), 386p.*
THORNE, Leon
Out of the ashes: the story of a survivor *(New York: Rosebern 1961), 203p.*
VRBA, Rudolf *and* BESTIC, Alan
I cannot forgive [Auschwitz] *(London: Sidgwick & Jackson & Gibbs & Phillips [1964]), 278p.*
WAREN, Helen
The buried are screaming *(New York: Beechhurst 1948), 9–186p.*
WEINSTOCK, Eugene
Beyond the last path *(New York: Boni & Gaer 1947), 281p.*
WEISS, Reska
Journey through hell: a woman's account of her experiences at the hands of the Nazis *(London: Vallentine, Mitchell [1961]), 255p.*
WELLS, Leon W
The Janowska Road *(New York: Macmillan 1963), [12], 307p.*
WIESEL, Elie
Night *(London: MacGibbon & Kee 1960), 139p.*
WIESENTHAL, Simon
The murderers among us *(London: Heinemann 1967), [7], 312p.*
ZYWULSKA, Krystyna
I came back [Auschwitz] *(London: Dobson [1951]), 246p.*
[*see also* GERMANY, GESTAPO, JEWS, POLAND]

CONFERENCES

ROOSEVELT, Elliott
As he saw it *(New York: Duell 1946), 270p.*
US DEPARTMENT OF STATE
The Conferences at Cairo and Teheran, 1943 *(Washington DC: Government Printing Office 1961), 932p.*
The Conferences at Malta and Yalta, 1945 *(Washington DC: Government Printing Office 1955), 1032p.*
[*see also* ATLANTIC CHARTER, CASABLANCA, POTSDAM, YALTA]

CONGRESSIONAL MEDAL OF HONOR

BRAUN, Saul M
Seven heroes: Medal of Honor stories of the war in the Pacific *(New York: Putnam 1965), 224p.*
SCOTT, Jay (pseud)
America's war heroes: dramatic true tales of courageous Marines, Army, Air Force, and Navy men whose exploits won them the Congressional Medal of Honor *(Derby, Conn: Monarch 1961), 143p.*

CONSCIENTIOUS OBJECTORS

BLISHEN, Edward
A cack-handed war *(London: Thames & Hudson 1972), 238p.*
CATLIN, George E G *and others*
Above all nations: an anthology *(London: Gollancz 1945), 87p.*
HAYES, Denis
Challenge of conscience: the story of the conscientious objectors of 1939–1949 *(London: Allen & Unwin 1949), 406p.*
SIBLEY, Mulford Q *and* JACOBS, Philip E
Conscription of conscience: the American state and the conscientious objector, 1940–1947 *(Ithaca, NY: Cornell UP 1952), 580p.*

CONTRABAND

LOMAX, *Sir* John
The diplomatic smuggler *(London: Barker [1965]), 288p.*

CONVOYS

BLAKE, Alfred E
Convoy to India *(New York: Triton 1953), 214p.*
BLOND, Georges
Ordeal below zero: the heroic story of the Arctic convoys in World War II *(London: Souvenir 1956), 199p.*
BROOME, Jack
Convoy to scatter *(London: Kimber 1972), 232p.*
BROWN, Maurice
We sailed in convoy *(London: Hutchinson 1942), x, 11-128p.*
CAMERON, Ian
Red duster, white ensign: the story of the Malta convoys *(London: Muller 1959), 218p; later published as:* Five days to hell.

CAMPBELL, Sir Ian *and* MACINTYRE, Donald
The Kola run: a record of Arctic convoys, 1941-1945 *(London: Muller 1958), 254p.*

CARSE, Robert
A cold corner of hell: the story of the Murmansk convoys, 1941-45 *(New York: Doubleday 1969), 268p.*

CREIGHTON, *Sir* Kenhelm
Convoy commodore *(London: Kimber 1956), 205p.*

FRANCIS, Eric V
The battle for supplies *(London: Cape 1942), 184p.*

GIBSON, Charles D
The ordeal of Convoy NY 119: a detailed accounting of one of the strangest World War II convoys ever to cross the North Atlantic *(New York: Seaport Port Museum 1973), 178p.*

GRETTON, *Sir* Peter
Convoy escort commander *(London: Cassell 1964),* [15], *224p.*
Crisis convoy: the story of HX 231 *(London: Davies 1974),* [*10*], *182p, bib.*

HARRIS, Murray G
Lifelines of victory *(New York: Putnam 1942), 160p.*

HERMAN, Frederick S
Dynamite cargo: convoy to Russia *(London: Cassell 1943), 103p.*

HUGHES, Robert
Through the waters: a gunnery officer in H.M.S. Scylla, 1942-43 *(London: Kimber 1956), 202p; US title:* Flagship to Murmansk.

IRVING, David
The destruction of P.Q.17 *(London: Cassell 1968), xiii, 337p.*

KNOX, Collie
Atlantic battle *(London: Methuen 1941), vii, 103p.*

LUND, Paul *and* LUDLAM, Harry
PQ 17 - convoy to hell: the survivors' story *(London: Foulsham 1968), 240p.*

PAWLOWICZ, Bohdan
O.R.P. Garland in convoy to Russia: the record of a Polish destroyer on her journey from Great Britain to Murmansk and Archangel in the Spring of 1942 *(London: Umcistowski 1943), 79p.*

RUSSELL, *Sir* Herbert
Sea shepherds: wardens of our food flocks *(London: Murray 1941), vii, 247p.*

RUTTER, Owen
Red ensign: a history of convoy *(London: Hale 1942), 214p.*
SCHOFIELD, Brian B
The Russian convoys *(London: Batsford 1964), xv, 237p, bib.*
SCHOFIELD, William G
Eastward the convoys *(Chicago, Ill: Rand McNally 1965), 239p.*
SETH, Ronald
The fiercest battle: the story of North Atlantic Convoy ON 5, 22nd April–7th May, 1943 *(London: Hutchinson 1961), 208p, bib.*
SHANKLAND, Peter *and* HUNTER, Anthony
Malta convoy *(London: Collins 1961), 256p, bib.*
SHAW, Frank H
The convoy goes through *(London: W H Allen 1942), 64p.*
SMITH, Peter C
Pedestal: the Malta convoy of August 1942 *(London: Kimber 1970), 208p.*
THOMPSON, D S E
Our ocean lifeline *(London: Dent 1941), 64p.*
WINN, Godfrey H
P.Q.17: a story of a ship *(London: Hutchinson 1947), 219p.*
[*see also* MERCHANT NAVY, NORTH ATLANTIC, ROYAL NAVY, U-BOATS]

CORAL SEA BATTLE

MILLOT, Bernard
The battle of the Coral Sea *(London: Allan 1974), 166p, bib.*
[*see also* AIRCRAFT CARRIERS, PACIFIC]

CORREGIDOR

BELOTE, James H *and* BELOTE, W M
Corregidor: the saga of a fortress *(New York: Harper 1967), 272p.*
WHITCOMB, Edgar D
Escape from Corregidor *(Chicago, Ill: Regnery 1958), xiii, 274p.*
WILLOUGHBY, *Mrs* Amea
I was on Corregidor: the experiences of an American official's wife in war-torn Philippines *(New York: Harper 1943), v, 249p.*
[*see also* BATAAN, PACIFIC, PHILIPPINES]

CORVETTES

MONSARRAT, Nicholas
H.M. Corvette *(London: Cassell 1942), 92p.*
Three corvettes: 'H.M. Corvette', 'East Coast Corvette', 'Corvette command' *(London: Cassell 1945), viii, 248p.*

COVENTRY

CLITHEROE, Graham
Coventry under fire: an impression of the great raids on Coventry in 1940 and 1941 *(Gloucester: British 1942), 2nd rev. ed., 64p.*
HOBBS, Ernest
The battle of the three spires: impressions of a blind citizen *(Gloucester: British 1943), 32p.*

CRETE

CLARKE, Alan
The fall of Crete *(London: Blond 1962), 206p, bib.*
COMEAU, Marcel G
Operation Mercury: an airman in the battle of Crete *(London: Kimber 1961), 160p.*
DAVIN, Daniel M
Crete *(London: Oxford UP 1953), xvii, 547p, bib.*
HETHERINGTON, John A
Airborne invasion: the story of the battle of Crete *(New York: Duell 1943), xii, 178p.*
HEYDTE, Friedrich A, *Baron von de*
Daedalus returned: Crete, 1941 *(London: Hutchinson 1958), 186p.*
LIND, L J
Escape from Crete *(London: Australasian 1944), 100p.*
LONG, Gavin
Greece, Crete and Syria *(Canberra: Australian War Memorial 1953), xiv, 587p.*
MOSS, William S
Ill met by moonlight *(London: Harrap 1950), 192p.*
PACK, Stanley W C
The battle for Crete *(London: Allan 1973), 144p, bib.*
PSYCHOUNDAKIS, George
The Cretan runner: his story of the German occupation *(London: Murray 1955), xi, 242p.*
RENDEL, Alexander M
Appointment in Crete: the story of a British agent *(London: Wingate 1953), 240p.*

SPENCER, John H
Battle for Crete *(London: Heinemann 1962), xii, 306p, bib.*
STEPHANIDES, Theodore
Climax in Crete *(London: Faber 1946), 166p.*
STEWART, Ian M G
The struggle for Crete, 20 May–1 June 1941: a story of lost opportunity *(London: Oxford UP 1966), xiii, 518p.*
THOMAS, David A
Crete 1941, the battle at sea *(London: Deutsch 1972), 224p, bib; US title:* Nazi victory.
[*see also* AIRBORNE FORCES, GREECE, MEDITERRANEAN]

CROYDON

CROYDON courageous: the story of Croydon's ordeal and triumph, 1939–1945 *(Croydon: Croydon Times 1945), 92p.*
SAYERS, William C B
Croydon and the Second World War: the official history of the war work of the Borough and its citizens from 1939 to 1945 *(Croydon: Croydon Corporation 1949), 581p.*

CRUISERS

HARKER, Jack S
Well done 'Leander' *(Auckland: Collins 1971), 316p.*
HOLMAN, Gordon
The King's cruisers: the story of the unending vigil of H.M. cruisers *(London: Hodder & Stoughton 1947), 264p.*
MORRIS, Colton G *and* CAVE, H B
The fightin'est ship: the story of the cruiser Helena *(New York: Dodd 1944), 192p.*
SIMS, George
H.M.S. Coventry, anti-aircraft cruiser *(London: HMS Coventry Old Hands 1972), vi, 137p.*
USS LOUISVILLE
Man of war: the log of the United States heavy cruiser Louisville *(Philadelphia, Pa: Dunlap 1946), 212p.*
USS PENSACOLA
A history of the U.S.S. Pensacola, with emphasis on the years she served in the Pacific against the Japanese during World War II *(San Francisco, Calif: Phillips & Van Orden 1946), 108p.*
[*see also* PACIFIC, ROYAL NAVY, US NAVY]

CZECHOSLOVAKIA

BENES, Bohus (ed)
Wings in exile: life and work of the Czechoslovakian airmen in France and Great Britain *(London: Czechoslovak 1942), 166p.*

BENES, Edouard
From Munich to new war and new victory *(London: Allen & Unwin 1954), 346p.*

BURGESS, Alan
Seven men at daybreak *(London: Evans 1960), xii, 13-231p.*

CRIMINALS on the bench: documents concerning crimes committed on the occupied territory of Czechoslovakia by the 230 Nazi judges and public prosecutors who today hold legal posts in Western Germany *(Prague: Orbis 1960), 138p.*

CZECHOSLOVAKIA fights back *(New York: American Council on Public Affairs 1943), 210p.*

CZECHOSLOVAKIA. Ministerstvo Zahrunicnich veci
Four fighting years *(London: Hutchinson 1943), 202p.*

ERDELY, Eugene V
Germany's first European protectorate: the fate of the Czechs and Slovaks *(London: Hale 1942), 242p.*
Prague braves the hangman *(London: Czechoslovak Independent Weekly 1942), 11-126p.*

GRANT DUFF, Sheila
German protectorate: the Czechs under Nazi rule *(New York: Macmillan 1942), viii, 295p.*

HEROES and victims *(London: Czechoslovak Ministry of Foreign Affairs 1945), 158p.*

HIRSCHMANN, Maria A
Hansi: the girl who loved the Swastika *(Wheaton, Ill: Tyndale House 1973), 243p.*

HRONEK, Jiri
Volcano under Hitler: the underground war in Czechoslovakia *(London: Czechoslovakia Independent Weekly 1941), 13-141p.*

KORBEL, Josef
The communist subversion of Czechoslovakia, 1938-1948: the failure of coexistence *(Princeton, NJ: Princeton UP 1959), 258p.*

KRAL, Vaclav (ed)
Lesson from history: documents concerning Nazi policies for Germanization and extermination in Czechoslovakia *(Prague: Orbis 1961), 168p.*

KUNSCHKE, Paul
Night over Czechoslovakia *(London: New Europe 1943), 31p.*

MACKWORTH, *Mrs* Cecily
Czechoslovakia fights back *(London: Drummond 1942), 117p.*
MASARYK, Jan G
Speaking to my country *(London: Lincolns-Prager 1944), 151p.*
MASTNY, Vojtech
The Czechs under Nazi rule: the failure of national resistance, 1939–1942 *(New York: Columbia UP 1971), xiii, 274p, bib.*
PANETH, Philip
Edouard Benes: a leader of democracy *(London: Alliance 1945), 127p.*
STRANSKY, Jan
East wind over Prague *(London: Hollis & Carter 1950), vii, 244p.*
TOMAN, Peter
Round the world to Britain *(London: Trinity 1946), 200p; later published as:* I fought for my country.
WECHSBERG, Joseph
Home coming *(New York: Knopf 1946), 117p.*

DANZIG

LEONHARDT, Hans L
The Nazi conquest of Danzig *(Chicago, Ill: Chicago UP 1942), xvi, 363p.*
[*see also* POLAND]

DARWIN

GRIFFITHS, Owen E
Darwin drama *(Sydney: L.C. 1947), 14–218p.*
LOCKWOOD, Douglas
Australia's Pearl Harbour: Darwin, 1942 *(London: Cassell 1966), xv, 232p, bib.*
[*see also* AUSTRALIA]

D-DAY [see NORMANDY]

DEAL (KENT)

PAIN, E C
Deal and the Downs in the war of liberation, 1939–1945 *(Deal: Pain 1948), 174p.*

DECORATIONS AND MEDALS

SAWICKI, James A
Nazi decorations and medals, 1933–1945 *(Rochester, NY: Babin 1958), 75p.*

DECOY SHIPS

HAMPSHIRE, Arthur C
The phantom fleet *(London: Kimber 1960), 208p.*

DEMOBILIZATION

MOCK, James R *and* THURBER, E W
Report on demobilisation *(Norman, Okl: Oklahoma UP 1944), xi, 257p.*

PRATT, George K
Soldier to civilian: problems of readjustment *(New York: McGraw-Hill 1944), xii, 233p.*

SPARROW, John C
History of personnel demobilisation in the United States Army *(Washington DC: Department of the Army 1951), 525p.*

DENMARK

BENNETT, Jeremy
British broadcasting and the Danish resistance movement, 1940–1945: a study of wartime broadcasting of the B.B.C. Danish service *(Cambridge: Cambridge UP 1966), xvi, 266p, bib.*

BERTELSEN, Aage
October '43 *(New York: Putnam 1954), 246p.*

FLENDER, Harold
Rescue in Denmark *(New York: Simon & Schuster 1963), 281p.*

GUDME, Sten
Denmark: Hitler's model protectorate *(London: Gollancz 1942), 168p.*

HALCK, Jorgen
Strictly confidential *(London: Cape 1961), 175p.*

LAMPE, David
The savage canary: the story of resistance in Denmark *(London: Transworld 1959), 284p; US title:* The Danish resistance.

MALTHE-BRUUN, Kim
Heroic heart: diary and letters, 1941–1945 *(New York: Random House 1955), 177p.*

MENTZE, Ernst (ed)
5 years: the occupation of Denmark in pictures *(New York: Bonnier 1946), 230p.*

MICHELSEN, Kaj C B
They died for us: in memory of Allied airmen who lost their lives in Denmark during the Second World War *(Chicago, Ill: Scandinavian 1946), 56p.*

MUUS, Flemming B
The spark and the flame *(London: Museum 1957), 172p.*

OUTZE, Borge (ed)
Denmark during the German occupation *(Chicago, Ill: Scandinavian 1946), 155p.*

PALMER, Paul
Denmark in Nazi chains *(London: Drummond 1942), 128p.*

TRIUMPH in disaster: Denmark's fight against Germany *(London: HMSO 1945), 64p.*

WERSTEIN, Irving
That Denmark might live: the saga of the Danish resistance in World War II *(Philadelphia, Pa: Macrae-Smith 1967), 143p.*

YAHIL, Leni
The rescue of Danish Jewry: test of a democracy *(Philadelphia, Pa: Hebrew 1969), xx, 536p.*
[*see also* RESISTANCE]

DESTROYERS

ABERCROMBIE, Laurence A *and* PRATT, F
My life to the destroyers *(New York: Holt 1945), xi, 157p.*

BELL, Frederick J
Condition red: destroyer action in the South Pacific *(New York: Longmans Green 1943), xiv, 274p.*

BRICE, Martin H
The Tribals: biography of a destroyer class *(London: Allan 1971), 64p.*

BROOKES, Ewart
Destroyer *(London: Jarrolds 1962), 212p, bib.*

CAIN, T J
H.M.S. Electra *(London: Muller 1959), ix, 282p.*

DAVIES, John
Lower deck *(London: Macmillan 1945), 159p.*

DIVINE, Arthur D
Destroyer's war: a million miles by the Eighth Flotilla *(London: Murray 1942), vi, 166p; US title:* Firedrake.

ELLIOTT, Peter
American destroyer escorts of World War II *(London: Almark 1974), 128p.*

EXTON, William Jr
He's in the destroyers now *(New York: McBride 1944), 5-224p.*

FORBES, Donald
Two small ships *(London: Hutchinson 1957), 208p.*

HODGINSON, Hugh
Before the tide turned: the Mediterranean experiences of a British destroyer officer *(London: Harrap 1944), 242p.*
HORAN, James D
Action tonight: the story of the destroyer O'Brannon in the Pacific *(New York: Putnam 1945), 171p.*
JONES, Ken
Destroyer Squadron 23: combat exploits of Arleigh Burke's gallant force *(Philadelphia, Pa: Chitton 1959), 283p.*
KEMP, Peter K
H.M. destroyers *(London: Jenkins 1956), 237p.*
POOLMAN, Kenneth
The 'Kelly' *(London: Kimber 1954), xii, 13-219p.*
PRESTON, Anthony
'V and W' class destroyers, 1917-1945 *(London: Macdonald 1971), 138p, bib.*
PUGSLEY, Anthony F
Destroyer man *(London: Weidenfeld & Nicolson 1957), 224p.*
ROSCOE, Theodore
United States destroyer operations in World War II *(Annapolis, Md: US Naval Institute 1953), 581p.*
SMITH, Peter C
Destroyer leader: the story of 'H.M.S. Faulknor' *(London: Kimber 1968), 191p.*
STITT, George
H.M.S. Wideawake: destroyer and preserver *(London: Allen & Unwin 1943), 164p.*
THOMAS, David A
With ensigns flying: the story of H.M. destroyers at war *(London: Kimber 1958), 216p.*
[*see also* ROYAL NAVY, US NAVY]

DIEPPE

AUSTIN, Alexander B
We landed at dawn: the story of the Dieppe raid *(London: Gollancz 1943), 158p.*
MAGUIRE, Eric
Dieppe, August 19, 1942 *(London: Cape 1963), 205p, bib.*
MORDAL, Jacques
Dieppe: the dawn of decision *(London: Souvenir 1963), 285p.*

REYBURN, Wallace
Rehearsal for invasion: story of Dieppe raid *(London: Harrap 1943), 126p; later published as:* Dawn landing; *US title:* Glorious chapter.

REYNOLDS, Quentin J
Dress rehearsal: the story of Dieppe *(London: Angus & Robertson 1943), x, 199p.*

ROBERTSON, Terence
The shame and the glory: Dieppe *(Toronto: McClelland & Stewart 1962), 432p.*

STUEBING, Doug
Dieppe 1942 *(Toronto: Clarke Irwin 1968), unp., bib.*

THOMPSON, Reginald W
Dieppe at dawn: the story of the Dieppe raid *(London: Hutchinson 1956), 215p; US title:* At whatever cost.

DIPLOMATIC HISTORY

ALFIERI, Dino
Dictators face to face *(London: Elek 1954), x, 307p.*

ALSOP, Joseph W *and* KINTNER, Robert
The American White Paper: the story of American diplomacy and the Second World War *(New York: Simon & Schuster 1940), 107p, (including postscript* What our policy-makers plan to do if Germany wins immediately).

BEITZELL, Robert E
The uneasy alliance: America, Britain and Russia, 1941–1943 *(New York: Knopf 1972), 404p.*

BUCHANAN, Albert R (ed)
The United States and World War II: military and diplomatic documents *(Columbia, SC: South Carolina UP 1972), 303p.*

CALLENDER, Harold
Preface to peace *(London: Allen & Unwin 1944), xi, 288, vip.*

CIECHANOWSKI, Jan
Defeat in victory *(New York: Doubleday 1947), xvi, 397p.*

DALLIN, David J
The big three: the United States, Britain, Russia *(New Haven, Conn: Yale UP 1945), 202p.*

DEANE, John R
The strange alliance: the story of our efforts at wartime co-operation with Russia *(Bloomington, Ind: Indiana UP 1973), 344p.*

DENNETT, Raymond *and* JOHNSON, Joseph E (eds)
Negotiating with the Russians *(Boston, Mass: World Peace Foundation 1951), 310p.*

DEROUSSY DE SALES, Raoul
The making of yesterday *(New York: Reynal & Hitchcock 1947), 310p.*

DIRKSEN, Herbert von
Moscow, Tokyo, London: twenty years of German foreign policy *(London: Hutchinson 1951), 288p.*

FARAGO, Ladislas
The broken seal: the story of 'Operation Magic' and the Pearl Harbor disaster *(London: Barker 1967), [10], 441p, bib.*

FISCHER, Louis
The road to Yalta: Soviet foreign relations, 1941-1945 *(New York: Harper 1972), 238p.*

FOX, Annette B
The power of small states: diplomacy in World War II *(Chicago, Ill: Chicago UP 1959), xi, 212p, bib.*

FRANCE. Ministry of Foreign Affairs
The French Yellow Book: diplomatic documents concerning the events and negotiations which preceded the opening of hostilities between Germany on the one hand and Poland, Great Britain and France on the other *(London: Hutchinson 1940), xxxvi, 368p.*

FUNK, Arthur Layton
The politics of TORCH: the Allied landings and the Algiers putsch 1942 *(Lawrence: Kansas UP 1974), 322p.*

GAFENCU, Grigory
The last days of Europe: a diplomatic journey in 1939 *(New Haven, Conn: Yale UP 1948), 239p.*
Prelude to the Russian campaign; from the Moscow Pact (August 21, 1939) to the opening of hostilities in Russia (June 22, 1941) *(London: Muller 1945), 348p.*

GANTENBEIN, James W (ed)
Documentary background of World War II, 1931 to 1941 *(New York: Columbia UP 1948), xxxiii, 1122p.*

GERMANY. Auswartiges amt
German White Book: documents concerning the last phase of the German-Polish crisis *(New York: German Library of Information 1939), 48p.*

GOODHART, Philip C
Fifty ships that saved the world: the foundation of the Anglo-American Alliance *(London: Heinemann 1965), 267p.*

GRAHAM-MURRAY, James
The sword and the umbrella *(Douglas, IoM: Times 1964), 254p, bib.*

GREAT BRITAIN. Foreign Office
British War Blue Book: documents concerning German-Polish relations and the outbreak of hostilities between Great Britain and Germany on Sept. 3 1939 *(New York: Farrar 1939), xxxiv, 251p.*

HARE, Judith, *Countess Listowel*
Crusader in the secret war *(London: Johnson 1952), 287p.*

HERZOG, James H
Closing the open door: American-Japanese diplomatic negotiations, 1936–1941 *(Annapolis, Md: Naval Institute 1973), 295p.*

HIRSZOWICZ, Lukasz
The Third Reich and the Arab East *(London: Routledge & Kegan Paul 1966), xi, 403p, bib.*

HOETTL, Wilhelm
The secret front: the story of Nazi political espionage *(London: Weidenfeld & Nicolson 1953), 335p.*

HUGESSEN, *Sir* Hugh M K
Diplomat in peace and war *(London: Murray 1949), 270p.*

KASE, Toshikazu
Journey to the Missouri *(New Haven, Conn: Yale UP 1950), xiv, 282p; UK title:* Eclipse of the Rising Sun.

KLEIST, Peter
The European tragedy *(London: Gibbs & Phillips 1965), 201p.*

KOLKO, Gabriel
The politics of war: Allied diplomacy and the world crisis of 1943–1945 *(New York: Random House 1969), x, 685p.*

LANGSAM, Walter C (ed)
Historic documents of World War 2 *(Princeton, NJ: Princeton UP 1958), 191p.*

LAUNAY, Jacques de
Secret diplomacy of World War II *(New York: Simmons-Boardman 1963), 175p.*

McCANN, Frank D
The Brazilian-American alliance in World War II, 1937–1945 *(Princeton, NJ: Princeton UP 1973), 527p.*

McNeil, Harry
Survey of international affairs: America, Britain and Russia: their co-operation and conflict, 1941-1946 *(London: Oxford UP 1953), xviii, 819p.*

Muggeridge, Malcolm (ed)
Ciano's diplomatic papers: being a record of nearly 200 conversations held during the years 1936–42 with Hitler, Mussolini, Franco, Goering, Ribbentrop, Chamberlain, Eden, Sumner Wells, Schuschnigg, Lord Perth, François-Poncet, and many other world diplomatic and political figures *(London: Odhams 1948), 490p.*

Namier, Lewis B
Diplomatic prelude, 1938–39 *(London: Macmillan 1948), xviii, 502p.*

Netherlands Orange Book: summary of the principal matters dealt with . . . in connection with the state of war up till Nov. 1939 *(New York: Columbia UP 194–), 31p.*

Neumann, William L
After victory: Churchill, Roosevelt, Stalin and the making of peace *(New York: Harper 1967), xii, 212p, bib.*
Making the peace, 1941-1945: the diplomacy of the wartime conferences *(Washington DC: Foundation for Foreign Affairs 1950), 101p.*

Newman, Bernard
The captured archives: the story of Nazi-Soviet documents *(London: Latimer House 1948), 222p.*

O'Connor, Raymond G
Diplomacy for victory: FDR and unconditional surrender *(New York: Norton 1971), 143p.*

Pendar, Kenneth W
Adventure in diplomacy: our French dilemma *(New York: Dodd 1945), 280p*

Rei, August (comp)
Nazi-Soviet conspiracy and the Baltic States: diplomatic documents and other evidence *(London: Boreas 1948), 61p.*

Rossi, Angelo (pseud)
The Russo-German Alliance, August 1939–June 1941 *(London: Chapman & Hall 1959), 218p.*

Rozek, Edward J
Allied wartime diplomacy: pattern in Poland *(London: Chapman & Hall 1958), xix, 481p, bib.*

SCHUMAN, Frederick L
Design for power: the struggle for the world *(New York: Knopf 1942), 324p.*
Night over Europe: the diplomacy of Nemesis, 1939–1940 *(New York: Knopf 1941), xv, 600p.*

SCHWARTZ, Andrew J
America and the Russo-Finnish war *(Washington DC: Public Affairs 1960), 103p.*

SEABURY, Paul
The Wilhelmstrasse: a study of German diplomats under the Nazi regime *(Berkeley, Calif: California UP 1954), 217p.*

SHELTON, John B
A night in Little Park Street *(London: Britannicus Liber 1950), 31p.*

SMITH, Gaddis
American diplomacy during the Second World War, 1941–1945 *(New York: Wiley [1965]), xii, 194p, bib.*

SNELL, John L
Illusion and necessity: the diplomacy of global war, 1939–1945 *(Boston, Mass: Houghton Mifflin 1963), 229p.*
Wartime origins of the East-West dilemma over Germany *(New Orleans, La: Hauser 1962), 268p.*

THOMSON, David
The proposal for Anglo-French union in 1940 *(Oxford: Clarendon 1966), 28p.*

TOYE, Hugh
The springing tiger: a study of a revolutionary [Subhas Chandra Bose] *(London: Cassell 1959), xx, 238p, bib.*

UMIASTOWSKI, Roman *and* ALDRIDGE, Joanna M
Poland, Russia and Great Britain, 1941–1945: a study of evidence *(London: Hollis & Carter 1946), 544p.*

VIORST, Milton
Hostile allies: FDR and Charles de Gaulle *(New York: Macmillan 1965), 280p.*

WANDYCZ, Piotr S
Czechoslovak-Polish confederation and the Great Powers, 1940–43 *(Bloomington, Ind: Indiana UP 1956), 152p.*

WEINBERG, Gerhard L
Germany and the Soviet Union, 1939–1941 *(Leiden, Holl: Brill 1954), 218p.*

WHITE, Dorothy S
Seeds of discord: De Gaulle, Free France and the Allies *(Syracuse, NY: Syracuse UP 1964), 471p.*

WILSON, Hugh R
A career diplomat; the third chapter: The Third Reich *(New York: Vantage 1961), 112p.*
WOODWARD, *Sir* Llewellyn
British foreign policy in the Second World War *(London: HMSO 1962–71, 3 vols.*
ZINK, Harold *and* COLE, Taylor (eds)
Government in wartime Europe *(New York: Reynal 1941), x, 249p.*
[*see also* HISTORY(general), INDIVIDUAL COUNTRIES]

DISPLACED PERSONS

COBB, Alice
War's unconquered children speak *(Boston, Mass: Beacon 1953), 244p.*
COLLIS, William R F
The ultimate value *(London: Methuen 1951), 183p; US title:* The lost and the found.
SCHECHTMAN, Joseph B
European population transfers, 1939–1945 *(New York: Russell & Russell 1971), 532p.*
[*see also* EVACUEES, REFUGEES]

DIVERS AND DIVING

CRAWFORD, Carl H
Salvage diver: United States Navy salvage divers at work and play in the European theatre of war *(New York: Pamphlet 1946), 7-80p.*
KARNEKE, Joseph S
Navy diver *(New York: Putnam 1962), 256p.*
[*see also* SALVAGE]

DOVER

FOSTER, Reginald F
Dover front: a searchlight reporter book *(London: Secker & Warburg 1941), 158p.*
ILLINGWORTH, Frank
Britain under shellfire *(London: Hutchinson 1942), 64p.*

DRESDEN

IRVING, David
The destruction of Dresden *(London: Kimber 1963), 255p, bib.*

DUNKIRK

BECKLES, Gordon
Dunkirk—and after, May 10th-June 17th, 1940 *(London: Hutchinson 1940), 255p.*

BLAXLAND, Gregory
Destination Dunkirk *(London: Kimber 1973), xii, 436p.*

BUTLER, Ewan *and* BRADFORD, J S
Keep the memory green *(London: Hutchinson 1950), 192p; later published as:* The story of Dunkirk.

COLLIER, Richard
The sands of Dunkirk *(London: Collins 1961), 319p, bib.*

DIVINE, Arthur D
Dunkirk *(London: Faber 1945), 307p.*
The nine days of Dunkirk *(London: Faber 1959), 308p.*

FRANKLYN, *Sir* Harold E
The story of one Green Howard in the Dunkirk campaign *(Richmond, Yorks: Reg. HQ, Green Howards 1966), 43p.*

MASEFIELD, John
The twenty-five days *(London: Heinemann 1972), x, 173p.*

SMYTH, *Sir* John
Before the dawn: a story of two historic retreats *(London: Cassell 1957), xv, 220p.*

WILLIAMS, Douglas (comp)
New contemptibles *(London: Murray 1940), 90p; US title:* Retreat from Dunkirk.

DUXFORD

BOWEN, I H *and others* (eds)
Duxford diary, 1942-1945 [for American units stationed there] *(Cambridge: Heffer 1945), 151p.*

EAST AFRICA

BIRKBY, Carel
It's a long way to Addis *(London: Muller 1942), xii, 308p.*

ELLSBERG, Edward
Under the Red Sea sun *(New York: Dodd 1949), 500p.*

GLASFURD, Alexander L
Voyage to Berbera *(London: Sheppard 1947), 133p.*

INDIA AND PAKISTAN. Combined Inter-Services Historical Section. East Africa campaign, 1940–41 *(Bombay: Longmans 1963), xxiv, 180p.*

ORPEN, Neil D
East African and Abyssinian campaigns *(London: Purnell 1969), 390p.*

ROSENTHAL, Eric
The fall of Italian East Africa *(London: Hutchinson 1942), 86p.*
[*see also* ABYSSINIA, ERITREA]

EASTERN EUROPE (RUSSO-GERMAN FRONT)

ALLEN, William E D *and* MARATOFF, Paul
The Russian campaigns of 1944–45 *(London: Penguin 1946), 332p.*

ANDERS, Wladyslaw
Hitler's defeat in Russia *(Chicago, Ill: Regnery 1953), 267p.*

THE BATTLE of Orel, July 1943 *(London: Hutchinson 1944), 95p.*

BAURDZHAM, Momysh-Uly
Volokolamish highway *(Moscow: Foreign Languages 195–), 329p.*

BEHIND the front lines: being an account of the military activities, exploits, adventures, and day to day life of the Soviet guerillas operating behind German lines from the Finnish-Karelian front to the Crimea *(London: Hutchinson 1945), 160p.*

BLAU, George E
The German campaign in Russia: planning and operations, 1940–1942 *(Washington DC: Department of Army 1955), 187p.*

BONGARTZ, Heinz
Flight in winter: Russia conquers, January to May 1945 *(New York: Pantheon 1951), 318p.*

CARELL, Paul (pseud)
Hitler's war on Russia: the story of German defeat in the East *(London: Harrap 1964), 640p, bib; US title:* Hitler moves East, 1941-1943.
Hitler's war on Russia *(London: Harrap 1970), vol. 2:* Scorched earth, *556p, bib.*

CHUIKOV, Vasilii I
The beginning of the road *(London: MacGibbon & Kee 1963), 388p; US title:* The battle for Stalingrad.
The end of the Third Reich *(London: MacGibbon & Kee 1967), 261p.*

CLARK, Alan
Barbarossa: the Russian-German conflict, 1941-1945 *(London: Hutchinson 1965), xxiii, 444p, bib.*

DANISHEVSKY, I (comp)
The road of battle and glory *(Moscow: Foreign Languages 1964), 306p.*

DEVILLIERS, Catherine
Lieutenant Katia *(London: Constable 1964), 5-256p.*

EFFECTS of climate on combat in European Russia *(Washington DC: Department of Army 1952), 81p.*

EHRENBURG, Il'ia G
The war, 1941-1945 *(Cleveland, Ohio: World 1964), 198p.*

EREMENKO, Andrei I
The arduous beginning *(New York: Universal 1966), 329p.*

FERNAU, Joachim
Captain Pax: a report on the terribleness and greatness of men *(London: Constable 1960), 134p.*

GERMAN defence tactics against Russian break-throughs: historical study *(Washington DC: Department of Army 1951), 80p.*

GROSSMAN, Vasilii S
With the Red Army in Poland and Byelorussia *(London: Hutchinson 1945), 52p.*

HAAPE, Heinrich
Moscow tram stop: a doctor's experiences with the German spearhead in Russia *(London: Collins 1957), 384p.*

HASSEL, Sven (pseud)
The legion of the damned *(London: Allen & Unwin 1957), 298p.*
Wheels of terror *(London: Souvenir [1960]), 287p.*

JUKES, Geoffrey
Kursk: the clash of armour *(New York: Ballantine 1968), 160p, bib.*

KEEGAN, John
Barbarossa: invasion of Russia 1941 *(New York: Ballantine 1971), 160p.*

KERN, Erich (pseud)
Dance of death *(London: Collins 1951), 255p.*

KRIGER, Evgenii G
From Moscow to the Prussian frontier *(London: Hutchinson 1945), 136p.*

LETTERS from the dead: last letters from Soviet men and women who died fighting the Nazis, 1941-1945 *(Moscow: Progress 1965), 236p.*

MALAPARTE, Curzio (pseud)
The Volga rises in Europe *(London: Redman 1957), 281p.*

MANSTEIN, Erich von
Lost victories *(London: Methuen [1958]), 574p.*

MILITARY improvisations during Russian campaign: historical study *(Washington DC: Department of Army 1951), 110p.*

OPERATIONS of encircled forces: German experiences in Russia: historical study *(Washington DC: Department of Army 1952), 74p.*

NEUMANN, Peter
Other men's graves *(London: Weidenfeld & Nicolson 1958), 286p; US title:* Black March.

PABST, Helmut
The outermost frontier: a German soldier in the Russian campaign *(London: Kimber 1957), 204p.*

POLEVOI, Boris N
From Belgorod to the Carpathians: from a Soviet war correspondent's notebook *(New York: Universal 1947), 164p.*

RIGONI, Stern M
The sergeant in the snow *(London: MacGibbon & Kee 1954), 158p.*

RUSSIAN combat methods in World War II: historical study *(Washington DC: Department of Army 1950), 116p.*

RUSSIANS tell the story: sketches of the war on the Soviet-German front *(London: Hutchinson 1944), 146p.*

SAJER, Guy
The forgotten soldier *(New York: Harper 1971), xi, 465p.*

SCHEIBERT, Horst
Panzers in Russia; German armoured forces on the Eastern Front, 1941–44: a pictorial history *(London: Altmark* [*1974*]*), 237p.*

SEATON, Albert
The battle for Moscow, 1941-1942 *(London: Hart-Davis 1971), 320p, bib.*
The Russo-German war, 1941–45 *(London: Barker 1971), xix, 628p, bib.*

SETH, Ronald S
Operation Barbarossa: the battle for Moscow *(London: Blond 1964), 191p.*

SMALL unit actions during the German campaign in Russia: historical study *(Washington DC: Department of Army 1953), 289p.*

SMIRNOV, Sergei S
Heroes of Brest fortress *(Moscow: Foreign Languages 1957), 211p.*

TERRAIN factors in the Russian campaign *(Washington DC: Department of Army 1950), 104p.*

THORWALD, Jurgen
Flight in the winter: Russia conquers—January to May 1945 *(New York: Pantheon 1951), 318p.*

TRUE to type: a selection from letters and diaries of the German soldiers and civilians collected on the Soviet-German front *(London: Hutchinson 1945), 160p.*

US Military Academy, West Point
Operations of the Russian front *(New York: West Point, 1945-6), 3 vols in I.*

VONKONRAT, G
Assault from within *(London: Wingate 1970), 286p.*

WHALEY, Barton
Codeword BARBAROSSA *(Cambridge, Mass: MIT 1973), 376p.*

ZHUKOV, Georgii K
Marshal Zhukov's greatest battles *(New York: Harper 1969), xi, 304p.*

ZIEMKE, Earl F
The German northern theater of operations, 1940–1945 *(Washington DC: US Government Printing Office 1960), 342p.*

ZIESER, Benno
In their shallow graves *(London: Elek 1956), 208p; US title:* Road to Stalingrad.
[*see also* LENINGRAD, MOSCOW, STALINGRAD, ZHUKOV]

ECONOMICS

ARGONAUT (pseud)
Give us the tools: a study of the hindrances to full war production and how to end them *(London: Secker & Warburg 1942), 7-191p.*

ASHWORTH, William
Contracts and finance *(London: HMSO 1953), 309p.*

BASCH, Antonin
New economic warfare *(New York: Columbia UP 1941), xvi, 190p.*

BEALS, Carleton
Pan America *(Boston, Mass: Houghton Mifflin 1940), xiv, 545p.*

BELLAMY, Francis R
Blood money: the story of U.S. Treasury agents *(New York: Dutton 1947), 257p.*

BEVIN, Ernest
Balance sheet of the future *(New York: McBride 1941), xii, 15-303p; US title:* The job to be done.

BISSON, Thomas A
Japan's war economy *(New York: Macmillan 1945), 267p.*

BOYAN, Edwin A
Handbook of war production *(New York: McGraw-Hill 1942), xiii, 368p.*

BRANDT, K *and others*
Management of agriculture and food in the German occupied and other areas of Fortress Europe *(Stanford, Calif: Stanford UP 1953), 742p.*
BRUNN, Geoffrey *and* LEE, Dwight E
The Second World War and after *(Boston, Mass: Houghton Mifflin 1964), 200p.*
CAMPBELL, Robert F
The history of basic metals price control in World War II *(New York: Columbia UP 1948), 7-263p.*
CASSINGTON, John (ed)
A metal man's wartime diary, Aug. 1939-Feb. 1941 *(London: Quin 1941), 116p.*
CHANDLER, Lester V
Inflation in the United States, 1940-1948 *(New York: Harper 1951), 402p.*
CHERNE, Leo M
Your business goes to war *(Boston, Mass: Houghton Mifflin 1942), viii, 496p.*
CHESTER, Daniel N (ed)
Lessons of the British war economy *(Cambridge: Cambridge UP 1951), 260p.*
CLARK, John M
Demobilization of wartime economic controls *(New York: McGraw-Hill 1944), xiii, 219p.*
COHEN, Jerome B
The Japanese war economy 1937-1945 *(Minneapolis, Minn: Minnesota UP 1949), 545p.*
COLES, Jessie V
Consumers can help win the war *(Berkeley, Calif: California UP 1943), v, 121p.*
CRAF, John R
Survey of the American economy, 1940-1946 *(New York: North River 1947), xiii, 217p.*
CROWTHER, Geoffrey
The ways and means of war *(London: Oxford UP 1940), vi, 184p.*
DAMERON, Kenneth (ed)
Consumer problems in wartime *(New York: McGraw-Hill 1944), xi, 672p.*
DAVENPORT, Nicholas E H
Vested interests or common pool? *(London: Gollancz 1942), 184p.*
DOBB, Maurice H
Soviet economy and the war *(London: Routledge 1941), v, 88p.*

DUNLOP, John T *and* HILL, Arthur D
The wage adjustment board: wartime stabilization in the building and construction industry *(Cambridge, Mass: Harvard UP 1950), 166p.*

EINZIG, Paul
Economic warfare, 1939–1940 *(New York: Macmillan 1941), x, 150p.*

GEMMILL, Paul *and* BLODGETT, R H
American economy in wartime *(New York: 1942), 72p.*

GORDON, David L *and* DANGERFIELD, Royden
The hidden weapon: the story of economic warfare *(New York: Harper 1947), 238p.*

GROSS, Feliks
The Polish worker: a study of a social stratum *(New York: Roy 1945), 274p.*

HALL, H Duncan
North American supply *(London: HMSO 1955), 559p.*

HALL, H Duncan *and* WRIGLEY, C C
Studies in overseas supply *(London: HMSO 1956), 537p.*

HANCOCK, William K *and* GOWING, M M
British war economy *(London: HMSO 1949), 583p.*

HANSON, Alice C
Family spending and saving in wartime *(Washington DC: US Department of Labour 1945), 218p.*

HARRIS, Seymour E
Economics of America at war *(New York: Norton 1943), 418p.*
Economics of American defense *(New York: Norton 1941), 7-350p.*
Inflation and the American economy *(New York: McGraw-Hill 1945), 559p.*

HART, Albert G *and* ALLEN, E D
Paying for defense *(Philadelphia, Pa: Blakiston 1941), viii, 275p.*

HAVIGHURST, Robert J *and* MORGAN, H G
The social history of a war-boom community *(Westport, Conn: Greenwood 1968), 356p.*

HESSEL, *Mrs* Mary S *and others*
Strategic materials in hemisphere defense *(Toronto: Saunders 1942), xviii, 235p.*

HIRSCH, Julius
Price control in the war economy *(New York: Harper 1943), xvii, 311p.*

HOLMANS, Arthur J
Agricultural wage stabilization in World War II *(Washington DC: US Bureau of Agricultural Economics 1950), 140p.*

HOLMES, Harry N
Strategic materials and national strength *(Toronto: Macmillan 1942), 106p.*

HOETTL, Wilhelm
Hitler's paper weapon *(London: Hart-Davis 1955), 187p.*

HOUSE, Frank H
Timber at war: an account of the organization and activities of the Timber Control 1939–1945 *(London: Benn 1965), 332p.*

INGOT (pseud)
The economic aspect of war *(London: Allen & Unwin 1940), 7-251p.*

JAMES, Robert W
Wartime economic co-operation: a study of relations between Canada and the United States *(Toronto: Ryerson 1949), xiii, 415p.*

JANEWAY, Eliot
Struggle for survival: a chronicle of economic mobilization in World War II *(New Haven, Conn: Yale UP 1951), ix, 382p.*

JONES, Drummond
The role of the Office of Civilian Requirements in the Office of Production Management and War Production Board, January 1941 to November 1945 *(Washington DC: War Production Board 1946), 351p.*

KEYNES, John M
How to pay for the war: a radical plan for the Chancellor of the Exchequer *(London: Macmillan 1940), vii, 88p.*

KLEIN, Burton H
Germany's economic preparations for war *(Cambridge, Mass: Harvard UP 1959), 272p.*

KUCZYNSKI, Jurgen *and* WITT, M
Economics of barbarism: Hitler's new economic order in Europe *(London: Muller 1942), 5-64p.*

LAMER, Mirke
World fertilizer economy [in the Second World War] *(Stanford, Calif: Stanford UP 1957), 715p.*

LEAGUE OF NATIONS
Money and banking 1942/44 *(London: Allen & Unwin 1945), 224p.*
Wartime rationing and consumption *(London: Allen & Unwin 1942), 7-87p.*
World economic survey, 1931-1944 *(Geneva 1932-45), 11 vols.*

LORWIN, Lewis L
The economic consequences of the Second World War *(New York: Random House 1941), xvii, 510p.*

LUMER, Hyman
War economy and crisis *(New York: International 1954), 256p.*

MASS OBSERVATION
Enquiry into British war production *(London: Murray 1942), 420p.*

MEDLICOTT, William N
The economic blockade *(London: HMSO 1952-1959), 2 vols.*

MILLER, Douglas P
You can't do business with Hitler *(Boston, Mass: Little, Brown 1941), 229p.*

MILWARD, Alan S
The German economy at war *(London: Athlone 1965), 214p.*

MOODY, Blair
Boom or bust *(New York: Duell 1941), 336p.*

MOSS, William S
Gold is where you hide it: what happened to the Reichbank treasure? *(London: Deutsch 1956), 191p.*

MURPHY, Henry C
The national debt in war and transition *(New York: McGraw-Hill 1950), 295p.*

MURPHY, Mary E
British war economy, 1939-1943 *(New York: Professional & Technical 1943), xiv, 403p.*

OWEN, Jack
War in the workshops *(London: Lawrence & Wishart 1942), 72p.*

OXFORD UNIVERSITY. Institute of Statistics
Studies in war economics *(New York: Macmillan 1947), vii, 410p.*

PARKINSON, Joseph F (ed)
Canadian war economics *(London: Oxford UP 1941), vii, 191p.*

PATERSON, Thomas T
Morale in war and work: an experiment in the management of men *(London: Parrish 1955), 256p.*

PIED PIPER (pseud)
Rats! big business, big finance and war *(London: Gollancz 1941), 11-219p.*

POSTAN, Michael M *and others*
Design and development of weapons; studies in government and industrial organization *(London: HMSO 1964), 579p.*

PREST, A R
War economics of primary producing countries *(Cambridge: Cambridge UP 1948), 308p.*

RUNDELL, Walter
Black market money: the collapse of U.S. military currency control in World War II *(Baton Rouge, La: Louisiana State UP 1964), 125p.*

SAYERS, Richard S
Financial policy, 1939–45 *(London: HMSO 1956), 608p.*

SHIOMI, Saburo
Japanese and taxation, 1940–1956 *(New York: Columbia UP 1957), 190p.*

SOUTHARD, Frank A
The finances of European liberation, with special reference to Italy *(New York: King's Crown 1946), 206p.*

SPIEGEL, Henry W
Economics of total war *(New York: Appleton 1942), xiv, 410p.*

STEIN, Emanuel *and* BACKMAN, Jules
War economics *(New York: Farrar 1942), x, 501p.*

STEINER, George A (ed)
Economic problems of war *(New York: Wiley 1942), 692p.*

STERNBERG, Fritz
From Nazi sources: why Hitler can't win *(New York: Alliance 1943), xiv, 208p.*

STETTINIUS, Edward R
Lend-lease, weapon for victory *(New York: Macmillan 1944), xiv, 358p.*

STEVENS, Alden
Arms and the people *(New York: Harper 1942), ix, 262p.*

STRYKER, Perrin
Arms and the aftermath *(Boston, Mass: Houghton Mifflin 1942), viii, 157p.*

UNITED NATIONS
Proceedings and documents [of the Monetary and Financial Conference, Bretton Woods, New Hampshire, 1944.] *(Washington DC: Government Printing Office 1948), 2 vols.*

VAN VALKENBURG, Samuel (ed)
America at war: a geographical analysis *(New York: Prentice-Hall 1942), xiv, 296p.*

VOZNESENSKII, Nikolai A
The economy of the USSR during World War II *(Washington DC: Public Affairs 1948), 115p.*

WARE, Caroline F
The consumer goes to war: a guide to victory on the home front *(New York: Funk 1942), viii, 300p.*

WEBB, Maurice
Britain's industrial front *(London: Odhams 1943), 64p.*

WEEKS, *Sir* Ronald M
Organization and equipment for war *(Cambridge: Cambridge UP 1950), [II], 132p.*

WORSLEY, R H M
Europe versus America: implications of the new order *(London: Cape 1942), 204p.*

WORSLEY, Thomas B
Wartime economic stabilization and the efficiency of government procurement: a critical analysis of certain experiences of the United States in World War II *(Washington DC: National Security Resources Board 1949), 422p.*
[*see also* FINANCE]

EDUCATION

DENT, Harold C
Education in transition: a sociological study of the impact of war on English education, 1939-1944 *(Westport, Conn: Greenwood 1973), 244p.*

KANDEL, Isaac Leon
The impact of the war on American education *(Westport, Conn: Greenwood 1974), 285p.*

MILLER, Joseph H *and* BROOKS, D
The role of higher education in war and after *(New York: Harper 1944), xii, 222p.*

STANFORD UNIVERSITY. School of Education
Education in wartime and after *(New York: Appleton 1943), x, 465p.*

US OFFICE OF EDUCATION
Education under enemy occupation in Belgium, China, Czechoslovakia, France, Greece, Luxembourg, Netherlands, Norway, Poland *(Washington DC: 1945), 71p.*

WOLF, Abraham
Higher education in German-occupied countries *(London: Methuen 1945), 133p.*

EGYPT

BARKER, *Mrs* Gabriella
Desert angels: the story of a concert-party in Egypt during the war, 1939–1945 *(London: G.Barker 1956), 93p.*

HUGHES, Pennethorne
While Shepheard's watched *(London: Chatto & Windus 1949), 207p.*

LUGOL, Jean
Egypt and World War II: the anti-Axis campaigns in the Middle East *(Cairo: Societé Orientale de Publicité 1945), 402p.*

SCOULLAR, Joseph L
The battle for Egypt: the summer of 1942 *(London: Oxford UP 1956), 401p.*

WARNER, Denis
Written in sand *(London: Angus & Robertson 1944), viii, 193p.*

[*see also* MIDDLE EAST, NORTH AFRICA]

EICHMANN

ARENDT, Hannah
Eichmann in Jerusalem: a report on the banality of evil *(London: Faber 1963), [7], 275p, bib.*

BRAHAM, Randolph L
Eichmann and the destruction of Hungarian Jewry *(New York: Twayne 1961), 969p.*

CLARKE, Comer
Eichmann: the man and his crimes *(New York: Ballantine 1960), 153p.*

DONOVAN, John
Eichmann: man of slaughter *(New York: Avon 1960), 100p.*

GOLLANCZ, Victor
The case of Adolf Eichmann *(London: Gollancz 1961), 61p.*

HAUSNER, Gideon
Justice in Jerusalem *(London: Nelson 1967), xiii, 528p, bib.*

HULL, William L
The struggle for a soul *(New York: Doubleday 1963), 175p.*

LINZE, Dervey A
The trial of Adolf Eichmann *(Los Angeles: Holloway 1961), 224p.*

MUSMANNO, Michael A
The Eichmann kommandos *(Philadelphia, Pa: Macrae Smith 1961), 263p.*
PANETH, Philip
Eichmann: technician of death *(New York: Speller 1960), 239p.*
PAPADATOS, Peter
The Eichmann trial *(London: Stevens [1964]), x, 129p, bib.*
PEARLMAN, Moshe
The capture of Adolf Eichmann *(London: Weidenfeld & Nicolson [1961]), [5], 182p.*
The capture and trial of Adolf Eichmann *(London: Weidenfeld & Nicolson 1963), [5], 666p.*
REYNOLDS, Quentin J
Minister of death: the Adolf Eichmann story *(London: Cassell 1961), x, 264p, bib.*
ROBINSON, Jacob
And the crooked shall be made straight: the Eichmann trial, the Jewish catastrophe, and Hannah Arendt's narrative *(New York: Macmillan [1965]), ix, 406p, bib.*
RUSSELL, Edward F L, *2nd baron Russell of Liverpool*
The trial of Adolf Eichmann *(London: Heinemann 1962), xxviii, 324p.*
WIGHTON, Charles
Eichmann: his career and crimes *(London: Odhams 1961), 288p.*
ZEIGER, Henry A (ed)
The case against Adolf Eichmann *(New York: New American Library 1960), 192p.*
[*see also* CONCENTRATION CAMPS, GERMANY, JEWS, WAR CRIMES]

EISENHOWER

ALLIED FORCES Supreme Headquarters
Eisenhower's own story of the war: the complete record by the Supreme Commander . . . on the war in Europe from the day of invasion to the day of victory *(New York: Arco 1946), 122p.*
AMBROSE, Stephen E
Eisenhower and Berlin; 1945: the decision to halt at the Elbe *(New York: Norton 1967), 119p.*
The Supreme Commander: the war years of General Dwight D. Eisenhower *(New York: Doubleday 1969), xi, 732p.*
BLUMENSON, Martin
Eisenhower *(New York: Ballantine 1972), 160p, bib.*

BUTCHER, Harry C
My three years with Eisenhower *(New York: Simon & Schuster 1946), 911p.*
CHANDLER, Alfred D
The papers of Dwight David Eisenhower *(Baltimore, Md: Johns Hopkins 1970), 5 vols.*
EISENHOWER, Dwight D
Crusade in Europe *(London: Heinemann 1948), xiv, 582p.*
Eisenhower's wartime letters to Marshall *(Baltimore, Md: Johns Hopkins 1971), ix, 255p, bib.*
GUNTHER, John
Eisenhower: the man and the symbol *(London: Hamilton 1952),* [7], *184p, bib.*
McCANN, Kevin
America's man of destiny: an intimate biography of General Eisenhower *(London: Heinemann 1952), ix, 201p.*
McKEOGH, Michael J *and* LOCKRIDGE, Richard
Sergeant Mickey and General Ike *(New York: Putnam 1946), 185p.*
SIXSMITH, Eric K G
Eisenhower as military commander *(London: Batsford 1973), xiii, 248p, bib.*
SMITH, Walter B
Eisenhower's six great decisions *(Toronto: Longmans 1956), 237p.*
SUMMERSBY, Kathleen
Eisenhower was my boss *(New York: Prentice-Hall 1948), 302p.*

EL ALAMEIN

BARNETT, Correlli
The battle of El Alamein: decision in the desert *(New York: Macmillan* [*1964*]*),* [*6*], *90p, bib.*
CACCIA-DOMINIONI, Paolo *conte di Sillavengo*
Alamein, 1933–1962: an Italian story *(London: Allen & Unwin 1966), 3–289p.*
CARVER, Michael
El Alamein *(London: Batsford 1962), 3–216p.*
DENHOLM-YOUNG, Clement P S
Men of Alamein *(Cairo: Schindler 1943), 233p.*
DOUGLAS, Keith
Alamein to Zem Zem *(London: Editions Poetry 1946), 3–152p.*
JEWELL, Derek (ed)
Alamein and the desert war *(London: Sphere 1967), 208p.*

MAJDALANY, Fred
The battle of El Alamein *(London: Weidenfeld & Nicolson 1965), ix, 164p, bib.*
PHILLIPS, Cecil E L
Alamein *(London: Heinemann 1962), xii, 434p.*
THOMAS, Robert C W
The battles of Alam Halfa and El Alamein *(London: Clowes 1952), 56p.*
[*see also* BRITISH ARMY *(Eighth Army),* MONTGOMERY, NORTH AFRICA]

ENTERTAINMENT

DEAN, Basil
The theatre at war *(London: Harrap 1956), 573p.*
HOPE, Bob
I never left home *(New York: Simon & Schuster 1944), 207p.*
LEVIS, Carroll
A showman goes East *(London: Macdonald 1945), v, 7-223p.*
[*see also* EGYPT]

ERITREA

BARKER, Arthur J
Eritrea 1941 *(London: Faber 1966), 3-248p, bib.*
DOODY, John
The burning coast *(London: Joseph 1955), 255p.*
[*see also* ABYSSINIA, EAST AFRICA]

ESCAPES

AGUIRRE, Jose A
Escape via Berlin *(New York: Macmillan 1944), 361p; UK title:* Freedom was flesh and blood
ALLAN, James
No citation *(London: Angus & Robertson 1955), 222p.*
ARKWRIGHT, Albert S B
Return journey: escape from Oflag VIB *(London: Seeley 1948), 239p.*
ASTON, Walter H
. . . Nor iron bars a cage *(London: Macmillan 1946), 160p.*
BARLOW, Randle
Hit or miss: being the adventures of Driver Randle Barlow *(London: Wingate 1954), 223p.*

BAUER, Josef
As far as my feet will carry me *(London: Deutsch 1957), 254p.*

BELLEGARDE, Carlo de
African escape *(London: Kimpton 1957), 203p.*

BLACKMAN, Michael
By the hunter's moon *(London: Hodder & Stoughton 1956), 191p.*

BRICKHILL, Paul
Escape-or die: authentic stories of the R.A.F. Escaping Society *(London: Evans 1952), 223p.*
The great escape *(London: Faber 1951), 263p.*

BRICKHILL, Paul *and* NORTON, Conrad
Escape to danger *(London: Faber 1946), 341p.*

BRILHAC, Jean
The road to liberty: the story of 186 men who escaped *(London: Davies 1945), 215p.*

BRUDENELL-BRUCE, Chandos S C, *earl of Cardigan*
I walked alone *(London: Routledge 1950), viii, 206p.*

BURT, Kendal *and* LEASOR, James
The one that got away *(London: Collins 1956), 255p.*

CAMINADA, Jerome
My purpose holds *(London: Cape 1952), 221p.*

CHRISP, John
The tunnellers of Sandborstal *(London: Hale 1959), 172p; later published as:* Escape.

CLAIRE (pseud)
Escape from France *(London: Hale 1941), 117p.*

COLLINS, Douglas
P.O.W. [10 World War II escapes] *(New York: Norton 1968), 310p.*

CRAWLEY, Aidan
Escape from Germany: a history of R.A.F. escapes during the war *(London: Collins 1956), 318p.*

DAVIES, Tony
When the moon rises: an escape through wartime Italy *(London: Cooper 1973), ix, 165p.*

DEANE-DRUMMOND, Anthony
Return ticket *(London: Collins 1953), 256p.*

DELMAYNE, Anthony
Sahara desert escape *(London: Jarrolds 1958), 255p.*

DERRY, Sam
The Rome escape line: the story of the British organization in Rome for assisting escaped prisoners-of-war, 1943–44 *(London: Harrap 1960), 239p.*

DEVIGNY, Andre
Escape from Montluc *(London: Dobson 1957), 223p; US title:* A man escaped.

DEWET, Hugh O
The valley of the shadow *(Edinburgh: Blackwood 1949), 192p.*

DOMINY, John
The sergeant escapers: [the story of W. O. George Grimson who succeeded in establishing an escape route within Nazi Germany] *(London: Allan 1974), 144p.*

DUNBAR, John
Escape through the Pyrenees *(New York: Norton 1955), 176p.*

DUNCAN, Michael
Underground from Posen *(London: Kimber 1954), 192p.*

EVANS, Alfred J
Escape and liberation, 1940–45 *(London: Hodder & Stoughton 1945), 238p.*

FANCY, John
Tunnelling to freedom *(London: Hamilton 1957), 192p.*

FURMAN, John
Be not fearful *(London: Blond 1959), 225p.*

GALLAGHER, Joseph P
Scarlet Pimpernel of the Vatican *(London: Souvenir 1967), 184p.*

GARRAD-COLE, E
Single to Rome *(London: Wingate 1955), 143p.*

GIBBS, Patrick
It's further via Gibraltar *(London: Faber 1961), 144p.*

HARGEST, James
Farewell Campo 12 *(London: Joseph 1945),* [*II*], *206p.*

HARRIS, G H
Prisoner of war and fugitive *(Aldershot, Hants: Gale & Polden 1948), 70p.*

HELION, Jean
They shall not have me: the capture, forced labor and escape of a French prisoner of war *(New York: Dutton, 1943), 11–435p.*

HORSMAN, Jack
A thousand miles to freedom *(London: Drummond 1942), 64p.*

HUTTON, Clayton
The hidden catch *(London: Elek 1955), 176p.*
Official secret: the remarkable story of escape aids—their invention, production—and the sequel *(London: Parrish 1960),* [*8*], *196p.*

JACKSON, Robert
A taste of freedom: stories of the German and Italian prisoners who escaped from camps in Britain during World War 2 *(London: Barker* [*1964*], *208p.*
When freedom calls: great escapes of the Second World War *(London: Barker 1973), 190p.*

JAMES, David
A prisoner's progress *(London: Blackwood 1947), xi, 176p; US title:* Escaper's progress.

JOLLY, Cyril
The vengeance of Private Pooley *(London: Heinemann 1956), x, 237p.*

JONES, Ewart C
Germans under my bed *(London: Barker 1957), 222p.*

JONES, Francis S
Escape to nowhere *(London: Lane 1952), 267p.*

JONES, W A
Prisoner of the Kormoran *(London: Harrap 1945), 192p.*

KOPP, Hans
Himalaya shuttle cock *(London: Hutchinson 1957), 191p.*

KRIGE, Uys
The way out *(London: Collins 1946),* [22], *260p.*

LANG, *Sir* Derek
Return to St. Valery: the story of an escape through wartime France and Spain *(London: Cooper 1974), 192p.*

LANGLEY, James M
Fight another day *(London: Collins 1974), 254p.*

MACADAM, John
Minus the man from Cook's: record of an escape from wartime Britain *(London: Jarrolds 1944), 86p.*

MCCOY, Melvyn H *and* MELLNIK, S M
Ten escape from Tojo *(New York: Farrar 1944), 106p.*

MAGENER, Rolf
Prisoner's bluff *(London: Hart-Davis 1954), 239p.*

MAKUCEWICZ, Peter
I escaped from Germany *(London: Maxlove 1944), 125p.*

MEDD, Peter
The long walk home: an escape through Italy *(London: Lehmann 1951), xx, 21-176p.*

MEYNELL, Laurence
Airmen on the run: true stories of evasion and escape by British airmen of World War II *(London: Odhams 1963), 160p.*

MILLAR, George
Horned pigeon *(London: Heinemann 1946),* [*4*], *443p.*
MONSEY, Derek
The hero observed *(London: Gollancz 1960), 162p.*
MURRAY, Mary
Escape: a thousand miles to freedom *(London: Angus & Robertson 1965), 260p.*
NEAVE, Airey
Saturday at M.I.9: a history of underground escape lines in North-West Europe in 1940–5 by a leading organizer at M.I.9 *(London: Hodder & Stoughton 1969), 327p; US title:* The escape room.
They have their exits *(London: Hodder & Stoughton* [*1953*]*), 192p.*
NEILSON, William A (ed)
We escaped: twelve personal narratives of the flight to America *(New York: Macmillan 1941), vii, 258p.*
PAPE, Richard
Boldness be my friend *(London: Elek 1953),* [*6*], *314p.*
Sequel to boldness: the astonishing follow-on story to one of the greatest war books ever written *(London: Odhams* [*1959*]*), 256p.*
PHILPOT, Oliver
Stolen journey *(London: Hodder & Stoughton* [*1950*]*), 412p.*
PRITTIE, Terence C F *and* EDWARDS, William E
Escape to freedom *(London: Hutchinson 1953),* [*4*], *400p; previously published as:* South to freedom.
REID, Ian D
Prisoner at large: the story of five escapes *(London: Gollancz 1947), 305p.*
REID, Patrick R
The Colditz story *(London: Hodder & Stoughton* [*1952*]*), 288p; US title:* Men of Colditz.
The latter days: Colditz Castle, 1942–1945 *(London: Hodder & Stoughton* [*1953*]*), 300p.*
RICHARDSON, Anthony
Wingless victory: the story of Sir Basil Embry's escape from occupied France in the summer of 1940 *(London: Odhams* [*1950*]*), 256p; US title:* Alone he went.
ROFE, Cyril
Against the wind *(London: Hodder & Stoughton* [*1956*]*), 319p.*
ROOSENBURG, Henriette
The walls came tumbling down *(London: Secker & Warburg 1957), 222p.*

RAF Flying Review
They got back: the best escape stories from the R.A.F. Flying Review *(London: Jenkins 1961), 143p.*

SCHRIRE, I
Stalag doctor *(London: Wingate 1956), 209p.*

SEXTON, Winton K
We fought for freedom *(Kansas City, Kan: Burton 1948), 116p.*

SMITH, Sydney
Wings Day: the man who led the R.A.F.'s epic battle in German captivity *(London: Collins 1968), 3-252p: US title:* Mission escape.

SPENSER, James (pseud)
The awkward Marine *(London: Longmans Green 1948), 251p.*

TAYLOR, Geoff
Piece of cake *(London: Davies 1956), [9], 273p.*

TURNER, John F
Prisoner at large *(London: Staples 1957), 171p.*

TUTE, Warren
Escape route green *(London: Dent 1971), ix, 175p.*

VINCENT, Adrian
The long way home *(London: Allen & Unwin 1956), 208p.*

WARRACK, Graeme
Travel by dark after Arnhem *(London: Harvill [1963]), 256p.*

WEINTZEL, Fritz
Single or return?: the story of a German P.O.W. in British camps and the escape of Lieutenant Franz von Werra *(London: Kimber 1954), viii, 9-172p.*

WILLIAMS, Eric (comp)
Great escape stories *(London: Weidenfeld & Nicolson 1958), 256p.*
The tunnel *(London: Collins 1951), 255p.*

YOUNGER, Calton
No flight from the cage *(London: Muller 1956), 255p.*
[*see also* ESPIONAGE, INTELLIGENCE, SECRET SERVICES]

ESSEX

BENHAM, Hervey (ed)
Essex at war *(Colchester: Benham 1945), 154p.*

EVACUEES

BARNET HOUSE STUDY GROUP
London children in war-time Oxford *(London: Oxford UP 1947), 126p.*

BELL, Caroline D *and* BELL, E A B
Thank you twice; or, How we like America *(New York: Harcourt 1941), vi, 112p.*

BODY, Alfred H
Children in flight: some pictures of the evacuation *(London: London UP 1940), 95p.*

BOYD, William (ed)
Evacuation in Scotland: a record of events and experiments *(London: London UP 1944), xvi, 224p.*

BRADBEER, Grace
The land changed its face: the evacuation of Devon's South Hams, 1943–1944 *(Newton Abbot, Devon: David & Charles 1973), 144p.*

DADE, Harry A
To his refugee son *(Albuquerque, NM: New Mexico UP 1942), 191p.*

HARBINSON, Robert
Song of Erne *(London: Faber 1960), 244p.*

ISAACS, Mrs Susan S (ed)
The Cambridge evacuation survey: a wartime study in social welfare and education *(London: Methuen 1941), ix, 235p.*

JOHNSON, Bryan S
The evacuees *(London: Gollancz 1968), 288p; bib.*

LEIGHTON, Alexander H
The governing of men: general principles and recommendations based on experience at a Japanese relocation camp *(Princeton, NJ: Princeton UP 1945), 404p.*

LORIMER, Jean
Pilgrim children *(London: Muller 1942), 154p.*

PADLEY, Richard *and* COLE, M I P
Evacuation survey: a report to the Fabian Society *(London: Routledge 1940), 296p.*

POOLEY, Richard
The evacuee *(Hull: Anglo-American Publicity Services 1972), [3], 54p.*

WHITE, William L
Journey for Margaret *(New York: Harcourt 1941), 256p.*
[*see also* CHILDREN, INTERNMENT]

EXETER

HOARE, M C B
This jewel remains: illustrated record of the Baedeker raid on Exeter, the cathedral capital of the West, on May 4th, 1942 *(Exeter: Western Times 1947), 67p.*

FAR EAST

BLACKATER, C F
Gods without reason *(London: Eyre & Spottiswoode 1948), 214p.*

BRALY, William C
The hard way home *(Washington DC: Infantry Journal Press 1947), 282p.*

BROUGHTON, Douglas G
Mongolian plains and Japanese prison *(London: Pickering & Inglis 1947), 71p.*

BROWN, Cecil
Suez to Singapore *(New York: Random House 1942), xi, 545p.*

BROWN, Robert M
I solemnly swear: the story of a GI named Brown *(New York: Vantage 1957), 203p; UK title:* A GI named Brown.

BRYAN, Joseph *and* REED, Philip
Mission beyond darkness *(New York: Duell 1945), 133p.*

CATES, Tressa R
Drainpipe diary *(New York: Vantage 1957), 273p.*

COLLIER, Basil
The war in the Far East, 1941-1945: a military history *(London: Heinemann 1969), xiii, 530p, bib.*

CONGDON, Don (comp)
Combat: the war with Japan *(London: Mayflower 1963), 384p.*

DUPUY, Trevor N
Asiatic land battles: the expansion of Japan in Asia *(New York: Watts 1963),* [4], 68p.

EVANS, *Sir* Geoffrey
The desert and the jungle *(London: Kimber 1959), 206p.*

EYRE, Donald C *and* BOWLER, Douglas
The soul and the sea *(London: Hale* [*1959*]*), 192p.*

GALLAGHER, O'Dowd
Retreat in the East: a war book *(London: Harrap 1942), 192p.*

JONES, F C *and others*
Survey of international affairs 1939-1946: the Far East, 1942-1946 *(London: Oxford UP 1955), xiv, 589p.*

KEETON, George W
China, the Far East and the future *(London: Cape 1943), 296p.*
KEPHART, Rodney
Wake, war and waiting *(New York: Exposition 1950), 84p.*
KIRBY, Stanley W *and others*
The war against Japan *(London: HMSO 1957–8), 2 vols.*
MORRISON, Ian
This war against Japan: thoughts on the present conflict in the Far East *(London: Faber 1943), 112p; US title:* Our Japanese foe.
PHILLIPS, G D R
Russia, Japan and Mongolia *(London: Muller 1942), 104p.*
QUIGLEY, Harold S
Far Eastern war, 1937–1941 *(Boston, Mass: World Peace 1942), xi, 369p.*
SHRIDHARANI, Krishnaial J
Warning to the West *(New York: Duell 1942), ix, 274p.*
TOLAND, John
But not in shame: the six months after Pearl Harbour *(London: Gibbs & Phillips 1962), 443p.*
WAGG, Alfred
A million died: war in the Far East *(London: Nicholson & Watson 1943), 192p.*
[*see also* CHINA, JAPAN, PACIFIC, PHILIPPINES]

FERRY PILOTS

CURTIS, Lettice
The forgotten pilots: a story of the Air Transport Auxiliary 1939–45 *(London: Foulis 1971), xv, 337p.*
GREAT BRITAIN. Air Ministry
Atlantic bridge: the official account of R.A.F.'s Transport Command's ocean ferry *(London: HMSO 1945), 75p.*
KING, Alison
Golden wings: the story of some of the women ferry pilots of Air Transport Auxiliary *(London: Pearson [1956]), x, 11–191p.*
WATT, Sholto
I'll take the high road: a history of the beginning of the Atlantic air ferry in war-time *(Fredericton, New Brunswick: Brunswick 1960), 169p.*

FIGHTERS

AUSTIN, Alexander B
Fighter Command *(London: Gollancz 1941), 248p.*

AYLING, Keith

Combat aviation *(Harrisburg, Pa: Military Service 1943), 253p.*

Flying furies *(New York: Nelson 1942), 7-42p.*

R.A.F.; the story of a British fighter pilot *(New York: Holt 1941), xiv, 332p.*

They fly for victory *(New York: Nelson 1943), 215p.*

BADER, Douglas

Fight for the sky: the story of the Spitfire and the Hurricane *(London: Sidgwick & Jackson 1973), 190p.*

BAILEY, Jim

The sky suspended *(London: Hodder & Stoughton 1965), 166p.*

BAKER, Edgar C R

The fighter aces of the R.A.F., 1939-1945 *(London: Kimber 1962), 208p, bib.*

Pattle—supreme fighter in the air *(London: Kimber 1965), 207p.*

BINDER, Jenane

One crowded hour: the saga of an American boy *(New York: William-Frederick 1946), 171p.*

BLOND, Georges

Born to fly: exploits of the war's great fighter aces *(London: Souvenir 1956), 208p.*

CLOSTERMANN, Pierre

The big show: some experiences of a French fighter pilot in the R.A.F. *(London: Chatto & Windus 1951), 256p.*

CROOK, David M

Spitfire pilot *(London: Faber 1942), 104p.*

DEERE, Alan C

Nine lives *(London: Hodder & Stoughton 1959), 262p.*

DONAHUE, Arthur G

Tally-ho! Yankee in a Spitfire *(New York: Macmillan 1941), 190p.*

ELLAN, B J (pseud)

Spitfire! the experiences of a fighter pilot *(London: Murray 1942), xi, 99p.*

FALKOWSKI, Jan P

With the wind in my face: the story of a Polish fighter pilot in the R.A.F. *(Whitby, Ontario: Canada Yearbook Services 1966), 166p.*

FIEDLER, Arkady

Squadron 303: the story of the Polish fighter squadron with the R.A.F. *(London: Davies 1942), 116p.*

FORBES, Athol S *and* ALLEN, H R
Ten fighter boys *(London: Collins 1942), 176p.*
FORRESTER, Larry
Fly for your life: the story of R. R. Stanford Tuck, D.S.O., D.F.C. and two bars *(London: Muller [1956]), 367p.*
FREEMAN, Roger A
Mustang at war *(London: Allan 1974), 160p.*
FRIEDHEIM, Eric *and* TAYLOR, Samuel W
Fighters up: the story of American fighter pilots in the battle of Europe *(Philadelphia, Pa: Macrea Smith 1945), 275p.*
GALLICO, Paul
The Hurricane story *(London: Joseph 1959), 143p.*
GLEED, Ian R
Arise to conquer *(London: Gollancz 1942), 111p.*
GODFREY, John T
The look of eagles *(New York: Random House 1958), 245p.*
GREEN, William
Famous fighters of the Second World War *(London: Macdonald 1962), 2 vols.*
Rocket fighter *(New York: Ballantine 1971), 159p.*
GREY, Charles G
British fighter planes *(London: Faber 1941), xvi, 200p.*
HALL, Grover C
1000 destroyed: the life and times of the 4th Fighter Group *(Montgomery, Ala: Brown 1946), [12], 286p.*
HESS, William N
Famous airmen: the Allied aces of World War II *(New York: Arco 1967), 64p.*
Pacific sweep: the 5th and 13th Fighter Commands in World War II *(New York: Doubleday 1974), 278p.*
HILLARY, Richard H
Last enemy *(London: Macmillan 1942), vii, 220p; US title:* Falling through space.
HIRSCH, Phil (ed)
Fighting aces *(New York: Pyramid Books 1965), 173p.*
HOUSTON, Karl H *and* CARPENTER, Newt
66th Fighter wing in Europe *(Cambridge: Cambridge UP 1945), 1 vol.*
JAMES, Stefan (pseud)
Bitter monsoon: the memoirs of a fighter pilot *(London: Hale 1955), 192p.*
JOHNSON, James E (Johnnie)
Wing leader *(London: Chatto & Windus 1956), 320p.*

KENNERLY, Byron
Eagles roar! *(New York: Harper 1942), xviii, 271p.*

LALLEMANT, Raymond
Rendezvous with fate *(London: Macdonald [1964]), 3-192p.*

LANCHBERRY, Edward
Against the gun: the story of Wing Commander Roland Beaumont, pilot of the Canberra and the P.I. *(London: Cassell 1955), 270p.*

LOOMIS, Robert D
Great American fighter pilots of World War II *(New York: Random House 1961), 208p.*

MASON, Ernest M
Imshi: a fighter pilot's letters to his mother *(London: W. H. Allen 1943), 168p.*

MASON, Francis K
The Hawker Hurricane *(London: Macdonald 1962), 175p.*

MASON, Herbert M
Duel for the sky: fighter planes and fighter pilots of World War II *(New York: Grosset 1970), 148p.*

MOUCHOTTE, Rene
The Mouchotte diaries, 1940–1943 *(London: Staples 1956), 221p.*

OLMSTED, Merie C
The Yoxford Boys: the 357th fighter group on escort over Europe and Russia *(Fallbrook, Calif: Aero 1971), 103p.*

PEARL, Jack
Aerial dogfights of World War II *(Derby, Conn: Monarch 1962), 138p.*

POKRYSHKIN, Aleksandr I
Red air ace *(London: Soviet War News 1945), 55p.*

PRINGLE, Patrick
Fighting pilots *(London: Evans 1961), 207p, bib.*

R.A.F. CASUALTY (pseud)
I had a row with a German *(London: Macmillan 1941), xiii, 108p.*

REED, Arthur *and* BEAMONT, Roland
Typhoon and Tempest at war *(London: Allan 1974), 176p.*

RICHEY, Paul H M
Fighter pilot: a personal record of the campaign in France, 1939–1940 *(London: Pan rev. ed. 1969), xii, 147p.*

ROBERTSON, Bruce
Spitfire: the story of a famous fighter *(Harleyford, Herts: Harborough 1960), 211p.*

RUST, Kean C *and* HESS, W N
The Slybird Group: the 353rd Fighter Group on escort and ground attack operations *(Fallbrook, Calif: Aero 1968), 95p.*

SHORES, Christopher F *and* RING, Hans
Fighters over the desert: the air battles in the Western Desert, June 1940 to December, 1942 *(London: Spearman 1969), 256p.*

SHORES, Christopher F *and* WILLIAMS, Clive
Aces high: the fighter aces of the British and Commonwealth air forces in World War II *(London: Spearman 1966), 335p, bib.*

SIMS, Edward H
American aces in great fighter battles, of World War II *(New York: Harper 1958), xvi, 17-318p; UK title:* American aces of World War 2.

The fighter pilots: a comparative study of the Royal Air Force, the Luftwaffe and the United States Army Air Force in Europe and North Africa, 1939-1945 *(London: Cassell 1967), x, 294p, bib.*

The greatest aces *(New York: Harper 1967), 294p.*

The greatest fighter missions of the top Navy and Marine aces of World War II *(New York: Harper 1962), xxii, 250p.*

TAYLOR, John W R *and* ALLWARD, Maurice F
Spitfire *(Leicester: Drysdale 1946), 119p.*

TIDY, Douglas
I fear no man: the story of N.74 (Fighter) squadron, Royal Flying Corps and Royal Air Force (the Tigers) *(London: Macdonald 1972), xv, 239p.*

TURNER, Richard E
Big friend, little friend: memoirs of a World War II fighter pilot *(New York: Doubleday 1969), 176p; US title:* Mustang pilot.

ULANOFF, Stanley M (ed)
Fighter pilot *(New York: Doubleday 1962), 430p.*

VADER, John
Spitfire *(New York: Ballantine 1970), 160p, bib.*

WALKER, John B
War in the air: fighter planes and pilots in action *(New York: Random House 1941), 7-74p.*

WILSON, A J
Sky sweepers: the story of Fighter Command's offensive operations against the enemy in 1941 and the Spring of 1942, and the battle with the German night bombers over Britain *(London: Jarrolds 1942), 128p.*

WINSTON, Robert
Aces wild *(New York: Holiday 1941), 9-320p.*

ZIEGLER, Herman E
Rocket fighter: the story of the Me 163 *(London: Macdonald 1963), 161p.*

FIJI

HOWLETT, Robert A (comp)
The history of the Fiji military forces, 1939–1945 *(London: Crown Agents for the Colonies 1948), 267p.*

FINANCE

CRUM, William L *and others*
Fiscal planning for total war *(New York: National Bureau of Economic Resources 1942), xxv, 358p.*

DONN, Albert I
World War II prisoner of war script of the United States *(Iola, Wis: Krause 1970), 112p.*

KATONA, George
War without inflation: the psychological approach to problems of war economy *(London: Oxford UP 1942), x, 213p.*

TOY, Raymond S *and* MEYER, R E
Axis military currency: all known issues are listed *(El Cagon, Calif: Toy 1967), 98p.*

VOORHIS, Horace J
Out of debt, out of danger: proposals for war finance and to-morrow's money *(New York: Devin-Adair 1943), 238p.*
[*see also* ECONOMICS]

FINLAND

CHEW, Allen F
The white death: the epic of the Soviet-Finnish winter war *(East Lansing, Mich: Michigan State UP 1971), 313p.*

CLARK, Douglas
Three days to catastrophe *(London: Hammond [1966]), 228p.*

COATES, William P *and* COATES, Z K
Soviet-Finnish campaign, military and political, 1939–1940 *(London: Eldon 1942), 172p.*

CONDON, Richard W
The winter war: Russia against Finland *(New York: Ballantine 1972), 160p, bib.*

COX, Geoffrey
The Red Army moves *(London: Gollancz 1941), 278p.*

ELLISTON, Herbert B
Finland fights *(London: Harrap 1940), 398p.*
ENGLE, Eloise *and* PAANANEN, Lauri
The winter war: the Russo-Finnish conflict, 1939-40 *(New York: Scribner 1973), xv, 176p, bib.*
FINLAND and World War II, 1939-1944 *(New York: Ronald 1948), 228p.*
FINLAND reveals her secret documents on Soviet policy, March, 1940-June, 1941 *(New York: Funk 1941), 122p.*
JAKOBSON, Max
The diplomacy of the winter war: an account of the Russo-Finnish war, 1939-1940 *(Cambridge, Mass: Harvard UP 1961),* [*9*], *281p.*
KROSBY, H P
Finland, Germany and the Soviet Union, 1940-1941: the Petsamo dispute *(Madison, Wis: Wisconsin UP 1968), 276p.*
LANGDON-DAVIES, John
Finland: the first total war *(London: Routledge 1940), ix, 202p; US title:* Invasion in the snow.
LUNDIN, Leonard
Finland in the Second World War *(Bloomington, Ind: Indiana UP 1957), 303p.*
LUUKKANEN, Eino A
Fighter over Finland: the memoirs of a fighter pilot *(London: Macdonald 1963), 254p.*
STRODE, Hudson
Finland forever *(New York: Harcourt 1941), xix, 443p.*
TANNER, Vaino
The winter war: Finland against Russia, 1939-1940 *(Stanford, Calif: Stanford UP 1957), x, 274p.*
UPTON, Anthony F
Finland, 1939-1940 *(London: Davis-Poynter 1974), 174p, bib.*
Finland in crisis, 1940-1941: a study in small-power politics *(London: Faber 1964), 3-318p, bib.*
WARD, Edward H H
Despatches from Finland, Jan.-Apr. 1940 *(London: Lane 1940), 160p.*

FLEET AIR ARM

CAMERON, Ian
Wings of morning: the story of the Fleet Air Arm in the Second World War *(London: Hodder & Stoughton 1962), 288p, bib.*

GREAT BRITAIN. Admiralty
Fleet Air Arm *(London: HMSO 1942), 128p.*

HORSLEY, Terence
Find, fix and strike: the work of the Fleet Air Arm *(London: Eyre & Spottiswoode 1945), 144p.*

MACINTYRE, Donald
Wings of Neptune: the story of naval aviation *(London: Davies 1963), x, 269p, bib.*

MOORE, John C
Fleet Air Arm: a short account of its history and achievements *(London: Chapman & Hall 1943), 140p.*

POPHAM, Hugh
Sea flight: a Fleet Air Arm pilot's story *(London: Kimber 1954), 200p.*

RAWLINGS, John D R
Pictorial history of the Fleet Air Arm *(London: Allan 1973), 208p.*

RUTTER, Owen
The British Navy's air arm: the official story of the British Navy's air operations *(Washington DC: Infantry Journal Press 1944), 248p.*

TOWNEND, John M
Overture to life *(London: Rich & Cowan 1944), 150p.*
[*see also* AIRCRAFT CARRIERS, ROYAL NAVY]

FLORENCE

TUTAEV, David
The consul of Florence *(London: Secker & Warburg 1966), xiv, 303p, bib; US title:* The man who saved Florence.

FLYING BOATS

BROWN, Winifred
No distress signals *(London: Davies 1952), 248p.*

KAMMEN, Michael G
Operational history of the flying boat, open sea and seadrome aspects, selected campaigns, World War II *(Washington DC: Bureau of Aeronautics, Navy Department 1959), 133p.*

POOLMAN, Kenneth
Flying boat: the story of the 'Sunderland' *(London: Kimber 1962), 208p.*

FLYING BOMBS

IRVING, David
The mare's nest *(London: Kimber [1964]), 320p.*

NEWMAN, Bernard
They saved London *(London: Laurie 1952), 192p.*
[*see also* ROCKETS]

FLYING CONTROL

BULLMORE, Francis T K
The dark haven *(London: Cape 1956), 192p.*

FOOD

BAKER, Benjamin
Wartime food procurement and production *(New York: King's Crown 1951), 219p.*
BLACK, John D
Food enough *(Lancaster, Pa: Cattell 1943), vii, 269p.*
BOURNE, Geoffrey
Nutrition and the war *(Cambridge: Cambridge UP 1940), xii, 126p.*
EYLES, Margaret L
Eat well in war-time *(London: Gollancz 1940), 158p.*
FOWLER, Bertram B
Food: a weapon for victory *(Boston, Mass: Little, Brown 1942), 185p.*
GENUNG, Albert B
Food policies during World War II: a historical account of American food production, price, and control operations during the Second World War, 1941–1946 *(Ithaca, NY: Northeast Farm Foundation 1951), 81p.*
GREAT BRITAIN. Ministry of Food
How Britain was fed in war time: food control, 1939–1945 *(London: HMSO 1946), 66p.*
HAMMOND, Richard J
Food *(London: HMSO 1951–62), 3 vols.*
Food and agriculture in Britain, 1939–45: aspects of wartime control *(Stanford, Calif: Stanford UP 1954), 246p.*
HENDRICKSON, Roy F
Food crisis *(New York: Doubleday 1943), xi, 274p.*
INTERNATIONAL LABOR OFFICE
Food control in Great Britain *(London: King 1942), vi, 272p.*
JOHNSTON, Bruce F *and others*
Japanese food management in World War II *(Stanford, Calif: Stanford UP 1953), 283p.*

KNIGHT, *Sir* Henry F
Food administration in India, 1939-1947 *(Stanford, Calif: Stanford UP 1954), 323p.*

LEAGUE OF NATIONS
Food, famine and relief 1940-1946 *(London: Allen & Unwin 1946), 162p.*

LLOYD, Edward M H
Food and inflation in the Middle East. 1940-45 *(Stanford, Calif: Stanford UP 1956), 375p.*

MARRACK, John R
Food and planning *(London: Gollancz 1942), 285p.*

ORR, *Sir* John B
Fighting for what? *(London: Macmillan 1942), xiv, 89p.*

PEARSON, Frank A *and* PAARLBERG, Don
Food *(New York: Knopf 1944), xi, 239p.*

POTIPHAR (pseud)
They must not starve *(London: Gollancz 1945), 107p.*

PRENTICE, Ezra P
Food, war and the future *(New York: Harper 1944), xii, 164p.*

ROLL, Erich
Combined food board: a study of wartime international planning *(Stanford, Calif: Stanford UP 1956), 385p.*

RUSSELL, Judith *and* FANTIN, Renee
Studies in food rationing *(Washington DC: Office of Price Administration 1948), 404p.*

STEWART, Leslie
Protection and salvage of food in wartime *(London: Jordan 1942), 64p.*

TOLLEY, Howard R
Farmer citizen at war *(Toronto: Macmillan 1943), xi, 318p.*

WALKER, Roy
Famine over Europe: the problem of controlled food relief *(London: Dakers 1941), 185p.*

WALWORTH, George
Feeding the nation in peace and war *(London: Allen & Unwin 1942), 548p.*

[*see also* AGRICULTURE, EARL WOOLTON'S MEMOIRS]

FRANCE

ARENSTAM, Arved
Tapestry of a debacle from Paris to Vichy: a book of contracts *(London: Constable 1942), v, 194p.*

ARMSTRONG, Hamilton F
Chronology of failure: the last days of the French Republic *(New York: Macmillan 1940), viii, 202p.*

ARON, Robert
De Gaulle before Paris: the liberation of France, June–August, 1944 *(London: Putnam [1963]), vii, 312p.*
De Gaulle triumphant: the liberation of France, August 1944–May 1945 *(London: Putnam 1964), [7], 360p. bib.*
France reborn: the history of the liberation, June 1944–May 1945 *(New York: Scribner 1964), 490p.*

AUREN, Sven A G
The tricolour flies again *(London: Hammond 1946), 200p.*

BATCHELLER, *Mrs* Tryphosa
France in sunshine and shadow *(New York: Brentano 1944), II–202p.*

BEAUFRE, Andre
1940: the fall of France *(London: Cassell 1967), xxii, 228p.*

BENOIST-MECHIN, Jacques
Sixty days that shook the West: the fall of France, 1940 *(London: Cape 1963), 559p, bib.*

BIDAULT, Georges
Resistance: the political autobiography of Georges Bidault *(London: Weidenfeld & Nicholson [1967]), xx, 348p.*

BLOCH, Marc L B
Strange defeat: a statement of evidence written in 1940 *(Toronto: Oxford UP 1949), xxii, 178p.*

BLUM, Leon
Leon Blum before his judges at the Supreme Court of Riom, March 11th–12th, 1942 *(London: Routledge 1943), viii, 159p.*

BOIS, Elie J
The truth on the tragedy of France *(London: Hodder & Stoughton 1941), 416p.*

BROOKS, Howard L
Prisoners of hope: a report on a mission *(New York: Fischer 1942), 319p.*

CHAMBRUN, Rene, *comte de*
I saw France fall; will she rise again? *(New York: Morrow 1940), 11–216p.*

CHAPMAN, Guy
Why France collapsed *(London: Cassell 1968), iii–xiv, 403p, bib.*

COT, Pierre
The triumph of treason *(New York: Ziff-Davis 1944), 432p.*

Cotnareanu, Leon
Alternative-culture and peace *(New York: Dodd 1941), xi, 78p.*

Curie, Eve *and others* (eds)
They speak for a nation: letters from France *(New York: Doubleday 1941), xxv, 238p.*

Dank, Milton
The French against the French: collaboration and resistance *(Philadelphia, Pa: Lippincott 1974), 365p.*

DeMontmorency, Alec
The enigma of Admiral Darlan *(New York: Dutton 1943), 5-194p.*

DePolnay, Peter
Death and to-morrow: adventures in occupied and unoccupied France *(London: Secker & Warburg 1942), 299p.*

Deporte, A W
De Gaulle's foreign policy, 1944–1946 *(Cambridge, Mass: Harvard UP 1968), xvii, 327p, bib.*

Downing, Rupert
If I laugh: the chronicle of my strange adventures in the great Paris exodus - June 1940 *(London: Harrap 1940), 191p.*

Draper, Theodore
Six weeks war: France, May 10–June 25, 1940 *(New York: Viking 1944), vi, 346p.*

Dutourd, Jean
The taxis of the Marne *(London: Secker & Warburg 1957), 192p.*

Fernand-Laurent, Camille J
Gallic charter: foundations of tomorrow's France *(Boston, Mass: Little, Brown 1944), 280p.*

Feutchwanger, Leon
The devil in France: my encounter with him in the summer of 1940 *(New York: Viking 1941), 265p.*

Fontaine, Peter
Last to leave Paris: the diary of an odyssey of 5,000 to escape from France *(London: Chaterson 1941), xi, 148p.*

Fonvielle-Alquier, Francois
The French and the phoney war, 1939–40 *(London: Stacey 1973), 218p.*

Fortune, G *and* Fortune, W (pseuds)
Hitler divided France: a factual account of conditions in occupied France and unoccupied France from the armistice of June 1940 up to the total occupation in Nov. 1942 *(London: Macmillan 1943), vii, 134p.*

France and the war *(London: Muller 1944), 96p.*

FRANCE during the German occupation, 1940–1944: a collection of 292 statements on the government of Marechal Petain and Pierre Laval *(Stanford, Calif: Stanford UP 1959), 3 vols.*

FREEMAN, C D *and* COOPER, Douglas
The road to Bordeaux *(London: Cresset 1940), 408p.*

FRENCH, Herbert E
My Yankee Paris *(New York: Vanguard 1945), 260p.*

FRY, Varian
Surrender on demand *(New York: Random House 1945), xii, 243p.*

GROULT, Benoitre *and* GROULT, Flora
Diary in duo *(London: Barrie & Rockliff 1965), 350p.*

HENREY, *Mrs* Robert
Madeleine, young wife: the autobiography of a French girl *(New York: Dutton 1954), 380p.*
The return to the farm *(London: Davies 1947), 173p.*

HORNE, Alistair
To lose a battle: France 1940 *(London: Macmillan 1969), xxvii, 556p, bib.*

HUDDLESTON, Sisley
France: the tragic years; an eyewitness account of war, occupation and liberation *(New York: Devin-Adair 1954), xxiv, 360p.*

HUSTON, James A
Across the face of France: liberation and recovery, 1944–1963 *(West Lafayette, Ind: Purdue University Studies 1963), 251p.*

KERNAN, Thomas
France on Berlin time *(Philadelphia, Pa: Lippincott 1941), 11-312p.*

LEITH-ROSS, *Mrs* Sylvia
Cocks in the dawn *(London: Hutchinson 1944), 80p.*

LEVERRIER, Madeleine G
France in torment *(London: Hamilton 1942), 167p.*

LIEBLING, Abbot J
The republic of silence *(New York: Harcourt 1947), 522p.*

LORRAINE, Jacques
Behind the battle of France *(Oxford: Oxford UP 1943), vi, 136p.*
The Germans in France *(London: Hutchinson 1947), 192p.*

LYTTON, Neville S
Life in unoccupied France *(London: Macmillan 1942), viii, 94p.*

MCCALLUM, Ronald B
England and France 1939–1943 *(London: Hamilton 1944), 189p.*

MACKAY, *Mrs* Helen G
With love for France *(New York: Scribner 1942), 139p.*

MACKWORTH, Cecily
I came out of France *(London: Routledge 1941), v, 248p.*

MALAQUAIS, Jean
War diary *(New York: Doubleday 1944), 246p.*

MARITAIN, Jacques
France, my country, through the disaster *(New York: Longmans 1941), ix, 117p.*
Messages, 1941-1944 *(New York: Maison-Française 1945), 221p.*

MARLOW, James
De Gaulle's France and the key to the coming invasion of Germany *(London: Simpkin Marshall 1940), 95p.*

MARTY, André P
The trial of the French communist deputies: a contribution to the history of a crime *(London: Lawrence & Wishart 1941), viii, 9-126p.*

MAUROIS, Andre
The battle of France *(London: Lane 1940), 210p.*
Tragedy in France *(New York: Harper 1940), viii, 250p; UK title:* Why France fell.

MENDES-FRANCE, Pierre
The pursuit of freedom *(London: Longmans Green 1956), 256p.*

MORROW, Elizabeth R (ed)
All Gaul is divided . . . letters from occupied France *(London: Gollancz 1941), 119p.*

MUIR, Peter
War without music *(New York: Scribner 1940), viii, 262p.*

NATTAGES, Francois
Escape to danger *(London: Harrap 1943), 148p.*

NIVELLE, Robert
And yet France smiled *(London: Continental 1944), 64p.*

ODIC, Charles J
Stepchildren of France *(New York: Roy 1945), 181p.*

OSGOOD, Samuel M (comp)
The fall of France, 1940: causes and responsibilities *(Boston, Mass: Heath [1966]), xii, 80p, bib.*

PAUL, Oscar (pseud)
Farewell France!: an eye-witnesses account of her tragedy *(London: Gollancz 1941), 224p.*

PERTINAX (pseud)
Gravediggers, Reynaud, Petain and Laval; military defeat, armistice and counter revolution *(New York: Doubleday 1944), xi, 612p.*

PHILIP, Percy J
France in defeat *(London: Muller 1941), 96p.*

PICKLES, Dorothy M
France between the republics *(London: Contact 1946), 247p.*

POL, Heinz
The suicide of a democracy *(New York: Reynal 1940), xii, 296p.*

PORTER, Roy P
Uncensored France: an eye-witnesses account of France under the occupation *(New York: Dial 1942), viii, 9–305p.*

PRITT, Denis N
The fall of the French Republic *(London: Muller 1941), 177p.*

REITHINGER, Anton
Why France lost the war: a biologic and economic survey *(New York: Veritas 1940), 75p.*

REYNAUD, Paul
In the thick of the fight, 1930–1945 *(London: Cassell 1955), xi, 689p, bib.*

RIEBER, Alfred
Stalin and the French Communist Party, 1941–1947 *(New York: Columbia UP 1962), 395p.*

ROBICHON, Jacques
The second D-Day *(London: Barker 1969), x, 314p, bib.*

ROUCHARD, Martine
The time of our lives *(New York: Pantheon 1946), xi, 322p.*

ROWE, Vivian
The great wall of France: the triumph of the Maginot Line *(New York: Putnam 1959), 328p.*

STEXUPERY, Consuelo de
Kingdom of the rocks: memories of Oppede *(New York: Random House 1946), 305p.*

SAINTJEAN, Robert de
France speaking *(New York: Dutton 1941), 7–335p.*

SALIÈGE, Jules G, *cardinal*
Who shall bear the flame? *(Chicago, Ill: Fides 1949), 191p.*

SAURAT, Denis
Spirit of France *(London: Dent 1940), 75p.*
Watch over Africa *(London: Dent 1941), vii, 167p.*

SHIRER, William L
The collapse of the Third Republic: an inquiry into the fall of France in 1940 *(New York: Simon & Schuster 1969), xv, 1045p, bib.*

SIMON, Paul
One enemy only – the invader: a record of French resistance *(London: Hodder & Stoughton 1942), 167p.*

SIMON, Yves
The march to liberation *(Milwaukee, Wis: Tower 1942), 102p.*

SIMONE, Andre (pseud)
J'accuse! the men who betrayed France *(New York: Dial 1940), 7-354p.*

SPEARS, *Sir* Edward L
Assignment to catastrophe *(London: Heinemann 1954), 2 vols.*

STEIN, Gertrude
Wars I have seen *(New York: Random House 1945), 259p.*

TARTIERE, Dorothy *and* WERNER, Morris R
The house near Paris: an American woman's story of traffic in patriots *(New York: Simon & Schuster 1946), 326p.*

TEISSIERDUCROS, Janet
Divided loyalties *(London: Hamilton 1962), 329p.*

THOMSON, David
Two Frenchmen: Pierre Laval and Charles de Gaulle *(London: Cresset 1951), 256p.*

TISSIER, Pierre
I worked with Laval *(London: Harrap 1942), 128p.*

TOMPKINS, Peter
The murder of Admiral Darlan: a study in conspiracy *(London: Weidenfeld & Nicolson 1965), 287p.*

TOURNOUX, Jean R
Petain and de Gaulle *(London: Heinemann 1966), ix, 245p, bib.*

TREAT, Ida
The anchored heart: a Brittany island during the Second World War *(New York: Harcourt 1941), 314p; UK title:* Rock of France.

VIGNERAS, Marcel
Rearming the French *(Washington DC: Department of Army 1957), 444p.*

VOMECOURT, Philippe de
Who lived to see the day: France in arms, 1940–1945 *(London: Hutchinson 1961), 288p; US title:* An army of amateurs.

WARNER, Geoffrey
Pierre Laval and the eclipse of France *(London: Eyre & Spottiswoode 1968), xv, 245p, bib.*

WATERFIELD, Gordon
What happened to France *(London: Murray 1940), 160p.*

WERTH, Alexander
The twilight of France, 1933–1940 *(New York: Ferlig 1966), xxii, 368p.*

WEYGAND, M *and* WEYGAND, J
The role of General Weygand *(London: Eyre & Spottiswoode 1948), 192p.*

WILLIAMS, John
France; summer 1940 *(New York: Ballantine 1969), 160p, bib.*
The Ides of May: the defeat of France, May–June 1940 *(London: Constable 1968), 416p, bib.*

WINTER, Gustav
This is not the end of France *(London: Allen & Unwin 1942), 299p.*
[*see also* RESISTANCE, WESTERN EUROPE *1939–40, 1944–5*]

FREE FRENCH FORCES

AGHION, Raoul
Fighting French *(New York: Holt 1943), 315p.*

BURMAN, Ben L
Miracle on the Congo: report from the Free French front *(New York: Day 1942), 13–153p.*

DAVIS, Hassoldt
Half past when!: an American with the fighting French *(Philadelphia, Pa: Lippincott 1944), 9–283p.*

HASEY, John F
Yankee fighter: the story of an American in the Free French Foreign Legion *(Boston, Mass: Little, Brown 1942), 293p.*

MAULE, Henry
Out of the sand: the epic story of General Leclerc and the fighting Free French *(London: Odhams 1966), 288p.*
[*see also* NORTH AFRICA, WESTERN EUROPE *1944–5*]

FRENCH ARMY

BARLONE, D
A French officer's diary (23 August 1939–1 October, 1940) *(Cambridge: Cambridge UP 1942), viii, 156p.*

GERARD, Robert M
Tank-fighter team *(Washington DC: Infantry Journal Press 1942), x, 83p.*

GOUTARD, Adolphe
The battle of France, 1940 *(London: Muller 1958), 280p, bib.*

De Lattre de Tassigny, Jean
The history of the French First Army *(London: Allen & Unwin 1952), 532p.*

Greenwall, Harry J
When France fell *(London: Wingate 1958), xii, 13–188p.*

FRENCH NAVY

Auphan, Paul *and* Cras, Herve
The French Navy in World War II *(Annapolis, Md: US Naval Institute 1959), 413p.*

Couhat, Jean L
French warships of World War II *(London: Allan 1971), 176p.*

Heckstall-Smith, Anthony
The fleet that faced both ways *(London: Blond 1963)*, [7], *232p, bib.*

Jubelin, Andre
The flying sailor *(London: Hurst & Blackett 1953), 276p.*

LeMasson, Henri
The French Navy *(London: Macdonald 1969), 2 vols.*

Vader, John
The fleet without a friend *(London: New English Library 1971), 160p, bib.*

FROGMEN

Bekker, Cajus D (pseud)
K-men: the story of German frogmen and midget submarines *(London: Kimber 1955), 202p.*

Brou, Willy
The war beneath the sea *(London: Muller 1958), 239p.*

Fane, Francis D *and* Moore, Don
The naked warriors *(London: Wingate 1957), 223p.*

Fraser, Ian
Frogman, V.C. *(London: Angus & Robertson 1957), 216p.*

Higgins, Edward T
Web footed warriors: the story of a frogman in the [U.S.] Navy during World War II *(New York: Exposition 1955), 172p.*

Pugh, Marshall
Commander Crabb *(London: Macmillan 1956), 166p; US title:* Frogman.

Waldron, Thomas J *and* Gleeson, James
The frogmen: the story of the wartime underwater operators *(London: Evans 1950), 191p.*

WRIGHT, Bruce S
The frogmen of Burma: the story of the Sea Reconnaissance Unit *(Toronto: Clarke, Irwin 1968), 168p, bib.*

FUEL

COURT, W H S
Coal *(London: HMSO 1951), xii, 422p.*
FUEL RESEARCH STATION
Fuel research, 1939–1946 *(London: HMSO 1950), 76p.*

GAULLE, CHARLES de

CROZIER, Brian
De Gaulle the warrior *(London: Eyre & Spottiswoode 1973), xv, 395p.*
FUNK, Arthur L
Charles de Gaulle: the crucial years, 1943–1944 *(Norman, Okl: Oklahoma UP 1959), 336p.*
GAULLE, Charles de
The complete war memoirs *(London: Weidenfeld & Nicolson 1955–60), 3 vols.*
GRINNELL-MILNE, Duncan
The triumph of integrity: a portrait of Charles de Gaulle *(London: Bodley Head 1961), 320p.*
KERILLES, Henri de
I accuse De Gaulle *(New York: Harcourt 1946), 270p.*
MAURIAC, Francois
De Gaulle *(New York: Doubleday 1966),* [4], *229p.*
PENDAR, Kenneth W
Adventure in diplomacy: the emergence of General de Gaulle in North Africa *(London: Cassell 1966), 382p.*
SCHOENBRUN, David
The three lives of Charles de Gaulle *(New York: Atheneum 1965), xviii, 365p.*

GEORGE CROSS

HARE-SCOTT, Kenneth B
For gallantry: the George Cross *(London: Garnett 1951), xiv, 168p.*

GERMANY

ABRAHAMS, Gerald
Retribution *(London: W H Allen 1941), 128p.*

ALLEN, Charles R
Heusinger of the Fourth Reich *(New York: Marzani & Munsell 1963), 320p.*

ALMOND, Gabriel A (ed)
The struggle for democracy in Germany *(New York: Russell & Russell 1965), 245p.*

ANGOLIA, John R
Insignia of the Third Reich *(London: Ducimus 1974), 144p.*

BALFOUR, Michael
Helmuth von Moltke: a leader against Hitler *(London: Macmillan 1972), xii, 388p.*

BANNISTER, Sybil
I lived under Hitler: an Englishwoman's story *(London: Rockliff [1957]), 264p.*

BAYLES, William D
Postmarked Berlin *(London: Jarrolds 1942), 144p.*

BECKER, Karl
Zero hour for Germany *(London: ING 1944), 80p.*

BENGTSON, John R
Nazi war aims: the plans for the thousand year Reich *(Rock Island, Ill: Augustana College Library 1962), 155p.*

BERADT, Charlotte
The Third Reich of dreams *(Chicago, Ill: Quadrangle 1968), 177p.*

BERNADOTTE OF WISBURG, *count*
The curtain falls: the last days of the Third Reich *(New York: Knopf 1945), 154p.*

BIELENBURG, Christabel
The past is myself *(London: Chatto & Windus 1968), 285p.*

BLOND, Georges
The death of Hitler's Germany *(New York: Macmillan 1954), ix, 302p, bib.*

BLOOD-RYAN, H W
The great German conspiracy *(London: Drummond 1943), 276p.*

BOEHM, Eric H (ed)
We survived: the stories of fourteen of the hidden and hunted of Nazi Germany *(New Haven, Conn: Yale UP 1949), xiii, 308p.*

BONHOEFFER, Dietrich
Letters and papers from prison *(London: SCM Press 1953), 190p; US title:* Prisoner for God.

BORKENAU, Franz
Totalitarian enemy *(London: Faber 1940), 254p.*

BRACHER, Karl D
The German dictatorship: the origins, structure and effects of National Socialism *(New York: Praeger 1970), 685p.*

BUCHHEIM, Hans
The Third Reich, it's beginning, it's development, it's end *(London: Wolff 1961), 98p.*

BURDICK, Charles B
Germany's military strategy and Spain in World War II *(Syracuse, NY: Syracuse UP 1968), 228p.*

CHESNEY, Inga L
A time of rape *(New York: Prentice-Hall 1972), 255p.*

COLLINS, Sarah M
Alien years: being the autobiography of an Englishwoman in Germany and Austria, 1938–1946 *(London: Hodder & Stoughton 1949), 222p.*

DAVID, Claude
Hitler's Germany *(New York: Walker 1963), 154p.*

DEJONG, L
The German fifth column and the Second World War *(London: Routledge 1956), 322p.*

DEMENDELSSOHN, Peter
The Nuremberg documents: some aspects of German war policy, 1939–45 *(London: Allen & Unwin 1946), 291p.*

DEUTSCH, Harold C
The conspiracy against Hitler in the twilight war *(Minneapolis, Minn: Minnesota UP 1968), xii, 394p, bib.*

DONOHOE, James
Hitler's conservative opponents in Bavaria, 1939–1945: a study of Catholic Monarchist, and Separatist anti-Nazi activities *(Leiden, Belgium: Brill 1961), 348p.*

DOUGLAS-SMITH, Aubrey E
Guilty Germans? *(London: Gollancz 1942), 240p.*

DULLES, Allen W
Germany's underground *(London: Macmillan 1947), 207p.*

ESSAME, Hubert
The battle for Germany *(London: Batsford 1969), xii, 228p, bib.*

FEST, Joachim C
The face of the Third Reich *(London: Weidenfeld & Nicolson 1970), xii, 402p, bib.*

FLANNERY, Harry W
Assignment to Berlin *(London: Joseph 1942), 439p.*

FOERSTER, Friedrich W

Europe and the German question *(New York: Sheed & Ward 1940), xviii, 474p.*

FRAENKEL, Heinrich

The German people versus Hitler *(London: Allen & Unwin 1940), 7-370p.*

The other Germany *(London: Drummond 1942), 144p.*

FREIDIN, Seymour *and* RICHARDSON, William (eds)

Fatal decision *(London: Joseph 1956), 261p.*

FRISCHAUER, Willi

The Nazis at war *(London: Gollancz 1940), 283p.*

FURMANSKI, H R R

Life can be cruel *(New York: Vantage 1960), 61p.*

GALLIN, Mary A

Ethical and religious factors in the German resistance to Hitler *(Washington DC: Catholic University of America 1955), 231p; later published as:* German resistance to Hitler.

GERMANY. Auswärtiges Amt

Documents on German foreign policy, 1918-1945 *(Washington DC: Department of State 1949-66), 13 vols.*

German policy in Turkey, 1941-1943 *(Moscow: Foreign Languages 1948), 126p.*

Nazi-Soviet relations, 1939-1941, from the archives of the German Foreign Office *(Washington DC: Department of State 1948), 362p.*

GISEVIUS, Hans B

To the bitter end *(Boston, Mass: Houghton Mifflin 1947), 600p.*

GOLDSTON, Robert

The life and death of Nazi Germany *(Indianapolis, Ind: Bobbs-Merrill 1967), 224p, bib.*

GOLLWITZER, Helmeut *and others*

Dying we live: the final messages and records of some Germans who defied Hitler *(London: Harvill 1956), 224p.*

HAFFNER, Sebastian

Germany: Jekyll and Hyde *(London: Secker & Warburg 1940), [13], 318p.*

HAGEN, Paul

Will Germany crack?: a factual report on Germany from within *(London: Gollancz 1942), xv, 283p.*

HANSER, Richard (comp)

True tales of Hitler's Reich *(Greenwich, Conn: Fawcett 1962), 192p.*

HARSCH, Joseph C
Pattern of conquest *(New York: Doubleday 1941), ix, 309p.*
HESS, Tisa, *Countess Schulenburg*
The last days and the first *(London: Harvill 1948), 32p.*
HIGGINS, Trumbull
Hitler and Russia: the Third Reich in a two-front war, 1937–1943 *(New York: Macmillan 1966), 310p.*
HILL, Helen D *and* AGAR, Herbert
Beyond German victory *(New York: Reynal 1940), viii, 117p.*
HINDUS, Maurice G
Hitler cannot conquer Russia *(New York: Doubleday 1942), xvi, 299p.*
HITLER doomed to madness: smuggled ms reveals secrets of new Nazi horrors; uncensored photographs *(Greenwich, Conn: Country 1940), 66p.*
HOEMBERG, Elisabeth S
Thy people, my people *(New York: Crowell 1950), 314p.*
HOMZE, Edward L
Foreign labor in Nazi Germany *(Princeton, NJ: Princeton UP 1967), 350p.*
INTERNATIONAL COUNCIL FOR PHILOSOPHY AND HUMANISTIC STUDIES
The Third Reich *(London: Weidenfeld & Nicolson 1955), xv, 910p, bib.*
JACKH, Ernst
The war for man's soul *(New York: Farrar 1943), x, 303p.*
JARMAN, Thomas L
The rise and fall of Nazi Germany *(London: Grosset 1955), 388p.*
JOFFROY, Pierre
A spy for God: the ordeal of Kurt Gerstein *(London: Collins 1971), 319p, bib.*
JONG, Louis de
The German fifth column in the Second World War *(London: Routledge 1956), 308p.*
KALOW, Gert
The shadow of Hitler: a critique of political consciousness *(London: Rapp & Whiting 1968), xii, 144p.*
KAPS, Johannes (ed)
The martyrdom and heroism of the women of East Germany: an excerpt from the Silesian Passion, 1945–1946 *(Munich: 'Christ Unterwegs' 1955), 155p.*
The tragedy of Silesia, 1945–46: a documentary account with a special survey of the Archdiocese of Breslau *(Munich: 'Christ Unterwegs', 1952–3), 576p.*

KERN, Erich
Dance of death *(New York, Scribner 1951), 11-255p.*

KESSEL, Joseph
The magic touch *(London: Hart-Davis 1961), 254p.*

KOEHL, Robert L
RKFDV: German resettlement and population policy, 1939–1945: a history of the Reich Commission for the strengthening of Germandom *(Cambridge, Mass: Harvard UP 1957), 263p.*

KRUK, Zofia
The taste of fear: a Polish childhood in Germany, 1939–46 *(London: Hutchinson 1973), 208p.*

KURTH, Karl O (comp)
Documents of humanity during the mass expulsions *(New York: Harper 1954), 184p.*

LEBER, Annedore (comp)
Conscience in revolt: sixty-four stories of resistance in Germany, 1933–1945 *(London: Vallentine, Mitchell 1957), 270p.*

LEISER, Erwin
A pictorial history of Nazi Germany *(Harmondsworth, Herts 1962), 204p.*

LERNER, Adolph R
The march of evil: a history of the rise and fall of Fascist evil *(New York: FFF 1945), 79p.*

LERNER, Daniel
The Nazi elite *(Stanford, Calif: Stanford UP 1951), 112p.*

LESSNER, Erwin C
Blitzkrieg and bluff: the legend of Nazi invincibility *(New York: Putnam 1943), vii, 246p.*
Phantom victory: the Fourth Reich, 1945–1960 *(New York: Putnam 1944), 227p.*

LEUNER, Heinz D
When compassion was a crime: Germany's silent heroes, 1933–45 *(London: Wolff 1966), 164p, bib.*

LOCHNER, Louis P
What about Germany? *(New York: Dodd 1942), xiv, 395p.*

MCKEE, Ilse
Tomorrow the world *(London: Dent 1960), 199p.*

MANN, Thomas
This war *(London: Secker & Warburg 1940), 66p.*

MASCHMANN, Melita
Account rendered: a dossier on my former self *(New York: Abelard-Schuman 1964), 223p.*

MAU, Hermann *and* KRAUSNICK, Helmut
German history, 1933–45: an assessment by German historians *(London: Wolff 1959), 157p.*

MAYER, Milton
They thought they were free: the Germans, 1933–1945 *(Chicago, Ill: Chicago UP 1955), xxii, 346p.*

MEINECKE, Friedrich
The German catastrophe: reflection and recollections *(Cambridge, Mass: Harvard UP 1950), 121p.*

MERKER, Paul F
Germany today . . . and Germany tomorrow *(London: ING 1943), 57p.*

MINOTT, Rodney G
The fortress that never was: the myth of Hitler's Bavarian stronghold *(New York: Holt 1964), 208p.*

MUSMANNO, Michael A
Ten days to die *(New York: Doubleday 1950), 276p.*

NAMIER, *Sir* Lewis B
In the Nazi era *(London: Macmillan 1952), vii, 204p.*

NEUMANN, Robert
The pictorial history of the Third Reich *(New York: Bantam 1962), 224p.*

NORDEN, Albert
Thugs of Europe: the truth about the German people and its rulers *(New York: German American League for Culture 1943), 6–85p.*

OECHSNER, Frederick C *and others*
This is the enemy *(Boston, Mass: Little, Brown 1942), 364p.*

PANETH, Philip
Reshaping Germany's future *(London: Alliance 1943), 104p.*

PAQUIN, Grete *and* HAGEN, Renate
Two women and a war: diary and pillar of fire *(Philadelphia, Pa: Muhlensberg 1953), 233p.*

PIHL, Gunnar T
Germany: the last phase *(New York: Knopf 1944), 322p.*

PRITTIE, Terence C F
Germans against Hitler *(London: Hutchinson 1964), 292p. bib.*

RALEIGH, John M
Behind the Nazi front *(New York: Dodd 1940), vii, 307p.*

RAUSCHNING, Hermann
The beast from the abyss *(London: Heinemann 1941), 170p; US title:* Redemption of democracy.
Makers of destruction: meetings and talks in revolutionary Germany *(London: Eyre & Spottiswoode 1942), 362p; US title:* Men of chaos.
RECK-MALLECZEWEN, Fritz P
Diary of a man in despair *(New York: Macmillan 1970), 219p.*
RIESS, Curt
The invasion of Germany *(New York: Putnam 1943), xvi, 206p.*
The Nazis go underground *(London: Boardman 1945), 224p.*
RITTER, G
The German resistance: Carl Goerdeler's struggle against tyranny *(London: Allen & Unwin 1958), 330p.*
RODENHAUSER, Reiner *and* NAPP, R R
Breaking down the barrier: a human document on war *(Durham, NC: Seeman Printery 1961), 148p.*
ROON, Ger van
German resistance to Hitler: Count von Moltke and the Kreisan Circle *(New York: Van Nostrand Reinhold 1971), xii, 400p, bib.*
ROTHFELS, Hans
The German opposition to Hitler: an appraisal *(London: Hinsdale, Regnery 1948), 166p.*
ROYCE, Hans (ed)
Germans against Hitler, July 20, 1944 *(Bonn: Press & Information Office 1964), 360p.*
RUMPF, Hans
The bombing of Germany *(London: Muller 1963), 256p.*
RUSSELL, Frank M
The Saar: battleground and pawn *(New York: Russell & Russell 1970), 204p.*
SAVA, George (pseud)
School for war *(London: Faber 1942), 176p.*
SAYERS, Michael A K
Plot against peace: Nazi Germany plans for future wars *(New York: Dial 1945), 258p.*
SAYRE, Joel
The house without a roof *(New York: Farrar 1948), 214p.*
SCHLABRENDORFF, Fabian von
Revolt against Hitler: the personal account of Fabian von Schlabrendorff *(London: Eyre & Spottiswoode 1948), 176p.*
The secret war against Hitler *(New York: Putnam 1965), x, 438p.*

SCHLOTTERBECK, Friedrich
The darker the night; the lighter the stars: a German worker remembers *(London: Gollancz 1947), 250p.*

SCHOENBERGER, Franz
The inside story of an outsider *(New York: Macmillan 1949), xi, 273p.*

SCHUTZ, William W
Pens under the Swastika: a study in recent German writing *(London: SCM Press 1946), 110p.*

SCHUTZ, William W *and* SEVIN, Barbara de
The German home front *(London: Gollancz 1943), x, 11-312p.*

SEGER, Gerhart
Dictatorship, war, disaster: history of the Nazi regime *(Oberaudorf, Bavaria: Schoenstein 1957), 300 photos.*

SEGER, Gerhart *and* MARCK, S K
Germany, to be or not to be? *(New York: Rand School 1943), 7-190p.*

SEYDEWITZ, Max
Civil life in wartime Germany: the story of the home front *(New York: Viking 1945), 448p.*

SHIRER, William L
The rise and fall of the Third Reich: a history of Nazi Germany *(London: Secker & Warburg 1960), xii, 1247p, bib.*

SMITH, Howard K
Last train from Berlin *(London: Cresset 1942), 267p.*

STEINERT, M G
Capitulation, 1945: the story of the Donitz regime *(London: Constable 1969), ix, 326p; US title:* 23 days.

STEPHENS, Frederick J
Hitler Youth: history, organization, uniforms and insignias *(London: Almark 1973), 88p, bib.*

STERN, James
The hidden damage *(New York: Harcourt 1947), 406p.*

STODDARD, Theodore L
Into the darkness: Nazi Germany, today *(New York: Duell 1940), 11-311p.*

STRADLER, Kurt (pseud)
Death to Hitler . . . rare smuggled photos: revolt against Nazis revealed by a fugitive Gestapo captain *(Greenwich, Conn: Country 1941), 66p.*

STRAUSS, Harold
The division and dismemberment of Germany, from the Casablanca Conference (January 1943) to the establishment of the East German Republic (October 1949) *(Ambilly, Switz: Cooperative 'Les Presses de Savoie' 1952), 240p.*

THORNTON, Michael J
Nazism, 1918–1945 *(London: Pergamon 1966), viii, 181p, bib.*

TOLISCHUS, Otto D
They wanted war *(London: Hamilton 1940), viii, 340p.*

TORRES, Henry
Campaign of treachery *(New York: Dodd 1942), 256p.*

TOSEVIC, Dimitrije J
Not Nazi but Germans *(Boston, Mass: Humphries 1944), x, 306p.*

TREFOUSSE, Hans L
Germany and American neutrality, 1939–1941 *(New York: Bookman 1951), 9–247p.*

TROUGHTON, Ernest R
It's happening again *(London: Gifford 1944), 111p.*

VALLANCE, Ute
A girl survives *(London: MacGibbon & Kee 1958), 298p.*

VILLARD, Oswald G
Inside Germany; with an epilogue: England at war *(London: Constable 1939), 86p; US title:* Within Germany.

WAHLE, Anne
Ordeal by fire: an American woman's terror-filled trek through war-torn Germany *(New York: World 1966), 152p.*

WENDEL, Else
Hausfrau at war: a German woman's account of life in Hitler's Reich *(London: Odhams 1957), 255p.*

WETZEL, Friedrich
They called me Alfred *(London: Ronald 1959), 237p.*

WILLIAMS, Wythe *and* PARRY, Albert
The riddle of the Reich *(London: Hurst & Blackett 1941), 207p.*

ZELLER, Eberhard
The flame of freedom: the German struggle against Hitler *(London: Wolff 1967), 471p, bib.*

ZIFF, William B
The coming battle of Germany *(London: Hamilton 1942), xxiii, 280p.*
[*see also* HITLER]

GERMAN AIR FORCE (LUFTWAFFE)

BARTZ, Karl
Swastika in the air: the struggle and defeat of the German Air Force, 1939–1945 *(London: Kimber 1956), viii, 9–204p.*

BAUMBACH, Werner
Broken Swastika: the defeat of the Luftwaffe *(London: Hale 1960), 224p.*

BEKKER, Cajus D
The Luftwaffe war diaries *(London: Macdonald 1967), 399p, bib.*

BENDER, Roger J
Air organizations of the Third Reich *(London: Scott 1967), 192p.*

BLOEMERTZ, Gunther
Heaven next stop: impressions of a German fighter pilot *(London: Kimber 1953), 189p.*

CAIDIN, Martin
Me 109: Willy Messerschmitt's peerless fighter *(New York: Ballantine 1969), 160p, bib.*

CONSTABLE, Trevor J *and* TOLIVER, Raymond
Horrido! fighter aces of the Luftwaffe *(London: Barker 1968), xv, 348p.*

DEICHMANN, Paul
German Air Force operations in support of the Army *(New York: Arco 1968), 210p.*

FEUCHTER, Georg W
Der Luftkrieg *(London: Scott 1967), 403p.*

GALLAND, Adolf
The first and the last: the German fighter force in World War II *(London: Methuen 1955), xii, 368p.*
The Luftwaffe at war, 1939–1945 *(London: Allan 1972), 247p.*

GREY, Charles G
Luftwaffe *(London: Faber 1944), 251p.*

HEILMANN, Willi
Alert in the West *(London: Kimber 1955), x, 11–202p.*

HENN, Peter
The last battle *(London: Kimber 1954), 214p.*

JOHNEN, Wilhelm
Duel under the stars: a German night fighter pilot in the Second World War *(London: Kimber 1957), 202p.*

KILLEN, John
The Luftwaffe: a history *(London: Muller 1967), x, 310p, bib.*

KNOKE, Heinz
I flew for the Fuhrer: the story of a German airman *(London: Evans 1953), x, 11-187p.*

LEE, Asher
The German Air Force *(London: Duckworth 1946), 284p.*

LESKE, Gottfried
I was a Nazi flier *(New York: Dial 1941), 5-351p.*

MORZIK, Fritz
German Air Force airlift operations *(New York: Arno 1961). xxvi, 416p.*

OBERMAIER, Ernst
Luftwaffe holders of the Knight's Cross *(London: Scott 1966), vol. I:* Fighter pilots, 1939-1945, 256p.

PLOCHER, Hermann
The German Air Force versus Russia, 1941 *(Maxwell Air Force Base, Ala: Air University 1965), 335p.*

PRICE, Alfred
Luftwaffe: birth, life and death of an air force *(New York: Ballantine 1969), 160p, bib.*
Pictorial history of the Luftwaffe, 1933-1945 *(London: Allan 1969), 64p.*

RUDEL, Hans
Stuka pilot *(Dublin: Euphorion 1952), 259p.*

SHULMAN, Milton
Defeat in the West *(London: Secker & Warburg 1947), xvi, 336p.*

SMITH, John R *and* KAY, A L
German aircraft of the Second World War *(London: Putnam 1972), 745p.*

SMITH, Peter C
The Stuka at war *(London: Allan 1971), 192p.*

SUCHENWIRTH, Richard
Historical turning points in the German Air Force war effort *(New York: Arno 1968), 143p.*

TANTUM, William H *and* HOFFSCHMIDT, E J (eds)
The rise and fall of the German Air Force, 1933-1945 *(Old Greenwich: WE 1969), 422p.*

TISCHER, Werner
And so we bombed Moscow alone: the exciting personal story of one man's experience in the German Luftwaffe *(New York: Greenwich 1961), 94p.*

US Air Force
German aviation medicine, World War II *(Washington DC: Department of Air Force 1950), 2 vols.*
Windrow, Martin C
Luftwaffe airborne and field units *(Reading, Berks: Osprey 1972), 40p.*
Luftwaffe colour schemes and markings, 1939-1945 *(Reading, Berks: Osprey 1971), 2 vols.*

GERMAN ARMY

Bahnemann, Gunther
I deserted Rommel *(London: Jarrolds 1961), 256p.*
Bender, Roger J *and* Taylor, Hugh P
Uniforms; organization and history of the Waffen SS *(London: Scott 1969–71), 2 vols, bib.*
Chamberlain, Peter
Panzer-Grenadiers: German infantry, 1939–45 *(London: Almark 1972), 32p.*
Davies, William J K
German Army handbook, 1939-1945 *(London: Allan 1973), 176p, bib.*
Edwards, Roger
German airborne troops *(London: Macdonald & Janes 1974), 160p.*
Fried, Hans E
The guilt of the German Army *(New York: Macmillan 1942), xi, 426p.*
Germany. Oberkommando der Wehrmacht
Hitler directs his war: the secret records of his daily military conferences *(New York: Oxford UP 1951), xxxiii, 187p, bib.*
Guderian, Heinz
Panzer leader *(London: Joseph 1952), 528p.*
Hohne, Heinz
The Order of the Death's Head: the story of Hitler's SS *(London: Secker & Warburg 1969), xxx, 655p, bib.*
Humble, Richard
Hitler's Generals *(New York: Doubleday 1974), 167p.*
Keegan, John
Waffen SS: the asphalt soldiers *(New York: Ballantine 1970), 160p, bib.*
Kramarz, Joachim
Stauffenberg: the life and death of an officer, 15th November 1907-20th July 1944 *(London: Deutsch 1967), 255p.*

LIDDELL-HART, Basil H
The other side of the hill *(London: Cassell 1948), 346p; US title:* German Generals talk.
MACKSEY, Kenneth J
Panzer division *(New York: Ballantine 1968), 160p, bib.*
MARSHALL, Samuel L A
Armies on wheels *(New York: Morrow 1941), 5-251p.*
Blitzkrieg: its history, strategy, economics and the challenge to America *(New York: Morrow 1940), 7-185p.*
MELLENTHIN, Friedrich W von
Panzer battles, 1939-1945: a study of the employment of armour in the Second World War *(London: Cassell 1955), xix, 371p.*
MILSOM, John
German military transport of World War 2 *(London: Arms & Armour 1974), 224p.*
PRULLER, Wilhelm
Diary of a German soldier *(London: Faber 1963), 200p.*
RICHARDSON, William *and* FREIDIN, Seymour (eds)
The fatal decisions *(London: Joseph 1956), xii, 261p.*
RIESS, Curt
The self-betrayed: glory and doom of the German Generals *(New York: Putnam 1942), xvi, 402p.*
SCHMIDT, Heinz W
With Rommel in the desert *(London: Harrap 1951), 240p.*
SCHRAMM, Wilhelm
Conspiracy among Generals *(London: Allen & Unwin 1956), 215p.*
STEIN, George H
The Waffen SS: Hitler's elite guard at war, 1939-1945 *(Ithaca, NY: Cornell UP 1966), xxxv, 330p, bib.*
TAYLOR, Telford
Sword and Swastika: the Wehrmacht in the Third Reich *(New York: Simon & Schuster 1952), 413p.*
US WAR DEPARTMENT
The German replacement army, Ersatzheer *(Washington DC: War Department 1954), 504p.*
WESTPHAL, Siegfried
The German Army in the West *(London: Cassell* [*1952*]*), ix, 222p.*
WHEELER-BENNETT, John
Nemesis of power: the German Army in politics, 1918-1945 *(London: Macmillan 1953), xvi, 839p, bib.*

WINDROW, Martin C
The Panzer divisions *(Reading, Berks: Osprey 1973), 40p.*
Waffen-SS *(Reading, Berks: Osprey 1971), 40p.*
[*see also* AFRIKA KORPS]

GERMAN NAVY

BEKKER, Cajus
Hitler's naval war *(London: Macdonald 1974), 400p, bib.*
Swastika at sea: the struggle and destruction of the German Navy, 1939-1945 *(London: Kimber [1953]), 207p; later published as:* The German Navy, 1939-1945.
BRENNECKE, Hans J
The hunters and the hunted *(London: Burke 1958), 320p.*
BUSCH, Fritz O
The story of the 'Prince Eugen' *(London: Hale 1960), 190p.*
FEHLER, Johann H
Dynamite for hire: the story of Hein Fehler *(London: Laurie 1956), vi, 7-264p.*
GERMANY. Kriegsmarine Oberkommando
Fuehrer conferences on matters dealing with the German Navy, 1939-1945 *(London: HMSO 1947), 7 vols in 9.*
HUMBLE, Richard
Hitler's high seas fleet *(New York: Ballantine 1971), 160p, bib.*
JONES, Geoffrey P
Under three flags: the story of Nordmark and the armoured supply ships of the German Navy *(London: Kimber 1973), 256p.*
MARTIENSSEN, Anthony
Hitler and his admirals *(London: Secker & Warburg 1948), x, 275p.*
RAEDER, Erich
Struggle for the sea *(London: Kimber 1959), 270p.*
TULEJA, Thadeus V
Twilight of the sea gods *(New York: Dutton 1958), 284p, bib; UK title:* Eclipse of the German Navy.
VON DER PORTEN, Edward P
The German Navy in World War II *(New York: Crowell 1969), xiii, 274p, bib.*
[*see also* U-BOATS]

GERMAN SURFACE RAIDERS

ALEXANDER, Roy
Sea prison and shore hell: the cruise of the raider Atlantis, from the diary of Jim Creagh *(London: Angus & Robertson 1942), ix, 199p.*

BRENNECKE, Hans J
Ghost cruiser H.K.33 *(London: Kimber 1954), 208p; US title:* Cruise of the raider.
CHATTERTON, Edward K
Commerce raiders *(London: Hurst & Blackett 1943), 128p.*
DETMERS, Theodor
The raider Kormoran *(London: Kimber 1959), 206p.*
DIVINE, Arthur D
Wake of the raiders *(London: Murray 1940), 161p.*
HOYT, Edwin P
Raider 16 *(New York: World 1970), 255p.*
MOHR, Ulrich
Atlantis: the story of a German surface raider *(London: Laurie 1955), xx, 246p.*
ROGGE, Bernhard *and* FRANK, Wolfgang
The German raider Atlantis *(New York: Ballantine 1956), 216p; UK title:* Under ten flags.
WEYHER, Kurt *and* EHRLICH, H J
The black raider *(London: Elek 1955), 200p.*
WHEELER, Harold F B
War with the sea wolves *(London: Nelson 1940), 251p.*
WOODWARD, David
The secret raiders: the story of the operations of the German armed merchant raiders in the Second World War *(London: Kimber 1955), xii, 13–236p.*
[*see also* MERCHANT NAVY]

GESTAPO

CRANKSHAW, Edward
Gestapo: instrument of tyranny *(New York: Viking 1956), 275p.*
DELARUE, Jacques
The history of the Gestapo *(London: Macdonald 1964), 416p; US title:* The Gestapo.
KENNARD, *Sir* Coleridge A F
Gestapo France, 1943–1945 *(London: Grant Richards 1947), 208p.*
MANVELL, Roger
S.S. and Gestapo: rule by terror *(New York: Ballantine 1969), 160p, bib.*
NORDEN, Peter
Madam Kitty: a true story *(London: Abelard-Schuman 1974), 223p.*

REITLINGER, Gerald R
The S.S.: alibi of a nation, 1922–1945 *(London: Heinemann 1956), 502p.*

SINOKOP, N
Letters from the dead: letters and documents written in the last minutes of their lives in a Gestapo cell, 1941 and 1945 *(New York: Universal 1965), 233p.*
[*see also* WAR CRIMES]

GIBRALTAR

MONKS, Noel
That day at Gibraltar *(London: Muller [1957]), xii, 192p.*

GLIDER PILOTS

CHATTERTON, George
The wings of Pegasus *(London: Macdonald 1962), xi, 282p.*

SETH, Ronald
Lion with blue wings: the story of the Glider Pilot Regiment, 1942–1945 *(London: Gollancz 1955), 245p.*

WRIGHT, Lawrence
The wooden sword *(London: Elek [1967]), xii, 258p.*
[*see also* ARNHEM, NORMANDY]

GOEBBELS

BOELCKE, Willi A (ed)
The secret conferences of Dr. Goebbels: the Nazi propaganda war, 1939–1943 *(New York: Dutton 1970), xiii, 364p.*

EBERMAYER, Erich *and* MEISSNER, Hans O
Evil genius *(London: Wingate 1954), 207p.*

HEIBER, Helmut
Goebbels *(New York: Hawthorn 1972), ix, 387p, bib.*

LOCHNER, L P (ed)
The Goebbels diaries, 1942–1943 *(New York: Doubleday 1948), 496p.*

MANVELL, Roger *and* FRAENKEL, Heinrich
Doctor Goebbels: his life and death *(London: Heinemann 1960), 329p.*

RIESS, Curt
Joseph Goebbels: a biography *(London: Hollis & Carter 1949), 460p.*

SEMMLER, Rudolf
Goebbels - the man next to Hitler *(London: Westhouse 1947), 234p.*

WYKES, Alan
Goebbels *(New York: Ballantine 1973), 160p.*

GOERING

BEWLEY, Charles H
Hermann Goring and the Third Reich: a biography based on family and official records *(New York: Devin-Adair 1962), 517p.*

BUTLER, Ewan *and* YOUNG, Gordon
Marshal without glory *(London: Hodder & Stoughton 1951), 251p.*

FRISCHAUER, Willi
Goering *(London: Odhams [1951]), 304p, bib; US title:* The rise and fall of Hermann Goering.

LEE, Asher
Goering, air leader *(London: Duckworth 1972), 256p, bib.*

MANVELL, Roger *and* FRAENKEL, Heinrich
Hermann Goring *(London: Heinemann 1962), 283p; US title:* Goering.

MOSLEY, Leonard
The Reich Marshal: a biography of Hermann Goering *(London: Weidenfeld & Nicolson 1974), xiii, 394p.*

GRAF SPEE

BENNETT, Geoffrey
Battle of the River Plate *(London: Allan 1972), 96p, bib.*

DOVE, Patrick
I was Graf Spee's prisoner *(London: Withey Grove 1940), 160p.*

LANDSBOROUGH, Gordon
The battle of the River Plate *(London: Hamilton [1956]), 160p.*

MILLINGTON-DRAKE, *Sir* Eugen (comp)
The drama of Graf Spee and the Battle of the Plate: a documentary anthology, 1914–1964 *(London: Davies 1964), xxvi, 510p, bib.*

POPE, Dudley
The battle of the River Plate *(London: Kimber 1956), xviii, 19–259p; US title:* Graf Spee.

POWELL, Michael
Graf Spee *(London: Hodder & Stoughton 1956), 224p; US title:* Death in the South Atlantic.

STRABOLGI, Joseph M K, *16th baron*
The battle of the River Plate *(London: Hutchinson 1940), xxxvi, 238p.*
[*see also* BATTLESHIPS, GERMAN NAVY, ROYAL NAVY]

GREECE

AGRAFIOTIS, Cris J (comp)
Was Churchill right in Greece? *(Manchester, NH: Granite 1945), 152p.*
AMYNTOR (pseud)
Victors in chains *(London: Hutchinson 1943), 7-80p.*
ARCHER, Laird
Balkan journal *(New York: Norton 1942), 7-254p.*
ARGENTI, Philip P
The occupation of Chios by the Germans and their administration of the island described in contemporary documents *(Cambridge: Cambridge UP 1966), xiv, 375p.*
ATHENIAN (pseud)
Greek miracle *(London: Chapman & Hall 1942), 144p.*
BUCKLEY, Christopher
Greece and Crete, 1941 *(London: HMSO 1952), viii, 311p.*
BYFORD-JONES, W
The Greek triology (resistance - liberation - revolution) *(London: Hutchinson 1945), 270p.*
CASE study in guerrilla war: Greece during World War II *(Washington DC: American University 1961), 338p.*
CASSON, Stanley
Greece against the Axis *(London: Hamilton 1942), 207p.*
CERVI, Mario
The hollow legions: Mussolini's blunder in Greece, 1940-1941 *(New York: Doubleday 1971), xv, 336p, bib.*
CRISP, Robert
The gods were neutral *(London: Muller 1960), 221p.*
DAVIS, Homer W (ed)
Greece fights: the people behind the front *(New York: American Friends of Greece 1942), 7-96p.*
DEMETRIADES, Phokion
Shadow over Athens *(New York: Rinehart 1946), 155p.*
EUDES, Dominique
The Kapetanios partisans and civil war in Greece, 1943-1949 *(London: NLB 1972), xxv, 381p.*

FIELDING, Xan
Hide and seek: the story of a war-time agent *(London: Secker & Warburg 1954), 255p.*

GAGE, Jack
Greek adventure *(Beperb, Cape Town: Unie-Volkspers 1950), 110p.*

GANDER, Leonard M
Long road to Leros *(London: Macdonald 1945), 215p.*

HAMSON, Denys
We fell among Greeks *(London: Cape 1946), 224p.*

HECKSTALL-SMITH, Anthony *and* BAILLIE-GROHMAN, Harold
Greek tragedy *(London: Blond 1961), 240p, bib.*

HOWELL, Edward
Escape to live *(London: Longmans Green 1947), 230p.*

JECCHINIS, Chris
Beyond Olympus: the thrilling story of the 'train-busters' in Nazi-occupied Greece *(London: Harrap 1960), 219p.*

JORDAN, Fritz
Escape *(London: Yoseloff 1970), 278p.*

JORDAN, William
Conquest without victory *(London: Hodder & Stoughton 1969), 256p.*

KARAMANOS, Georgios J (ed)
Lest we forget that noble and immortal nation, Greece *(New York: Greek War Relief Association 1943), 320p.*

KOUSOULAS, Dimitrios G
The price of freedom: Greece in world affairs, 1939–1953 *(Syracuse, NY: Syracuse UP 1953), 210p.*

LINCOLN, John (pseud)
Achilles and the tortoise: an Eastern Aegean exploit *(London: Heinemann 1958), 256p.*

MACKENZIE, Compton
Wind of freedom: the history of the invasion of Greece by the Axis Powers, 1940–1941 *(London: Chatto & Windus 1943), xi, 275p.*

MCNEILL, William H
The Greek dilemma: war and aftermath *(London: Gollancz 1947), 240p.*

MATTHEWS, Kenneth
Memories of a mountain war: Greece, 1944–1949 *(London: Longmans 1972), 3–284p.*

MICHALOPOULOS, Andre
Greek fire *(London: Joseph 1943), 182p.*

MYERS, Edmund C W
Greek entanglement *(London: Hart-Davis 1955), 290p.*

NOEL-BAKER, Francis E
Greece: the whole story *(London: Hutchinson 1946), 64p.*

PANETH, Philip
The glory that is Greece *(London: Alliance 1945), 138p.*

PAPAGOS, Alexandros
The battle of Greece, 1940–1941 *(Athens: Scazikis 1949), 406p.*

PEZAS, Mikia
The price of liberty *(New York: Washburn 1945), 261p.*

POWELL, Dilys
Remember Greece *(London: Hodder & Stoughton 1941), 190p.*

REID, Francis
I was in Noah's ark *(London: Chambers 1957), 143p; later published as:* Resistance fighter.

RODINUS, P
The fight in Greece *(London: Europe 1943), vi, 7-77p.*

SARAFIS, Stefanos
Greek resistance army: the story of ELAS *(London: Birch 1951), xxvii, 324p.*

SMITH, Peter C *and* WALKER, Edwin
War in the Aegean *(London: Kimber 1974), 304p, bib.*

SWEET-ESCOTT, Bickham
Greece: a political and economic survey, 1939-1953 *(London: Royal Institute of International Affairs 1954), 206p.*

SYMMACHOS (pseud)
Greece fights on *(London: Drummond 1943), 143p.*

THOMAS, Walter B
Dare to be free *(London: Wingate 1951), 256p.*

WASON, Elizabeth
Miracle in Hellas: the Greeks fight on *(London: Museum 1943), 263p.*

WOODHOUSE, Christopher M
Apple of discord: a survey of recent Greek politics in the international setting *(London: Hutchinson 1948), 320p.*

WRIGHT, Colin
A British soldier in Greece *(London: Universal 1946), xii, 74p.*

XYDIS, Stephen G
Greece and the great powers, 1944–1947: prelude to the 'Truman doctrine' *(Thessalonika: Institute for Balkan Studies 1963), 758p.*

ZITRIDOU, Pipitsa C *and* Psimeno, H
Women of Greece, World War II, 1940–1944 *(Athens: Aetos 1950), 199p.*

ZOTOS, Stephanos
Greece: the struggle for freedom *(New York: Crowell 1967), 194p.*
[*see also* BALKANS, CRETE]

GREENLAND

BALCHEN, Bernt *and others*
War below zero: the battle for Greenland *(Boston, Mass: Houghton Mifflin 1944), 127p.*

HOWARTH, David
The sledge patrol *(London: Collins 1957), 257p.*

GUADALCANAL

ANDREWS, Stan
Close-up of Guadalcanal *(Wellington, NZ: Progressive 1944), 54p.*

COGGINS, Jack
The campaign for Guadalcanal: a battle that made history *(New York: Doubleday 1972), 208p.*

COOK, Charles
The battle of Cape Esperance: encounter at Guadalcanal *(New York: Crowell 1968), 156p.*

GALLANT, Thomas G
On valor's side *(New York: Doubleday 1963), 364p.*

GEORGE, John B
Shots fired in anger: a rifleman's eye view of the activities on the Island of Guadalcanal in the Solomons, during the elimination of the Japanese forces there *(Georgetown, SC: Small Arms 1947), xi, 421p.*

GRIFFITH, Samuel B
The battle for Guadalcanal *(Philadelphia, Pa: Lippincott 1963), 282p.*

KENT, Graeme
Guadalcanal, island ordeal *(New York: Ballantine 1971), 161p, bib.*

LECKIE, Robert
Challenge for the Pacific: Guadalcanal—the turning point of the war *(New York: Doubleday 1965), xii, 372p, bib.*

MERILLAT, Herbert L
Island: a history of the First Marine Division on Guadalcanal, Aug 7-Dec 9, 1942 *(Boston, Mass: Houghton Mifflin 1944), xii, 283p.*

MILLER, John
Guadalcanal: the first offensive *(Washington DC: Department of Army 1949), 413p.*

MILLER, Thomas G
The cactus air force *(New York: Harper 1969), 242p.*

NEWCOMB, Richard F
Savo: the incredible naval debacle off Guadalcanal *(New York: Holt 1961), xv, 237p, bib.*

TREGASKIS, Richard W
Guadalcanal diary *(New York: Random House 1955), 180p.*

US MARINE CORPS
The Guadalcanal campaign August 1942 to February 1943 *(Washington DC: USMC 1949), 189p.*

WERSTEIN, Irving
Guadalcanal *(New York: Crowell 1963), 186p.*
[*see also* PACIFIC, SOLOMON ISLANDS, US MARINES]

GUAM

ITO MASASHI
The Emperor's last soldiers: the grim story of two Japanese who hid for sixteen years in the Guam jungle *(London: Souvenir 1967), 191p.*

TWEED, George R
Robinson Crusoe, U.S.N.: the adventures of George R. Tweed in Jap-held Guam *(New York: McGraw-Hill 1945), 267p.*

US MARINE CORPS
The recapture of Guam *(Washington DC: USMC 1954), 214p.*

US WAR DEPARTMENT
Guam: operators of the 77th Division, 21 July-10 Aug 1944 *(Washington DC: War Department, 1946), 136p.*
[*see also* PACIFIC, US MARINES]

GUERILLAS

BAND, C *and* BAND, W
Dragon fangs *(London: Allen & Unwin 1948), 347p.*

CECH, Jan
Death stalks the forest *(London: Drummond 1943), 75p.*

HEILBRUNN, Otto *and* DIXON, Cecil A
Communist guerilla warfare *(London: Allen & Unwin 1954), xviii, 229p.*
PEERS, William R *and* BRELIS, Dean
Behind the Burma Road: the story of America's most successful guerilla force *(Boston, Mass: Little, Brown 1963), 246p.*
ROGERS, Lindsay S
Guerilla surgeon *(London: Collins 1953), 256p.*
SMITH, Douglas M *and* CARNES, Cecil
American guerrilla fighting behind the enemy lines *(Indianapolis, Ind: Bobbs-Merrill 1943), 11-316p.*
SPENCER, Louis R
Guerilla wife *(New York: Crowell 1945), 209p.*
TAURAS K V (pseud)
Guerilla warfare on the amber coast *(New York: Voyages 1962), 110p.*
[*see also* BALKANS, BURMA, CHINA, EASTERN EUROPE, RESISTANCE]

GURKHAS

NEILD, Eric
With Pegasus in India: the story of 153 Gurkha Parachute Battalion *(Aldershot, Hants: Neild [1970]), iv, 110p.*

GYPSIES

ADLER, Marta
My life with the gipsies *(London: Souvenir 1960), 204p.*
YOORS, Jan
Crossing: a journal of survival and resistance in World War II *(New York: Simon & Schuster 1971), 224p.*

HAMBURG

CAIDIN, Martin
The night Hamburg died *(New York: Ballantine 1960), 158p.*

HAWAII

ALLEN, Gwenfread E
Hawaii's war years, 1941-1945 *(Hawaii: Hawaii UP 1950), xiii, 418p.*

ALLEN, Riley H (ed)
Hawaii at war: 74 pictures and running story of attack on Pearl Harbor and events up to Mar. 15, 1942 *(Honolulu: Star Bulletin 1942), 64p.*
ANTHONY, Joseph G
Hawaii under Army rule *(Stanford, Calif: Stanford UP 1955), 203p.*
LEMON, *Sister* Adele M
To you from Hawaii *(Albany, NY: Fort Orange 1950), xv, 377p.*
LIND, Andrew W
Hawaii's Japanese: an experiment in democracy *(Princeton, NJ: Princeton UP 1946), 264p.*
MACDONALD, Alexander W
Revolt in paradise: the social revolution in Hawaii after Pearl Harbor *(Brattleboro, Vt: Daye 1944), xi, 288p.*
MACLEOD, Alexander S
The spirit of Hawaii before and after Pearl Harbor *(New York: Harper 1943), 142p.*
MURPHY, Thomas D
Ambassadors in arms: the story of Hawaii's 100th Battalion *(Honolulu: Hawaii UP 1954), 315p.*
RADEMAKER, John A
These are Americans: the Japanese Americans in Hawaii in World War II *(Palo Alto, Calif: Pacific 1951), viii, 278p.*
[*see also* PEARL HARBOR]

HEAVY WATER

DRUMMOND, John D
But for these men: how eleven Commandos saved Western Civilisation *(London: W H Allen 1962), 205p.*
[*see also* ATOM BOMB, COMMANDOS, NORWAY]

HESS

DOUGLAS-HAMILTON, James
Motive for a mission: the story behind Hess's flight to Britain *(London: Macmillan 1971), 290p, bib.*
HESS, Rudolf
Prisoner of peace *(London: Britons 1954), 151p.*
HUTTON, Joseph B
Hess: the man and his mission *(London: David Bruce & Watson 1970), [15], 262p.*

LEASOR, James
Rudolf Hess: the uninvited envoy *(London: Allen & Unwin 1962), 239p, bib; US title:* The uninvited envoy

MANVELL, Roger
Hess: a biography *(London: MacGibbon & Kee 1971), 256p, bib.*

REES, John R (ed)
The case of Rudolf Hess: a problem in diagnosis and forensic psychiatry *(London: Heinemann 1947), 224p.*

HEYDRICH

WIENER, Jan G
The assassination of Heydrich *(New York: Grossman 1969), 177p.*

WIGHTON, Charles
Heydrich: Hitler's most evil henchman *(London: Odhams 1962), 288p.*

WYKES, Alan
Heydrich *(New York: Ballantine 1973), 160p.*

X, - FORMER GESTAPO OFFICER (pseud)
Heydrich the murderer *(London: Quality 1942), 62p.*
[*see also* CZECHOSLAVAKIA, GESTAPO]

HIMMLER

FRISCHAUER, Willi
Himmler: the evil genius of the Third Reich *(London: Odhams 1953), 270p, bib.*

WYKES, Alan
Himmler *(New York: Ballantine 1972), 160p.*
[*see also* CONCENTRATION CAMPS, GESTAPO]

HISTORY (general)

ADAMS, Henry H
The year that doomed the Axis *(New York: McKay 1967), 522p.*
Years of deadly peril *(New York: McKay 1969), 559p.*
Years of expectation: Guadalcanal to Normandy *(New York: McKay 1973), 430p.*

AMERICAN HERITAGE
The American Heritage picture history of World War II *(New York: American Heritage 1966), 640p.*

ARNOLD-FORSTER, Mark
The world at war *(London: Collins 1973), x, 340p, bib.*

AUGE, J N (ed)
With the British and U.S. Forces at war: a military reader *(Paris: Didier 1948), 2 vols.*

BALDWIN, Hanson W
Battles lost and won: great campaigns of World War II *(New York: Harper 1966), xi, 532p, bib.*
Great mistakes of the war *(London: Redman 1950),* [5], *105p, bib.*

BALL, Adrian
The last day of the old world: 3rd September 1939 *(London: Muller 1963),* [II], *292p, bib.*

BAYNE-JARDINE, Colin C
World War Two *(London: Longmans 1968),* [8], *143p, bib.*

BERNANOS, Georges
Plea for liberty *(New York: Pantheon 1944), 136p.*

BLIVEN, Bruce
From Casablanca to Berlin: the war in North Africa and Europe, 1942–1945 *(New York: Random House 1965), 180p.*

BROOKHOUSE, Frank (ed)
This was your war: an anthology of great writings from World War II *(New York: Doubleday 1960), 498p.*

BROWNE, Harry
The Second World War *(London: Faber 1968), 112p, bib.*

BRYANT, *Sir* Arthur
The turn of the tide, 1939–1943: a study based on the diaries and autobiographical notes of Field-Marshal the Viscount Alanbrooke, K.G., O.M. *(London: Collins 1957), 766p.*

CALVOCORESSI, Peter
Total war: causes and courses of the Second World War *(London: Lane 1972), xv, 959p, bib.*

CHURCHILL, *Sir* Winston S
The Second World War *(London: Cassell 1948–54), 6 vols; later edition: abridgement, 1065p.*

COLLIER, Basil
A short history of the Second World War *(London: Collins 1967), 3–638p, bib.*

COLLIER'S photographic history of World War II: action and events in all theaters *(New York: Collier 1946), 5–272p.*

COMMAGER, Henry S (ed)
The story of the Second World War *(Boston, Mass: Little, Brown, 1945), 578p.*

COOPER, Alfred D
Second World War: first phase *(New York: Scribner 1939), 7-346p.*

COWIE, Donald
The campaigns of Wavell: the inner story of the Empire in action *(London: Chapman & Hall 1941-2), 2 vols.*

CUFF, Samuel H
The face of the war, 1931-1942 *(New York: Messner 1942), 290p.*

DAILY TELEGRAPH (Newspaper)
The story of the war *(London: Hodder & Stoughton 1945), 6 vols.*

DANIELL, David S
World War 2: an illustrated history *(London: Benn 1966), 128p, bib.*

DE GRUCHY, Francis A L
War diary: an overall war picture, 1939-1945 *(Aldershot, Hants: Gale & Polden 1949), vii, 187p.*

DENNIS, Geoffrey (ed)
The world at war: a history dealing with every phase of World War II on land, at sea, and in the air, including events which led up to the outbreak of hostilities *(London: Caxton 1951), 4 vols.*

DETZER, Karl W
The mightiest army *(Pleasantville, NY: Reader's Digest 1945), 168p.*

DOLLINGER, Hans
The decline and fall of Nazi Germany and Imperial Japan: a pictorial history of the final days of World War II *(London: Odhams 1968), 432p, bib.*

DORF, Philip
This war: a survey of world conflict *(New York: Oxford Book 1941), 124p.*

DUPUY, Richard E
World War II: a compact history *(New York: Hawthorn 1969), 334p.*

DUTCH, Oswald (pseud)
Pall over Europe *(London: Gollancz 1942), 144p.*

EARLE, Hubert P
Blackout: the human side of Europe's march to war *(Philadelphia, Pa: Lippincott 1939), 11-290p.*

ENSOR, Robert C K
A miniature history of the war down to the liberation of Paris *(New York: Oxford UP 1945), 153p.*

ESPOSITO, Vincent J
A concise history of World War 2 *(New York: Praeger 1964), xiv, 434p, bib.*

FALLS, Cyril
The Second World War: a short history *(London: Methuen 1950), 3rd rev ed, xiv, 312p.*

FARRAR-HOCKLEY, Anthony
The true book about the Second World War *(London: Muller [1959]), 143p.*

FENSTON, Joseph
Victory cavalcade *(London: Heath Cranton 1950), xv, 304p.*

FLOWER, Desmond *and* REEVES, James (comps)
The war, 1939–1945 *(London: Cassell 1960), xv, 1120p; US title:* Taste of courage.

FORTUNE, Charles H
The war in retrospect: a day-to-day record of World War II *(Dunedin, NZ: Evening Star 1944–5), 2 vols.*

FULLER, John F C
The Second World War, 1939–1945: a strategical and tactical history *(London: Eyre & Spottiswoode 1948), 431p.*

GALLAGHER, Matthew P
The Soviet history of World War 2: myths, memories and realities *(New York: Praeger [1963]), xvi, 205p, bib.*

GARDNER, Brian
The wasted hour: the tragedy of 1945 *(London: Cassell 1963), xiii, 356p, bib; US title:* The year that changed the world.

GILBERT, Martin
The Second World War *(London: Chatto & Windus 1970), 108p, bib.*

GLEESON, James J *and* WALDRON, Thomas J
Now it can be told *(London: Elek 1952), 188p.*

GRAVES, Charles
War over peace *(London: Hutchinson 1940), 256p.*

GROTH, John
Studio: Europe *(New York: Vanguard 1945), 282p.*

HALL, Walter P
Iron out of cavalry: an interpretive history of the Second World War *(New York: Appleton 1946), 389p.*

HANSEN, Harold A *and others* (eds)
Fighting for freedom: historic documents *(Philadelphia, Pa: Winston 1947), 502p.*

HARDY, Alfred C
Everyman's history of the war *(London: Nicholson & Watson 1948-55), 3 vols.*

HASLUCK, Eugene L
The Second World War *(London: Blackie 1948), 358p.*

HAY, Ian (pseud)
Arms and the men *(London: HMSO 1950), 330p.*

HEIFERMAN, Ron
World War II *(London: Octopus 1973), 256p.*

HENDERSON, Harry B *and* MORRIS, H C
War in our time: a comprehensive and analytical history in pictures and text of the first eleven years of World War II *(New York: Doubleday 1942), 6-416p.*

HENDERSON, *Sir* Nevile
Failure of a mission *(London: Hodder & Stoughton 1940), 318p.*

HOARE, Robert J
World War Two: an illustrated history in colour, 1939-1945 *(London: Macdonald 1973), 64p, bib.*

HOBSON, Harold
The first three years of the war: a day-by-day record *(London: Hutchinson 1942), 260p.*

HOLT, Edgar
The world at war, 1939-45 *(London: Putnam 1956), 272p, bib.*

HOPKINS, John A H (comp)
Diary of world events, being a chronological record of the Second World War *(Baltimore, Md: National Advertising 1942-8), 54 vols.*

HOWE, Quincy
Ashes of victory: World War II and its aftermath *(New York: Simon & Schuster 1972), 542p.*

HOYLE, Martha B
A world in flames: a history of World War II *(New York: Atheneum 1970), xxi, 356p, bib.*

HUSTED, H H
A thumb-nail history of World War II *(Boston, Mass: Humphries 1948), 7-442p.*

HUTCHINSON, Walter (ed)
Pictorial history of the war: a complete and authentic record in text and pictures *(London: Hutchinson 1939-45), 26 vols.*

'ILLUSTRATED, book of World War II: the first record in full colour photographs *(London: Sidgwick & Jackson 1972), 128p.*

INGERSOLL, Ralph McA
Top secret *(London: Partridge 1946), 285p.*

JACOBSEN, Hans A *and* ROHWER, Jurgen
Decisive battles of World War 2: the German view *(London: Deutsch 1965), 509p, bib.*

JORDAN, Max
Beyond all fronts: a bystander's notes on this thirty years' war *(Toronto: Ryerson 1944), xiv, 386p.*

KIMCHE, Jon
The unfought battle *(London: Weidenfeld & Nicolson 1968),* [7], *168p, bib.*

KING-HALL, Stephen
History of the war *(London: Hodder & Stoughton 1939–40), 3 vols.*
Total victory *(London: Faber 1941), xii, 306p.*

KINNAIRD, Clark (ed)
It happened in 1945 *(New York: Duell 1946), 464p.*

LAMB, Geoffrey F
Great exploits of the Second World War *(London: Harrap 1959), 24p, bib.*

LANGSAM, Walter C (ed)
Historic documents of World War II *(Princeton, NJ: Princeton UP 1958), 192p.*

LEVIEN, Jack *and* LORD, John
The valiant years: a dramatic narrative of the Second World War *(London: Harrap 1962), 216p.*

LEWIN, Ronald
The war on land, 1939–1945: an anthology of personal experiences *(London: Hutchinson 1969), xvi, 339p, bib.*

LIDDELL HART, Basil H
History of the Second World War *(London: Cassell 1970), xvi, 766p, bib.*
The current of war *(London: Hutchinson 1941), 415p.*
This expanding war *(London: Faber 1942), 278p.*

LIGON, L D
The three longest days: Sicily, Salerno, Normandy *(New York: Vantage 1972), 136p.*

LORD, Louis E
Thucydides and the World War *(New York: Russell & Russell 1967), 300p.*

LUNN, Arnold H M
Whither Europe? *(London: Hutchinson 1940), 7-270p.*

MCINNES, Edgar
The war *(London: Oxford UP 1940–5), 6 vols.*

MAJDALANY, Fred
The fall of fortress Europe *(New York: Doubleday 1968), xi, 442p, bib.*

MARCH, Anthony (ed)
Darkness over Europe: first-person accounts of life in Europe during the war years, 1939–1945 *(Chicago, Ill: Rand McNally 1969), 271p.*

MAULE, Henry
The great battles of World War II *(London: Hamlyn 1972), 448p, bib.*

MEE, Arthur
Immortal dawn *(London: Hodder & Stoughton 1942), 224p.*
Wonderful year *(London: Hodder & Stoughton 1943), 148p.*

MICHEL, Henri
World War 2: a short history *(Farnborough, Hants: Saxon House 1973), xviii, 81p.*

MILLER, Francis T
History of World War II *(Philadelphia, Pa: Winston 1945), 966p.*

MILWARD, Alan S
World War II *(Milton Keynes, Bucks: Open University 1973), 101p.*

MODLEY, Rudolf
History of the war in maps, in pictographs, in words *(Washington DC: Infantry Journal Press 1943), x, 177p.*

MORRIS, Herman C *and* HENDERSON, Harry B (eds)
World War II in pictures *(New York: Journal of Living Publishing 1945), 3 vols.*

MOWAT, Robert C
Ruin and resurgence, 1939–1965 *(London: Blandford 1966), xvi, 406p, bib.*

NAMIER, Lewis B
Europe in decay: a study in disintegration, 1936–1940 *(London: Macmillan 1950), 329p.*

NECKER, Wilhelm
This bewildering war *(London: Drummond 1940), 344p.*

NEILSON, Francis
Tragedy of Europe: a day by day commentary on the Second World War *(Appleton, Wis.: Nelson 1940–6), 5 vols.*

NEWSWEEK (periodical)
The month that made history: a Newsweek report *(New York: Newsweek 1945), 64p.*

NICOLL, Peter H
Britain's blunder: an objective study of the Second World War, its cause, conduct and consequence *(Lawrencekirk, Kincardineshire: Nicoll 1949), vii, 134p.*

ODHAMS History of the Second World War *(London: Odhams 1951), 2 vols.*

OLECK, Howard L (comp)
Heroic battles of World War II *(New York: Belmont 1962), 189p.*

OLSSON, Carl
From hell to breakfast: epic operations of the last war *(London: Brown, Watson 1959), 157p.*

O'NEILL, Herbert C
Man of Destiny: being studies of the four who rode the war and made this precarious landfall *(London: Phoenix House 1953), 240p.*

PARKINSON, Roger
Blood, toil, tears and sweat: the war history from Dunkirk to Alamein, based on the War Cabinet papers of 1940–1942 *(London: Hart-Davis MacGibbon 1973), x, 539p, bib.*

A day's march nearer home: the war history from Alamein to VE Day based on the War Cabinet papers of 1942 to 1945 *(London: Hart-Davis MacGibbon 1974), xxvi, 551p, bib.*

PEIS, Gunter
The man who started the war *(London: Odhams 1960), 233p.*

PICTORIAL history of the Second World War: a photographic record of all theaters of action chronologically arranged *(New York: Wise 1944–9), 10 vols.*

PICTORIAL history of World War II: the graphic record of your Armed Forces in action throughout every phase of global conflict *(New York: Veterans of Foreign Wars Memorial Edition 1951), 2 vols.*

READER'S DIGEST (periodical)
Illustrated history of World War II *(New York: Reader's Digest 1969), 528p.*

RECORD of the war: first-tenth quarters, Sept-Nov 1939 to Jan-Mar 1942 *(London: Hutchinson 1940–2), 10 vols.*

REED, Douglas
From smoke to smother, 1935-1948: a sequel to Insanity Fair *(London: Cape 1948), 317p.*

REEDER, Russell P
The story of the Second World War *(Des Moines, Iowa: Meredith 1969), 2 vols.*

ROONEY, Andrew A
The fortunes of war: four great battles of World War II *(Boston, Mass: Little, Brown 1962), 236p.*

ROOT, Waverly L
The secret history of the war *(New York: Scribner 1945–6), 3 vols.*

ROTHBERG, Abraham
Eyewitness history of World War II *(New York: Bantam 1962), 4 vols.*

ROYAL INSTITUTE OF INTERNATIONAL AFFAIRS
Chronology of the Second World War *(London: RIIA 1947), 374p.*

SAVAGE, Katharine
A state of war, Europe, 1939–1945 *(London: Blond 1964), 72p, bib.*
The story of the Second World War *(London: Oxford UP 1957), 230p.*

SELBY, John M
The Second World War *(London: Allen & Unwin 1967), 112p.*

SELLMAN, Roger R
The Second World War *(London: Methuen 1964), 111p.*

SETH, Ronald S
The day war broke out: the story of the 3rd September, 1939 *(London: Spearman 1963), 175p.*

SHUGG, Roger W *and* DEWEERD, H A
World War II: a concise history *(Washington DC: Infantry Journal Press 1946), 538p.*

SNOW, Edgar
Glory and bondage *(London: Gollancz 1945), 263p.*

SNYDER, Louis L
The first book of World War 2 *(New York: Watts [1958]), 96p.*
The war: a concise history, 1939–1945 *(New York: Messner 1960), xiii, 594p, bib.*

STEWART, *Sir* James P
Over military age: a war-time commentary on the first two years' war *(London: Allen & Unwin 1942), vi, 226p.*

STORRS, Ronald *and* GRAVES, Philip
A record of the war *(London: Hutchinson 1940–7), 24 vols.*

STRATEGICUS (pseud)
Foothold in Europe: the campaigns in Sicily, Italy, the Far East and Russia between July 1943 and May 1944 *(London: Faber 1945), 243p.*
From Tobruk to Smolensk *(London: Faber 1941), 9–308p.*

Strategicus (pseud) *(cont.)*

A short history of the Second World War, and its social and political significance *(London: Faber 1950), 345p.*
The tide turns: the battles of Stalingrad, Alamein and Tunisia (23 Aug 1942–14 May 1943) *(London: Faber 1944), 244p.*
To Stalingrad and Alamein *(London: Faber 1943), 237p.*

SULZBERGER, Cyrus L
World War II *(New York: American Heritage 1970), 386p.*

SURVEY OF INTERNATIONAL AFFAIRS
The wartime series for 1939–46 *(London: Oxford UP 1952), 7 vols.*

TABORI, Paul
Twenty tremendous years: World War II and after *(New York: McBride Books 1962), 288p.*

TAYLOR, Alan J P (ed)
History of World War II *(London: Octopus 1974), 2–287p.*

THOMPSON, Laurence
1940: year of legend, year of history *(London: Collins 1966), 254p, bib.*

THOMSON, George M
Vote of censure *(London: Secker & Warburg 1968), 3–253p, bib.*

TOLAND, John
The last 100 days *(New York: Random House 1966), x, 622p.*

US WAR DEPARTMENT
The world at war, 1939–1944: a brief history of World War II *(Washington DC: Infantry Journal Press 1945), 416p.*

VAN SINDEREN, Adrian
Four years: a chronicle of the war by months [Sept 1939–Sept 1943] *(New York: Coward-McCann 1944), xvi, 206p.*
The story of the six years of global war *(New York: Price 1946), 393p.*

VERNI, Vicente
Twenty war fronts: a Latin vision of World War II *(Mexico City 1945), 193p.*

VICTORY on the march: reports on the progress of the war by Franklin D. Roosevelt, Winston Churchill, Geo. C. Marshall and the U.S. Navy *(New York: National Education Alliance 1944), viii, 200p.*

WAR of 1939: a history dealing with every phase of the war on land, sea and in the air *(London: Caxton), 10 vols, n.d.*

THE WAR reports of General of the Army George C. Marshall, Chief of Staff; General of the Army H. H. Arnold, Commanding General Army Air Forces; and Fleet Admiral Ernest J. King, Commander-in-Chief, United States Fleet and Chief of Naval operations *(Philadelphia, Pa: Lippincott 1947), 801p.*

WATTS, Franklin *and others* (eds)
Voices of history: great speeches and papers of the year, 1941, 1942–43 to 1945–46 *(New York: Gramercy 1942–6), 5 vols.*

WELLES, Sumner
Seven decisions that shaped history *(New York: Harper 1951), 236p; UK title:* Seven major decisions.

WEYR, Thomas
World War II *(Folkestone, Kent: Bailey & Swinfen 1970), 224p, bib.*

WIENER LIBRARY
On the track of tyranny: essays presented to Leonard Montefiore *(London: Valentine, Mitchell 1960), 232p.*

WILMOT, Chester
The struggle for Europe *(London: Collins 1952), 766p, bib.*

WRIGHT, Gordon
The ordeal of total war, 1939–1945 *(New York: Harper 1968), iii-xix, 314p, bib.*

WYKES, Alan
1942 - the turning point *(London: Macdonald 1972), xiii, 194p, bib.*

YOUNG, Arthur P
The 'X' documents *(London: Deutsch 1974), 253p.*

YOUNG, Peter (comp)
Decisive battles of the Second World War: an anthology *(London: Barker [1967]), 439p.*
World War, 1939–45: a short history *(London: Barker [1966]), 447p, bib.*

YUST, Walter (ed)
Ten eventful years: a record of events of the years preceding, including and following World War II, 1937 through 1946 *(Chicago, Ill: Encyclopaedia Britannica 1947), 4 vols.*

HITLER

BAXTER, Richard
Hitler's darkest secret: what he has in store for Britain *(New York: Universal 1941), xii, 13–157p.*

BEZYMENSKI, Lev
The death of Adolf Hitler: unknown documents from Soviet archives *(London: Joseph 1968), [10], 114p.*

BOLDT, Gerhard
Hitler's last days: an eye-witness account *(London: Sphere 1973), 188p.*
In the shelter with Hitler *(London: Citadel 1948), 78p.*

BULLOCK, Allan
Hitler: a study in tyranny *(London: Odhams 1952), 776p, bib.*

BUNTING, James
Adolf Hitler *(Folkestone, Kent: Bailey & Swinfen 1973), 3-157p, bib.*

CROSS, Colin
Adolf Hitler *(London: Hodder & Stoughton 1973), 348p, bib.*

DIETRICH, Otto
Hitler *(Chicago, Ill: Regnery 1955), 227p; UK title:* The Hitler I knew.

ELLIOTT, Brendan L
Hitler and Germany *(London: Longmans 1966), viii, 176p, bib.*

FITZGIBBON, Constantine
To kill Hitler *(London: Stacey 1972), 288p; originally published as:* The shirt of Nessus; *US title:* 20 July.

GENOUD, François (ed)
The testament of Adolf Hitler: the Hitler-Bormann documents, Feb–Apr. 1945 *(London: Cassell 1961), 115p.*

HALDER, Franz
Hitler as war lord *(London: Putnam 1950), ix, 70p.*

HEIBER, Helmut
Adolf Hitler: a short biography *(London: Wolff 1961), 192p, bib.*

HESSE, Fritz
Hitler and the English *(London: Wingate 1954), 218p.*

HINSLEY, Francis H
Hitler's strategy: the naval evidence *(Cambridge: Cambridge UP 1951), xii, 254p.*

HITLER, Adolf
Hitler's secret book *(New York: Grove 1962), xxv, 230p.*
Hitler's table talk, 1941-1944 *(London: Weidenfeld & Nicolson 1953), 746p; US title:* Secret conversations 1941-1944.

HITLER'S war directives, 1939–1945 *(London: Sidgwick & Jackson 1964), xxvii, 229p; US title:* Blitzkrieg to defeat.
My new order *(New York: Reynal & Hitchcock 1941), xv, 1008p.*

HOFFMANN, Heinrich
The Hitler phenomenon: an intimate portrait of Hitler and his entourage *(Newton Abbot, Devon: David & Charles 1974), 223p.*
Hitler was my friend *(London: Burke 1955), 256p.*

LANGER, Walter C
The mind of Adolf Hitler *(New York: Basic 1972), ix, 269p, bib.*

MANVELL, Roger
The conspirators: 20th July 1944 *(New York: Ballantine 1971), 160p, bib.*

MANVELL, Roger *and* FRAENKEL, Heinrich
The July plot: the attempt in 1944 on Hitler's life and the men behind it *(London: Bodley Head 1964), 272p, bib; US title:* The men who tried to kill Hitler.

MASER, Werner
Hitler *(London: Lane 1973), ii–xv, 433p, bib.*
Hitler's letters and notes *(London: Heinemann 1974), viii, 390p.*

PAYNE, Robert
The life and death of Adolf Hitler *(London: Cape 1973), xiv, 623p, bib.*

RAUSCHNING, Hermann
Hitler's aims in war and peace *(London: Heinemann 1940), xix, 131p.*

RICH, Norman
Hitler's war aims *(London: Deutsch 1974), xvii, 548p, bib.*

ROBERTSON, Esmonde M
Hitler's pre-war policy and military plans, 1933–1939 *(London: Longmans Green 1963), 207p.*

SCHLABRENDORFF, Fabian von
They almost killed Hitler *(New York: Macmillan 1947), x, 150p; UK title:* Revolt against Hitler.

SCHMIDT, Paul
Hitler's interpreter *(London: Heinemann 1951), 286p.*

SCHRAMM, Percy E
Hitler: the man and the military leader *(London: Lane 1972), x, 214p.*

SHIRER, William L
The rise and fall of Adolf Hitler *(New York: Random House 1961), 185p.*

SNYDER, Louis L
Hitler and Nazism *(New York: Watts 1961), [8], 151p.*

STEED, Henry W
That bad man: a tale for the young of all ages *(London: Macmillan 1942), 200p.*

STRASSER, Otto
Hitler and I *(London: Cape 1940), 249p.*
STRAWSON, John
Hitler as military commander *(London: Batsford 1971), 256p, bib.*
THYSSEN, Fritz
I paid Hitler *(London: Hodder & Stoughton 1941), xxix, 281p.*
TREVOR-ROPER, Hugh R
The last days of Hitler *(London: Macmillan 1971), 4th ed., lxiii, 286p.*
WAITE, Robert G L (ed)
Hitler and Nazi Germany *(New York: Holt 1965),* [5], *122p, bib.*
WALDMAN, Morris D
Sieg Heil!: the story of Adolf Hitler *(New York: Oceana 1962), 318p.*
WARLIMONT, Walter
Inside Hitler's headquarters, 1939–45 *(London: Weidenfeld & Nicolson* [*1964*]*), xi, 658p, bib.*
WYKES, Alan
Hitler *(New York: Ballantine 1970),* [2], *160p, bib.*
Hitler's bodyguards: Leibstandarte Division *(New York: Ballantine 1974), 160p.*

HOLLAND

ASHTON, H S (pseud)
The Netherlands at war *(London: Routledge 1941), xxi, 130p.*
BLOKZIJL, Jan
Captain Blokzijl and the Nazis *(Philadelphia, Pa: Dorrance 1971), 308p.*
BOAS, J H
Religious resistance in Holland *(London: Allen & Unwin 1945), 64p.*
BOOM, Corrie ten
The hiding place *(New York: Chosen Books 1971), 219p.*
BURGHERS, Nelly M
Holland under the Nazi heel: letters from Hollanders to their countrymen in South Africa, written after the war *(Ilfracombe, Devon: Stockwell* [*1958*]*), 94p.*
DE GAULLE, A J N (pseud)
Desperate carnival *(London: Muller 1955), 288p.*
DE JONG, Louis
Holland fights the Nazis *(London: Drummond 1941), 138p.*

DONKER, P A
. . . Winter '44–'45 in Holland: a winter never to be forgotten *(Antwerp: Donker 1945), 72p.*

FRANK, Anne
The diary of a young girl *(London: Vallentine, Mitchell 1952), xvii, 281p.*

GANIER-RAYMOND, Philippe
The tangled web *(London: Barker 1968), 203p.*

HAZELHOFF, Erik
Soldier of Orange *(London: Hodder & Stoughton 1972), 222p.*

KLEFFENS, Eelco N van
Rape of the Netherlands *(London: Hodder & Stoughton 1940), 253p; US title:* Juggernaut over Holland.

KONIJNENBURG, Emile van
Organized robbery *(The Hague: Netherlands Government Printing & Publishing Office 1949), 242p.*

KROESE, A
The Dutch Navy at war *(London: Allen & Unwin 1945), 131p.*

LAURENS, Anne
The Lindemans affair *(London: Allan Wingate 1971), 191p.*

MAASS, Walter B
The Netherlands at war, 1940–1945 *(London: Abelard-Schuman 1970), 264p, bib.*

MALNUTRITION and starvation in Western Netherlands, September 1944–July 1945 *(The Hague: General State Printing Office 1948), 2 vols.*

MARTENS, Allard
The silent war: glimpses of the Dutch underground and views on the battle of Arnhem *(London: Hodder & Stoughton 1961), 318p, bib.*

MASON, Henry L
The purge of Dutch Quislings: emergency justice in the Netherlands *(The Hague: Nijhoff 1952), 199p.*

MEERLOO, Joost A M
Total war and the human mind: a psychologist's experiences in occupied Holland *(New York: International Universities Press 1945), 78p.*

MINCO, Marga
Bitter herbs: a little chronicle *(London: Oxford UP 1960),* [7], *116p.*

POSTHUMUS, H W (ed)
The Netherlands during German occupation *(Philadelphia, Pa: American Academy of Political & Social Science 1946), 231p.*

PRESSER, Jacob
Ashes in the wind: the destruction of Dutch Jewry *(London: Souvenir 1968), 556p; US title:* The destruction of the Dutch Jews.

SCHNABEL, Ernst
Anne Frank: a portrait in courage *(New York: Harcourt 1958), 192p; UK title:* The footsteps of Anne Frank.

SCHREURS, Johannes J
My country in trouble *(New York: Carlton 1962), 52p.*

SOMEREN, Liesje van
Escape from Holland *(London: Jenkins 1942), 121p.*

VAN PAASSEN, Pierre
Earth could be fair: a chronicle *(New York: Dial 1946), 509p.*

VANWOERDAN, Peter
In the secret place: a story of Dutch underground *(Wheaton, Ill: Van Kampen Press 1954), 64p.*

WALT, Harrp P van
The night is far spent *(Philadelphia, Pa: Dorrance 1945), 221p.*

WARMBRUNN, Werner
The Dutch under German occupation, 1940–1945 *(Stanford, Calif: Stanford UP 1963), xiv, 338p, bib.*

WOODRUFF, John H
Relations between the Netherlands Government-in-exile and occupied Holland during World War II *(Boston, Mass: Boston University Bookstore 1964), 146p.*

[*see also* ARNHEM, JEWS, RESISTANCE, WESTERN EUROPE 1939–40; WESTERN EUROPE 1944–5]

HOME GUARD

FINCH, Peter
Warmen courageous: the story of the Essex Home Guard *(Southend-on-Sea, Essex: Burrows [1952]), [14], 351p.*

GRAVES, Charles
Home Guard of Britain: comprehensive history of the Home Guard movement, 1940–1943 *(London: Hutchinson 1943), 364p.*

HISTORY of the Cheshire Home Guard from L.D.V. formation to stand-down, 1940–1944 *(Aldershot, Hants: Gale & Polden 1950), xiii, 158p.*

LONGMATE, Norman
The real Dad's Army *(London: Arrow 1974), 128p.*

MCGEOCH, W P
The triumphs and tragedies of a Home Guard (Factory) Company, B Company 41st Warwickshire (Birmingham) Battalion Home Guard *(Birmingham: Tuckey 1946), 188p.*

OGILVY-DALGLEISH, James W
The Rutland Home Guard of 1940–44 *(Springfield, Rutland: the author 1955), 68p.*

SHIRLAW, Gerald B *and* TROKE, Clifford
Medicine versus invasion: the Home Guard medical service in action *(London: Secker & Warburg 1941), xx, 208p.*

SLATER, Hugh
Home Guard for victory *(London: Gollancz 1941), 120p.*

STREET, Arthur G
From dusk till dawn *(London: Harrap 1943), 136p.*

HONG KONG

BROWN, Wenzell
Hong Kong aftermath *(New York: Smith & Durrell 1943), 283p.*

CAREW, Tim
The fall of Hong Kong *(London: Blond 1960), 228p, bib.*

DEW, Gwen
Prisoner of the Japs *(New York: Knopf 1943), viii, 309p.*

FIELD, Helen
Twilight in Hong Kong *(London: Muller 1960), 232p.*

GOODWIN, Ralph B
Hongkong escape *(London: Barker 1953), 223p, later published as:* Passport to eternity.

GUEST, Freddie
Escape from the bloodied sun *(London: Jarrolds 1956), 192p.*

HAHN, Emily
Hong Kong holiday *(New York: Doubleday 1946), viii, 305p.*

HAMMOND, Robert B
Bondservants of the Japanese *(Pasadena, Calif: Hammond 1943), 7–87p.*

HARROP, Phyllis
Hong Kong incident *(London: Eyre & Spottiswoode 1943), 192p.*

LAN, Yu Shi *and* WANG, Mayling
We flee from Hong Kong *(Grand Rapids, Mich: Zondervan 1944), 125p.*

MARSMAN, Jan H
I escaped from Hong Kong *(New York: Reynal 1942), 249p.*

PROUIX, Benjamin A
Underground from Hong Kong *(New York: Dutton 1943), 9–214p.*

RYAN, Thomas F (comp)
Jesuits under fire in the siege of Hong Kong, 1941: a composite narrative *(London: Burns & Gates 1944), 188p.*

WRIGHT, Robert J
I was a hell camp prisoner *(London: Brown, Watson 1963), 160p.*
[*see also* JAPAN PRISON CAMPS, PRISONER OF WAR CAMPS]

HOSPITALS

BAMM, Peter
The invisible flag: a report *(London: Faber 1956), 229p.*
CURNOCK, George C (ed)
Hospitals under fire - but the lamp still burns *(London: Allen & Unwin 1941), 148p.*
[*see also* MEDICAL, NURSES]

HUNGARY

ARNOTHY, Christine
I am fifteen and do not want to die *(London: Collins 1956), 128p.*
BISS, Andreas
A million Jews to save: check to the final solution *(London: Hutchinson 1973), 272p.*
BOLDIZSAR, Ivan
The other Hungary *(Budapest: 'New Hungary' 1946), 76p.*
BRAHAM, Randolph L
The destruction of Hungarian Jewry: a documentary account *(New York: Pro Arte 1963), 2 vols.*
The Hungarian Jewish catastrophe: a selected and annotated bibliography *(New York: Yivo Institute for Jewish Research 1962), 86p.*
CZEBE, Jeno *and* PETHO, Tibor
Hungary in World War II: a military history of the years of war *(Budapest: 'New Hungary' 1946), 74p.*
DREISZIGER, Nandor A F
Hungary's way to World War II *(Astor Park, Fla: Danubian 1969), 239p.*
FABER, W S
Hungary's alibi *(London: Lincolns-Praeger 1944), 48p.*
FENYO, Mario D
Hitler, Horthy and Hungary: German-Hungarian relations, 1941-1944 *(New Haven, Conn: Yale UP 1972), xii, 279p, bib.*
GALANTAI, Maria
The changing of the guard: the siege of Budapest 1944-5 *(London: Pall Mall 1961), 224p.*
HEIMER, Eugene
Night of the mist *(New York: Vanguard 1959), 191p.*

KALLAY, Nicholas
Hungarian premier: a personal account of a nation's struggle in the Second World War *(New York: Columbia UP 1954), xxxvii, 518p.*

KERTESZ, Istvan
Diplomacy in a whirlpool: Hungary between Nazi Germany and Soviet Russia *(Notre Dame, Ind: Notre Dame UP 1953), 273p.*

KOBR, Milos A
Hungary's war *(London: New Europe 1943), 56p.*

LEVAI, Jeno
Black book on the martyrdom of Hungarian Jewry *(Zurich: Central European Times 1948), 475p.*
Hungarian Jewry and the Papacy: Pope Pius XII did not remain silent *(London: Sands 1968), xii, 132p.*

MACARTNEY, Carlile A
A history of Hungary, 1929–1945 *(New York: Praeger 1956–57), 2 vols; UK title:* October Fifteenth.

MASTERS, Anthony
The summer that bled: the biography of Hannah Senesh *(London: Joseph 1972), 349p, bib.*

MONKS, Noel
Fighter squadrons: the epic story of two Hungarian squadrons in France *(London: Angus & Robertson 1941), xii, 243p.*

NADANYI, Paul
Hungary at the crossroads of invasions *(New York: Amerikai magyar nepszava 1943), 94p.*

ORME, Alexandra (pseud)
From Christmas to Easter: a guide to a Russian occupation *(London: Hodge 1949), 343p; US title:* Comes the comrade.

PARKER, Robert B
Headquarters Budapest *(New York: Farrar 1944), 345p.*

WHITE book, concerning the status of Hungarian prisoners of war illegally detained by the Soviet Union and of Hungarian civilians forcefully deported by Soviet authorities *(Munich: Edition Hungaria 1951), 116p.*

[*see also* CATHOLICISM, JEWS]

ICELAND

CHAMBERLIN, William C
Economic development of Iceland through World War II *(New York: Columbia UP 1947), 141p.*

GOODELL, Jane
They sent me to Iceland *(New York: Washburn 1943), 248p.*
LINKLATER, Eric
Northern garrisons: the defense of Iceland and the Faeroe, Orkney and Shetland Islands *(New York: Garden City 1941), vii, 71p.*
WATKINS, Ernest S
No depression in Iceland *(London: Allen & Unwin 1942), vii, 9–83p.*

INDIA

BARTON, *Sir* William
India's fateful hour *(London: Murray 1942), 157p.*
BRAILSFORD, Henry N
Subject India *(London: Gollancz 1943), 223p.*
CLARE, Thomas H
Lookin' eastward, a G.I. salaam to India *(New York: Macmillan 1945), 321p.*
CLUNE, Frank P
Song of India *(Sydney: Invincible 1946), 350p.*
COMBINED INTER-SERVICES HISTORICAL SECTION INDIA AND PAKISTAN
Defence of India: policy and plans *(Bombay: Longmans 1963), xvii, 278p.*
DEB, J N
Blood and tears *(Bombay: Hind Kitabs 1945), 244p.*
FISCHER, Louis
A week with Gandhi *(New York: Duell 1942), 122p.*
GANDHI, Mohandas K
My appeal to the British *(New York: Day 1942), 5–79p. UK title:* I ask every Briton.
GUPTA, S C
History of the Indian Air Force, 1933–45 *(Delhi: Combined Inter-Services Historical Section 1961), 194p.*
HUNTINGDON, Francis J C, *15th earl of Hastings*
Commonsense about India *(London: Heinemann 1942), 80p.*
JOG, N G
Will war come to India: a week-by-week record of the first two years of World War II *(Bombay: New 1941), 299p.*
KARAKA, Dosoo F
I've shed my tears: a candid view of resurgent India *(New York: Appleton 1947), 280p.*

KHAN, Shah N
My memories of I.N.A. and its Netaji *(Delhi: Rajkarnal 1946), 283p.*
MACKENZIE, DeWitt
India's problem can be solved *(New York: Doubleday 1943), x, 265p.*
MITCHELL, Kate L
India and the war: an analysis of the Cripps mission and its aftermath *(New York: Amerasia 1942), 48p.*
India without fable: a 1942 survey *(New York: Knopf 1943), vii, 296p.*
MUIR, Peter
This is India *(New York: Doubleday 1943), 237p.*
PALTA, Krishnan R
My adventures with the I.N.A. *(Lahore: Lion 1946), viii, 215p.*
PRITT, Denis N
India our ally *(London: Muller 1942), 54p.*
THE ROYAL Indian Air Force at war: an account of air operations against the Japanese in South East Asia *(New Delhi: Sabharwall at Roxy Printing 1945), 120p.*
SIVARAM, M
The road to Delhi *(Rutland, Vt: Tuttle 1967), 264p.*
THOMAS, John
Line of communication: railway to victory in the East *(London: Locomotive 1947), 10-86p.*
THOMPSON, Edward J
Enlist India for freedom! *(London: Gollancz 1940), 120p.*
VAIDYA, Suresh
Over there *(Bombay: Hind Kitabs 1945), 102p.*
WADE, Harry F
Five miles closer to heaven: an adventure by parachute over the jungles of India *(Oconomowoc, Wis: Liguerian Pamphlet Office 1945), 60p.*
YEATS-BROWN, Francis C C
Martial India *(London: Eyre & Spottiswoode 1945), 200p.*

INDIAN ARMY

BAINES, Frank
Officer boy *(London: Eyre & Spottiswoode 1971), 207p.*
BRETT-JAMES, Antony
Ball of fire: the Fifth Indian Division in the Second World War *(Aldershot, Hants: Gale & Polden 1951), xiv, 481p.*
Report my signals *(London: Locke 1948), 352p.*

DHARM, Pal
Campaign in Western Asia *(London: Longmans, Green 1956), xxii, 570p.*
DOULTON, Alfred J F
The fighting cock: being the history of the 23rd Indian Division, 1942-1947 *(Aldershot, Hants: Gale & Polden 1951), xvi, 318p.*
ELLIOTT, James G
A roll of honour: the story of the Indian Army, 1939-1945 *(London: Cassell 1965), [15], 392p, bib; US title:* Unfading honor.
GRAHAM, Cuthbert A L
The history of the Indian Mountain Artillery *(Aldershot, Hants: Gale & Polden 1957), 470p.*
MACKENZIE, Compton
Eastern epic *(London: Chatto & Windus 1951), vol. I: September 1939-March 1943, xxiv, 623p.*
PRASAD, Nandan
Expansion of the armed forces and defence organization, 1939-1945 *(London: Longmans, Green 1956), xxxiv, 546p.*
The reconquest of Burma *(London: Longmans, Green 1958), 2 vols.*
The retreat from Burma *(London: Longmans, Green 1952), 501p.*
ROBERTS, Michael R
Golden arrow: the story of the 7th Indian Division in the Second World War, 1939-1945 *(Aldershot, Hants: Gale & Polden 1952), xxii, 304p.*
ROSS, John *and* HAILES, Walter L
War services of the 9th Jat Regiment *(Redhill, Surrey: Becher 1965), vol. 2: 1937-48.*
SANDES, Edward W C
The Indian Engineers, 1939-47 *(Kirkee, India: Institute of Military Engineering 1956), 534p.*
[*see also* BURMA]

INDONESIA

BENDA, Harry J
The crescent and the rising sun: Indonesian Islam under the Japanese occupation, 1942-1945 *(The Hague: Hoeve 1958), 320p.*
BENDA, Harry J *and others* (eds)
Japanese military administration in Indonesia: selected documents *(New Haven, Conn: Yale UP 1965), 279p.*

MOOK, Hubertus J van
The Netherlands Indies and Japan: their relations, 1940-41 *(London: Allen & Unwin 1944), 5-138p.*
[*see also* SOUTHEAST ASIA]

INDUSTRY

THE BATTLE of steel: a record of the British iron and steel industry at war *(London: British Iron & Steel Federation 1945), 52p.*

BORTH, Christy
Masters of mass production *(Indianapolis, Ind: Bobbs-Merrill 1945), 290p.*

CAMPBELL, Levin H
The industry-ordnance team *(New York: McGraw-Hill 1946), 461p.*

CONNERY, Robert H
The Navy and the industrial mobilization in World War II *(Princeton, NJ: Princeton UP 1951), xiii, 527p.*

FISHER, Douglas A
Steel in the war *(New York: US Steel Corporation 1946), 164p.*

HARGREAVES, Eric L *and* GOWING, M M
Civil industry and trade *(London: HMSO 1952), 678p.*

HORNBY, William
Factories and plant *(London: HMSO 1958), 421p.*

HURSTFIELD, J
The control of raw materials *(London: HMSO 1953), 530p.*

INMAN, Peggy
Labour in the munitions industries *(London: HMSO 1957), 461p.*

KOHAN, C M
Works and buildings *(London: HMSO 1952), 540p.*

MEIGGS, Russell
Home timber production, 1939-1945 *(London: Lockwood 1949), 277p.*

NATIONAL BUREAU FOR INDUSTRIAL PROTECTION
A history of the National Bureau for Industrial Protection, Washington, D.C., organized February 3, 1941, disbanded September 1, 1945 *(Washington DC 1945), 157p.*

NELSON, Donald M
Arsenal of democracy: the story of American war production *(New York: Harcourt 1946), 439p.*

NOVICK, David *and others*
Wartime production controls *(New York: Columbia UP 1949), 441p.*

POSTAN, Michael M
British war production *(London: HMSO 1952), 512p.*
SCOTT, John D *and* HUGHES, Richard
The administration of war production *(London: HMSO 1955), 544p.*
STOUGHTON, Bradley
History of the tools division, War Production Board *(New York: McGraw-Hill 1949), 154p.*
THE TIMES (newspaper)
British war production, 1939–1945: a record compiled by The Times *(London: The Times 1945), 240p.*
WALTON, Francis
The miracle of World War II: how American industry made victory possible *(New York: Macmillan 1956), 575p.*
WALTON, Frank L
Thread of victory: the conversion and conservation of textiles, clothing and leather for the world's biggest war program *(New York: Fairchild 1945), 272p.*
WOODBURY, David O
Battlefronts of industry: Westinghouse in World War II *(New York: Wiley 1948), 342p.*
[*see also* ECONOMICS]

INTELLIGENCE

ASTLEY, Joan B
The inner circle: a view of war at the top *(London: Hutchinson 1971), 228p.*
BARNES, Derek G
Cloud cover: recollections of an intelligence officer *(London: Rich & Cowan 1943), 176p.*
CROFT-COOKE, Rupert
The licentious soldiery *(London: W H Allen 1971), 173p.*
FARAGO, Ladislas
The game of the foxes: British and German intelligence operations and personalities which changed the course of the Second World War *(New York: McKay 1971), xxi, 696p, bib.*
The war of wits: the anatomy of espionage and intelligence *(New York: Funk 1954), 379p.*
FELSTEAD, Sidney T
Intelligence: an indictment of a colossal failure *(London: Hutchinson 1941), 253p.*

IND, Allison
Allied intelligence bureaux: our secret weapon in the war against Japan *(New York: McKay 1958), 305p; UK title:* Spy ring Pacific.

KIRKPATRICK, Lyman B
Captains without eyes: intelligence failures in World War II *(New York: Macmillan 1969), 303p.*

KOCH, Oscar W *and* HAYS, R G
G-2: intelligence for Patton *(Philadelphia, Pa: Whitmore 1972), 167p.*

LEUERKUEHN, Paul
German military intelligence *(London: Weidenfeld & Nicolson 1954), vii, 209p.*

MASTERMAN, *Sir* John C
The double-cross system in the war of 1939 to 1945 *(New Haven, Conn: Yale UP 1972), xix, 203p.*

ROWAN, Richard W
Terror in our time: the secret service of surprise attack *(Toronto: Longmans 1941), ix, 438p.*

SCHULZE-HOLTHUS, [Bernardt]
Daybreak in Iran: a story of the German Intelligence Service *(London: Staples 1954), 319p.*

STRONG, *Sir* Kenneth
Intelligence at the top: the recollections of an intelligence officer *(London: Cassell 1968), 271p.*
Men of intelligence: a study of the roles and decisions of Chiefs of Intelligence from World War I to the present day *(London: Cassell 1970), 183p, bib.*

US ARMY
History of technical intelligence: South West and Western Pacific areas, 1942–1945 *(Tokyo: US Army, Technical Intelligence Center 1945), 2 vols.*

US COUNTER-INTELLIGENCE CORPS SCHOOL
History and mission of the counter-intelligence corps in World War II *(Baltimore, Md: CIC School 1951), 83p.*

WILLIAMS, Wythe *and* NARVIG, W van
Secret sources: the story behind some famous scoops *(New York: Ziff-Davis 1943), 5–326p.*

WINTERBOTHAM, Frederick W
The ultra secret *(London: Weidenfeld & Nicolson 1974), xiii, 199p.*

ZACHARIAS, Ellis M
Secret missions: the story of an intelligence officer *(London: Putnam 1946), 433p.*
[*see also* SECRET SERVICES]

INTERNATIONAL LAW

BAR-ZOHAR, Michel
The avengers *(London: Barker 1968), 287p.*
MCNAIR, *Sir* Arnold D
The legal effects of war *(Cambridge: Cambridge UP 1948), 458p.*
SMITH, Herbert A
The crisis in the law of nations *(London: Stevens 1947), 102p.*
[*see also* WAR TRIALS]

INTERNEES

BARNHART, Edward N
Japanese American evacuation and resettlement: catalog of material in the general library *(Berkeley, Calif: California UP 1958), 177p.*
BROOM, Leonard *and* KITSUSE, John I
Managed casualty: the Japanese-American family in World War II *(Berkeley, Calif: California UP 1956), 226p.*
BROOM, Leonard *and* RIEMER, Ruth
Removal and return: the socio-economic effects of the war on Japanese Americans *(Berkeley, Calif: California UP 1949), x, 259p.*
THE CASE for the Nisei: brief of the Japanese evacuation *(Salt Lake City, Utah: Japanese American Citizens' League 1945), 193p.*
CONRAT, Maisie *and* CONRAT, Richard
Executive Order 9066: the internment of 110,000 Japanese Americans *(Cambridge, Mass: MIT 1972), 120p.*
DANIELS, Roger
Concentration camps USA: Japanese Americans and World War II *(New York: Holt 1971), xiv, [14], 188p.*
FISHER, Anne M R
Exile of race: a history of the forcible removal and imprisonment by the Army of the 115,000 citizens and alien Japanese who were living on the West Coast in the Spring of 1942 *(Sydney: BC 1965), 245p.*

GIOVANNELLI, Nickolay L
Paper hero: at His majesty's pleasure!: an account of life as a Manx internee during World War II *(Douglas, IoM: Island Development Company 1971), 90p.*

GIRDNER, Audrie *and* LOFTIS, Ann
The great betrayal: the evacuation of the Japanese-Americans during World War II *(New York: Macmillan 1969), 562p.*

GRODZINS, Morton
Americans betrayed: politics and the Japanese evacuation *(Cambridge: Cambridge UP 1949), 445p.*

KITAGAWA, Daisuke
Issei and Nisei: the internment years *(New York: Seabury 1967), 174p.*

LAURENT, Livia
A tale of internment *(London: Allen & Unwin 1942), 7-127p.*

MYER, Dillon S
Uprooted Americans: the Japanese Americans and the war relocation authority during World War II *(Tucson, Ariz: Arizona UP 1971), 360p.*

OKUBO, Mine
Citizen 13660 *(New York: Columbia UP 1946), 209p.*

RENNE, Louis O
Our day of Empire: war and the exile of Japanese-Americans *(Glasgow: Strickland Press 1954), 224p.*

THOMAS, Dorothy S *and* NISHIMOTO, R S
The spoilage: Japanese-American evacuation and resettlement during World War II *(Berkeley, Calif: California UP 1969), xx, 388p.*

IRAN

HAMZAVI, Abdol H
Persia and the Powers: an account of diplomatic relations 1941–1946 *(London: Hutchinson 1946), 125p.*

SKRINE, *Sir* Clarmont
World war in Iran *(London: Constable 1962), xxiv, 267p.*
[*see also* MIDDLE EAST]

IRELAND

BLAKE, John W
Northern Ireland in the Second World War *(Belfast: HMSO 1956), xv, 569p.*

DE VALERA, Eamonn
Ireland's stand: being a selection of speeches during the war, 1939–45 *(Dublin: Gill 1946), 102p.*
HARRISON, Henry
The neutrality of Ireland: why it was inevitable *(London: Hale 1942), 192p.*
MITCHELL, Mairin
The Atlantic battle and the future of Ireland *(London: Muller 1941), 72p.*
O'CALLAGHAN, Sean
The jackboot in Ireland *(London: Wingate 1958), 157p.*
PHELAN, James L
Churchill can unite Ireland *(London: Gollancz 1940), 120p.*
Ireland-Atlantic gateway *(London: Lane 1941), 96p.*
STEPHAN, Otto
Spies in Ireland *(London: Macdonald 1963), xiii, 15–311p, bib.*

ITALY

ADDIS ABABA, Pietro B, *'duca d'*
Italy in the Second World War, memories and documents *(London: Oxford UP 1948), x, 234p.*
ALESSANDRO, Giuletta d'
The child across the river *(New York: McDowell Obolensky 1958), 209p.*
BATESON, Henry
First into Italy *(London: Jarrolds 1944), 104p.*
BOJANO, Filippe
In the wake of the goose step *(London: Cassell 1944), 287p.*
BOKUN, Branko
Spy in the Vatican, 1941–45 *(London: Stacey 1973), [12], 259p.*
CARTER, Barbara B
Italy speaks *(London: Gollancz 1947), 195p.*
CROCE, Benedetto
Croce, the King and the Allies: extracts from a diary by Benedetto Croce, July 1943–June 1944 *(London: Allen & Unwin 1950), 158p.*
DEAKIN, Frederick W
The brutal friendship: Mussolini, Hitler and the fall of Italian Fascism *(London: Penguin 1966), rev. ed., 575p, bib.*
GAYRE, George R
Italy in transition: extracts from the private journal of G. R. Gayre *(London: Faber 1946), 254p.*

GUARESCHI, Giovanni
My secret diary, 1943–1945 *(London: Gollancz 1958), 199p.*

HAMBLOCH, Ernest
Italy militant *(London: Duckworth 1941), 293p.*

HELLER, Frank (pseud)
Twilight of the gladiators: Italy and the Italians, 1939–1943 *(New York: Putnam 1944), 146p.*

HOOD, Stuart
Pebbles from my skull *(London: Hutchinson 1963), 153p.*

INFIELD, Glenn B
Disaster at Bari *(New York: Macmillan 1971), 301p.*

K, S
Agent in Italy *(New York: Doubleday 1942), viii, 331p.*

KOGAN, Norman
Italy and the Allies *(Cambridge, Mass: Harvard UP 1956), 246p.*

LETT, Gordon
Rossano: an adventure of the Italian resistance *(London: Hodder & Stoughton* [*1955*]*), 223p.*

LOMBROSO, Silvia
No time for silence *(New York: Roy 1945), 165p.*

LUZZATTO, Riccardo
The unknown war in Italy *(London: New Europe 1946), 135p.*

MACGREGOR-HASTIE, Roy
The day of the lion: the life and death of Fascist Italy, 1922–1945 *(London: Macdonald 1963), x, 11–395p, bib.*

McMILLAN, Richard
Twenty angels over Rome: the story of Fascist Italy's fall *(London: Jarrolds 1945), 160p.*

MALAPARTE, Curzio
Kaputt *(New York: Dutton 1946), 5–407p.*

MASSOCK, Richard G
Italy from within *(London: Macmillan 1943), vii, 352p.*

ORIGO, Iris
War in Val D'Orcia: a diary *(London: Cape 1947), 253p.*

PACKARD, Reynolds *and* PACKARD, Eleanor
Balcony empire: Fascist Italy at war *(Toronto: Oxford UP 1942), 380p.*

PESCE, Giovanni
And no quarter: an Italian partisan in World War II *(Athens, Ohio: Ohio UP 1972), 292p.*

STARK, Flora
An Italian diary *(London: Murray 1945), 50p.*

TOMPKINS, Peter
Italy betrayed *(New York: Simon & Schuster 1966), 352p.*
TUTAEV, David
The consul of Florence *(London: Secker & Warburg 1966), xiv, 303p, bib.*
VILLARI, Luigi
The liberation of Italy, 1943–1947 *(London: Holborn 1959), xxiii, 265p.*
WAGG, Alfred *and* BROWN, David
No spaghetti for breakfast *(London: Nicholson & Watson 1944), 231p.*
[*see also* AXIS, MUSSOLINI, RESISTANCE]

ITALIAN AIR FORCE

BONCIANI, Carlo
F squadron *(London: Dent 1948), 211p.*

ITALIAN ARMY

MAUGHERI, Franco
From the ashes of disgrace *(New York: Harcourt 1948), viii, 376p.*
RIGONI, Stern M
The sergeant in the snow *(London: MacGibbon & Kee 1954), 158p.*

ITALIAN NAVY

BORGHESE, Junio V
Sea devils *(London: Melrose 1952), 263p.*
BRAGADIN, Marc' A
The Italian Navy in World War II *(Annapolis, Md: US Naval Institute 1957), 380p.*
COCCHIA, Aldo
Submarines attacking: adventures of Italian naval forces *(London: Kimber 1956), 204p; US title:* Hunters and the hunted.
[*see also* CAPEMATAPAN, TARANTO]

ITALIAN CAMPAIGN

ADLEMAN, Robert H
The devil's brigade *(Philadelphia, Pa: Chilton 1966), [13], 240p.*

ALEXANDER, Harold R L G, *1st earl Alexander of Tunis*
Report by the Supreme Allied Commander, Mediterranean . . . to the Combined Chiefs of Staff on the Italian Campaign, 12th December 1944 to 2nd May 1945 *(London: HMSO 1951), 66p.*

BALL, Edmund F
Staff officer with the Eighth Army: Sicily, Salerno and Anzio *(New York: Exposition 1958), 365p.*

BLUMENSON, Martin
Bloody river: prelude to the battle of Cassino *(Boston, Mass: Houghton Mifflin 1970), viii, 150p, bib.*

BOWLBY, Alex
Recollections of Rifleman Bowlby; Italy 1944 *(London: Cooper 1969), 220p.*

BUCKLEY, Christopher
The road to Rome *(London: Hodder & Stoughton 1945), 333p.*

THE CAMERONIANS in Sicily *(Hamilton, Scot: Covenanter 1944), 40p.*

CARLISLE, John M
Red arrow men: stories about the 32nd Division on the Villa Verde *(Detroit, Mich: Powers 1946), 215p.*

COX, Geoffrey
The road to Trieste *(London: Heinemann 1947), 249p.*

DAVIS, Melton S
Who defends Rome?: the forty-five days, July 25–September 8, 1943 *(London: Allen & Unwin 1972), xiv, 560p, bib.*

DELANEY, John P
The Blue devils in Italy: a history of the 88th Infantry Division in World War II *(Washington DC: Infantry Journal Press 1947), 359p.*

FINITO!: the Po Valley campaign, 1945 *(Milan: Rizzoli 1945), 62p.*

JACKSON, William G F
The battle for Italy *(London: Batsford 1967),* [3], *372p, bib.*

KEUN, Odette
The trumpets bray *(London: Constable 1943), 152p.*

LINKLATER, Eric
The campaign in Italy *(London: HMSO 1951),* [9], *480p.*

MCCALLUM, Neil
Journey with a pistol *(London: Gollancz 1959), 160p.*

MELLING, Leonard
With the Eighth in Italy *(Manchester: Torch 1955), 172p.*

MEPHAM, Clement R
With the Eighth Army in Italy *(Ilfracombe, Devon: Stockwell 1951), 117p.*

NANCE, Curtis H
The final campaign across North-West Italy, 14 April–2 May 1945 *(Milan: US Army IV Corps 1945), 119p.*

19 DAYS from the Apennines to the Alps: the story of the Po Valley campaign of the U.S. Fifth Army *(Milan 1945), 90p.*

OLSEN, Jack
Silence on Monte Sole *(London: Barker 1969), xii, 330p.*

ORGILL, Douglas
The Gothic Line: the autumn campaign in Italy, 1944 *(London: Heinemann 1967), xiii, 257p, bib.*

ROBSON, Walter
Letters from a soldier *(London: Faber 1960), 3–192p.*

SHAPIRO, Lionel S B
They left the back door open: a chronicle of the Allied campaign in Sicily and Italy *(London: Jarrolds 1945), 191p.*

SHEPPERD, Gilbert A
The Italian campaign 1943–45: a political and military re-assessment *(London: Barker 1968), xiii, 450p, bib.*

STARR, Chester G (ed)
From Salerno to the Alps: a history of the Fifth Army, 1943–1945 *(Washington DC: Infantry Journal 1948), 529p.*

STRABOLGI, Joseph M K, *10th baron*
The conquest of Italy *(London: Hutchinson 1944), 185p.*

STRAHL, Fred M
The monuments, the mountains and the towns: a pictorial record of the campaign for the Apennines *(Glendale, Calif 1946), 50p.*

STURSBERG, Peter
Journey into victory: up the Alaskan highway and to Sicily and Italy *(London: Harrap 1944), 160p.*

SWIECICKI, Marek
Seven rivers to Bologna *(London: Rolls 1946), 115p.*

THE TIGER triumphs: the story of the three great Indian Divisions in Italy *(London: HMSO 1946), 212p.*

TREGASKIS, Richard W
Invasion diary [July 9, 1943 to January 13, 1944] *(New York: Random House 1944), 245p.*

US MILITARY ACADEMY WEST POINT
Operations in Sicily and Italy, July 1943 to December 1944 *(New York: West Point 1945), 85p.*

US War Department
Fifth Army at winter line, 15 November 1943–15 January 1944 *(Washington DC: Government Printing Office 1945), 117p.*
From the Volturno to the winter line, 6 October–15 November, 1943 *(Washington DC: Government Printing Office 1945), 119p.*
Valentine, Archibald W
We landed in Sicily and Italy: a story of the Devons *(Aldershot, Hants: Gale & Polden 1944), 55p*
Wagner, Robert L
The Texas army: a history of the 36th Division in the Italian campaign *(Austin, Tex: Wagner 1972), 285p.*
Warren, Charles *and* Benson, James
The broken column: the story of James Frederick Wilde's adventures with the Italian partisans *(London: Harrap 1966), 207p.*
White, Margaret B
They called it Purple Heart Valley: a combat report of the war in Italy *(New York: Simon & Schuster 1944), viii, 182p; later published as* Purple Heart Valley.
Yunnie, Park
Warriors on wheels *(London: Hutchinson 1959), 384p.*
[*see also* ANZIO, BRITISH ARMY, EIGHTH ARMY, CASSINO, ROME, SALERNO, US ARMY]

IWO JIMA

Henri, Raymond
Iwo Jima: springboard to final victory *(New York: US Camera 1945), 95p.*
Newcomb, Richard F
Iwo Jima *(New York: Holt 1965), 338p.*
US Marine Corps
Iwo Jima: amphibious epic *(Washington DC: US Marine Corps 1954), 253p.*
[*see also* PACIFIC, US MARINE CORPS]

JAPAN

Aikawa, Takaaki
Unwilling patriot *(Toronto: Burns & McEachern 1960), 150p.*
Alcott, Carroll D
My war with Japan *(New York: Holt 1943), 368p.*
Barber, Noel
How strong is Japan? *(London: Harrap 1942), 132p.*

BERGAMINI, David
Japan's imperial conspiracy *(New York: Morrow 1971), xxxviii, 1239p.*
BRETT, Homer
Blue print for victory *(New York: Appleton 1942), v, 215p.*
BROOKS, Lester
Behind Japan's surrender: the secret struggle that ended an Empire *(New York: McGraw-Hill 1968), 428p.*
BROWNE, Courtney
Tojo: the last banzai *(London: Angus & Robertson 1967), x, 245p, bib.*
BUSH, Lewis W
Clutch of circumstance *(Tokyo: Okuyama 1956), 263p.*
The road to Inamura *(London: Hale 1961), 238p.*
BUTOW, Robert J C
Japan's decision to surrender *(Stanford, Calif: Stanford UP 1954), xi, 259p, bib.*
Tojo and the coming of the war *(Princeton, NJ: Princeton UP 1961), 584p.*
BYAS, Hugh
Government by assassination *(New York: Knopf 1942), x, 369, viiip.*
The Japanese enemy, his power and his vulnerability *(New York: Knopf 1942), ix, 107p.*
CANT, Gilbert
War on Japan *(New York: American Council, Institute of Pacific Relations 1945), 64p.*
CHEN, Jack
Japan and the Pacific theatre of war *(London: Lawrence & Wishart 1942), 76p.*
COFFEY, Thomas M
Imperial tragedy: Japan in World War II, the first days and the last *(New York: World 1970), 531p.*
COOX, Alvin
Japan: the final agony *(New York: Ballantine 1970), 160p, bib.*
CRAIG, William
The fall of Japan *(New York: Dial 1967), xv, 368p, bib.*
ELSBREE, Willard H
Japan's role in Southeast Asian nationalist movements, 1940–1945 *(London: Allen & Unwin 1953), 182p.*
GOETTE, John A
Japan fights for Asia *(New York: Harcourt 1943), 248p.*

GORDON, Gary
The rise and fall of the Japanese Empire *(Derby, Conn: Monarch 1962), 236p.*

HARMAN, Phillip
Hellions of Hirohito *(Los Angeles, Calif: De Vorss 1944), 213p.*

HAUGHLAND, Vern
The AAF against Japan *(New York: Harper 1948), xvii, 515p.*

HAVEN, Violet S
Gentlemen of Japan: a study in rapist diplomacy *(New York: Ziff-Davis 1944), 321p.*

HUNTER, Kenneth E *and* TACKLEY, Margaret E (comps)
The war against Japan *(Washington DC: Department of Army, 1952), 471p.*

IKE, Nobutaka (ed)
Japan's decision for war: records of the 1941 conferences *(Stanford, Calif: Stanford UP 1967), 306p.*

JAMES, David H
The rise and fall of the Japanese Empire *(London: Allen & Unwin 1951), 409p.*

JAPAN'S longest day *(Tokyo: Kodansha 1968), 339p.*

JONES, Francis C
Japan's new order in East Asia: its rise and fall, 1937–45 *(Toronto: Oxford UP 1954), 498p.*

KARIG, Walter *and others*
Battle report *(New York: Rinehart 1948), vol 4:* The end of an Empire *xii, 5–532p.*

KASE, Toshikazu
Eclipse of the Rising Sun *(London: Cape 1951), vi, 282p; US title:* Journey to the Missouri.

KATO, Masuo
The lost war: a Japanese reporter's inside story *(New York: Knopf 1946), 282p.*

KAWAI, Michi
Sliding doors *(Tokyo: Keisen-jo-gaku-en 1950), 201p.*

KIRBY, S W *and others*
The war against Japan *(London: HMSO 1957–69), 5 vols.*

KODAMA, Yoshio
I was defeated *(Rutland, Vt: Tuttle 1951), 223p.*

KONOYE, Fumimaro, *prince*
The memoirs of Prince Fumimaro Konoye *(Tokyo: Okuyama Service 195–), 62p.*

MAKI, John M
Japanese militarism: its cause and cure *(New York: Knopf 1945), x, 258p.*
MATSUO, Kinoaki
How Japan plans to win *(London: Harrap 1942), 240p.*
MAXON, Yale C
Control of Japanese foreign policy: a study of civil-military rivalry, 1930–1945 *(Cambridge: Cambridge UP 1957), 286p.*
MISHIMA, Sumie S
The broader way: a woman's life in new Japan *(London: Gollancz 1954), vii, 247p.*
MISSELWITZ, Henry F
Japan commits hari-kiri: a sketchbook *(San Mateo, Calif: Paulson 1945), 151p.*
MORRIS, John
A traveller from Tokyo *(London: Cresset 1943), 163p.*
NEWMAN, Barclay M
Japan's secret weapon *(New York: Current 1944), 223p.*
PACIFIC WAR RESEARCH
Japan's longest day *(London: Souvenir 1968), 279p.*
PANETH, Philip
Sunset over Japan *(London: Alliance 1943), 228p.*
RANDAU, Carl *and* ZUGSMITH, Leane
The setting sun of Japan *(New York: Random House 1942), vii, 342p.*
ROSENFARB, Joseph
Highway to Tokyo *(Boston, Mass: Little, Brown 1943), 117p.*
ROSENTHAL, Eric
Japan's bid for Africa; including the story of the Madagascar campaign *(Johannesburg: Central News 1944), 127p.*
SATO, Tasuku *and* TENNIEN, Mark
I remember flores *(New York: Farrar 1957), xxv, 129p.*
SCHOENBERGER, Walter S
Decisions of destiny *(Athens, Ohio: Ohio UP 1970), 330p.*
SHIGEMITSU, Mamoru
Japan and her destiny *(London: Hutchinson 1958), 364p.*
TERASAKI, Gwen H
Bridge of the sun *(Chapel Hill, NC: North Carolina UP 1957), 260p.*
TIMPERLEY, Harold J
Japan: a world problem *(New York: Day 1942), ix, 150p.*
TOGO, Shigenori
The cause of Japan *(New York: Simon & Schuster 1956), 372p.*

TOLAND, John
The rising sun: the decline and fall of the Japanese Empire, 1936-1945 *(New York: Random House 1970), xxxv, 954p, bib.*

TOLISCHUS, Otto D
Through Japanese eyes *(New York: Reynal & Hitchcock 1945), 182p.*

TSUJI, Masanobu
Underground escape *(Tokyo: Booth & Fukuda 1952), 298p.*

US ARMY AIR FORCE
Mission accomplished: interrogations of Japanese industrial, military and civil leaders of World War II *(Washington DC: Government Printing Office 1946), 110p.*

US WAR DEPARTMENT
Japanese recruiting and replacement system *(Washington DC: War Department 1945), 366p.*

WARD, Robert S
Asia for the Asiatics: the techniques of Japanese occupation *(Chicago, Ill: Chicago UP 1945), 204p.*

JAPANESE AIR FORCE

CAIDIN, Martin
Zero fighter *(New York: Ballantine 1969), 160p, bib.*

DAVIS, Burke
Get Yamamoto *(New York: Random House 1969),* [5], *231p.*

FRANCILLON, Rene J
Japanese aircraft of the Pacific war *(London: Putnam 1970), 570p.*

OKUMIYA, Masatake *and* HORIKOSHI, Jiro
Zero! *(New York: Dutton 1956), 424p.*

SAKAI, Saburo
Samurai *(New York: Dutton 1957), 206p.*

JAPANESE ARMY

DILLEY, Roy
Japanese army uniforms and equipment, 1939-1945 *(London: Almark 1970), 48p.*

HAYASHI, Saburo
Kogun: the Japanese Army in the Pacific war *(Quantico, Va: Marine Corps 1959), 249p.*

KELEN, Stephen
Jackals in the jungle *(Sydney: Mingay 1942), 151p.*

POTTER, John D
A soldier must hang: a biography of an oriental general *(London: Muller 1963), 210p.*

SWINSON, Arthur
Four samurai: a quartet of Japanese Army commanders in the Second World War *(London: Hutchinson 1968), 266p, bib.*
THOMPSON, Paul W *and others*
How the Jap Army fights *(Washington DC: Infantry Journal Press 1942), 142p.*
WARNER, Philip
Japanese Army of World War II *(Reading, Berks: Osprey 1973), 40p.*

JAPANESE NAVY

ALBAS, Andrieu D'
Death of a navy: the fleets of the Mikado in the Second World War, 1941-1945 *(London: Hale 1957), 224p, bib.*
BUESCHEL, Richard M
Mitsubishi Nakajima G3MI/2/3, Kusho 63YI/2 in Japanese Naval service *(Reading, Berks: Osprey 1972), [51p.]*
HARA, Tameichi *and others*
Japanese destroyer captain *(New York: Ballantine [1961]), 312p.*
HOUGH, Richard
The fleet that had to die *(London: Hamilton 1958), 208p.*
HUMBLE, Richard
Japanese high seas fleet *(London: Pan 1974), 160p.*
ITO, Masanori
The end of the Imperial Japanese Navy *(New York: Norton 1962), 240p.*
THE JAPANESE Navy in World War II: an anthology of articles by former officers of the Imperial Japanese Navy and Air Defence Force *(Annapolis, Md: US Naval Institute 1969), 147p.*
US ARMY
The Imperial Japanese Navy in World War II: a graphic presentation of the Japanese naval organization and list of combatant and non-combatant vessels lost or damaged in the war *(Tokyo: Far East Command 1952), 279p.*
WATTS, Anthony J
Japanese warships of World War II *(London: Allan 1967), 400p.*
[*see also* PACIFIC, TOKYO]

JAPANESE PRISONS

ADAMS, Geoffrey P
No time for geishas *(London: Cooper 1973), 217p.*

ARMSTRONG, Colin N
Life without ladies *(Wellington, NZ: Whitcombe & Tombs 1947), 264p.*

BANCROFT, Arthur *and* ROBERTS, R G
The Mikado's guests: a story of Japanese captivity *(Perth, WA: Patersons 1945), 171p.*

BARNARD, John T
The endless years: a personal record of the experiences of a British officer as a prisoner of war in Japanese hands from the fall of Singapore to his liberation *(London: Chantry 1950), xii, 160p.*

FITZGERALD, Earl A
Voices in the night [messages from prisoners-of-war in Japan] *(Bellingham, Wash: Fitzgerald 1948), 203p.*

FLETCHER-COOKE, *Sir* John
The Emperor's guest, 1942–45 *(London: Hutchinson 1971), xviii, 318p.*

GARCIA, Robert L *and* BEALL, E J
Americans you die *(New York: Vantage 1968), 453p.*

GUIREY, E L
Laughter in hell: being the true experiences of Lt. E. L. Guirey, USN, and Technical Sergt. H. C. Nixon, USMC, and their comrades in the Japanese prison camps in Osaka and Tsuruga *(Caldwell, Idaho: Caxton 1954), 256p.*

HARING, Douglas G
Blood on the rising sun *(New York: Macrae, Smith 1943), xii, 15–239p.*

HEASLETT, Samuel, *bishop*
From a Japanese prison *(London: SCM Press 1943), 64p.*

HILL, M
Exchange ship *(New York: Farrar 1942), 312p.*

JOHNSTON, Doris R
Bread and rice *(New York: Thurston Macauley 1947), 235p.*

KAHN, Ely J
The stragglers *(New York: Random House 1962), 176p.*

KEITH, Billy
Days of anguish, days of hope *(New York: Doubleday 1972), 214p.*

KENT-HUGHES, Wilfrid S
Slaves of the Samurai *(Melbourne, Aust: Oxford UP 1947), 296p.*

LONG, Frances
Half a world away: from boarding school to Jap prison *(New York: Farrar 1943), 243p.*

MOODY, Samuel B *and* ALLEN, Maury
Reprieve from hell *(New York: Pageant 1961), 213p.*
MOULE, William R
God's arms around us *(New York: Vantage 1960), 399p.*
MYERS, Hugh H
Prisoner of war, World War II *(Portland, Ore: Metropolitan 1965), 200p.*
NANSEN, Odd
From day to day *(New York: Putnam 1949), 485p.*
NOLAN, Liam
Small man of Nanataki: the true story of a Japanese who risked his life to provide comfort for his enemies *(London: Davies 1966), 162p.*
PARKIN, Ray
The sword and the blossom *(London: Hogarth 1968), xx, 266p.*
PRIESTWOOD, *Mrs* Gwen
Through Japanese barbed wire *(New York: Appleton 1943), 197p.*
RIVETT, Rohan D
Behind bamboo: an inside story of the Japanese prison camps *(Sydney: Angus & Robertson 1947), 335p.*
SIMONS, Jessie E
While history passed: the story of the Australian nurses who were prisoners of the Japanese for 3½ years *(London: Heinemann 1954), xviii, 131p; later published as:* In the arms of the Japanese.
STEVENS, Frederic H
Santo Tomas internment camp *(New York: Stratford 1946), 569p.*
WEEDON, Martin
The guest of an Emperor *(London: Barker 1948), 223p.*
WHITECROSS, Roy H
Slaves of the sun of heaven: the personal story of an Australian prisoner-of-war of the Japanese during the years, 1942–1945 *(Sydney: Dymock's 1951), 246p.*
WHITNEY, Hans
Guest of the fallen sun, in the prisoner-of-war camps in Japan and China *(New York: Exposition 1951), 69p.*
[*see also* MALAYSIA, SINGAPORE, SOUTH EAST ASIA, SUMATRA, THAILAND]

JAVA

CARMER, Carl L
The Jesse James of the Java Sea *(New York: Farrar 1945), 119p.*

COOPER, George
Ordeal in the sun *(London: Hale 1963), 192p.*
GANDASUBRATA, S M
An account of the Japanese occupation of Banjumas Residency, Java, March 1942 to August 1945 *(Ithaca, NY: Cornell UP 1953), 21p.*
JOHNS, William E *and* KELLY, R A
No surrender: the story of William E. Johns, D.S.M., Chief Ordnance Artificer, and how he survived after the eventual sinking of H.M.S. Exeter in the Java Sea in March 1942 *(London: Harrap 1969), 224p.*
McDOUGALL, William H
Six bells off Java: a narrative of one man's private miracle *(New York: Scribner 1948), 222p.*
PARKIN, Ray
Out of the smoke: the story of a sail *(London: Hogarth 1960), xx, 311p.*
PUSAT TENAGA RAKJAT
The Putera reports: problems in Indonesian-Japanese wartime co-operation *(Ithaca, NY: Cornell UP 1971), 114p.*
THOMAS, David A
Battle of the Java Sea *(London: Deutsch 1968), 260p, bib.*
THOMPSON, John
Hubbub in Java *(New York: Universal 1946), viii, 95p.*
VAN DER GRIFT, Cornelius *and* LANSING, E H
Escape from Java *(New York: Crowell 1943), 166p.*
VAN DER POST, Laurens
The night of the new moon *(London: Hogarth 1970), 157p; US title:* The prisoner and the bomb.
WHITING, George F
Japanese bondage *(London: Brown, Watson 1957), 160p.*

JEWS

BAR-ADON, Dorothy R
Seven who fell *(Tel-Aviv: Lion the Printer 1947), 198p.*
BARTOSZEWSKI, Wladyslaw
Righteous among nations: how Poles helped the Jews, 1939–1945 *(London: Earlscourt 1969), iii–lxxxvii, 834p.*
BARTOSZEWSKI, Wladyslaw *and* LEWINOWNA, Zofia
The samaritans: heroes of the holocaust *(New York: Twayne 1970), 442p.*
BENTWICH, Norman de M
A wanderer in war 1939–1945 *(London: Gollancz 1946), 196p.*

BERKOWITZ, Sarah B
Where are my brothers? *(New York: Helios 1965), 127p.*
BLACKBOOK of localities whose Jewish population was exterminated by the Nazis *(Jerusalem: Yad va-shem 1965), 439p.*
THE BLACK BOOK: the Nazi crime against the Jewish people *(New York: Duell 1946), 560p.*
BRAND, Joel
Advocate for the dead *(London: Deutsch 1958), 255p; US title:* Desperate mission.
CHARY, Frederick B
The Bulgarian Jews and the final solution, 1940–1944 *(Pittsburgh: Pittsburgh UP 1972), xiv, 246p, bib.*
COHEN, Israel
The Jews in the war *(London: Muller 1942), 80p.*
DAVIS, Mac
Jews fight too *(New York: Jordan 1945), 221p.*
DRIBBEN, Judith S
A girl called Judith Strick *(Chicago, Ill: Cowles 1970), 340p.*
ELKINS, Michael
Forged in fury *(New York: Ballantine 1971), 312p.*
FEINGOLD, Henry L
The politics of rescue: the Roosevelt administration and the holocaust, 1938–1945 *(New Brunswick, NJ: Rutgers UP 1970), 394p.*
FISHER, Julius S
Transnistria: the forgotten cemetery *(London: Yoseloff 1969), 161p, bib.*
FRIEDMAN, Philip
The Jewish ghettos of the Nazi era *(New York: Conference on Jewish relations 1954), 88p.*
Their brothers' keepers *(New York: Crown 1957), 224p.*
FRIEDMAN, Tuvia
The hunter *(London: Gibbs & Phillips 1961), 301p.*
HARWOOD, Richard
Did six million really die?: the truth at last *(Richmond, Surrey: Historical Review [1974]), 28p.*
HILBERG, Raul
The destruction of the European Jews *(London: W H Allen 1961), xi, 788p.*
Documents of destruction: Germany and Jewry, 1933–1945 *(Chicago, Ill: Quadrangle 1971), xii, 243p.*
HILSENRAD, Helen
Brown was the Danube *(New York: Yoseloff 1966), 492p.*

HOROWITZ, P
The Jews, the war and after *(London: Cole 1943), 144p.*

IRANEK-OSMECKI, Kazimierz
He who saves one life *(New York: Crown 1971), 336p.*

JABOTINSKY, Y
The Jewish war front *(London: Allen & Unwin 1940), 255p; US title:* The war and the Jew.

JAWORSKI, Leon
After fifteen years *(Houston, Tex: Gulf 1961), 154p.*

THE JEWS in Europe, their martyrdom and their future *(London: Board of Deputies of British Jews 1945), 64p.*

KAUFMAN, Isador
American Jews in World War II: the story of 550,000 fighters for freedom *(New York: Dial 1947), 2 vols.*

KINNAIRD, Clark
This must not happen again!: the black book of Fascist horror *(New York: Howell Soskin 1945), 157p.*

KLUGER, Ruth *and* MANN, Peggy
The last escape: the launching of the largest secret rescue movement of all time *(New York: Doubleday 1973), 518p.*

KOWALSKI, Isaac
A secret press in Nazi Europe: the story of Jewish united partisan organization *(New York: Central Guide 1969), 416p.*

KUCHLER-SILBERMAN, Lena
My hundred children *(London: Souvenir 1961), 285p; US title:* One hundred children.

KULKIELKO, Renya
Escape from the pit *(New York: Sharon 1947), xii, 189p.*

LEBOUCHER, Fernande
The incredible mission of Father Benoit *(New York: Doubleday 1969), 192p.*

LEFTWICH, Joseph
Calling all Jews to action *(London: Jewish Fund for Soviet Russia 1943), 112p; later published as:* Russian Jews in the war.

LESTSCHINSKY, Jacob
Balance sheet of extermination *(New York: Office of Jewish Information 1946), 2 vols.*

LEVIN, Nora
The holocaust: the destruction of European Jewry 1933–1945 *(New York: Crowell 1968), 768p.*

MARX, Hugo
The case of the German Jews vs. Germany: a legal basis for the claims of the German Jews against Germany *(New York: Egmont 1944), 11-124p.*

MORSE, Arthur D
While six million died *(London: Secker & Warburg 1968), x, 420p.*

NADICH, Judah
Eisenhower and the Jews *(New York: Twayne 1953), 271p.*

NAZI Germany's war against the Jews *(New York: American Jewish Conference 1947), 857p.*

POLIAKOV, Leon
Harvest of hate: the Nazi programme for the destruction of the Jews of Europe *(London: Elek 1956), 338p.*

POLIAKOV, Leon *and* SABRILLO, Jacques
Jews under the Italian occupation *(Paris: Editions du Centre 1955), 207p.*

RABINOWITZ, Louis I
Soldiers from Judaea: Palestinian Jewish units in the Middle East, 1941-1943 *(London: Gollancz 1944), 79p.*

RANDALL, *Sir* Alec
The Pope, the Jews and the Nazis *(London: Catholic Trust Society [1963]), [I], 23p, bib.*

REISS, Johanna
The upstairs room *(New York: Crowell 1972), [10], 138p.*

REITLINGER, Gerald
The final solution: the attempt to exterminate the Jews of Europe, 1939-1945 *(London: Vallentine, Mitchell 1953), 622p.*

ROBINSON, Jacob *and* FRIEDMAN, Philip
Guide to Jewish history under Nazi impact *(New York: Yivo Institute for Jewish Research 1960), 425p.*

RONTCH, Isaac
Jewish youth at war: letters from American soldiers *(New York: Marstin 1945), 304p.*

ROSEN, Donia
The forest, my friend *(New York: Bergen-Belsen Memorial 1971), 117p.*

SCHWARZ, Leo W
The root and the bough: the epic of an enduring people *(New York: Rinehart 1949), xviii, 362p.*

SMOLIAR, Hersh
Resistance in Minsk *(Berkeley, Calif: Judah L. Magues Memorial Museum 1966), 109p.*

SUHL, Yuri
They fought back: the story of the Jewish resistance in Nazi Europe *(London: MacGibbon & Kee 1968), 360p.*

SYRKIN, Marie
Blessed is the match: the story of Jewish resistance *(New York: Knopf 1947), 361p.*

SZENDE, Stefan
The promise Hitler kept *(London: Gollancz 1945), 280p.*

SZOSKIIS, Henryk J
No traveller returns *(New York: Doubleday 1945), 267p.*

TRUNK, Isaiah
Judenrat: the Jewish councils in Eastern Europe under Nazi occupation *(New York: Macmillan 1972), xxxv, 664p.*

TUSHNET, Leonard
The uses of adversity *(New York: Yoseloff [1966]), 108p, bib.*

UNSDORFER, S B
The yellow star *(New York: Yoseloff 1961), 205p.*

VIDA, George
From doom to dawn: a Jewish chaplain's story of displaced persons *(New York: David 1967), 146p.*

WACHSMAN, Z H (ed)
The Jews in post war Europe: the governments in exile and their attitude towards the Jews *(New York: Glanz 1944), 111p.*

WEISSBERG, Alexander C
Advocate for the dead: the story of Joel Brand *(London: Deutsch 1958), 255p.*

YOUTH amid the ruins: a chronicle of Jewish youth in the war *(New York: Hashomer Latzair Organization of North America 1941), 11-117p.*

ZUCKERMAN, Isaac *and* BASAK, Moshe (eds)
The fighting ghettos *(Philadelphia, Pa: Lippincott 1962), 407p.*
[*see also* CONCENTRATION CAMPS, INDIVIDUAL COUNTRIES, RESISTANCE]

KAMIKAZES

BARKER, Arthur J
Suicide weapon *(New York: Ballantine 1971), 160p, bib.*

INOGUCHI, Rikihei *and others*
Divine wind: Japan's Kamikaze force in World War II *(Annapolis, Md: US Naval Institute 1958), xxii, 240p.*

LARTEGUY, Jean (ed)
The sun goes down: last letters from Japanese suicide-pilots and soldiers *(London: Kimber 1956), 183p.*

MILLOT, Bernard
Divine thunder: the life and death of the Kamikazes *(New York: McCall 1971), vii, 243p, bib.*
NAGASUKA, Ryuji
I was a Kamikaze: the knights of the divine wind *(London: Abelard-Schuman 1973), 212p.*
[*see also* JAPANESE AIR FORCE]

KATYN WOOD

THE CRIME of Katyn: facts and documents *(London: Polish Cultural Foundation 1965), xvi, 303p.*
FITZGIBBON, Louis
Katyn *(London: Stacey 1971), 285p, bib.*
The Katyn cover-up *(London: Stacey 1972), [17], 185p.*
KOMOROWSKI, Eugenfusz A
Night never ending *(London: Abelard-Schuman 1974), 272p.*
MACKIEWICZ, Joseph
The Katyn Wood murders *(London: Hollis & Carter 1951), vii, 252p.*
WITTLIN, Tadeusz
Time stopped at 6.30 *(Indianapolis, Ind: Bobbs-Merrill 1965), 317p.*
ZAWODNY, Janusz K
Death in the forest: the story of the Katyn Forest massacre *(Notre Dame, Ind: Notre Dame UP 1962), xvii, 235p.*
[*see also* POLAND, RUSSIA]

KENNEDY

DONOVAN, Robert J
PT 109: John F. Kennedy in World War II *(New York: McGraw-Hill 1961), 247p.*
The wartime adventures of President John F. Kennedy *(London: Gibbs 1962), 160p.*
WHIPPLE, Chandler
Lt. John F. Kennedy - expendable! *(New York: Universal 1962), 160p.*

KENT

BANNER, Hubert
Kentish fire *(London: Hurst & Blackett 1944), 124p.*

BOORMAN, Henry R P
Hell's corner, 1940: Kent becomes the battlefield of Britain *(Maidstone, Kent: Kent Messenger and Maidstone Telegraph 1942), vi, 7-128p.*
Kent unconquered *(Maidstone, Kent: Kent Messenger 1951), 217p.*
[*see also* DEAL, DOVER, RAMSGATE]

LACONIA

PEILLARD, Leonce
U-boats to the rescue: the 'Laconia' incident *(London: Cape 1963), 3-270p; US title:* The Laconia affair.

LANCASTRIA

BOND, Geoffrey
'Lancastria' *(London: Oldbourne 1959), 256p.*

LANDING CRAFT

BLORE, Trevor
Commissioned barges: the story of the landing craft *(London: Hutchinson 1946), 216p.*

LANGUAGE

HUNT, John L *and* PRINGLE, A G (eds)
Service slang: a first selection *(London: Faber 1943), 72p.*
KENDALL, Park (comp)
A dictionary of service slang *(New York: Mill 1944), 64p.*
PARTRIDGE, Eric
A dictionary of Forces' slang, 1939-1945 *(London: Secker & Warburg 1948), 212p.*
A dictionary of R.A.F. slang *(London: Joseph 1945), 64p.*
TAYLOR, Anna M (comp)
The language of World War II: abbreviations, captions, quotations, slogans, titles and other terms and phrases *(New York: Wilson 1944), 94p.*
WARD-JACKSON, C H
It's a piece of cake, or, R.A.F. slang made easy *(London: Simpkin Marshall 1943), 64p.*

LATVIA

BILMANIS, Alfreds
Baltic States and world peace and security organization, facts in review *(Washington DC: Latvian Legation 1945), 67p.*
Between the anvil and the hammer *(Washington DC: Latvian Legation 1945), 64p.*
FELD, Mischa J (pseud)
The hug of the bear *(New York: Holt 1961), 305p.*
LATVIA in 1939–1942: background, Bolshevik and Nazi occupation, hopes for the future *(Washington DC: Latvian Legation 1942), 137p.*
MERCER, Asja
One woman's war *(London: Wingate 1958), 220p.*
THESE names accuse: nominal list of Latvians deported to Soviet Russia in 1940–41 *(Stockholm: Latvian National Fund in Scandinavian Countries 1951), 547p.*
[*see also* BALTIC]

LAW

DOMKE, Martin
Trading with the enemy in World War II *(New York: Central Book 1943), xv, 640p.*
HOWARD, Francis C
Trading with the enemy *(London: Butterworth 1943), xix, 119p.*
SCHWARZENBERGER, Georg
International law and totalitarian lawlessness *(London: Cape 1943), 168p.*
[*see also* INTERNATIONAL LAW]

LEAGUE OF NATIONS

LEAGUE OF NATIONS
Report on the work of the League during the war *(Geneva: League of Nations 1945), 167p.*

LEND-LEASE

JONES, Robert H
The roads to Russia: U.S. lend-lease to the Soviet Union *(Norman, Okl: Oklahoma UP 1969), 326p.*
KIMBALL, Warren F
The most unsordid act: lend-lease, 1939–1941 *(Baltimore, Md: Johns Hopkins 1969), 281p.*

LENINGRAD

FADEEV, Aleksander A
Leningrad in the days of the blockade *(Westport, Conn: Greenwood 1971), 104p.*

GOURE, Leon
The siege of Leningrad *(Stanford, Calif: Stanford UP 1962), xiv, 363p, bib.*
Soviet administrative controls during the siege of Leningrad *(Santa Monica, Calif: Rand 1957), 73p.*

INBER, Vera
Leningrad diary *(London: Hutchinson 1971), 207p.*

NIKITIN, M N *and* VAGIN, P L
The crimes of the German Fascists in the Leningrad region: materials and documents *(London: Hutchinson 1946), 128p.*

PAVLOV, Dmitri V
Leningrad 1941: the blockade *(Chicago, Ill: Chicago UP 1965), xxiv, 186p.*

SALISBURY, Harrison E
The 900 days *(New York: Harper 1969), xv, 635p, bib; UK title:* The siege of Leningrad.

SKOMOROVSKY, Boris A
The siege of Leningrad: the saga of the greatest siege of all time *(New York: Dutton 1944), 9–196p.*

TIKHONOV, Nikolai S *and others*
The defence of Leningrad: eye-witness accounts of the siege *(London: Hutchinson 1943), 136p.*

WYKES, Alan
The siege of Leningrad: epic of survival *(New York: Ballantine 1970), 160p, bib.*
[*see also* EASTERN EUROPE, RUSSIA]

LEYTE

CANNON, M H
Leyte: the return to the Philippines *(Washington DC: Department of Army 1954), 420p.*

FALK, Stanley L
Decision at Leyte *(New York: Norton 1966), 330p.*

FIELD, James A
The Japanese at Leyte Gulf: the Sho-operation *(Princeton, NJ: Princeton UP 1947), 162p.*

MACINTYRE, Donald
Leyte Gulf: armada in the Pacific *(New York: Ballantine 1969), 160p, bib.*

ST JOHN, Joseph F
Leyte calling *(New York: Vanguard 1945), 220p.*
SMITH, Stanley F
The battle of Leyte Gulf *(New York: Belmont 1961), 174p.*
WOODWARD, Comer V
The battle of Leyte Gulf *(New York: Macmillan 1947), 192p.*
[*see also* PACIFIC, PHILIPPINES, US NAVY]

LIBRARIES

BALLOU, Robert O
A history of the Council of Books in wartime, 1942–1946 *(New York: Council of Books in wartime 1946), 126p.*
BUTLER, Pierce (ed)
Books and libraries in wartime *(Chicago, Ill: Chicago UP 1945), 159p.*
JAMIESON, John
Books for the Army: the Army library service in the Second World War *(New York: Columbia UP 1950), xv, 335p, bib.*

LIDICE

HUTAK, Jakub B
With blood and with iron: the Lidice story *(London: Hale 1957), 160p.*
TRINKA, Z'dena
A little village called Lidice: the story of the return of the women and children of Lidice . . . *(Ludgerwood, ND: International 1947), 128p.*
[*see also* CZECHOSLOVAKIA, HEYDRICH]

LITHUANIA

HARRISON, Ernest J
Lithuania's fight for freedom *(New York: Lithuanian American Information Center 1952), 95p.*
IN the name of the Lithuanian people *(Wolfberg, Aust: Perkunas 1945), 71p.*
NOREM, Owen J
Timeless Lithuania *(Cleveland, Ohio: League for the Liberation of Lithuania 1943), 299p.*
PAKSTAS, Kazys
The Lithuanian situation *(New York: Lithuanian Cultural Institute 1941), 5-61p.*
[*see also* BALTIC]

LIVERPOOL

PORT at war: being the story of the Port of Liverpool, its ordeals and achievements during the World War, 1939–1945 *(Liverpool: Mersey Docks & Harbour Board 1946), 64p.*

LOGISTICS

BALLANTINE, Duncan S
U.S. Naval logistics in the Second World War *(Princeton, NJ: Princeton UP 1947), 308p.*

CARTER, Worrall R
Beans, bullets, and black oil: the story of fleet logistics afloat in Pacific during World War II *(Washington DC: Department of the Navy 1953), 482p.*

CARTER, Worrall R *and* DUVALL, Elmer E
Ships, salvage, and sinews of war: the story of fleet logistics afloat in Atlantic and Mediterranean waters during World War II *(Washington DC: Department of the Navy 1954), 533p.*

RICHARDSON, Endora R *and* ALLAN, Sherman
Quartermaster supply in the European theater of operations in World War II *(Camp Lee, Va: Quartermaster School 1948), 10 vols.*

RUPPENTHAL, Roland G
Logistical support of the Armies *(Washington DC: Department of Army 1953–8), 2 vols.*

STORAGE and distribution of Quartermaster supplies in the European theater of operations in World War II *(Fort Lee, Va: Quartermaster School 1962), 291p.*

US ARMY
Logistical history of NATOUSA, MTOUSA *(London: Naples 1945), 486p.*

WEEKS, *Sir* Ronald M
Organization and equipment for war *(Cambridge: Cambridge UP 1950), 132p.*

LONDON

BAKER, Richard B
The year of the buzz bomb: a journal of London, 1944 *(New York: Exposition 1952), 118p.*

BATO, Joseph
Defiant city *(London: Gollancz 1942), 108p.*

BEATON, Cecil
History under fire: 52 photographs of air raid damage to London buildings, 1940–41 *(London: Batsford 1941), viii, 117p.*

BOLITHO, Hector
War in the Strand: a notebook of the first two and a half years in London *(London: Eyre & Spottiswoode 1942), v, 9–185p.*

BROMLEY, Gordon
London goes to war, 1939 *(London: Joseph 1974), 128p.*

BRYHER
The days of Mars: a memoir, 1940–1946 *(London: Calder & Boyars 1972), iii–xii, 190p.*

BUTLER, Arthur S G
Recording ruin *(London: Constable 1942), 148p.*

CALDER, Peter R
Carry on London *(London: English UP 1941), xv, 17–163p.*
The lesson of London *(London: Secker & Warburg 1941), 127p.*

COLLIER, Richard
The city that wouldn't die: London, May 10–11, 1941 *(London: Collins 1959), 256p.*

EVENING NEWS (newspaper)
Hitler passed this way: 170 pictures *(London: Alabaster, Passmore 1945).*

FARSON, Negley
Bomber's moon *(London: Gollancz 1941), 7–160p.*

FAVIELL, Frances
A Chelsea concerto *(London: Cassell 1959), ix, 259p.*

FITZGIBBON, Constantine
The blitz *(London: Wingate 1957), xv, 272p; US title:* The winter of bombs.
London's burning *(New York: Ballantine 1970), 160p, bib.*

FORBES-ROBERTSON, Diana
The battle of Waterloo Road *(New York: Random House 1941), 124p.*

GARVIN, Viola G
London's glory: 20 paintings of the city's ruins by Wanda Ostrowska *(London: Allen & Unwin 1945), 51p.*

GRAVES, Charles
A Londoner's life *(London: Hutchinson 1942), 172p.*

HENREY, *Mrs* Robert
The incredible city *(London: Dent 1944), 195p.*
London under fire, 1940–45 *(London: Dent 1969), 255p.*
The siege of London *(London: Dent 1946), 200p.*
A village in Piccadilly *(London: Dent 1942), 163p.*

HOWGRAVE-GRAHAM, Hamilton M
The Metropolitan Police at war *(London: HMSO 1947), 89p.*

IDLE, Emily D
War over West Ham: a study of community adjustment *(London: Faber 1943), 136p.*

JESSE, F Tennyson *and* HARWOOD, H M
London front: letters written to America, 1939–1940 *(London: Constable 1940), viii, 469p.*
While London burns: letters written to America (July 1940–June 1941) *(London: Constable 1942), 384p.*

JONES, Sydney R
London triumphant *(London: Studio 1942), 5–278p.*

KENT, William
The lost treasures of London *(London: Phoenix House 1947), 150p.*

LEWEY, Frank R
Cockney campaign *(London: Paul 1944), 144p.*

LONDON Fire Brigade
Fire fighters of London in action *(New York: Garden City 1942), 58p.*

LONDON'S hour: an illustrated pictorial taken from the original drawings of firemen artists during the blitz *(London: Staples 1942), 52p.*

MATTHEWS, Walter R
Saint Paul's Cathedral in wartime, 1939–1945 *(London: Hutchinson 1946), 104p.*

MENGIN, Robert
No laurels for de Gaulle *(New York: Farrar 1966), 360p.*

MIDDLE TEMPLE ordeal: an account of what World War II meant to the Inn *(London: Butterworth 1948), 55p.*

MORDAUNT, Evelyn M
Here too is valour *(London: Muller 1941), 128p.*
This was our life *(London: Hutchinson 1942), 174p.*

MOSLEY, Leonard
Backs to the wall: London under fire, 1939–45 *(London: Weidenfeld & Nicolson 1971), xiv, 397p.*

MURROW, Edward R
This is London *(London: Cassell 1941), 278p.*

PANTER-DOWNES, Mollie
London war notes, 1939–1945 *(New York: Farrar 1971), 378p.*

PERRY, Colin
Boy in the blitz *(London: Cooper 1972), [8], 220p.*

PLASTOW, Norman
Safe as houses: Wimbledon 1939-1945 *(London: John Evelyn 1972), [4], 92p.*

RESPECTFULLY yours, Annie: letters from a London cook *(New York: Dutton 1942), 11-230p.*

REYNOLDS, Quentin J
London diary *(New York: Random House 1941), 304p.*

RICHARDSON, Maurice L
London's burning *(London: Hale 1941), vii, 9-184p.*

ROBBINS, Gordon
Fleet Street blitzkrieg diary *(London: Benn 1944), 64p.*

SANSOM, William
Westminster in war *(London: Faber 1947), 209p.*

SAVA, George (pseud)
They stayed in London *(London: Faber 1941), xv, 231p.*

STEDMAN, Henry W
The battle of the flames *(London: Jarrolds 1942), 80p.*

TINTON, Ben T
War comes to the docks *(London: Marshall, Morgan & Scott 1942), ix, 11-124p.*

WHITNELL, Lewis
Engines over London *(London: Carroll & Nicolson 1949), 164p.*

WILSON, Herbert A
East window *(London: Mowbray 1946), 146p.*

WOON, Basil
Hell came to London: a reportage of the blitz during 14 days *(London: Davies 1941), ix, 211p.*

[*see also* FLYING BOMBS, ROCKETS]

LONG-RANGE DESERT GROUP

CRICHTON-STUART, Michael
G patrol *(London: Kimber 1958), 206p.*

OWEN, David L
The desert my dwelling place *(London: Cassell 1957), 271p.*

SHAW, William B K
Long Range Desert Group: the story of its work in Libya, 1940-1943 *(London: Collins 1945), 192p.*

SWINSON, Arthur
The raiders: desert strike force *(New York: Ballantine 1968), 160p.*

[*see also* NORTH AFRICA]

LORD HAW-HAW

COLE, John A
Lord Haw-Haw and William Joyce: the full story *(London: Faber 1964), 3-316p.*
HALL, J W (ed)
The trial of William Joyce (Lord Haw-Haw) *(London: Hodge 1946), 312p.*
ROBERTS, C E B (ed)
Trial of William Joyce *(London: Jarrolds 1946), 191p.*

LOWESTOFT

JENKINS, Ford
Port war: Lowestoft, 1939–1945 *(London: Cowell 1946), 80p.*

LUXEMBURG

LUXEMBURG and the German invasion before and after *(London: Hutchinson 1942), 64p.*

MACARTHUR

HUNT, Frazier
MacArthur and the war against Japan *(New York: Scribner 1944), viii, 182p.*
LONG, Gavin
MacArthur as military commander *(London: Batsford 1969), xi, 243p, bib.*
MACARTHUR, Douglas
Reminiscences *(New York: McGraw-Hill 1964), viii, 438p.*
A soldier speaks: public papers *(New York: Praeger 1965), 367p.*
MAYER, Sydney L
MacArthur *(New York: Ballantine 1971),* [2], *160p, bib.*
MILLER, Francis T
General Douglas MacArthur *(Philadelphia, Pa: Winston 1945), 295p.*
WHITNEY, Courtney
MacArthur: his rendezvous with history *(New York: Knopf 1956), 547p.*
WILLOUGBY, Charles A *and* CHAMBERLAIN, John
MacArthur: 1941–1951; victory in the Pacific *(New York: McGraw-Hill 1954), 441p.*
WITTNER, Lawrence S
MacArthur *(Eaglewood Cliffs: Prentice-Hall 1971), vi, 186p, bib.*

MADAGASCAR

CROFT-COOKE, Rupert
The blood-red island *(London: Staples 1953), 248p.*

MAKIN ISLAND

JENKINS, Burrin A
Father Meany and the fighting 69th *(New York: Fell 1944), 11-61p.*
[*see also* PACIFIC, US MARINES]

MALAYSIA

ASSOCIATION OF BRITISH MALAYA
Civil defence of Malaya: a narrative of the part taken in it by civilian population of the country in the Japanese invasion *(London: Hutchinson 1944), 128p.*

BRYAN, John N L
The churches of the captivity in Malaya *(London: SPCK 1946), 72p.*

CHAPHEKAR, Shankarrao G
A brief study of the Malayan campaign, 1941–42 *(Poona: Maharashtra Militarisation Board 1960), 2nd rev. ed., 8, 121p.*

CHAPMAN, Frederick S
The jungle is neutral *(London: Chatto & Windus 1949), 351p.*

CHIN KEE ONN
Malaya upside down *(Singapore: Jitts 1946), 208p.*

COOMBES, J H H
Banpong express: being an account of the Malayan campaign, with some subsequent experiences as a guest of the Imperial Japanese Army *(London: Darlington, Coombes 1948), 153p.*

CRAWFORD, Hew T M
The long green tunnel *(London: Joseph 1967), 205p.*

CROSS, John
Red jungle *(London: Hale [1958]), 244p.*

DUFFY, James
An Australian in Malaya, and other tales of the Malayan campaign *(Sydney: Johnston 1943), 89p.*

EYRE, Donald C
The soul and the sea *(London: Hale 1959), 192p; later published as:* Ordeal by endurance.

GLOVER, Edwin M
In 70 days: the story of the Japanese campaign in British Malaya *(London: Muller 1946), 244p.*

GURCHAN SINGH
Singa: the lion of Malaya *(London: Quality 1949), 255p.*

HAMILTON, Thomas
Soldier surgeon in Malaya *(Sydney: Angus & Robertson 1958),* [6], *218p.*

HILL, Anthony
Diversion in Malaya: an incidental account of five years' residence in the Federated Malay States, 1937-1942 *(London: Collins 1948), 186p.*

HOLMAN, Dennis
The green torture: the ordeal of Robert Chrystal *(London: Hale 1962), 190p.*
Noone of the Ulu *(London: Heinemann 1958), 253p.*

KATHIGASU, Sybil
No dream of mercy *(London: Spearman 1954), 237p.*

LAMBERT, Eric
MacDougal's farm *(London: Muller 1965), 155p.*

MANT, Gilbert
Grim glory *(Sydney: Currawong 1955), 95p.*

MORRISON, Ian
Malayan postscript *(London: Faber 1942), 196p.*

PERCIVAL, Arthur E
The war in Malaya *(London: Eyre & Spottiswoode 1949), 336p.*

REID, Caroline
Malayan climax: experiences of an Australian girl in Malaya, 1940-1942 *(Hobart, Tas: Oldham 1942), 116p.*

ROWAN-ROBINSON, Henry
Jungle warfare *(London: Hutchinson 1944), 64p.*

SIM, Katharine
Malayan landscape *(London: Joseph 1946), 248p.*

STEWART, Athole
Let's get cracking *(Sydney: Johnston 1943), 151p.*

STEWART, I M
History of the Argyll & Sutherland Highlanders: 2nd Battalion (the Thin Red Line) Malayan campaign, 1941-42 *(London: Nelson 1947), xvii, 171p.*

THATCHER, Dorothy *and* CROSS, Robert
Pai Naa: the story of Nona Baker *(London: Constable 1959),* [7], *184p.*

THOMPSON, Virginia M
Postmortem on Malaya *(New York: Macmillan 1943), xix, 323p.*

TOMLINSON, Henry M
Malay waters: the story of little ships coasting out of Singapore and Penang in peace and war *(London: Hodder & Stoughton 1950), 199p.*
[*see also* SINGAPORE]

MALTA

BARNHAM, Denis
One man's window: an illustrated account of ten weeks at war, Malta, April 13th to June 21st 1942 *(London: Kimber 1956), 201p.*

BEURLING, George F *and* ROBERTS, Leslie
Malta Spitfire: the story of a fighter pilot *(Toronto: Oxford UP 1943), 235p.*

BRENNAN, Paul *and others*
Spitfires over Malta *(London: Jarrolds 1943), 96p.*

COFFIN, Howard M
Malta story *(New York: Dutton 1943), 15-222p.*

DOBBIE, Sybil
Grace under Malta *(London: Drummond 1944), 158p.*

THE EPIC of Malta *(London: Odhams 1943), 128p.*

GERARD, Francis
Malta magnificent *(London: Cassell 1943), 142p.*

GILCHRIST, R T
Malta strikes back: the story of 231 Infantry Brigade *(Aldershot, Hants: Gale & Polden 1946), 136p.*

GREAT BRITAIN. Ministry of Information
The air battle of Malta *(London: HMSO n.d.), 96p.*

GUNBUSTER (pseud)
Grand barrage *(London: Hodder & Stoughton 1944), 185p.*

HAY, Ian (pseud)
Unconquered isle: the story of Malta, G.C. *(London: Hodder & Stoughton 1943), 208p; US title:* Malta epic.

LLOYD, *Sir* Hugh P
Briefed to attack: Malta's part in African victory *(London: Hodder & Stoughton 1949), 230p.*

MARKS, Tamara
A woman in Malta *(Cairo: Schindler 1943), 107p.*

NORMAN, Kathleen
For gallantry: Malta's story *(Ilfracombe, Devon: Stockwell 1956), 208p.*

OLIVER, R L
Malta at bay: an eye-witness account *(London: Hutchinson 1942), 108p.*

PEROWNE, Stewart
The siege within the walls: Malta, 1940–1943 *(London: Hodder & Stoughton 1970), 192p, bib.*

POOLMAN, Kenneth
Faith, Hope and Charity: three planes against an Air Force *(London: Kimber 1954), 200p.*

TATTERED battlements: a Malta diary *(London: Davies 1943), 134p.*

MANPOWER

CORSON, John J
Manpower for victory: total mobilization for total war *(New York: Farrar 1943), xii, 299p.*

PARKER, Henry M D
Manpower: a study of war-time policy and administration *(London: HMSO 1957), 535p.*

MARIANAS

CROWL, Philip A
Campaign in the Marianas *(Washington DC: Department of Army 1960), 505p.*
Seizure of the Gilberts and Marshalls *(Washington DC: Department of Army 1955), 414p.*

MARSHALL, Samuel L A
Island victory *(Washington DC: Infantry Journal Press 1944), viii, 213p.*

MARUYAMA, Michiro
Anatahan *(Weidenfeld & Nicolson 1954), 191p.*

US MARINE CORPS
The Marshalls, increasing the tempo *(Washington DC: USMC 1954), 188p.*
[*see also* PACIFIC, US MARINES]

MEDICAL

AHNFELDT, Arnold L
Radiology in World War II *(Washington DC: Department of Army 1966), 1087p.*

ALLEN, Ted
The scalpel, the sword: the story of Dr. Norman Bethune *(Boston, Mass: Little, Brown 1952), 336p.*

ANDRUS, Edwin C *and others* (eds)
Advances in military medicine *(Boston, Mass: Little, Brown 1948), 2 vols.*

BEEBE, Gilbert W *and* DEBAKEY, Michael E
Battle casualties: incidence, mortality, and logistic considerations *(Springfield, Ill: Thomas 1952), 277p.*

BEECHER, Henry K
Resuscitation and anesthesia for wounded men *(Springfield, Ill: Thomas 1949), 161p.*

BLASSINGAME, Wyatt
Medical Corps heroes of World War II *(New York: Random House 1969), 177p.*

BONAPARTE, Marie
Myths of war *(London: Imago 1947), 161p.*

BORDEN, Mary
Journey down a blind alley *(London: Hutchinson 1946), 296p.*

BRASHEAR, Alton D
From Lee to Bari: the history of the Forty-Fifth General Hospital, 1940–1945 *(Richmond, Va: Whittet & Shipperson 1957), 468p.*

BUNNELL, Sterling
Hand surgery *(Washington DC: Department of Army 1955), 447p.*

COATES, John B (ed)
Internal medicine in World War II *(Washington DC: Department of Army 1961), 2 vols.*
Preventive medicine in World War II *(Washington DC: Department of Army 1955), vols 2, 4, 5, 7, pub.*
Thoracic surgery *(Washington DC: Department of Army 1963), 1 vol. pub.*
Wound ballistics *(Washington DC: Department of Army 1962), 883p.*

COATES, John B *and* CLEVELAND, Mather (eds)
Orthopedic surgery in the European Theater of operations *(Washington DC: Department of Army 1956), 397p.*

COATES, John B *and* WILTSE, Charles M (eds)
Organization and administration in World War II *(Washington DC: Department of Army 1963), 613p.*

COATES, John B *and others* (eds)
Activities of surgical consultants *(Washington DC: Department of Army 1962), 2 vols.*
Environmental hygiene *(Washington DC: Department of Army 1955), 404p.*
General surgery *(Washington DC: Department of Army 1955), 417p.*
Ophthalmology and otolaryngology *(Washington DC: Department of Army 1957), 605p.*

COLE, Howard N
On wings of healing: the story of Airborne medical services, 1940–1960 *(Edinburgh: Blackwood 1963), xviii, 227p, bib.*

COPE, *Sir* Zachary
Medicine and pathology *(London: HMSO 1952), 565p.*
Surgery *(London: HMSO 1953), 772p.*

COULTER, Jack L S (ed)
The Royal Naval Medical Service *(London: HMSO 1954–6), 2 vols.*

CREW, Francis A E
The Army Medical Services *(London: HMSO 1953–5), 2 vols.*
The Army Medical Services: campaigns *(London: HMSO 1956–1966), 5 vols.*

CUSHING, Emory C
The history of entomology in World War II *(Washington DC: Smithsonian Institute 1957), 117p.*

DUNN, Cuthbert L
The emergency medical services *(London: HMSO 1952–3) 2 vols.*

ELKIN, Daniel C *and* DEBAKEY, Michael E (eds)
Vascular surgery *(Washington DC: Department of Army 1955), 465p.*

FERGUSON, Ion
Doctor at war *(London: Johnson 1955), 223p.*

FISHBEIN, Morris (ed)
Doctors at war *(New York: Dutton 1945), 418p.*

GREAT BRITAIN. War Office
Statistical report on the health of the Army, 1939–1945 *(London: HMSO 1948), 204p.*

GREEN, Francis H R *and* COVELL, *Sir* Gordon (eds)
Medical research *(London: HMSO 1953), 387p.*

GRIFFIN, Alexander R
Out of carnage *(New York: Howell, Soskin 1945), 327p.*

HAMPTON, Oscar
Orthopedic surgery in the Mediterranean Theater of operations *(Washington DC: Department of Army 1957), 368p.*

HILL, Justina H
Silent enemies: the story of the diseases of war and their control *(New York: Putnam 1942), xii, 266p.*

HILLSMAN, John B
Eleven men and a scalpel *(Winnipeg, Manitoba 1949), 144p.*

HURST, *Sir* Arthur F *and others*
Medical diseases of war *(London: Arnold 1944), 4th ed., 507p.*

JEFFCOTT, George F
United States Army Dental Service in World War II *(Washington DC: Department of Army 1955), 362p.*

JUNOD, Marcel
A warrior without weapons *(New York: Macmillan 1951), xvi, 283p.*

KENDRICK, Douglas B
Blood program in World War II *(Washington DC: Department of Army 1964), 922p.*

LINK, Mae M *and* COLEMAN, Hubert A
Medical support of the Army Air Forces in World War II *(Washington DC: US Air Force 1955), 1027p.*

McMINN, John H *and* LEVIN, Max
Personnel in World War II *(Washington DC: Department of Army 1963), 548p.*

MACNALTY, *Sir* Arthur S
The civilian health and medical services *(London: HMSO 1953–5), 2 vols.*
Medical services in the war: the principal medical lessons of the Second World War: based on the official histories of the U.K., Canada, Australia, New Zealand and India *(London: HMSO 1968), xviii, 781p.*

MACNALTY, *Sir* Arthur S *and* MELLOR, W F
Health recovery in Europe *(London: Muller 1946), 180p.*

MAISEL, Albert Q
The wounded get back *(New York: Harcourt 1944), viii, 230p.*

MEDICAL science abused: German medical science as practised in concentration camps and in so-called Protectorate, reported by Czech doctors *(Prague: Orbis 1946), 81p.*

MELLOR, William F
Casualties and medical statistics *(London: HMSO 1972), xiv, 893p.*

MILBOURNE, Andrew R
Lease of life *(London: Museum 1952), 189p.*

MILLER, Everett B
U.S. Army Veterinary Service in World War II *(Washington DC: Department of Army 1961), 779p.*

PARSONS, Robert P
Mob three: a naval hospital in a South Sea jungle *(Indianapolis, Ind: Bobbs-Merrill 1945), 248p.*

PAUL, Daniel (pseud)
Surgeon at arms *(London: Heinemann 1956), 227p.*

THE PHYSIOLOGIC effects of wounds *(Washington DC: Department of Army 1952), 376p.*

R, J R
Memoirs of an army surgeon *(Edinburgh: Blackwood 1948), x, 354p.*

REXFORD-WELCH, Samuel C (ed)
The Royal Air Force medical services *(London: HMSO 1955–8), 3 vols.*

SAUNDERS, Hilary A St G
The Red Cross and the White: a short history of the front line organization of the British Red Cross Society and the Order of St. John of Jerusalem during the war, 1939–1945 *(London: Hollis & Carter 1949), 195p.*

SCRIVEN, Gordon J
Regimental stretcher bearers in action: being a true record of a British soldier's life in the battlefields of North-West Europe during World War II *(Weymouth, Dorset: Scriven 1951),* [2], *29p.*

SHARON, Henrietta
It's good to be alive *(New York: Dodd, Mead 1945), 150p.*

SIMPSON, William
I burned my fingers *(London: Putnam 1955), 283p.*

SLADEN, Frank J (ed)
Psychiatry and the war *(Springfield, Ill: Thomas 1943), xxii, 505p.*

SMITH, Clarence McK
The medical department; hospitalization and evacuation, zone of interior *(Washington DC: Department of Army 1956), 503p.*

SMITH, Dean A *and* WOODRUFF, Michael F A
Deficiency diseases in Japanese prison camps *(London: HMSO 1951), 209p.*

SOUTH, Oron P
Medical support in a combat air force: a study of medical leadership in World War II *(Maxwell Air Force Base, Ala: Air University 1956), 126p.*

SPURLING, R G *and* WOODHALL, Barnes (eds)
Neurosurgery *(Washington DC: Department of Army 1958–9), 2 vols.*

STEVENSON, Eleanor *and* MARTIN, Pete
I knew your soldier *(Washington DC: Infantry Journal Press 1945), 237p.*

TALIAFERRO, William H (ed)
Medicine and the war *(Chicago, Ill: Chicago UP 1944), vii, 193p.*

TIDY, Henry L (ed)
Inter-Allied conferences on war medicine, 1942–43, convened by the Royal Society of Medicine *(New York: Staples 1947), 531p.*

TREW, Cecil G
What are you doing here?: being the adventures of a surgical artist with the B.L.A. *(Edinburgh: International 1947), 128p.*

TSUCHIDA, William S
Wear it proudly: letters *(Berkeley, Calif: California UP 1947), 147p.*

TURVILLE, William H H
The story of the U.S. naval mobile hospital number 8 *(New York: Kelly 1945), 161p.*

US BUREAU OF MEDICINE AND SURGERY
The history of the medical department of the U.S. Navy in World War II *(Washington DC: US Government Printing Office 1950), 5 vols.*
US Naval medical department administrative history, 1941–1945 *(Washington DC: US Government Printing Office 1946), 2 vols in 8.*

WALKER, Arthur E *and* JACKSON, Seymour
A follow-up study of head wounds in World War II *(Washington DC: Government Printing Office 1961), 202p.*

WALLIS, Ralph R
Two red stripes: a naval surgeon at war *(London: Allan 1973), 144p.*

WATTS, John C
Surgeon at war *(London: Allen & Unwin 1955), 166p.*

WEINSTEIN, Alfred A
Barbed-wire surgeon *(New York: Macmillan 1948), x, 310p.*

WHAYNE, Tom F *and* DEBAKEY, Michael E
Cold, injury, ground type *(Washington DC: Department of Army 1958), 579p.*

WHEELER, Keith
We are the wounded *(New York: Dutton 1945), 224p.*

WOLFE, Don M (ed)
The purple testament: life stories of disabled veterans *(Harrisburg, Pa: Stackpole 1946), 361p.*

[*see also* HOSPITALS, NURSES]

MEDITERRANEAN

BRITAIN'S conquest of the Mediterranean: the first complete authoritative account of five years' fight for mastery in the critical Mediterranean theatre *(London: Burke 1944), 5-82p.*

CLARK, Mark
Calculated risk: his personal story of the war in North Africa and Italy *(New York: Harper 1950), 500p.*

CLUNE, Frank
Tobruk to Turkey: with the Army of the Nile in World War II *(Melbourne, Aust: Georgian House 1949), 308p.*

GREAT BRITAIN. Admiralty
The Mediterranean Fleet, Greece to Tripoli: the Admiralty account of operations April 1941-January 1943 *(London: HMSO [1944]), unp.*

GUNTHER, John
D Day *(London: Hamilton 1944), 200p.*

HATLEM, John C *and others* (comps)
The war against Germany and Italy: Mediterranean and adjacent areas *(Washington DC: Department of Army 1951), 465p.*

HUNT, *Sir* David
A don at war *(London: Kimber 1966), 288p.*

JACOB, Naomi E
Me and the Mediterranean *(London: Hutchinson 1945), 156p.*

LASSEN, Suzanne
Anders Lassen, V.C. *(London: Muller 1965), ix, 244p.*

PLAYFAIR, Ian S O
The Mediterranean and Middle East *(London: HMSO 1954-73), 5 vols.*

REID, Anthony
Laughter in the sun: a Mediterranean adventure *(London: Bles 1952), 223p.*

ROWAN-ROBINSON, Henry
From Tunisia to Normandy *(London: Hutchinson 1945), 176p.*

SANDFORD, Kenneth
Mark of the lion: the story of Capt. Charles Upham, V.C. and bar *(London: Hutchinson 1962), 287p.*

SHORES, Christopher F
A pictorial history of the Mediterranean air war *(London: Allan 1972–74), 3 vols.*

SMITH, Peter C
The battles of the Malta striking forces *(London: Allan 1974), 120p.*

STRABOLGI, Joseph M K, *10th baron*
From Gibraltar to Suez: the battle of the Middle Sea *(London: Hutchinson 1941), ix, 263p.*

THRUELSEN, Richard *and* ARNOLD, Elliott
Mediterranean sweep: air stories from El Alamein to Rome *(New York: Duell 1944), x, 278p.*

[*see also* MALTA, MIDDLE EAST, NORTH AFRICA, ROYAL AIR FORCE, ROYAL NAVY]

MEMOIRS

ACHESON, Dean
Present at the creation: my years in the State Department *(New York: Norton 1969), 798p.*

ADAMIC, Louis
Dinner at the White House *(New York: Harper 1946), 276p.*

ARNOLD, Henry H
Global mission *(London: Hutchinson 1951), 276p.*

ATTLEE, Clement R, *1st earl Attlee*
A Prime Minister remembers: the war and post-war memoirs of . . . *(London: Heinemann 1961), 269p; US title:* Twilight of Empire.
As it happened *(London: Heinemann 1954), 256p.*

(AUCHINLECK, *Sir* Claude) CONNELL, John
Auchinleck: a biography of Field Marshal Sir Claude Auchinleck *(London: Cassell 1959), xxiii, 975p.*

BAUDOUIN, Paul
The private diaries (March 1940 to January 1941) *(London: Eyre & Spottiswoode 1948), 308p.*

BEATON, Cecil
Far East *(London: Batsford 1945), 110p.*
The years between, diaries 1939–44 *(London: Weidenfeld & Nicolson 1965), 352p.*

BENES, Eduard
Memoirs of Dr. Eduard Benes, from Munich to new war and new victory *(London: Allen & Unwin 1954), xiii, 346p.*

BERENSON, Bernard
Rumour and reflection, 1941–1944 *(London: Constable 1952), 400p.*

BILAINKIN: George
Second diary of a diplomatic correspondent *(London: Sampson Low 1947), 423p.*

(BLAMEY, *Sir* Thomas) HETHERINGTON, John A
Blamey: the biography of Field Marshal Sir Thomas Blamey *(London: Angus & Robertson 1955), 277p.*

BRADLEY, Omar N
A soldier's story of the Allied campaigns from Tunis to the Elbe *(London: Eyre & Spottiswoode 1952), xix, 618p.*

BRERETON, Lewis H
The Brereton diaries: the war in the air in the Pacific, Middle East and Europe, 3 October 1941–8 May 1945 *(New York: Morrow 1946), 450p.*

BYRNES, James F
Speaking frankly *(New York: Harper 1947), 324p.*

CADOGAN, *Sir* Alexander
The diaries of Sir Alexander Cadogan, O.M., 1938–1945 *(London: Cassell 1971), [9], 881p, bib.*

CASEY, Richard G, *1st baron Casey*
Personal experience, 1939–1946 *(London: Constable 1962), xi, 256p.*

CHENNAULT, Claire L
The way of a fighter *(New York: Putnam 1949), xxii, 375p.*

(CIANO, Galeazzo) MUGGERIDGE, Malcolm (ed)
Ciano's diary *(London: Heinemann 1946), 592p.*

COOPER, Diana M, *countess Norwich*
Trumpets from the steep *(London: Hart-Davis 1960), 253p.*

(CUNNINGHAM, Andrew B), *1st viscount Cunningham of Hyndhope*
A sailor's odyssey *(London: Hutchinson 1951), 715p.*

PACK, Stanley W C
Cunningham the commander *(London: Batsford 1974), xi, 323p, bib.*

WARNER, Oliver
Cunningham of Hyndhope, Admiral of the Fleet: a memoir *(London: Murray [1967]), ix, 301p.*

DALTON, Hugh
The fateful years *(London: Muller 1957), 493p.*

(DE LATTRE DE TASSIGNY, Jean) SALISBURY-JONES, *Sir* Guy
So full a glory: a biography of Marshal de Lattre de Tassigny *(London: Weidenfeld & Nicolson 1954), 288p.*

DOENITZ, Karl
Memoirs: ten years and twenty days *(London: Weidenfeld & Nicolson [1959]), x, 500p.*

DOUGLAS, Sholto, *1st baron Douglas of Kirtleside*
Years of command: the 2nd volume of the autobiography *(London: Collins 1966), 382p.*

EDEN, *Sir* Anthony *1st earl of Avon*
Freedom and order: selected speeches, 1939-1946 *(Boston, Mass: Houghton Mifflin 1948), 436p.*

The reckoning: the Eden memoirs *(London: Cassell 1965), 623p.*

FORTESCUE, *Lady* Winifred
Beauty for ashes *(Edinburgh: Blackwood 1948), xiii, 318p.*

(FREYBERG, *Sir* Bernard, *1st baron Freyberg*) STEVENS, William G
Freyberg, V.C.: the man, 1939-1945 *(London: Jenkins 1965), 130p.*

GALE, *Sir* Richard N
Call to arms: an autobiography *(London: Hutchinson 1968), x, 230p.*

GIBBS, *Sir* Gerald
Survivor's story *(London: Hutchinson 1956), 182p.*

HALDER, Franz
The Halder diaries *(Washington DC: Infantry Journal Press 1950), 7 vols.*

HALSEY, William *and* BRYAN, J
Admiral Halsey's story *(New York: Whittlesey House 1947), 310p.*

HAMMERTON, *Sir* John A
As the days go by: leaves from my diary, 1939-1940 *(London: Cassell 1941), 285p.*

HASSELL, Ulrich von
The von Hassell diaries, 1938-44: the story of forces against Hitler inside Germany *(New York: Doubleday 1947), 400p.*

HENDERSON, *Sir* Nevile
Water under the bridge *(London: Hodder & Stoughton 1945), 228p.*

HEYST, Axel (pseud)
There shall be no victory: a diary of a European *(London: Gollancz 1947), 336p.*

(HOLLIS, *Sir* Leslie) LEASOR, James
War at the top; based on the experiences of General Sir Leslie Hollis, K.C.B., K.B.E. *(London: Joseph 1959), 306p; US title:* The clock with four hands.

(HOPKINS, Harry L) SHERWOOD, R E (ed)
The White House papers of Harry L. Hopkins *(London: Eyre & Spottiswoode 1948), 2 vols.*

HORROCKS, *Sir* Brian
A full life *(London: Collins 1960), 320p.*

(HORTON, *Sir* Max K) CHALMERS, William S
Max Horton and the Western Approaches; a biography of Admiral Sir Max Kennedy Horton *(London: Hodder & Stoughton 1954), 301p.*

HULL, Cordell
Memoirs *(New York: Macmillan 1948), 2 vols.*

ICKES, Harold L
The secret diary of Harold L Ickes *(New York: Simon & Schuster 1953–4), 3 vols.*

IRONSIDE, William E, *1st baron Ironside*
The Ironside diaries, 1937–1940 *(London: Constable 1962), 432p; US title:* The unguarded.

ISMAY, Hastings L, *1st baron Ismay*
The memoirs of General the Lord Ismay *(London: Heinemann 1960), xiii, 486p.*

KEITEL, Wilhelm
The memoirs of Field-Marshal Keitel *(London: Kimber 1965), 288p.*

KENNEDY, *Sir* John
The business of war: the war narrative of Major-General Sir John Kennedy *(London: Hutchinson 1957), xix, 371p.*

KERSTEN, Felix
The Kersten memoirs, 1940–1945 *(London: Hutchinson 1956), 314p.*

KESSELRING, Albert
The memoirs of Field Marshal Kesselring *(London: Kimber 1953), 319p.*

KIMMINS, Anthony M
Half-time *(London: Heinemann 1947), 290p.*

KING, Cecil H
With malice towards none: a war diary *(London: Sidgwick & Jackson 1970), viii, 343p.*

KING, Ernest J *and* WHITEHILL, W M
Fleet Admiral King: a naval record *(New York: Norton 1952), xv, 674p.*

KIPPENBERGER, *Sir* Howard
Infantry brigadier *(New York: Oxford UP 1949), 371p.*

KUNCEWICZOWA, Maria S
The keys: a journey through Europe at war *(London: Hutchinson 1945), 176p.*

LAVAL, Pierre
Diary *(New York: Scribner 1948), xv, 240p; UK title:* Unpublished diary.

LEAHY, William D
I was there: the personal story of the Chief of Staff to Presidents Roosevelt and Truman, based on his notes and diaries made at the time *(London: Gollancz 1950), 592p.*

(LINDEMANN, F A, *1st viscount Cherwell*) BIRKENHEAD, Frederick W F, *2nd earl*
The professor and the Prime Minister: the official life of Professor F. A. Lindemann, Viscount Cherwell *(Boston, Mass: Houghton Mifflin 1962), 400p.*

LINDBERGH, Charles A
The wartime journals of . . . *(New York: Harcourt 1970), xx, 1038p.*

LONG, Breckinridge
The war diary of . . . *(Lincoln, Neb: Nebraska UP 1966), xxv, 410p.*

MACMILLAN, Harold
The blast of war, 1939–1945 *(London: Macmillan 1967), xvi, 765p.*

MAISKII, Ivan M
Memoirs of a Soviet ambassador: the war, 1939–43 *(London: Hutchinson 1967), viii, 408p.*

MANNERHEIM, Carl G E
Memoirs *(London: Cassell 1954), 540p.*

(MARSHALL, George C)
Selected speeches and statements of General of the Army George C. Marshall *(Washington DC: Infantry Journal Press 1945), 324p.*

PAYNE, Robert
General Marshall: a study in loyalties *(London: Heinemann 1952), xii, 335p, bib.*

POGUE, P
George Marshall *(New York: Viking 1973), 2 vols.*

MARTEL, *Sir* Giffard L
Outspoken soldier: his views and memoirs *(London: Sifton 1949), x, 387p.*

(MESSERVY, *Sir* Frank) MAULE, Henry
Spearhead General: the epic story of General Sir Frank Messervy and his men in Eritrea, North Africa and Burma *(London: Odhams 1961), 384p.*

MORGAN, *Sir* Frederick
Peace and war: a soldier's life *(London: Hodder & Stoughton 1961), 320p.*

(MORGENTHAU, Henry) BLUM, John M
From the Morgenthau diaries: years of decision, 1938–1941 *(Boston, Mass: Houghton Mifflin 1964), 576p.*

MURPHY, Robert D
Diplomat among warriors *(New York: Doubleday 1964), 470p.*

(PAPEN, Franz von)
Memoirs *(London: Deutsch 1952), 640p.*
DUTCH, Oswald (pseud)
Errant diplomat: the life of Franz von Papen *(London: Arnold 1940), 291p.*

(PAULUS, Friedrich von) GORLITZ, Walter
Paulus and Stalingrad: a life of Field-Marshal Friedrich Paulus *(London: Methuen 1963), 301p.*

PETER II, *King of Jugoslavia*
A king's heritage: the memoirs of King Peter II of Jugoslavia *(London: Cassell 1955), xvi, 214p.*

POWNALL, *Sir* Henry
Chief of Staff *(London: Cooper 1972–4), 2 vols.*

(RAMSAY, *Sir* Bertram H) CHALMERS, William S
Full cycle: the biography of Admiral Sir Bertram Home Ramsay *(London: Hodder & Stoughton [1959]), 288p, bib.*

WOODWARD, David
Ramsay at war: the fighting life of Admiral Sir Bertram Ramsay *(London: Kimber 1957), 204p.*

RIBBENTROP, Joachim von
The Ribbentrop memoirs *(London: Weidenfeld & Nicolson 1954), xxiv, 216p.*

RIDGWAY, Matthew B
Soldier: the memoirs of Matthew B. Ridgway *(New York: Harper 1956), 371p.*

RUTTER, Owen (ed)
Allies in arms: the battle for freedom *(London: Allen & Unwin 1942), 175p.*

SCHELLENBERG, Walter
The Schellenberg memoirs *(London: Deutsch 1956), 479p; US title:* The labyrinth.

SHEEAN, Vincent
This house against this house *(New York: Random House 1946), 420p.*

(SOMERVILLE, Sir James) MACINTYRE, Donald
Fighting Admiral: the life of Admiral of the Fleet Sir James Somerville *(London: Evans 1961), 270p.*
(SPEER, Albert)
Inside the Third Reich: memoirs *(New York: Macmillan 1970), xxiv, 596p.*
HAMSHER, William
Albert Speer - victim of Nuremberg! *(London: Frewin 1970), 287p.*

STILWELL, Joseph W
Papers *(New York: Sloane 1948), xvi, 357p.*

STIMSON, H L *and* BUNDY, McG
On active service in war and peace *(New York: Harper 1948), 422p.*

TABORI, Paul
Restless summer: a personal record *(London: Sylvan 1946), 224p.*

TABUIS, *Mme* Genevieve
They called me Cassandra *(New York: Scribner 1942), xii, 436p.*

THAYER, Charles W
Hands across the caviar *(Philadelphia, Pa: Lippincott 1952), 251p.*

TRUMAN, Harry S
Memoirs *(London: Hodder & Stoughton 1955), vol. I:* Year of decisions, 1945, *526p.*

TRUSCOTT, Lucian K
Command missions: a personal story *(New York: Dutton 1954), 570p.*

WEDEMEYER, Albert C
Wedemeyer reports! *(New York: Holt 1958), 497p.*

WEIZACKER, Ernst H
Memoirs *(London: Gollancz 1951), 322p.*

WEYGAND, Maxime
Recalled to service: the memoirs of General Maxime Weygand *(London: Heinemann 1952), ix, 454p.*

WILSON, Henry M *1st baron Wilson*
Eight years overseas, 1939-1947 *(London: Hutchinson 1950), 285p.*

WINANT, John G
A letter from Grosvenor Square: an account of a stewardship *(London: Hodder & Stoughton 1947), 278p.*
Our greatest harvest: selected speeches, 1941-46 *(London: Hodder & Stoughton 1950), 228p.*

WOOLTON, Frederick J M, *1st earl Woolton*
Memoirs *(London: Cassell 1959), 452p.*

WRENCH, *Sir* Evelyn
Immortal years, 1937-1944, as viewed from five continents *(London: Hutchinson 1945), 232p.*

(YAMAMOTO) POTTER, John D
Admiral of the Pacific: the life of Yamamoto *(London: Heinemann 1965), 332p; US title:* Yamamoto: the man who menaced America

MERCHANT NAVY

ARMSTRONG, Warren
The battle of the oceans: the story of the British Merchant Marine *(London: Jarrolds 1943), xvii, 21-336p.*
Freedom of the seas *(London: Jarrolds 1943), 160p.*
Red duster at war *(London: Gollancz 1942), 192p.*

BEECHER, John
All the brave sailors: the story of the S.S. Broker T. Washington *(New York: Fisher 1945), 208p.*

BEHRENS, Catherine B A
Merchant shipping and the demands of war *(London: HMSO 1955), xxi, 499p.*

BEN LINE STEAMERS LTD
The Ben Line: the story of a merchant fleet at war, 1939-1943 *(London: Nelson 1946), 107p.*

BONE, *Sir* David W
Merchantman rearmed *(London: Chatto & Windus 1949), xx, 331p.*

BOWEN, Frank C
The flag of the Southern Cross, 1939-1945 *(London: Shaw, Savill & Albion 1947), 71p.*

BUSHELL, Thomas A
Eight bells: Royal Mail Lines war story, 1939-1945 *(London: Trade & Travel [1950]), xv, 207p.*

CAMPBELL, Archibald B
Salute the Red Duster *(London: Johnston 1952), 208p.*

CARSE, Robert
Lifeline: the ships and men of our Merchant Marine at war *(New York: Morrow 1943), 13-189p.*
The long haul: the U.S. Merchant Service in World War II *(New York: Norton 1965), 223p.*

COOKE, Kenneth
What cares the sea? *(London: Hutchinson 1960), 168p.*

DOUGLAS, John S *and* SALZ, Albert
He's in the Merchant Marine now *(New York: McBride 1943), 9–224p.*

GREAT BRITAIN. British Information Service
The British Merchant Navy *(New York: BIF 1945), 55p.*

GREAT BRITAIN. Ministry of War Transport
British merchantmen at war: official story of the Merchant Navy, 1939–1945 *(London: HMSO 1945), 142p.*

GRIBBLE, Leonard
Heroes of the Merchant Navy *(London: Harrap 1944), 204p.*

HALSTEAD, Ivor
Heroes of the Atlantic: a tribute to the Merchant Navy *(London: Drummond 1941), xii, 235p.*

HODSON, James L
British merchantmen at war: the official story of the Merchant Navy, 1939–1944 *(New York: Ziff-Davis 1945), 7–192p.*

HOPE, Stanton
Ocean odyssey: a record of the fighting Merchant Navy *(London: Eyre & Spottiswoode 1944), 220p.*

HURD, *Sir* Archibald S
The battle of the seas: the fighting merchantmen *(London: Hodder & Stoughton 1941), 160p.*

KERR, George F
Business in great waters: the war history of the P & O 1939–1945 *(London: Faber 1951), 196p.*

KERR, James L
Touching the adventures . . . of merchantmen in the Second World War *(London: Harrap 1953), 256p.*

LANE, Frederic C *and others*
Ships for victory: a history of ship-building under the U.S. Maritime Commission in World War II *(Baltimore, Md: Johns Hopkins 1951), 881p.*

LASKIER, Frank
A merchant seaman talks: my name is Frank *(London: Allen & Unwin 1941), 7–75p; US title:* My name is Frank.

LEE, Norman
Landlubber's log: 25,000 miles with the Merchant Navy *(London: Quality 1945), 98p.*

LINBAEK, Lise *and others*
Norway's new saga of the sea: the story of her Merchant Marine in World War II *(New York: Exposition 1969), 251p.*

McNeil, Calum
San Demetrio *(London: Angus & Robertson 1957), 241p.*

Masters, David
In peril on the sea: war exploits of Allied seamen *(London: Cresset 1960), 256p.*

O'Flaherty, Ferocious (pseud)
Abandoned convoy: the U.S. Merchant Marine in World War II *(New York: Exposition 1970), 87p.*

Palmer, Mary B
We fight with merchant ships *(Indianapolis, Ind: Bobbs-Merrill 1943), 5-307p.*

Pollock, George
The 'Jervis Bay' *(London: Kimber 1958), 206p, bib.*

Riesenberg, Felix
Sea war: the story of the U.S. Merchant Marine in World War II *(New York: Rinehart 1956), 320p.*

Roskill, Stephen W
A merchant fleet in war: Alfred Holt & Co., 1939-1945 *(London: Collins 1962), 352p.*

Ruge, Friedrich
Sea warfare, 1939-1945: a German view point *(London: Cassell 1957), xiv, 337p.*

Saunders, Hilary A St G
Valiant voyaging: a short history of the British India Steam Navigation Company in the Second World War, 1939-1945 *(London: Faber 1949), 136p.*

Sellwood, Arthur V
The damned don't cry *(London: Wingate 1973), 160p.*

Shaw, Frank H
The Merchant Navy at war *(London: Paul 1944), 136p.*
Under the Red Ensign *(London: Lane 1958), 207p.*

Standard Oil Company
Ships of the ESSO Fleet in World War II *(New York: Standard Oil Company 1946), 530p.*

Standby (pseud)
Little known in these waters *(Sydney: Dymock 1945), viii, 250p.*

Taffrail (pseud)
Blue Star Line at war 1939-1945 *(London: Foulsham 1973), 159, xiiip.*

Waters, Sydney
Ordeal by sea: the New Zealand Shipping Company in the Second World War, 1939-1945 *(London: Shipping Co 1949), 263p.*

WOON, Basil D
Atlantic front: the Merchant Navy in the war *(London: Davies 1941), xii, 324p.*
[*see also* CONVOYS, GERMAN SURFACE RAIDERS, U-BOATS]

MERS-EL-KEBIR

TUTE, Warren
The deadly stroke *(London: Collins 1973), 221p, bib.*
[*see also* FRENCH NAVY]

MIDDLE EAST

AGAR-HAMILTON, John A I *and* TURNER, Leonard C (eds)
Crisis in the desert, May - July 1942 *(London: Oxford UP 1952), 368p.*
The Sidi Rezeg battles *(London: Oxford UP 1957), 505p.*

BARCLAY, Cyril N
Against great odds: the story of the first offensive in Libya, in 1940–41, the first British victory in the Second World War *(London: Sifton Praed 1955), 112p.*

BUCKLEY, Christopher
Five ventures: Iraq-Syria-Persia-Madagascar-Dodecanese *(London: HMSO 1954), ix, 257p.*

COWARD, Noel P
Middle East diary *(London: Heinemann 1944), 119p.*

DIMBLEBY, Richard
The frontiers are green *(London: Hodder & Stoughton 1943), 278p.*

GRAHAM, Cormo
A space for delight: letters . . . to his wife during the years 1939 to 1942 *(London: Witherby 1954), xiv, 192p.*

GREAT BRITAIN. Central Office of Information
Paiforce: the official story of the Persian and Iraq Command, 1941-1946 *(London: HMSO 1948), 137p.*

GUEDALLA, Philip
Middle East, 1940-1942: a study in air power *(London: Hodder & Stoughton 1944), 236p.*

JOHN, Evan (pseud)
Time in the East: an entertainment *(London: Heinemann 1946), 230p.*

MOSENSON, Moshe
Letters from the desert *(New York: Sharon 1945), 222p.*
MOTTER, Thomas H V
The Persian corridor and aid to Russia *(Washington DC: Department of Army 1952), 545p.*
PHILLIPS, Norman C
Guns, drugs and deserters: the Special Investigation Branch in the Middle East *(London: Laurie 1954), 176p.*
SAYRE, Joel
Persian Gulf Command: some marvels on the road to Kazvin *(New York: Random House 1945), 140p.*
STARK, Freya M
East is West *(London: Murray 1945), xxii, 218p; US title:* Arab island, Middle East, 1939–1943.
STEVENS, William G
Bardia to Enfidaville *(Wellington, NZ: War Historical Branch, Department of Internal Affairs 1962), 416p.*
STRATEGICUS (pseud)
From Dunkirk to Benghazi *(London: Faber 1941), 9-295p.*
The war moves East *(London: Faber 1942), 236p.*
WARNER, Geoffrey
Iraq and Syria, 1941 *(London: Davis-Poynter 1974), 180p, bib.*
[*see also* MEDITERRANEAN, NORTH AFRICA]

MIDWAY ISLAND

BARKER, Arthur J
Midway: the turning point *(New York: Ballantine 1970), 160p, bib.*
COALE, Griffith B
Victory at Midway *(New York: Farrar 1944), xii, 178p.*
FUCHIDA, Mitsuo *and* OKUMIYA, Masatake
Midway: the battle that doomed Japan *(Annapolis, Md: US Naval Institute 1955), 263p.*
THE JAPANESE story of the battle of Midway *(Washington DC: Office of Naval Intelligence 1947), 68p.*
LORD, Walter
Incredible victory *(New York: Harper 1967), xv, 331p.*
SMITH, Chester L
Midway, 4 June 1942 *(London: Regency 1962), 67p.*
TULEJA, Thaddeus V
Climax at Midway *(London: Dent 1961), 248p, bib.*

US Marine Corps
Marines at Midway *(Washington DC: USMC 1948), 56p.*
Werstein, Irving
The battle of Midway *(New York: Crowell 1961), 145p.*
[*see also* PACIFIC, US MARINES, US NAVY]

MILITARY ENGINEERING

Bowman, Waldo G
American military engineering in Europe from Normandy to the Rhine *(New York: McGraw-Hill 1945), 102p.*
Building the Navy's bases in World War II: history of the Bureau of Yards and Docks and the Civil Engineer Corps, 1940–1946 *(Washington DC: Government Printing Office 1947), 2 vols.*
Patton, William
The scrap log of an engineer *(Ilfracombe, Devon: Stockwell 1952), 206p.*
Sill, Van R
American miracle: the story of war construction around the world *(New York: Odyssey 1947), 301p.*
Woodbury, David O
Builders for battle: how the Pacific naval bases were constructed *(New York: Dutton 1946), 415p.*
[*see also* MULBERRY]

MILITARY MARKINGS

Hodges, Peter
British military markings, 1939–1945 *(London: Almark 1971), 64p.*

MINES AND MINESWEEPING

Brookes, Ewart
Glory passed them by *(London: Jarrolds 1958), 176p.*
Connell, Brian
Return of the tiger *(London: Evans 1960), 207p.*
Cowie, J S
Mines, minelayers and mine laying *(Toronto: Oxford UP 1949), xiii, 216p.*

FANE, Robert (pseud)
Ships may proceed: more tales of a mine-sweeper *(London: W H Allen 1943), 63p.*
We clear the way *(London: W H Allen 1943), 64p.*

FISHER, Richard
With the French minesweepers *(London: Selwyn & Blount 1945), 175p.*

GIBSON, Charles
The ship with five names *(London: Abelard-Schuman [1965]), 159p.*

GROSVENOR, Joan *and* BATES, Leonard M
Open the ports: the story of human minesweepers *(London: Kimber 1956), xii, 13–199p.*

LANGMAID, Kenneth
The approaches are mined! *(London: Jarrolds 1965), 256p.*

LINCOLN, Fredman A
Secret naval investigator *(London: Kimber 1961), 207p.*

LOTT, Arnold S
Most dangerous sea: a history of mine warfare, and an account of U.S. Navy mine warfare operations in World War II and Korea *(Annapolis, Md: US Naval Institute 1959), 322p.*

MILLER, John
Saints and parachutes: two aspects of an adventure *(London: Constable 1951), 171p.*

SOUTHALL, Ivan
Softly tread the brave: a triumph over terror, devilry and death by mine disposal officers John Stuart Mould, G.C., G.M., and Hugh Randal Syme, G.C., G.M. and Bar *(Sydney: Angus & Robertson 1961), x, 293p.*

TURNER, John F
Service most silent: the Navy's fight against enemy mines *(London: Harrap 1955), 200p.*

MINING

COURT, William H B
Coal *(London: HMSO 1951), 422p.*

MORGAN, John D
The domestic mining industry of the United States in World War II: a critical study of the economic mobilization of the mineral base of national power *(Washington DC: Government Printing Office 1949), 500p.*

MISSIONARIES

BENSON, James
Prisoner's base and home again: the story of a missionary P.O.W. *(London: Hale 1957), 192p.*

LYNIP, G L
On good ground: missionary stories from the Philippines *(Grand Rapids, Mich: Eerdmans 1946), 149p.*

McMILLAN, Archibald M
For Christ in China *(Nashville, Tenn: Broadman 1949), 141p.*

SISTERS OF OUR LADY OF THE SACRED HEART
Red grew the harvest: missionary experiences during the Pacific war of 1941-45 *(Sydney: Pellegrini 1947), 185p.*

STRAELEN, Henricus van
A missionary in the war net *(London: Luzac 1944), 63p.*

SWANSON, Swan (ed)
Zamzam: the story of a strange missionary odyssey *(Rock Island, Ill: Augustana 1941), 149p.*

THROUGH toil and tribulation: missionary experiences in China during the war of 1937-1945 *(London: Carey 1947), 208p.*

MOBILIZATION

SMITH, Ralph E
The Army and economic mobilization *(Washington DC: Department of Army 1959), 749p.*

SOMERS, Herman M
Presidential Agency OWMR, the Office of War Mobilization and Reconversion *(Cambridge, Mass: Harvard UP 1950), 238p.*

MONTGOMERY

LEWIN, Ronald
Montgomery as military commander *(London: Batsford 1971), [13], 288p, bib.*

McGILL, Michael C *and* FLACKES, William D
Montgomery, Field Marshal: an Ulster tribute *(Belfast: Quota 1946), 122p.*

MONTGOMERY, Bernard L, *1st viscount Montgomery of Alamein*
Forward from victory: speeches and addresses *(London: Hutchinson 1948), 284p.*
The memoirs *(London: Collins 1958), 574p.*

MOOREHEAD, Alan
Montgomery *(London: Hamilton 1946), 255p.*
THOMPSON, Reginald W
Montgomery, the Field Marshal: a critical study of the generalship of Field-Marshal the Viscount Montgomery of Alamein, K.G., and of the campaign in North-West Europe, 1944/45 *(London: Allen & Unwin 1969), 3-344p, bib.*
The Montgomery legend *(London: Allen & Unwin 1967), 3-276p, bib; US title:* Churchill and the Montgomery myth.
WALKER, K A
Montgomery's sand blast *(Cairo: Schindler 1945), 111p.*

MORALS

MALKIN, Richard
Marriage, morals and war *(New York: Arden 1943), 11-245p.*
ROBINSON, Victor (ed)
Morals in wartime *(New York: Publishers Foundation 1943), xii, 205p.*

MOSCOW

CALDWELL, Erskine
Moscow under fire: a wartime diary 1941 *(London: Hutchinson 1942), 112p; US title:* All out on the road to Smolensk.
JACOB, Alaric
A window in Moscow, 1944–45 *(London: Collins 1946), 320p.*
JUKES, Geoffrey
The defence of Moscow *(New York: Ballantine 1970), 160p, bib.*
TURNEY, Alfred
Disaster at Moscow: Von Bock's campaigns 1941-1942 *(Albuquerque, NM: New Mexico UP 1970), xvii, 228p, bib.*
[*see also* EASTERN EUROPE, RUSSIA]

MOSQUITO

BISHOP, Edward
Mosquito, wooden wonder *(New York: Ballantine 1971), 160p, bib.*
BOWYER, Chaz
Mosquito at war *(London: Allan 1973), 144p.*
SHARP, Cecil M *and* BOWYER, Michael
Mosquito *(London: Faber 1967), 494p.*

MOTOR TORPEDO BOATS

BULKLEY, Robert J
At close quarters: PT boats in the U.S. Navy *(Washington DC: Department of Defense 1963),*

COOPER, Bryan
The battle of the torpedo boats *(London: Macdonald 1970), 296p.*
'P.T. boats' *(New York: Ballantine 1970), 160p, bib; UK title:* The buccaneers.

DICKENS, Peter
Night action: MTB Flotilla at war *(London: Davies 1974), 256p.*

DRUMMOND, John
Through hell and high water: with men of the little ships of the Royal Navy *(London: Sampson Low 1944), x, 146p.*

FARLEY, Edward I
PT patrol: wartime adventures in the Pacific and the story of PT's in World War II *(New York: Exposition 1957), 108p.*

GRANVILLE, Wilfred *and* KELLY, Robin A
Inshore heroes: the story of H.M. Motor Launches in two World Wars *(London: W H Allen 1961), 320p, bib.*

HAMPSHIRE, Arthur C
Armed with stings: the saga of a gunboat flotilla *(London: Kimber 1958), 203p.*
On hazardous service *(London: Kimber 1974), 256p.*

HICHENS, Robert
We fought them in gunboats *(London: Joseph 1944), 191p.*

HOLMAN, Gordon
Little ships *(London: Hodder & Stoughton 1943), 164p.*

KEATING, Bern
The mosquito fleet *(New York: Longmans 1963), 244p.*

REYNOLDS, Leonard C
Gunboat 658: the story of operations of a motor gunboat in the Mediterranean from the fall of Tunisia until the German surrender *(London: Kimber 1955), 246p.*

SCOTT, *Sir* Peter
The battle of the narrow seas: a history of the Light Coastal Forces in the Channel and North Sea 1939-1945 *(London: Country Life 1945), xii, 228p.*

THORBURN, Lois *and* THORBURN, Don
No tumult, no shouting: story of the PBY *(New York: Holt 1945), 148p.*

MOUNTBATTEN

SWINSON, Arthur
Mountbatten *(New York: Ballantine 1971), 2, 160p, bib.*

MULBERRY

STANFORD, Alfred B
Force Mulberry: the planning and installation of the artificial harbor off U.S. Normandy beaches in World War II *(New York: Morrow 1951), 7-240p.*
[*see also* NORMANDY]

MUSSOLINI

ARCHER, Jules
Twentieth century Caesar: Benito Mussolini *(New York: Messner 1964), 192p, bib.*

COLLIER, Richard
Duce!: the rise and fall of Benito Mussolini *(London: Collins 1971), 447p, bib.*

DABROWSKI, Roman
Mussolini, twilight and fall *(London: Heinemann 1956), 248p.*

DEAKIN, Frederick W
The last days of Mussolini *(London: Penguin 1966), rev. ed., 378p, bib.*

DELZELL, C F
Mussolini's enemies: the Italian anti-Fascist resistance *(Princeton, NJ: Princeton UP 1961), 640p.*

HIBBERT, Christopher
Benito Mussolini *(London: Longmans Green 1962), 367p; US title:* Il Duce.
Mussolini *(New York: Ballantine 1972), 160p, bib.*

KIRKPATRICK, *Sir* Ivone
Mussolini: a study of a demagogue *(London: Odhams 1964), 669p.*

MACARTNEY, Maxwell H H
One man alone: the history of Mussolini and the Axis *(London: Chatto & Windus 1944), vii, 183p.*

MUSSOLINI, Benito
The fall of Mussolini: his own story *(New York: Farrar 1948), 9-212p; UK title:* Memoirs, 1942-1943.

SAPORITI, Piero
Empty balcony *(London: Gollancz 1947), 128p.*

STELLE, Pier *and* LAZZARO, Urbano
Dongo - the last act *(London: Macdonald 1964), 187p.*

NARVIK

DICKENS, Peter
Narvik: battles in the fjords *(London: Allan 1974), 184p, bib.*

LAPIE, Pierre O
With the Foreign Legion at Narvik *(London: Murray 1941), xix, 138p.*

MACINTYRE, Donald
Narvik *(London: Evans 1959), 224p.*

POLISH troops in Norway: a photographic record of the Polish Highland Brigade's campaign at Narvik *(London: Kolin 1943), 160p.*

STRABOLGI, Joseph M K, *10th baron*
Narvik and after: a study of the Scandinavian campaign *(London: Hutchinson 1940), 13-216p.*

WAAGE, Johan
The Narvik campaign *(London: Harrap 1964), 190p.*

ZBYSZEWSKI, Karol
The fight for Narvik: impressions of the Polish campaign in Norway *(London: Drummond 1940), ix, 32p.*
[*see also* NORWAY]

NAVAL WARFARE (general)

ADAMS, James H
Ships in battledress *(Sydney: Currawong 1945), 9-155p.*

BLORE, Trevor
Turning point - 1943 *(London: Hutchinson 1945), 128p.*

COOK, Graeme
None but the valiant: stories of war at sea *(London: Hart-Davis 1972), 153p, bib.*

CRESWELL, John
Sea warfare, 1939-1945: a short history *(Toronto: Longmans 1950), xv, 344p.*

DIAMOND, Walker De W
Memoirs of ships and men *(New York: Vantage 1964), 256p.*

DIVINE, Arthur D
Navies in exile *(London: Murray 1944), vi, 194p.*

HARDY, Alfred C
Everyman's history of the sea war *(London: Nicholson & Watson 1948–55), 3 vols.*

LAND, Emory
Winning the war with ships *(New York: McBride 1958), 310p.*

LEEMING, Joseph
Brave ships of World War II *(New York: Nelson 1944), 9–238p.*

MASTERS, David
In peril on the sea: war exploits of Allied seamen *(London: Cresset 1960), 255p.*

MOTLEY, John J *and* KELLY, P R
Now hear this! *(Washington DC: Infantry Journal Press 1947), xii, 282p.*

POTTER, Elmer B *and* NIMITZ, Chester
The great sea war: the story of naval action in World War II *(New York: Prentice-Hall 1960), 468p.*

PRATT, Fletcher
Sea power and today's war *(New York: Harrison-Hilton 1939), x, 237p.*

PULESTON, William D
The influence of sea power in World War II *(New Haven, Conn: Yale UP 1947), 310p.*

ROGERS, Stanley R H
Enemy in sight! *(New York: Crowell 1943), 250p.*
Sailors at war *(London: Harrap 1942), 218p.*

RUSSELL, *Sir* Herbert
Sea warfare today *(London: Lane 1940), 119p.*

SALOMON, Henry *and* HANSER, Richard
Victory at sea *(New York: Doubleday 1959), 256p.*

SANDERS, Jacquin
The night before Christmas *(New York: Putnam 1963), 320p.*

SCHUBERT, Paul
Sea power in conflict *(New York: Coward-McCann 1942), vi, 252p.*

SCLATER, William
HAIDA *(Toronto: Oxford UP 1947), 221p.*

STIRLING, Yates
Why seapower will win the war *(New York: Fell 1944), 7–319p.*

STRABOLGI, Joseph M K, *10th baron*
Sea power in the Second World War *(London: Hutchinson 1943), 136p.*

TULEJA, Thaddeus V
The twilight of the sea gods *(New York: Norton 1958), 284p.*
TUNSTALL, William C B
Ocean power wins *(London: Secker & Warburg 1944), xi, 216p.*
World war at sea *(London: Secker & Warburg 1942), viii, 319p.*
TURNER, Leonard C F, *and others*
War in the southern oceans *(Toronto: Oxford UP 1961), 288p.*
WHITEHOUSE, Arthur G J
Squadrons of the sea *(New York: Doubleday 1962), 383p.*
[*see also* ROYAL NAVY, US NAVY]

NEGROES

FRANCIS, Charles E
The Tuskegee airmen: the story of the Negro in the U.S. Air Force *(Boston, Mass: Bruce Humphries 1956), 225p.*
FURR, Arthur
Democracy's negroes: a book of facts concerning the activities of negroes in World War II *(Boston, Mass: House of Edinboro 1947), 315p.*
PURDON, Eric
Black Company: the story of Subchaser 1264 *(Washington DC: Luce U972), 255p.*
SILVERA, J D
The Negro in World War II *(Baton Rouge, La: Military 1946), 1 vol.*
WATT, Donald C
World War II outside Europe *(Milton Keynes, Bucks: Open UP 1973), 77p, bib.*
WHITE, Walter F
A rising wind *(New York: Doubleday 1945), 155p.*
WILSON, Ruth
Jim Crow joins up: a study of Negroes in the Armed Forces of the United States *(New York: Press of W J Clark 1944), ix, 129p.*

NETHERLANDS [*see* HOLLAND]

NEUTRALS

NEUTRAL war aims: essays by representative writers of leading neutral countries *(London: Burns Oates 1940), 192p.*

YOUNG, George C
Outposts of peace *(London: Hodder & Stoughton 1945), 192p.* [*see also* SPAIN, SWITZERLAND]

NEW GUINEA

DAWES, Allan
A soldier superb *(Sydney: Johnston 1945), 102p.*

DEXTER, David
The New Guinea offensives *(Canberra: Australian War Memorial 1961), xx, 851p.*

JILLETT, Leslie
Moresby's few: being an account of the activities of No. 32 Squadron in New Guinea in 1942 *(Melbourne, Aus: Robertson & Mullens 1945), 107p.*

JOHNSTON, George H
The toughest fighting in the world *(New York: Duell 1943), xv, 240p; UK title:* New Guinea diary.

KAHN, Ely J
G.I. jungle: an American soldier in Australia and New Guinea *(New York: Simon & Schuster 1943), xiv, 150p.*

McCARTHY, Dudley
South-West Pacific area - first year: Kokoda to Wau *(Canberra: Australian War Memorial 1959), xiv, 656p.*

MANSFIELD, Alan (comp)
A brief history of the New Guinea Air Warning Wireless Company (A.I.F.) *(Melbourne, Aus: James 1961), 96p.*

MAYO, Lida
Bloody Buna *(New York: Doubleday 1974), 222p.*

MORESBY, Emily I
New Guinea, the sentinel *(Christchurch, NZ: Whitcombe & Tombs 1943), 126p.*

ON TARGET: with the American and Australian anti-aircraft brigade in New Guinea *(Sydney: Angus & Robertson 1943), 172p.*

PAVILL, Raymond
Retreat from Kokoda *(London: Heinemann 1958), xix, 319p.*

RYAN, Peter
Fear drive my feet *(London: Angus & Robertson 1960), ix, 251p.*

RHYS, Lloyd
Jungle Pimpernel: the story of a District Officer in Central Netherlands New Guinea *(London: Hodder & Stoughton 1947), 239p.*

ROBINSON, Bruce
Record of service: an Australian medical officer in the New Guinea campaign *(Melbourne, Aus: Macmillan 1944), x, 177p.*

ROBINSON, Pat
The fight for New Guinea: General MacArthur's first offensive *(New York: Random House 1943), 183p.*

ST. JOHN on the hill, Port Moresby, 1943-1944 *(Sydney: Penfold 1945), 63p.*

US MARINE CORPS
The campaign in New Britain *(Washington DC: USCM 1952), 220p.*

VADER, John
New Guinea: the tide is stemmed *(New York: Ballantine 1971), 160p, bib.*

WAR in New Guinea: the story of the battle for Australia told in official war photographs *(Sydney: Johnston 1943), 48p.*

WILCOX, Richard
Of men and battle *(New York: Howell, Soskin 1944), 8-124p.*
[*see also* PAPUA]

NEW HAMPSHIRE

GUYOL, Philip N
Democracy fights: a history of New Hampshire in World War II *(Hanover, NH: Dartmouth 1951), xix, 309p.*

NEW YORK CITY

LANUX, Pierre C
New York, 1939-1945 *(Paris: Hachette 1947), 223p.*

NEW YORK STATE

HARTZELL, Karl D
The Empire State at war: World War II *(Albany, NY: New York State Council 1949), 423p.*

NEW ZEALAND

ANSON, Thomas V
The New Zealand Dental Services *(Wellington, NZ: War History Branch, Department of Internal Affairs 1960), 422p.*

BAKER, John V T
The New Zealand people at war: war economy *(Wellington, NZ: Department of Internal Affairs 1965), 660p.*

BARNES-GRAHAM, John W
Up and over the hill *(Oxford: Ronald 1952), 166p.*

BASE wallahs: the story of the units of the Base organization, New Zealand Expeditionary Force in the Pacific *(Dunedin, NZ: Reed 1946), 256p.*

BATES, P W
Supply company *(Wellington, NZ: Department of Internal Affairs 1955), 371p.*

BERTRAM, James M
Beneath the shadow: a New Zealander in the Far East, 1939–46 *(New York: Day 1947), 308p.*

BICKERS, Emma P (comp)
Pakai tara Te Kopuru. (Te Kopuru's band of warriors) *(Dunedin, NZ: North Auckland Times 1947), 72p.*

BORMAN, C A
Divisional signals *(Christchurch, NZ: Whitcombe & Tombs 1954), 540p.*

BROAD, John E
Poor people, poor us *(Wellington, NZ: Tombs 1946), 277p.*

BURDON, Randal M
24 Battalion *(Wellington, NZ: Department of Internal Affairs 1953), 361p.*

COCKS, Edith M S
Kia Kaha: life at 3 New Zealand General Hospital, 1940–1946 *(Christchurch, NZ: Caxton 1958), 285p.*

CODY, Joseph F
New Zealand Engineers, Middle East *(Wellington, NZ: Department of Internal Affairs 1961), 774p.*
21 Battalion *(Wellington, NZ: Department of Internal Affairs 1953), 471p.*

DAWSON, William D
18 Battalion and Armoured Regiment *(Wellington, NZ: Department of Internal Affairs 1961), 676p.*

GILLESPIE, Olwen A
The Pacific *(Wellington, NZ: Department of Internal Affairs 1952), xii, 395p, bib.*

THE GUNNERS; an intimate record of units of the 3rd New Zealand Divisional Artillery in the Pacific from 1940 until 1945 *(Dunedin, NZ: Reed 1948), 290p.*

HEADQUARTERS: a brief outline of the activities of the Headquarters of the Third Division and the 8th and 14th Brigade during their service in the Pacific *(Dunedin, NZ: Reed 1947), 278p.*

HANCOCK, Kenneth R
New Zealand at war: an unofficial account of the Dominion's war effort overseas and at home, embracing the services in all theatres and the industrial and general domestic background during the period of hostilities, 1939–45 *(Wellington, NZ: Reed 1946), 351p.*

HENDERSON, James H
Gunner inglorious, 'no haughty feat of arms I tell' *(Wellington, NZ: Tombs 1945), 213p.*
RMT: official history of the 4th and 6th Reserve Mechanical Transport Companies 2 NZEF *(Wellington, NZ: Department of Internal Affairs 1954), 378p.*

HOBBS, Horace P
A Kiwi down the Strada *(Christchurch, NZ: Whitcombe & Tombs 1963), 122p.*

HUNT, Leslie
Defence until dawn: the story of 488 N.Z. Squadron; Church Fenton, 25th June 1942 to Gilze-Rijen, Holland, 26th April 1945 *(Southend-on-Sea, Essex: Washburn 1949), 104p.*

JACKSON, Francis
Air gunner: the adventures of Flying Officer H. Lyver *(Wellington, NZ: Reed 1944), 164p.*
Passage to Tobruk: the diary of a Kiwi in the Middle East *(Wellington, NZ: Reed 1943), 143p.*

KAY, Robin L
27th Machine Gun Battalion *(Wellington, NZ: Department of Internal Affairs 1958), 543p.*

KIDSON, Arthur L
Petrol company *(Wellington, NZ: Department of Internal Affairs 1961), 363p.*

LARSEN, Colin R
Pacific Commandos: New Zealanders and Fijians in action; a history of Southern Independent Commando and First Commando Fiji Guerillas *(Wellington, NZ: Reed 1946), 161p.*

McCLYMONT, W G
To Greece *(Wellington, NZ: Department of Internal Affairs 1959), 538p.*

McDonald, J D (ed)
The pitcher and the well *(London: Oldbourne 1963), 224p.*

Mason, Walter W
Prisoner of war *(Wellington, NZ: Department of Internal Affairs 1955), xxvi, 546p.*

Mitchell, Alan W
New Zealanders in the air war *(London: Harrap 1945), 192p.*

New Zealand. Department of Internal Affairs
Documents relating to New Zealand participation in the Second World War, 1939-45 *(Wellington, NZ: 1949), 3 vols.*
New Zealand in the Second World War, 1939-54, episodes and studies *(Wellington, NZ: 1948-54), 2 vols.*

Norton, Frazer D
26 Battalion *(Wellington, NZ: Department of Internal Affairs 1952), 554p.*

Pacific Kiwis: being the story of the service in the Pacific of the 30th Battalion, Third Division, Second N.Z. Expeditionary Force *(Wellington, NZ: Reed 1947), 150p.*

Pacific Pioneers: the story of the Engineers of the N.Z. Expeditionary Force in the Pacific *(Dunedin, NZ: Reed 1945), 168p.*

Pacific saga: the personal chronicle of the 37th Battalion and its part in the Third Division's campaign *(Wellington, NZ: Reed 1947), 114p.*

Pacific service: the story of the N.Z., A.S.C. Units with the Third Division in the Pacific *(Wellington, NZ: Reed 1948), 140p.*

Phillips, Neville C
Italy *(Wellington, NZ: Department of Internal Affairs 1957), 1 vol. pub.*

Pringle, Dave J C *and* Glue, W A
20 Battalion and Armoured Regiment *(Wellington, NZ: Department of Internal Affairs 1957), 631p.*

Ross, Angus
23 Battalion *(Wellington, NZ: Department of Internal Affairs 1959), 506p.*

Ross, J M S
The Royal New Zealand Air Force *(Wellington, NZ: Department of Internal Affairs 1955), 343p.*

Sinclair, Donald W
19 Battalion and Armoured Regiment *(Wellington, NZ: Department of Internal Affairs 1954), 559p.*

STARTUP, Robin McG
The mails went through: the story of New Zealand's Armed Forces Postal Services during the war years, 1939–1949 *(NZ: Masterton 1957), 169p.*

STEPPING stones to the Solomons: the unofficial history of the 29th Battalion with the Second N.Z. Expeditionary Force in the Pacific *(Wellington, NZ: Reed 1947), 121p.*

STEVENS, William G
Problems of 2 NZEF *(Wellington, NZ: Department of Internal Affairs 1958), 331p.*

STORY of the 34th: the unofficial history of a N.Z. Infantry Battalion with the Third Division in the Pacific *(Wellington, NZ: Reed 1947), 159p.*

STOUT, Thomas D McG
Medical services in New Zealand and the Pacific *(Christchurch, NZ: Whitcombe & Tombs 1958), 450p.*
New Zealand medical services in the Middle East and Italy *(Christchurch, NZ: Whitcombe & Tombs 1956), 721p.*
War surgery and medicine *(Christchurch, NZ: Whitcombe & Tombs 1954), 780p.*

THE TANKS: an official history of the activities of the Third N.Z. Division Tank Squadron in the Pacific *(Dunedin, NZ: Reed 1947), 227p.*

THE 35th Battalion: a record of service of the 35th Battalion with the Third Division in the Pacific *(Wellington, NZ: Reed 1947), 143p.*

THE 36th Battalion: a record of service of the 36th Battalion with the Third Division in the Pacific *(Wellington, NZ: Reed 1948), 129p.*

THOMPSON, Henry L
New Zealanders with the Royal Air Force *(London: Oxford UP 1953–59), 3 vols.*

THOMSON, Richard H
Captive Kiwi *(Christchurch, NZ: Whitcombe & Tombs 1964), 196p.*

WATERS, Sydney D
The Royal New Zealand Navy *(Wellington, NZ: Department of Internal Affairs 1956), 570p.*

WHEELER, Charles M
Kalimera Kiwi: to Olympus with the New Zealand Engineers *(Wellington, NZ: Reed 1946), 240p.*

WOOD, Frederick L W
The New Zealand people at war: political and external affairs *(Wellington, NZ: Department of Internal Affairs 1958), 395p.*
[*see also* EGYPT, MIDDLE EAST, PACIFIC]

NIGHT FIGHTERS

BRAHAM, John R D
Scramble *(London: Muller 1961), 256p; US title:* Night fighter.

BRANDON, Lewis
Night flyer *(London: Kimber 1961), 208p.*

RAWNSLEY, Cecil F *and* WRIGHT, Robert
Night fighter *(London: Collins 1957), 383p.*

SARGENT, Frederic O (comp)
Night fighters: an official history of the 415th Night Fighter Squadron *(Madison, Wis: 1946), 79p.*
[*see also* BOMBERS, GERMAN AIR FORCE, RAF, USAAF]

NORMANDY

BELFIELD, Eversley *and* ESSAME, Hubert
The battle for Normandy *(London: Batsford 1965), 239p, bib.*

BLIVEN, Bruce
The story of D-Day, June 6th, 1944 *(New York: Random House 1956), 180p.*

BOUSSEL, Patrice
D-Day beaches pocket guide *(London: Macdonald 1965), 227p.*

CARELL, Paul
Invasion - they're coming!: the German account of the Allied landing and the 80 days' battle for France *(London: Harrap [1962]), 288p, bib.*

CBS NEWS
D-Day *(New York: Watts 1967), 65p.*

COOPER, John St J
Invasion!: the D-Day story, June 6th, 1944 *(London: Beaverbrook Newspapers 1954),* [*122p.*]

EDWARDS, Kenneth
Operation Neptune *(London: Collins 1946), 319p.*

EISENHOWER FOUNDATION
D-Day: the Normandy invasion in retrospect *(Lawrence, Kan: Kansas UP 1971), 254p.*

ELLIS, Lionel F
Victory in the West *(London: HMSO 1962), vol. I:* the battle of Normandy, *xix, 595p.*

ELLSBERG, Edward
The far shore *(New York: Dodd 1960), 381p.*

ESSAME, Hubert
Normandy bridgehead *(New York: Ballantine 1970), 160p, bib.*

FLORENTIN, Eddy
Battle of the Falaise Gap *(London: Elek [1965]), 336p, bib.*

GALE, Sir Richard N
With the 6th Airborne Division in Normandy *(London: Sampson Low 1948), xv, 160p.*

HARRISON, Gordon A
Cross-channel attack *(Washington DC: Department of Army 1951), 519p.*

HARRISON, Michael
Mulberry: the return in triumph *(London: W H Allen 1965), 286p, bib.*

HOWARTH, David A
Dawn of D-Day *(London: Collins 1959), 255p; US title:* D-Day, the sixth of June, 1944.

HUNTER, R H
Battle coast: an illustrated history of D-Day, the sixth of June, 1944 *(London: Spurbooks 1973), 3–142p.*

JOHNS, Glover S
The clay pigeons of St. Lô *(Harrisburg, Pa: Military Service 1958), 224p; UK title:* The battle of St. Lô.

KOSKIMAKI, George E
D-Day with the Screaming Eagles *(New York: Vantage 1970), 416p.*

LERNER, Daniel
Sykewar: psychological warfare against Germany, D-Day *(New York: Stewart 1949), xxvii, 377p.*

LIEBLING, Abbot J
Normandy revisited *(New York: Simon & Schuster 1958), xi, 243p.*

LIPSCOMB, Frank W
D-Day story *(Southsea, Hants: Matthews 1965), 60p.*

MACCLOSKEY, Monro
Torch and the Twelfth Air Force *(New York: Richards Rosen 1971), 192p.*

MCELWEE, William
The battle of D-Day *(London: Faber 1965), 3–132p.*

MCKEE, Alexander
Caen: anvil of victory *(London: Souvenir 1964), 368p.*

MACKSEY, Kenneth John
Battle *(London: Macdonald & Janes 1974), 204p; US title:* Anatomy of a battle.

MARSHALL, Samuel L A
Night drop: the American air-borne invasion of Normandy *(Boston, Mass: Little, Brown 1962), iii–xxii, 425p.*
MASON, David
Breakout: drive to the Seine *(New York: Ballantine 1968), 160p, bib.*
MELVILLE, Alan (pseud)
First tide: D-Day invasion, June 6th, 1944 *(London: Skeffington 1945), 140p.*
MICHIE, Allan A
The invasion of Europe: the story behind D-Day *(New York: Dodd 1964), 203p.*
MORGAN, *Sir* Frederick
Overture to Overlord *(London: Hodder & Stoughton [1950]), 296p.*
NORMAN, Albert
Operation Overlord; design and reality: the Allied invasion of Western Europe *(Harrisburg, Pa: Military Service 1952), xiv, 230p.*
PERRAULT, Gilles
The secrets of D-Day *(London: Barker [1965]), 238p.*
RENAUD, Alexandre
Sainte Mere-Eglise: first American bridgehead in France, 6th June 1944 *(Monaco: Pathe 1964), 198p.*
REYBURN, Wallace
Dawn landing *(London: Brown, Watson 1958), 160p.*
ROWAN-ROBINSON, Henry
Onward from D-Day *(London: Hutchinson 1946), 175p.*
RYAN, Cornelius
The longest day: June 6th 1944 *(London: Gollancz 1960), 256p, bib.*
SAWYER, John
D-Day *(London: Landsborough 1960), 160p, bib.*
SCHOFIELD, Brian B
Operation Neptune *(London: Allan 1974), 168p, bib.*
SPEIDEL, Hans
We defended Normandy *(London: Jenkins 1951), 182p.*
STAGG, James M
Forecast for Overlord, June 6th, 1944 *(London: Allan 1971), 128p.*
STIMSON, Henry L
Prelude to invasion: an account based on official reports *(Washington DC: American Council on Public Affairs 1944), 332p.*

THOMPSON, Reginald W
D-Day: spearhead of invasion *(New York: Ballantine 1968), 160p, bib.*
The price of victory *(London: Constable [1960]), xii, 279p, bib.*
TOBIN, Richard L
Invasion journal *(New York: Dutton 1944), 7-223p.*
TURNER, John F
Invasion '44: the full story of D-Day *(London: Harrap 1959), 253p.*
TUTE, Warren *and others*
D-Day *(London: Sidgwick & Jackson 1974), 256p.*
UTAH Beach to Cherbourg, 6 June–27 June, 1944 *(Washington DC: Government Printing Office 1948), 213p.*
US MILITARY ACADEMY WEST POINT
The invasion of Western Europe *(New York: West Point 1946), 2 vols.*
US WAR DEPARTMENT
Omaha Beachhead, 6 June–13 June, 1944 *(Washington DC: Government Printing Office 1945), 167p.*
St-Lô, 7 July–19 July, 1944 *(Washington DC: War Department 1947), 128p.*
WATNEY, John B
The enemy within: a personal impression of the invasion of Normandy *(London: Hodder & Stoughton 1946), 254p.*
WERTENBAKER, Charles
Invasion *(New York: Appleton 1944), ix, 168p.*
[*see also* AIRBORNE FORCES, GLIDER PILOTS, MULBERRY, WESTERN EUROPE 1944–5]

NORTH AFRICA

AGHION, Raoul
War in the desert: the battle for Africa *(London: Hutchinson 1941), xvii, 300p.*
BARNETT, Correlli
The desert generals *(London: Kimber 1960), 320p.*
BARTIMUS (pseud)
The turn of the road: being the story of the part played by the R.N. and Merchant Navy in the landings in Algeria and French Morocco of combined British and U.S. Forces on 8th November 1942 and the final destruction of the Axis Forces in North Africa *(London: Chatto & Windus 1946), 122p.*

BERNSTEIN, B L
The tide turned at Alamein: impressions of the desert war with the South Africa Division and the Eighth Army, June 1941-Jan 1943 *(Johannesburg: Central News 1944), 144p.*

BHARUCHA, P C
The North African campaign, 1940-1943 *(London: Longmans Green 1956), xxx, 567p.*

BINGHAM, James K W *and* HAUPT, Werner
North African campaign, 1940-1943 *(London: Macdonald 1969), 160p.*

BLUMENSON, Martin
Rommel's last victory: the battle of Kasserine Pass *(London: Allen & Unwin 1968), x, 341p, bib.*

BRADDOCK, David W
The campaigns in Egypt and Libya, 1940-1942 *(Aldershot, Hants: Gale & Polden 1964), x, 184p, bib.*

CARELL, Paul
The foxes of the desert *(London: Macdonald 1960), [14], 370p.*

CLIFFORD, Alexander
Crusader *(London: Harrap 1942), 190p.*
Three against Rommel: the campaigns of Wavell, Auchinleck and Alexander *(London: Harrap 1943), 428p; US title:* Conquest of North Africa, 1940-1943.

THE CONQUEST of North Africa: the first complete authoritative account of the entire three years, North African campaign from Egypt to Tunisia *(London: Burke 1943), 5-78p.*

CRAWFORD, Kenneth G
Report on North Africa *(New York: Farrar 1943), xv, 206p.*

CRIMP, Reginald L
The diary of a desert rat *(London: Cooper 1971), [9], 210p.*

DASHIELL, Samuel
Victory through Africa *(New York: Smith & Durrell 1943), 320p.*

DUPUY, Trevor N
Land battles: North Africa, Sicily, and Italy *(New York: Watts 1962), [6], 90p.*

FARRAR-HOCKLEY, Anthony
The war in the desert *(London: Faber 1969), 128p, bib.*

GALLAGHER, Wesley
Back door to Berlin: the full story of the American coup in North Africa *(New York: Doubleday 1943), vii, 242p.*

GERVASI, Frank
But soldiers wondered why *(New York: Doubleday 1943), xvii, 267p.*

GOSSET, Renee P
Algiers; 1941-1943: a temporary expedient *(London: Cape 1945), 260p; US title:* Conspiracy in Algiers, 1942-1943.

GREAT BRITAIN. Ministry of Information
Eighth Army: from Alamein to Tripoli *(London: HMSO 1944), unp.*

HILL, Russell
Desert conquest *(London: Jarrolds 1944), 160p.*
Desert war *(London: Jarrolds 1943), 140p.*

HOLMES, Richard
Bir Hacheim: desert citadel *(New York: Ballantine 1971), 160p, bib.*

HORIZON (periodical)
Desert war in North Africa *(New York: American Heritage 1968), 151p.*

HOUART, Victor
Desert squadron *(London: Souvenir 1959), 167p.*

HOUGHTON, George W
They flew through sand: the notes and sketches of an R.A.F. officer in the Western Desert *(London: Jarrolds 1943), 120p.*

HOWE, George F
Northwest Africa: seizing the initiative in the West *(Washington DC: Department of Army 1957), 784p.*

JONES, Vincent
Operation Torch *(New York: Ballantine 1972), 159p.*

KINGHORN, Alan
The dynamic war: a study in military leadership in the British-German campaigns in North Africa, February 1941-January 1943 *(New York: Exposition 1967), 121p.*

MCDOWELL, Ernest R *and* HESS, W N
Checkertail clan: the 325th fighter group in North Africa and Italy *(Fallbrook, Calif: Aero 1969), 98p.*

MACKSEY, Kenneth J
Beda Fomm *(New York: Ballantine 1971), 160p. bib.*

MACMILLAN, Richard
Rendezvous with Rommel: the story of the Eighth Army *(London: Jarrolds 1943), 198p; US title:* Mediterranean assignment.

MCVANE, John
Journey into war: war and diplomacy in North Africa *(New York: Appleton 1943), xi, 330p; UK title:* War and diplomacy in North Africa.

MARSHALL, Howard P
Over to Tunis: the complete story of the North African campaign *(London: Eyre & Spottiswoode 1943), vi, 7-167p.*

MAUGHAM, Robin
Come to dust *(London: Chapman & Hall 1945), 191p.*

MONTGOMERY, Bernard L, *1st viscount Montgomery of Alamein*
El Alamein to the River Sangro *(London: Hutchinson 1948), 190p.*

MOOREHEAD, Alan
The desert war: the North African campaign, 1940-1943 *(London: Hamilton 1965), 279p.*
Eclipse *(London: Hamilton 1945), 255p.*
The end in Africa *(London: Hamilton 1943), 210p.*
Mediterranean front *(London: Hamilton 1941), 304p.*
A year of battle *(London: Hamilton 1943), 256p.*

MOYNET, Paul
Victory in the Fezzan *(London: Hutchinson 1944), 47p.*

OGILVIE, Eain G
Libyan log: Empire air forces Western Desert, July 1941-July 1942 *(Edinburgh: Oliver & Boyd 1943), 103p.*

ONSLOW, William A B, *6th earl of Onslow*
Men and sand *(London: St Catherine 1961), xi, 140p.*

PARRIS, John A *and* RUSSELL, Ned
Springboard to Berlin *(New York: Crowell 1943), 401p.*

PENDAR, Kenneth
Adventure in diplomacy: the emergence of General de Gaulle in North Africa *(London: Cassell 1966), xviii, 382p.*

POTTS, Charles
Soldier in the sand *(London: PRM [1962]), [7], 201p.*

PRICE, George W
Giraud and the African scene *(New York: Macmillan 1944), xi, 282p.*

PYLE, Ernest T
Here is your war *(New York: Holt 1943), 304p.*

RAMSEY, Guy H
One continent redeemed *(London: Harrap 1943), 256p.*

RANDLE, Edwin H
Safi adventure: the first operation of a famous regimental combat team *(Belleair, Fla: Eldnar [1969]), 2nd ed, 222p.*

RODGER, George
Desert journey *(London: Cresset 1944), 151p.*

ROWAN-ROBINSON, Henry
Auchinleck to Alexander *(London: Hutchinson 1943), 195p.*
RUTHERFORD, Ward
Kasserine: baptism of fire *(New York: Ballantine 1970), 160p, bib.*
STRATHERN, Robert F
Lest I forget: being the record of a tour through Northern Africa and part of the Middle East *(Durban, SA: Church 1947), 120p.*
STRAWSON, John
The battle for North Africa *(London: Batsford 1969), xiii, 226p, bib.*
TALBOT, Godfrey W
Speaking from the desert: a record of the Eighth Army in Africa *(London: Hutchinson 1944), 153p.*
TUNNELL, James M
Military installations in North Africa and the Middle East *(Washington DC: Government Printing Office 1945), 66p.*
US MILITARY ACADEMY WEST POINT
The war in North Africa *(New York, West Point 1945), 2 pts.*
WORDELL, Malcolm T *and* SEILER, E N
Wildcats over Casablanca *(Boston, Mass: Little, Brown 1943), x, 309p.*
[*see also* BRITISH ARMY (EIGHTH ARMY), EL ALAMEIN, MEDITERRANEAN, MIDDLE EAST, TUNISIA, US ARMY]

NORTH ATLANTIC

ALLEN, Kenneth
Battle of the Atlantic *(London: Wayland 1973), 96p, bib.*
EASTON, Alan
50 North: an Atlantic battleground *(London: Eyre & Spottiswoode 1963), 287p.*
GANDER, Leonard M
Atlantic battle: a personal narrative *(London: Hutchinson 1941), 95p.*
LANYARD (pseud)
Stand by to ram: a stirring and graphic account of dramatic episodes in the great battle of the Atlantic *(London: Crosby Lockwood 1943), v, 7-114, vii-viiip.*
MACINTYRE, Donald
Battle of the Atlantic 1939-1945 *(London: Lutterworth 1970), 80p.*
NIMITZ, Chester W *and others* (eds)
Triumph in the Atlantic: the naval struggle against the Axis *(New York: Prentice-Hall 1964), 188p.*

RAYNER, Denys A
Escort: the battle of the Atlantic *(London: Kimber 1955), 250p.*
WEYMSS, David E G
Relentless pursuit *(London: Kimber 1955), 128p.*
WOODROOFFE, Thomas
The battle of the Atlantic *(London: Faber 1965), 5-120p, bib.*
[*see also* CONVOYS, DESTROYERS, GERMAN NAVY, ROYAL NAVY, SUBMARINES, U-BOATS, US NAVY]

NORWAY

ADAMSON, Hans C *and* KLEM, Per
Blood on the midnight sun *(New York: Norton 1964), 282p.*
ASH, Bernard
Norway, 1940 *(London: Cassell 1964), 340p.*
ASTRUP, Helen *and* JACOT, Bernard L
Night has a thousand eyes *(London: Macdonald 1953), x, 11-221p; US title:* Oslo intrigue.
BROCH, Theodore
The mountains wait *(London: Joseph 1943), 191p.*
BROOKES, Ewart
Prologue to a war *(London: Jarrolds 1966), 192p, bib.*
BUCKLEY, Christopher
Norway, The Commandos, Dieppe *(London: HMSO 1952), viii, 276p.*
CHRISTENSEN, Synnove (pseud)
Norway is my country *(London: Collins 1943), 160p.*
COOK, Raymond A
Last boat from Bergen; or, Norway as it was and is now *(Newcastle-upon-Tyne: Reed 1943), 72p.*
CURTIS, Monica (ed)
Norway and the war: Sept 1939–Dec 1940 *(London: Oxford UP 1941), x, 154p.*
DERRY, Thomas K
The campaign in Norway *(London: HMSO 1952), xvi, 289p, bib.*
DYBWAD, Ejner
I saw the invader: the destiny of Norway *(London: Pilot 1940), 7-95p.*
EITINGER, Leo
Concentration camp survivors in Norway and Israel *(London: Allen & Unwin 1965), 199p, bib.*
FEN, Ake
Nazis in Norway *(London: Penguin 1943), 156p.*

FJELIBU, Arne
Memoirs from the war years *(Minneapolis, Minn: Augsburg 1947), 106p.*

FOLEY, Thomas
I was an Altmark prisoner *(London: Aldor 1940), 127p.*

FRIDTJOF (pseud)
Why Norway?: a contribution to the history of Germany's aggression against the North *(London: Hutchinson 1942), 76p.*

GUTTORMSON, Olga
Ships will sail again *(Minneapolis, Minn: Augsburg 1942), 7-96p.*

HAMBRO, Carl J
I saw it happen in Norway *(London: Hodder & Stoughton 1940), viii, 219p.*

HANNSON, Per
The greatest gamble *(London: Allen & Unwin 1967), 3-180p.*

HARRIMAN, Florence J
Mission to the North *(London: Harrap 1941), 240p.*

HAUGE, Eiliv O
Odds against Norway *(London: Drummond 1942), vi, 218p.*
Salt-water thief *(London: Duckworth 1958), 159p.*

HAUKELID, Knut
Skis against the atom *(London: Kimber 1954), 201p.*

HOVELSEN, Leif
Out of the evil night *(London: Blandsford 1959), 160p.*

HOWARTH, David A
Shetland bus *(London: Nelson 1951), 220p; US title:* Across to Norway.
We die alone *(London: Collins 1955), 256p.*

JOHN, Evan (pseud)
Lofoten letter *(London: Heinemann 1941), 67p.*

JOHNSON, Amanda
Norway - her invasion and occupation *(Milledgeville, Ga: Johnson 1948), x, 372p.*

KLEFOS, Brede
They came in the night: wartime experiences of a Norwegian American *(New York: Crown 1959), 206p.*

KOHT, Halvdan
Norway neutral and invaded *(London: Hutchinson 1941), 253p.*

LEHMKUHL, Dik
Journey to London: the story of the Norwegian Government at war *(London: Hutchinson 1946), 152p.*

LEHMKUHL, Herman K
Hitler attacks Norway *(London: Hodder & Stoughton 1943), 99p.*

MacClure, Victor
Gladiators over Norway *(London: W H Allen 1942), 5-46p.*

Manus, Max
Nine lives before thirty *(New York: Doubleday 1947), 328p.*
Underwater saboteur *(London: Kimber 1953), 239p.*

Moën, Lars
Under the iron heel *(London: Hale 1941), 285p.*

Moen, Petter
Diary *(New York: Farrar 1951), xii, 176p.*

Moulton, James L
The Norwegian campaign of 1940: a study of warfare in three dimensions *(London: Eyre & Spottiswoode 1966), 328p. bib.*

Myklebost, Tor
They came as friends *(London: Gollancz 1943), 204p.*

Norway does not yield: the story of the first year *(New York: American Friends of German Freedom 1941), 64p.*

Norway. Royal Norwegian Government Information Office
Arctic war: Norway's role in the Northern Front *(London: HMSO 1945), 64p.*
The Gestapo at work in Norway *(London 1942), 38p.*

Nyquist, Roi B
Fighting Norsemen *(London: Hutchinson 1944), 80p.*
Sons of the Vikings *(London: Hutchinson 1943), 128p.*

Olav, Hans *and* Gjesdal, Tor (eds)
Norway *(New York: Norwegian News 1941), 72p.*

Olsen, Oluf R
Two eggs on my plate *(London: Allen & Unwin 1952), 301p.*

Sharp, Gene
Tyranny could not quell them: how Norway's teachers defeated Quisling during the Nazi occupation *(London: Peace News [1959]), 23p.*

Sønsteby, Gunnar F T
Report from no. 24 *(New York: Stuart 1965), 192p.*

Vigness, Paul C
The German occupation of Norway *(New York: Vantage 1970), 285p.*

Walker, Roy
A people who loved peace: the Norwegian struggle against Nazism *(London: Gollancz 1946), 111p.*

Warbey, William
Look to Norway *(London: Secker & Warburg 1945), 242p.*

WORM-MÜLLER, Jacob S
Norway revolts against the Nazis *(London: Drummond 1941), unp.*
WRIGHT, Myrtle
Norwegian diary, 1940–1945 *(London: Friends Peace and International Relations Committee 1974), vi, 255p.*
[*see also* COMMANDOS, HEAVY WATER, NARVIK]

NORWICH

MOTTRAM, Ralph H
Assault upon Norwich: the official account of the air raids on the city *(Norwich, Norfolk: Soman-Wherry 1945), 38p.*

NOVA SCOTIA

NOVA SCOTIA helps the fighting man *(Halifax, NS: King's 1945), 64p.*

NUREMBERG (bombing)

CAMPBELL, James
The bombing of Nuremberg *(London: Allison & Busby 1973), iii–xii, 194p.*
MIDDLEBROOK, Martin
The Nuremberg raid, 30–31 March 1944 *(New York: Morrow 1974), 369p.*

NUREMBERG (trials)

ALEXANDER, Charles W
Justice at Nuernberg: a pictorial record of the trial of Nazi war criminals *(Chicago, Ill: Marvel 1946), 193p.*
ANDRUS, Burton C
The infamous of Nuremburg *(London: Frewin 1969), 211p.*
BENTON, Wilbourn E *and* GRIMM, Georg (eds)
Nuremberg: German views of the war trials *(Dallas, Tex: Southern Methodist UP 1955), 232p.*
BERNSTEIN, Victor H
Final judgment: the story of Nuremberg *(London: Latimer House 1947), 289p.*
BIDDLE, Francis B
In brief authority *(New York: Doubleday 1962), 494p.*
CALVOCORESSI, Peter
Nuremberg: the facts, the law and the consequences *(London: Chatto & Windus 1947), 176p.*

CBS NEWS
Trial at Nuremberg *(New York: Watts 1968), 66p.*

COOPER, B W
The Nuremberg trial *(London: Penguin 1947), 301p.*

DAVIDSON, Eugene
The trial of the Germans: an account of the twenty-two defendants before the International Military Tribunal at Nuremberg *(New York: Macmillan 1967), 636p.*

DUBOIS, Josiah E
Generals in grey suits: the directors of the International 'I.G. Farben' cartel, their conspiracy and trial at Nuremberg *(London: Lane 1953), x, 374p; US title:* The devil's chemists.

FISHMAN, Jack
The seven men of Spandau *(London: W H Allen 1954), 234p.*

FRITZSCHE, Hans
The sword in the scales *(London: Wingate 1953), 335p.*

GALLAGHER, Richard
Nuremberg: the Third Reich on trial *(New York: Avon 1961), 255p.*

GIBB, Andrew D
Perjury unlimited: a monograph on Nuremberg *(Edinburgh: Green 1954), 62p.*

GILBERT, Gustave M
Nuremberg diary *(New York: Farrar 1947), 430p.*

GLUECK, Sheldon
The Nuremberg trial and aggressive war *(New York: Knopf 1946), 121p.*

GREAT BRITAIN. War Office
The trials of German major war criminals *(London: HMSO 1948), 26 vols.*

HARRIS, Whitney R
Tyranny on trial: the evidence at Nuremberg *(Dallas, Tex: Southern Methodist UP 1954), xxxvii, 608p.*

HEYDECKER, Joe *and* LEEB, Johannes
The Nuremberg trials *(London: Heinemann [1962]), xii, 379p, bib.*

JACKSON, Robert H
The case against the Nazi war criminals: opening statement for the United States of America, and other documents *(New York: Knopf 1946), xiii, 216p.*
The Nurnberg case as presented by Robert H. Jackson, chief counsel for the United States, together with other documents *(New York: Knopf 1947), 268p.*

KELLEY, Douglas McG
22 cells in Nuremberg: a psychiatrist examines the Nazi criminals *(London: Allen & Unwin 1947), 245p.*

KNIERIEM, August von
The Nuremberg trials *(Chicago, Ill: Regnery 1959), xxii, 561p.*

TRIALS of war criminals before the Nuernberg Military Tribunals, October 1946–April 1949 *(Washington DC: US Government Printing Office 1949–53), 15 vols.*

US CHIEF OF COUNSEL for the Prosecution of Axis criminality
Nazi conspiracy and aggression *(Washington DC: US Government Printing Office 1946), 8 vols.*
Supplement A-B. *1947–48, 2 vols.*

WEST, Rebecca
A train of powder *(London: Macmillan 1955), 331p.*

WOETZEL, Robert K
The Nuremberg trials in international law *(London: Stevens 1960), 287p.*

NURSES AND NURSING

ARCHARD, Thersa
G.I. Nightingale: the story of an American Army nurse *(New York: Norton 1945), 187p.*

BARTLETT, Dorothy A
Nurse in war *(London: P. R. Macmillan 1961), 265p.*

BOWDEN, Jean
Grey touched with scarlet: the war experiences of the Army Nursing Sisters *(London: Hale [1959]), 189p.*

BRIGHT, Pamela
Life in our hands *(London: MacGibbon & Kee 1955), 208p.*

COOPER, Page
Navy nurse *(London: Whittlesey House 1946), 226p.*

EDGE, Catherine *and* JOHNSTON, Mary E
The ships of youth: the experiences of two Army Nursing Sisters on board the hospital carrier Leinster *(London: Hodder & Stoughton 1945), 124p.*

HARDISON, Irene
A nightingale in the jungle *(Philadelphia, Pa: Dorrance 1954), 133p.*

HARRISON, Ada M (ed)
Grey and scarlet: letters from the war areas by Army Sisters on active service *(London: Hodder & Stoughton 1944), 200p.*

HASKELL, Ruth G
Helmets and lipstick *(New York: Putnam 1944), 9–207p.*

LIM, Janet
Sold for silver *(London: Collins 1958), 255p.*

NEWCOMB, Ellsworth
Brave nurse: true stories of heroism *(New York: Appleton 1945), x, 176p.*

PETO, Marjorie
Women were not expected: an informal story of the nurses of 2nd General Hospital in the ETO *(Englewood, NJ: Peto 1948), 364p.*

SANDBACH, Betsy *and* EDGE, Geraldine
Prison life on Pacific raider: the adventures of nurse escorts to the first 50 children evacuated to Australia *(London: Hodder & Stoughton 1941), x, 13-222p.*

WARD, Irene
F.A.N.Y. Invicta *(London: Hutchinson 1955), 348p.*

OCCULT

AGATHANGELOS, Ieromahos
Prophecy of the war and the after effects with forecast for every year from 1939-1946; believed to have been written 500 years ago *(Boston, Mass: Gargilis 1941), 7-72p.*

BROWNVILLE, Charles G
Hitler's short day, and other revealing messages on world events *(Grand Rapids, Mich: Zondervan 1943), 113p.*

BYWATER, Hector C
The great Pacific war: a historic prophecy now being fulfilled *(Boston, Mass: Houghton Mifflin 1942), viii, 321p.*

HOWE, Ellic
Nostradamus and the Nazis: a footnote to the history of the Third Reich *(London: Arborfield 1965), 138p.*

REED, Clarence (comp)
Great prophecies about the war *(London: Faber 1941), 64p; US title:* Prophecies about the war in Europe.

SAVA, George (pseud)
Rasputin speaks *(London: Faber 1941), 323p.*

SPENCE, Lewis
Occult causes of the present war *(London: Rider 1940), 191p.*
Will Europe follow Atlantis *(London: Rider 1942), xiii, 15-197p.*

WOOD, Frederic H
Mediumship and war *(London: Rider 1942), xiii, 15-140p.*

ODER-NEISSE LINE

Jordan, Z
Oder-Neisse Line: a study of the political, economic and European significance of Poland's western frontier *(London: Polish Freedom Movement 1952), 141p.*

Rhode, Gotthold *and* Wagner, Wolfgang (eds)
The genesis of the Oder-Neisse Line in the diplomatic negotiations during World War II: sources and documents *(Stuttgart: Brentano-Verlag 1959), 287p.*

Szaz, Zoltan M
Germany's eastern frontiers: the problem of the Oder-Neisse Line *(Chicago, Ill: Regnery 1960), 256p.*

Wiskemann, Elizabeth
Germany's eastern neighbours: problems relating to the Oder-Neisse Line and the Czech frontier region *(London: Oxford UP 1956), 309p.*

OIL

Baker, Robert L
Oil, blood and sand *(New York: Appleton 1942), xvii, 300p.*

Friedwald, Eugene M
Oil and the war *(London: Heinemann 1941), 88p.*

Ickes, Harold L
Fightin' oil *(New York: Knopf 1943), x, 174p.*

Look (periodical)
Oil for victory: the story of petroleum in war and peace *(New York: McGraw-Hill 1946), 287p.*

Popple, Charles S
Standard Oil Company, New Jersey in World War II *(New York: Standard Oil Company 1952), 340p.*

OKINAWA

Appleman, Roy E *and others*
Okinawa: the last battle *(Rutland, Vt: Tuttle 1960), xxiii, 527p.*

Belote, James H *and* Belote, W M
Typhoon of steel: the battle for Okinawa *(New York: Harper 1970), 368p.*

Frank, Benis M
Okinawa: capstone to victory *(New York: Ballantine 1969), 160p, bib.*

US MARINE CORPS
Okinawa: victory in the Pacific *(Washington DC: US Marine Corps 1955), viii, 332p, bib.*
WERSTEIN, Irving
Okinawa: the last ordeal *(New York: Crowell 1968), 179p.*
[*see also* PACIFIC, US MARINES]

OPERATION SEA LION

ANSEL, Walter
Hitler confronts England *(Durham, NC: Duke UP 1960), xviii, 348p.*
CLARKE, Comer
England under Hitler *(New York: Ballantine 1961), 143p; UK title:* If the Nazis had come.
FLEMING, Peter
Invasion 1940: an account of the German preparations and British counter-measures *(London: Hart-Davis 1957), 323p; US title:* Operation Sea Lion.
GERMAN occupied Great Britain: ordinances of the military authorities *(London: Scott [1971]), 3-94p.*
GRINNELL-MILNE, Duncan
The silent victory; September 1940 *(London: Lane 1956), 208p, bib.*
LAMPE, David
The last ditch *(London: Cassell 1968), iii-xix, 219p.*
LONGMATE, Norman
If Britain had fallen *(London: BBC 1972), 276p, bib.*
NECKLER, Wilhelm
Hitler's war machine, and the invasion of Britain *(London: Drummond 1941), viii, 282p.*
This bewildering war *(London: Drummond 1940), 344p.*
STRATEGICUS (pseud)
Can Britain be invaded? *(London: Dent 1941), 63p.*
WHEATLEY, Ronald
Operation Sea Lion: German plans for the invasion of England, 1939-1942 *(Oxford: Clarendon 1958), xiv, 201p, bib.*

ORIGINS OF WAR

ANGELL, *Sir* Norman
Let the people know *(New York: Viking 1943), ix, 245p.*
ARMSTRONG, George G
Why another world war? how we missed collective security *(London: Allen & Unwin 1941), 224p.*

Aster, Sidney
1939: The making of the Second World War *(London: Deutsch 1973), 456p, bib.*

Bain, Leslie B
War of confusion *(New York: Mill 1942), 13–155p.*

Baker, Leonard
Roosevelt and Pearl Harbor *(New York: Macmillan 1970), 356p.*

Baynes, Helton G
Germany possessed *(London: Cape 1941), 305p.*

Benson, Oliver E
Through the diplomatic looking-glass: immediate origins of the war in Europe *(Norman, Okl: Oklahoma UP 1939), ix, 239p.*

Borgese, Guiseppe A
Common cause *(New York: Duell 1943), vi, 448p.*

Cave, Floyd A *and others*
Origins and consequences of World War II *(New York: Dryden 1948), xv, 820p.*

Clarkson, Alexander F K
Europe in eclipse *(London: Hale 1941), xi–xv, 346p.*

Colvin, Ian G
The Chamberlain Cabinet: how the meetings in 10 Downing Street, 1937-1939, led to the Second World War *(London: Gollancz 1971), 286p.*
Vansittart in office: an historical survey of the origins of the Second World War based on the papers of Sir Robert Vansittart *(London: Gollancz 1965), 360p; US title:* None so blind.

De Courcy, John
Behind the battle *(London: Eyre & Spottiswoode 1942), 262p.*

Divine, Robert A (ed)
Causes and consequences of World War II *(Chicago, Ill: Quadrangle 1969), 375p.*

Eimerl, Sarel
Hitler over Europe: the road to World War II *(Boston, Mass: Little, Brown 1971), 179p.*

Eubank, Keith
The origins of World War II *(New York: Crowell 1969), 194p.*
The road to World War II: a documentary history *(New York: Crowell 1973), 284p.*

Fisher, Herbert A L
The background and issues of the war: six lectures *(London: Oxford UP 1940), vi, 141p.*

FREEMAN, Kathleen
What they said at the time: a survey of the causes of the Second World War *(London: Muller 1945), 470p.*
FURNIA, Arthur H
The diplomacy of appeasement: Anglo-French relations and the prelude to World War II, 1931-1938 *(Washington: Washington UP 1960), 454p.*
GANTERBEIN, James W
Documentary background of World War II, 1931-1941 *(New York: Columbia UP 1948), 1112p.*
GERMANY. Auswärtiges Amt
Documents and materials relating to the eve of the Second World War *(New York: International 1948), 2 vols.*
GRENFELL, Russell
Unconditional hatred: German war guilt and the future of Europe *(New York: Devin-Adair 1953), 273p.*
GREW, Joseph C
Report from Tokyo: a message to the American people, *(New York: Simon & Schuster 1942), xxvii, 88p.*
Ten years in Japan: a contemporary record drawn from the diaries and private and official papers of Joseph C. Grew, United States ambassador to Japan, 1932-1942 *(Westport, Conn: Greenwood 1973), 554p.*
GUNTHER, John
The high cost of Hitler *(London: Hamilton 1939), 126p.*
HAINES, Charles G *and* HOFFMAN, R J S
The origins and background of the Second World War *(London: Oxford UP 1943), 659p.*
HELLER, Bernard
Dawn or dusk? *(New York: Bookman's 1962), 314p.*
HOFER, Walther
War premeditated, 1939 *(London: Thames & Hudson* [*1955*]*), 227p, bib.*
HOOPER, Sydney E (ed)
The deeper causes of the war and its issues *(Freeport NY: Books for Libraries 1970), 206p.*
KEITH, Arthur B
Causes of the war *(London: Nelson 1940), 573p.*
KERILLIS, Henri de *and* CARTIER, Raymond
Kerillis on the causes of the war *(London: Putnam 1939), 297p.*
KEUN, Odette
And hell followed . . . A European ally interprets the war for ordinary people like herself *(London: Constable 1942), 295p.*

KIRKCONNELL, Watson
Canada, Europe and Hitler *(London: Oxford UP 1940), vii, 213p.*
KLEINE-AHIBRANDT, William L (ed)
Appeasement of the dictators: crisis diplomacy *(New York: Holt 1970), 138p.*
KUHN, Helmut
Freedom forgotten and remembered *(London: Oxford UP 1943), 267p.*
LAFORE, Laurence D
The end of the glory: an interpretation of the origins of World War II *(Philadelphia, Pa: Lippincott 1970), 280p.*
LANDAU, Rom
We have seen evil: a background to war *(London: Faber 1941), 248p.*
LEE, Dwight E
Ten years: the world on the way to war, 1930–1940 *(Boston, Mass: Houghton Mifflin 1942), xviii, 443p.*
LOEWENHEIM, Francis L (ed)
Peace or appeasement? Hitler, Chamberlain, and the Munich crisis *(Boston, Mass: Houghton Mifflin 1965), 204p.*
LOUIS, William R
The origins of the Second World War - A. J. P. Taylor and his critics *(New York: Wiley 1972), x, 150p, bib.*
MCFARLANE, Charles T
The present war: its background and related developments *(New York: American 1940), 64p.*
War with the Axis: defending our freedom *(New York: American 1942), 136p.*
MARRIOTT, *Sir* John A R
The tragedy of Europe *(London: Blackie 1941), vii, 228p.*
MEE, Arthur
Why we had to go to war *(London: London UP 1939), 126p.*
MILLIS, Walter
Why Europe fights *(New York: Morrow 1940), vi, 277p.*
MOSLEY, Leonard
On borrowed time: how World War II began *(London: Weidenfeld & Nicolson 1969), xv, 509p, bib.*
MURRAY, Gilbert *and others*
The deeper causes of the war and its issues *(London: Allen & Unwin 1940), 206p.*
NEILSON, Francis
The makers of war *(Appleton, Wis: Nelson 1950), 240p.*

NOGUERES, Henri
Munich: peace for our time *(New York: McGraw-Hill 1965), 423p.*

OFFNER, Arnold A (ed)
America and the origins of World War II, 1933-1941 *(Boston, Mass: Houghton Mifflin 1971), 229p.*

PARKINSON, Roger
The origins of World War 2 *(London: Wayland 1970), 128p, bib.*

PETRIE, *Sir* Charles A
Twenty years armistice - and after: British foreign policy since 1918 *(London: Eyre & Spottiswoode 1940), vi, 296p.*

PREUSS, Ernst G
Merchants of death *(London: Hutchinson 1945), 80p.*

PRICE, Morgan P
Hitler's war and Eastern Europe *(London: Allen & Unwin 1940), 9-160p.*

RENOUVIN, Pierre
World War II and its origins: international relations, 1929-1945 *(New York: 1968), 402p.*

ROBERTSON, Esmonde M (ed)
The origins of the Second World War: historical interpretations *(London: Macmillan 1971), vii, 312p, bib.*

ROTHSTEIN, Andrew
Munich conspiracy *(London: Lawrence & Wishart 1958), 320p.*

ROWSE, Alfred L
Appeasement: a study in political decline, 1933-1939 *(New York: Norton 1961), 123p.*

SALVEMINI, Gaetano
Prelude to World War II *(London: Gollancz 1953), 519p.*

SANBORN, Frederic R
Design for war: a study of secret power politics, 1937-1941 *(New York: Devin-Adair 1951), 607p.*

SCANLON, John
But who has won? *(London: Allen & Unwin 1939), 11-282p.*

SLOSSON, Preston W
Why we are at war *(Boston, Mass: Houghton Mifflin 1942), vi, 90p.*

SNELL, John L
The outbreak of the Second World War: design or blunder *(Boston, Mass: Heath 1962), 107p.*

STRAUSZ-HUPE, Robert
Geopolitics: the struggle for space and power *(New York: Putnam 1942), xiii, 274p.*

TAYLOR, Alan J P
The origins of the Second World War *(London: Hamilton 1961), 296p, bib.*

THE TIMES (Newspaper)
Far East crisis: dream and reality *(London: The Times 1941), 125p.*

TRANSILL, Charles C
Backdoor to war: the Roosevelt foreign policy, 1933–1941 *(Chicago, Ill: Regnery 1952), 609p.*

TREFOUSSE, Hans L
Germany and American neutrality, 1939–1941 *(New York: Bookman 1951), 247p.*

WEGERER, Alfred von
The origins of World War II: a brief survey of the beginnings of the present war, on the basis of official documents *(New York: R R Smith 1941), viii, 13–128p.*

WHEELER-BENNETT, John W
Munich: prologue to tragedy *(London: Macmillan 1948), 507p.*

ZELOMEK, A W
This peculiar war *(New York: International Statistics Bureau 1940), xiv, 17–143p,*

OSS (OFFICE OF STRATEGIC SERVICE)

ALCORN, Robert H
No banners, no bands *(New York: McKay 1965), 192p; UK title:* Spies of the OSS.
No bugles for spies: tales of the OSS *(New York: McKay 1962), 209p.*

ALSOP, Stewart J S, *and* BRADEN, Thomas
Sub rosa: the OSS and American espionage *(New York: Harcourt 1964), 264p.*

BOOTH, Walter B
Mission Marcel-Proust: the story of an unusual OSS undertaking *(Philadelphia, Pa: Dorrance 1972), 168p.*

FORD, Corey
Donovan of O.S.S. *(Boston, Mass: Little, Brown 1970), iii–xvi, 366p, bib.*

FORD, Corey *and* MACBRAIN, Alastair
Cloak and dagger: the secret story of O.S.S. *(New York: Random House 1946), 216p.*

HALL, Roger
You're stepping on my cloak and dagger *(London: Kimber 1958), 205p.*

MORGAN, William J
The O.S.S. and I *(New York: Norton 1957), 281p.*
[*see also* SECRET SERVICES]

PACIFIC

ABEND, Hallett
Ramparts of the Pacific *(London: Lane 1942), xviii, 332p.*

BLIVEN, Bruce
From Pearl Harbor to Okinawa: the war in the Pacific, 1941–1945 *(New York: Random House 1960), 192p.*

CAIDIN, Martin *and* HYMOFF, Edward
The mission *(Philadelphia, Pa: Lippincott 1964), 208p.*

CANT, Gilbert
The great Pacific victory from the Solomons to Tokyo *(New York: Day 1946), 422p.*

CHAMBLISS, William C
The silent service *(London: Muller 1969), 158p.*

CLAUSEN, Walter B
Blood for the Emperor: a narrative history of the human side of the war in the Pacific *(New York: Appleton 1943), xii, 341p.*

CLIFFORD, L E
The leader of the crooks *(Melbourne, Ches: 1945), 221p.*

CONGDON, Don (comp)
Combat: war in the Pacific *(London: Mayflower 1965), 382p; US title:* Combat, the war with Japan.

CORKIN, Frank R
Pacific postmark: a series of letters from aboard a fighting destroyer in the war waters of the Pacific *(Meriden, Conn: Corking 1945), viii, 172p.*

DOS PASSOS, John
Tour of duty *(Boston, Mass: Houghton Mifflin 1946), 336p.*

DRISCOLL, Joseph
Pacific victory, 1945 *(Philadelphia, Pa: Lippincott 1949), 9–297p.*

DUPUY, Trevor N
The air war in the Pacific: victory in the air *(New York: Watts 1964), [6], 89p.*
Asiatic land battles: Japanese ambitions in the Pacific *(New York: Watts 1963), iv, 116p.*
The naval war in the Pacific: on to Tokyo *(New York: Watts 1964), [6], 90p.*
The rising sun of Nippon *(New York: Watts 1963), [6], 90p.*

EDMONDS, Walter D
They fought with what they had *(Boston, Mass: Little, Brown 1951), xxiii, 532p.*

EICHELBERGER. Robert L
Dear Miss Em: General Eichelberger's war in the Pacific, 1942–1945 *(Westport, Conn: Greenwood 1972), 322p.*
Jungle road to Tokyo *(London: Odhams 1951), 288p.*

ELLIS, Albert F
Mid-Pacific outposts *(Auckland, NZ: Brown & Stewart 1946), 303p.*

FAHEY, James J
Pacific war diary, 1942-1945 *(Boston: Mass: Houghton Mifflin 1963), 404p.*

FOSTER, John M
Hell in the heavens *(New York: Putnam 1961), 320p.*

FRANCILLON, Rene J
U.S. Army Air Forces in the Pacific *(Fallbrook, Calif: Aero 1969), 96p.*

GREAT BRITAIN. Colonial Office
Among those present: the official story of the Pacific Islands at war *(London: HMSO 1946), 95p.*

GREAT BRITAIN. (Ministry of Information)
Ocean front: the story of the war in the Pacific, 1941–44 *(London: HMSO 1945), 65p.*

GREAT BRITAIN. (War Office)
The official names of the battles, actions, engagements fought by the land forces of the Commonwealth during the Australian campaign in the 'South-West Pacific, 1942-1945, and the New Zealand campaign in the South Pacific, 1942-1944', and the Korean campaign 1950–1953 *(London: HMSO 1958), 18p.*

HAILEY, Foster B
Pacific battle line *(New York: Macmillan 1944), ix, 405p.*

HAMMER, David H
Lion six *(Annapolis, Md: US Naval Institute 1947), 107p.*

HODGE, Clarence L *and* BEFELER, Murray (eds)
Pearl Harbor to Tokyo *(Honolulu: Tongg 1945), 156p.*

HORAN, James D *and* FRANK, Gerold (eds)
Out in the boondocks: Marines in action in the Pacific *(New York: Putnam 1943), xi, 209p.*

HOUGH, Donald *and* ARNOLD, Elliott
Big distance *(New York: Duell 1945), 255p.*

HOWARD, Clive *and* WHITLEY, Joe
One damned island after another *(Chapel Hill, NC: Carolina UP 1946), 403p.*
HOWARD, Richard A
999 survived: an analysis of survival experiences in the Southwest Pacific *(Maxwell Air Force Base, Ala: Air University 1953), 60p.*
HOWLETT, Robert A
Battleground South Pacific *(Rutland, Vt: Tuttle 1970), 223p.*
HOYT, Edwin P
How they won the war in the Pacific: Nimitz and his admirals *(New York: Weybright & Talley 1970), 554p.*
HUIE, William B
From Omaha to Okinawa: the story of the 'Seabees' *(New York: Dutton 1945), 257p.*
JOHNSTON, George H
The battle of the seaways *(London: Angus & Robertson 1941), xi, 240p.*
Pacific partner *(London: Duell 1944), ix, 227p.*
JOHNSTON, Stanley F
The grim reapers *(London: Jarrolds 1945), 108p.*
JOSEPHY, Alvin M
The long and the short and the tall: the story of a Marine combat unit in the Pacific *(New York: Knopf 1946), xx, 221p.*
KENNEDY, Paul
Pacific onslaught: 7th Dec 1941–7th Feb 1943 *(New York: Ballantine 1972), 160p, bib.*
KENNEY, George C
General Kenney reports: a personal history of the Pacific war *(New York: Duell 1949), xiv, 594p.*
The saga of Pappy Gunn *(New York: Duell 1959), 133p.*
LARDNER, John
South-west passage: the Yanks in the Pacific *(Philadelphia, Pa: Lippincott 1943), 5–302p.*
LEE, Clark G
They call it Pacific: an eye-witness story of our war against Japan from Bataan to the Solomons *(London: Long 1943), 224p.*
LITZ, Leo M
Report from the Pacific *(Indianapolis, Ind: Indianapolis News 1946), 427p.*
LOVE, Edmund G
War is a private affair *(New York: Harcourt 1959), 192p.*
McCABE, Graeme
Pacific sunset *(Hobart, Tas: Oldham 1946), 108p.*

MACINTYRE, Donald
The battle for the Pacific *(London: Batsford 1966), 240p, bib.*

MARTIN, Ralph G
Boy from Nebraska: the story of Ben Kuroki *(New York: Harper 1946), 208p.*
World War II: a photographic record of the war in the Pacific from Pearl Harbor to V-J Day *(Greenwich, Conn: Fawcett 1965), 224p.*

MATTHEWS, Allen R
The assault *(New York: Simon & Schuster 1947), 216p.*

MIDLAM, Don S
Flight of the lucky lady *(Portland, Ore: Binfords & Mort 1954), 208p.*

MILLER, Max
It's tomorrow out here *(New York: McGraw-Hill 1945), 186p.*

MILLER, Norman M
I took the sky road *(New York: Dodd 1945), 212p.*

MOODY, Dallas D
Aerial gunner from Virginia: the letters of Don Moody to his family during 1944 *(Richmond, Va: Virginia State Library 1950), 366p.*

MORRILL, John H *and* MARTIN, W T
South from Corregidor *(New York: Simon & Schuster 1943), x, 252p.*

MUNTHE, Malcolm
Sweet is war *(London: Duckworth 1954), 185p.*

MURPHY, Thomas D
Ambassadors in arms *(Hawaii: Hawaii UP 1954), 315p.*

NAVY TIMES (periodical)
Operation victory: winning the Pacific war *(New York: Putnam 1968), 192p.*

NEW YORK Museum of Modern Art
Power in the Pacific *(New York: US Camera 1945), 144p.*

NORTON-TAYLOR, Duncan
With my heart in my mouth *(New York: Coward-McCann 1944), 156p; UK title:* I went to see for myself.

PEYTON, Green (pseud)
5,000 miles towards Tokyo *(Norman, Okl: Oklahoma UP 1945), 173p.*

POTTER, Elmer B *and* NIMITZ, Chester W (eds)
Triumph in the Pacific: the Navy's struggle against Japan *(New York: Prentice-Hall 1963), 186p.*

PRATT, Fletcher
The fleet against Japan *(New York: Harper 1946), 263p.*
The Marines' war: an account of the struggle for the Pacific from both American and Japanese sources *(New York: Sloane 1948), 456p.*
Night work: the story of Task Force 39 *(New York: Holt 1946), 267p.*

PRIDAY, H E L
The war from Coconut Square *(Wellington, NZ: Reed 1943), 144p.*

RALEIGH, John M
Pacific blackout *(New York: Dodd 1943), ix, 244p.*

REYNOLDS, Quentin J
70,000 to 1: the story of Lieutenant Gordon Manuel *(New York: Random House 1946), 217p.*

RIEGELMAN, Harold
The caves of Biak: an American officer's experiences in the Southwest Pacific *(New York: Dial 1955), 278p.*

SEASHOLES, Henry C
Adrift in the South Pacific; or, Six nights in the Coral Sea *(Boston, Mass: Baker 1951), 55p.*

SHANE, Ted
Heroes of the Pacific *(New York: Messner 1944), x, 373p.*

SHERROD, Robert L
On to westward!: war in the Central Pacific *(New York: Duell 1945), 333p.*

SMITH, Holland M *and* FINCH, Percy
Coral and brass *(New York: Scribner 1949), 289p.*

SMITH, Stanley E
The battle of Savo *(New York: MacFadden-Bartell 1962), 152p.*
13 against the Rising Sun *(New York: Belmont 1961), 140p.*

SNOWDEN, Rita F
Safety last: stirring tales of the Pacific *(London: Epworth 1946), 204p.*

STEICHEN, Edward (comp)
U.S. Navy war photographs, Pearl Harbor to Tokyo Harbour: a collection of official U.S. Navy, Marine Corps and Coast Guard photographs *(New York: US Camera 1946), 108p.*

STRATTON, Roy O
Saco, the rice paddy navy *(Pleasantville, NY: Palmer 1950), 408p.*

TAYLOR, George E
America in the new Pacific *(New York: Macmillan 1942), 160p.*

THORPE, Elliott R
East wind, rain: the intimate account of an intelligence officer in the Pacific, 1939-1949 *(Boston, Mass: Gambit 1969), xxi, 307p.*

US ARMY
Engineers of the Southwest Pacific, 1941-1945: reports of operations in the Far East, Southwest Pacific area, Army Forces, Pacific *(Washington DC: US Government Printing Office 1947), 1948, 8 vols.*
History of the Second Engineer Special Brigade, U.S. Army World War II *(Harrisburg, Pa: Telegraph 1946), 269p.*

US MARINE CORPS
Marines in action: a review of the U.S. Marine Corps' operations in the Pacific phase of World War II, from Samoa to Peleliu *(Washington DC: Marine Corps Institute 1945), 61p.*
Saipan; the beginning of the end *(Washington DC: USMC 1950), 286p.*
The seizure of Tinian *(Washington DC: USMC 1951), 169p.*

US Naval aviation in the Pacific *(Washington DC: Office of Naval Operations 1947), 56p.*

US WAR DEPARTMENT
The capture of Makin, 20 November-24 November 1943 *(Washington DC: War Department 1946), 136p.*

WEES, Marshall P
King-doctor of Ulithi: the true story of the war-time experiences *(New York: Macmillan 1950), viii, 128p.*

WHEELER, Keith
The Pacific is my beat *(New York: Dutton 1943), 17-383p.*

WHEELER, Richard
The bloody battle for Suribachi *(New York: Crowell 1965), 148p.*

WISTRAND, R B (ed)
Pacific sweep: a pictorial history of the Fifth Air Force Fighter Command *(Sydney: Johnston 1946), 112p.*

YOKOTA, Yutaka
The Kaiten weapon *(New York: Ballantine 1962), 255p.*
[*see also* AIRCRAFT CARRIERS, AUSTRALIAN ARMY, FAR EAST, JAPAN, NEW ZEALAND ARMY, ROYAL NAVY, US MARINES, US NAVY AIR FORCE]

PALESTINE

CONNELL, John (pseud)
The house by Herod's Gate *(London: Sampson Low 1947), 195p.*

PAPUA

MILLER, John
Cartwheel: the reduction of Rabaul *(Washington DC: Department of Army 1959), 418p.*

MILNER, Samuel
Victory in Papua *(Washington DC: Department of Army 1957), 409p.*

READING, Geoffrey
Papuan story *(London: Angus & Robertson 1946), 198p.*
[*see also* NEW GUINEA]

PARIS

COLLINS, Larry *and* LAPIERRE, Dominque
Is Paris burning? - Adolf Hitler, August 25th, 1944 *(London: Gollancz 1965), 376p, bib.*

JUCKER, Ninetta
Curfew in Paris: a record of the German occupation *(London: Hogarth 1960), 206p.*

ROY, Claude
Eight days that freed Paris *(London: Pilot 1945), 95p.*

THORNTON, Willis
The liberation of Paris *(New York: Harcourt 1962), 231p, bib.*

WALTER, Gerard
Paris under the occupation *(New York: Orion 1960), 209p.*

WERTH, Alexander
The last days of Paris: a journalist's diary *(London: Hamilton 1940), 274p.*
[*see also* FRANCE, RESISTANCE, WESTERN EUROPE]

PATHFINDERS

ANDERSON, William
Pathfinders *(New York: Jarrolds 1946), 111p.*

BENNETT, Donald C T
Pathfinder: a war autobiography *(London: Muller 1958), x, 11-287p.*

CUMMING, Michael
Pathfinder Cranswick *(London: Kimber [1962]), 208p.*
[*see also* MOSQUITO]

PATTON

ARMY TIMES (periodical)
Warrior: the story of General George S. Patton *(New York: Putnam 1967), 223p.*

AYER, Frederick
Before the colours fade: portrait of a soldier, George S. Patton *(Boston, Mass: Houghton Mifflin 1964), xvii, 266p.*

ESSAME, Hubert
Patton the commander *(London: Batsford 1974), viii, 280p, bib.*

FARAGO, Ladislas
Patton: ordeal and triumph *(New York: Obelensky 1964), 885p.*

HATCH, Alden
George Patton: general in spurs *(New York: Messner 1950), 184p.*

PATTON, George S
War as I knew it *(Boston, Mass: Houghton Mifflin 1947), xix, 425p.*

PEARL, Jack
Blood-and-guts Patton: the swashbuckling life story of America's most daring and controversial general *(Derby, Conn: Monarch 1961), 142p.*

SEMMES, Harry H
Portrait of Patton *(New York: Appleton 1955), 308p.*

WALLACE, Brenton G
Patton and his Third Army *(Harrisburg, Pa: Military Service 1946), 232p.*

WHITING, Charles
Patton *(New York: Ballantine 1970), [2], 160p.*

PEACE

ABEND, Hallett E
Reconquest: its results and responsibilities *(New York: Doubleday 1946), 305p.*

ANSHEN, Ruth N (ed)
Beyond victory *(New York: Harcourt 1943), 291p.*

BAKER, Albert E (ed)
The Christian basis for the post-war world: a commentary on the ten peace points *(New York: Morehouse 1942), 5-123p.*

BINGHAM, Alfred M
The practice of idealism *(New York: Duell 1944), 196p.*

BORNOW, Julian
Our road to power *(Cynthiana, Kty: Hobson 1944), viii, 216p.*

BRAILSFORD, Henry N
Our settlement with Germany *(New York: Day 1944), 160p.*

BRITTAIN, Vera M
War-time letters to peace lovers *(London: Peace 1940), 123p.*

BYNG, Edward J
Five-year peace plan: a schedule for peace building *(New York: Coward-McCann 1943), vii, 184p.*

CARR, Edward H
Conditions of peace *(London: Macmillan 1942), xxiv, 282p.*

CURTIS, Lionel
The way to peace *(London: Oxford UP 1944), 88p.*

DE ROUSSY DE SALES, Raoul
The making of tomorrow *(New York: Reynal 1942), 338p.*

DUNNING, Thomas G
Settlement with Germany *(London: SCM Press 1943), 100p.*

EINZIG, Paul
Appeasement: before, during and after the war *(London: Macmillan 1941), xii, 215p.*
Can we win the peace? *(London: Macmillan 1942), x, 148p.*

ELIOT, George F
The hour of triumph *(New York: Reynal 1944), x, 214p.*

EVANS, *Sir* Rowland
Prelude to peace *(London: Hutchinson 1943), 148p.*

FIKE, Linus R
No nation alone: a plan for organized peace *(New York: Philosophical Library 1943), 5-96p.*

FIORINO, Joaquin P
From cosmic war to universal peace *(New York: Helenson 1944), vii, 182p.*

FISCHER, Louis
Dawn of victory *(New York: Duell 1942), 270p.*

FRAENKEL, Heinrich
The winning of the peace *(London: Gollancz 1942), 95p.*

FREEMAN, Harrop A (ed)
Peace is the victory *(New York: Harper 1944), x, 253p.*

GARNETT, James C
Lasting peace *(London: Allen & Unwin 1940), 288p.*

GELBER, Lionel M
Peace by power: the plain man's guide to the key issue of the war and of the post-war world *(London: Oxford UP 1942), vii, 159p.*

GILMORE, Albert F
Christ at the peace table *(New York: Prentice-Hall 1943), xii, 264p.*

GOLDIN, Guthie B
The coming peace settlement with Germany: a study *(New York: Reklam 1943), 58p.*

GRABOWSKI, Zbigniew
Fear or security *(London: Maxlove 1945), 80p.*
GRIFFIN, Eldon
Clinching the victory *(Seattle, Wash: Wilberlilla 1943), 365p.*
HAMBRO, Carl J
How to win the peace *(Philadelphia, Pa: Lippincott 1942), 7-384p.*
HARRIS, Henry W
Problems of the peace *(New York: Macmillan 1944), xii, 116p.*
HERMENS, Ferdinand A
Tyrants' war and the people's peace *(Cambridge: Cambridge UP 1944), 249p.*
HEYST, Axel
After Hitler *(London: Minerva 1940), 228p.*
Wanted – a new vision *(London: Minerva 1941), 164p.*
HOLMES, John H
Out of darkness *(New York: Harper 1942), x, 151p.*
IVANYI-GRUNWOLD, Bela *and* BILL, Alan
Route to Potsdam: the story of the peace aims, 1939–1945 *(London: Wingate 1945), 111p.*
JACOBSON, Edmund
The peace we Americans need: a plea for clearer thinking about our Allies, our foes, ourselves and our future *(Chicago, Ill: Kroch 1944), 206p.*
JOHNSEN, Julia E (comp)
World peace plans *(New York: Wilson 1943), 281p.*
JOHNSON, Melvin M *and* HAVEN, C
For permanent victory: the case for an American arsenal of peace *(New York: Morrow 1942), 246p.*
KAZMAYER, Robert
Out of the clouds: a realistic approach to the problems of the post-war world *(New York: Macrae Smith 1944), vi, 99-255p.*
KING-HALL, Stephen
Britain's third chance: a book about post-war problems and the individual *(London: Faber 1943), 199p.*
Total victory *(London: Faber 1941), xii, 306p.*
KNICKERBOCKER, Hubert R
Is tomorrow Hitler's?: 200 questions on the battle of mankind *(New York: Reynal 1941), xviii, 382p.*
KNOX, *Sir* Geoffrey G
The last peace and the next *(London: Hutchinson 1943), 88p.*
LANGER, Felix
Stepping stones to peace *(London: Drummond 1943), viii, 183p.*

LEON, Maurice
How many world wars?: the warning of Foch *(New York: Dodd 1942), xvi, 164p.*

LIPPMANN, Walter
U.S. war aims *(London: Hamilton 1944), xi, 152p.*

LORIMER, *Mrs* Emily
What the German needs *(London: Allen & Unwin 1942), xiii, 14-129p.*

LUDWIG, Emil
How to beat the Germans *(London: Hutchinson 1944), 72p.*

MACCORMAC, John P
This time for keeps *(New York: Viking 1943), 196p.*

MACIVER, Robert M
Towards an abiding peace *(New York: Macmillan 1943), vi, 195p.*

MACNEIL, Neil
American peace *(New York: Scribner 1944), 276p.*

MALLERY, Otto T
Economic union and durable peace *(New York: Harper 1943), xvi, 183p.*

MATTHEWS, Walter R
Foundations of peace *(London: Eyre & Spottiswoode 1942), vi, 9-95p.*

MICHIE, Allan A
Keep the peace through air power *(London: Allen & Unwin 1944), 172p.*

MILLSPAUGH, Arthur C
Peace plans and American choices: the pros and cons of world order *(Washington DC: Brookings 1942), vii, 107p.*

MORGAN, Willard H
Aftermath of victory *(New York: Capper 1943), 11-79p.*

MOTHERWELL, Hiram
The peace we fight for *(New York: Harper 1943), x, 281p.*

MOULTON, Harold G *and* MARLIO, Louis
The control of Germany and Japan *(Washington DC: Brookings 1944), xi, 116p.*

NEUMANN, William L
After victory: Churchill, Roosevelt, Stalin and the making of the peace *(New York: Harper 1967), 212p.*
Making the peace, 1941-1945: the diplomacy of the wartime conferences *(Washington DC: Foundation for Foreign affairs 1950), 101p.*

NEWCOMB, Reginald S
From total war to total peace *(St Petersburg, Fla: Kingdom 1944), 136p.*
Total peace and the new Christian order *(Auckland, NZ: Gordon & Gotch 1943), 80p.*

NEWMAN, Bernard
The new Europe *(London: Hale 1942), 440p.*

PALMER, Frederick
It can be done this time *(New York: Scribner 1944), 307p.*

PARES, *Sir* Bernard
Russia and the peace *(New York: Macmillan 1944), xi, 293p.*

PEOPLE'S peace by representatives of the United Nations *(New York: Stewart 1943), 5–271p.*

P.E.P.
Building peace out of war *(London: Oxford UP 1944), 192p.*

PICK, Frank
Paths to peace: two essays in aims and methods *(London: Routledge 1941), vii, 96p.*

PICK, Frederick W
Peacemaking in perspective: from Potsdam to Paris *(Oxford: Pen-in-hand 1950), 251p.*

POL, Heinz
Hidden enemy: the German threat to post-war peace *(New York: Messner 1943), 281p.*

PRAGIER, Adam
Polish peace aims *(London: Maxlove 1944), 5–127p.*

PREFACES to peace: a symposium *(New York: Columbia UP 1943), xii, 473p.*

RANSHOFEN-WERTHEIMER, Egon F
Victory is not enough: the strategy for a lasting peace *(New York: Norton 1942), 9–322p.*

RAYMOND, Ernest *and* RAYMOND, Patrick
Back to humanity *(London: Cassell 1945), 89p.*

REVES, Emery
The anatomy of peace *(New York: Viking 1963), 293p.*

SADLER, William S
Prescription for permanent peace *(Chicago, Ill: Wilcox & Follett 1944), 202p.*

SCHWARZCHILD, Leopold
A primer of the coming world *(London: Hamilton 1944), 205p.*

SHIRLAW, Gerald B *and* JONES, L E
You and the peace *(New York: Macmillan 1944), vi, 176p.*

SPYKMAN, Nicholas J
Geography of the peace *(New York: Harcourt 1944), xii, 66p.*
STRASSER, Otto
Germany tomorrow *(London: Cape 1940), 7-254p.*
TEELING, William (ed)
After the war: a symposium of peace aims *(London: Sidgwick & Jackson 1940), viii, 198p.*
THOMAS, Elbert D
Four fears *(New York: Ziff-Davis 1944), xvi, 189p.*
VANSITTART, Robert G
Bones of contention *(New York: Knopf 1945), 157p.*
VISSON, Andre
The coming struggle for peace *(New York: Viking 1944), x, 301p.*
VOORHIS, Horace J
Beyond victory *(New York: Farrar 1944), xiv, 240p.*
WELLES, Sumner (ed)
The intelligent American's guide to the peace *(New York: Dryden 1945), vi, 370p.*
The world of the four freedoms *(Chicago, Ill: Chicago UP 1943), x, 121p.*
WHEELER-BENNETT, *Sir* John W *and* NICHOLLS, A J
The semblance of peace: the political settlement after the Second World War *(New York: Norton 1974), 706p.*
WOOLF, Leonard S
War for peace *(London: Routledge 1940), 244p.*
WURTELE, Allan R
When peace comes *(New Orleans, La: Pelican 1941), 325p.*

PEACE TREATIES

COHEN, Bernard C
The political process and foreign policy: the making of the Japanese peace settlement *(Princeton, NJ: Princeton UP 1957), xi, 293p.*
DUNN, Frederick S *and others*
Peace-making and the settlement with Japan *(Princeton, NJ: Princeton UP 1963), 210p.*
GREAT BRITAIN. Foreign Office
Draft peace treaty with Japan and Amendments *(London: HMSO 1951), 2 vols.*
Selected documents on Germany and the question of Berlin, 1944-1961 *(London: HMSO [1961]), xiii, 483p.*

KUKLICH, Bruce R
American policy and the division of Germany: the clash with Russia over reparations *(Ithaca, NY: Cornell UP 1972), 286p.*

LEISS, Amelia
European peace treaties after World War II: negotiations and texts of treaties with Italy, Bulgaria, Hungary, Rumania and Finland *(Boston, Mass: World Peace 1954), 341p.*

LONSDALE BRYANS, James
Blind victory: secret communications Halifax-Hassell *(London: Skeffington 1951), 191p.*

MAKING the peace treaties, 1941-1947: a history in the making of peace beginning with the Atlantic Charter, the Yalta and Potsdam Conferences, and culminating in the drafting of peace treaties with Italy, Bulgaria, Hungary, Rumania and Finland *(Washington DC: Department of State 1947), 150p.*

RATCHFORD, Benjamin U *and* ROSS, William D
Berlin reparations assignment: round one of the German peace settlement *(Chapel Hill, NC: North Carolina UP 1947), 259p.*

TREATY of peace with Japan, San Francisco 8th September, 1951 (with declarations and protocol) *(London: HMSO 1952), 120p.*

PEARL HARBOR

BARKER, Arthur J
Pearl Harbor *(New York: Ballantine 1969), 160p, bib.*

BURTNESS, Paul S *and* OBER, Warren V (eds)
The puzzle of Pearl Harbor *(Evanston, Ill: Row, Peterson 1962), 244p.*

CLARK, Thomas B
Remember Pearl Harbor *(Toronto: McCleod 1942), 7-127p; UK title:* Pearl Harbor.

KIMMEL, Husband E
Admiral Kimmel's story *(Chicago, Ill: Regnery 1955), 206p.*

LORD, Walter
Day of infamy *(New York: Holt 1957), [11], 243p.*

MILLIS, Walter
Pearl Harbor: the United States and Japan 1941 *(New York: Morrow 1947), 384p.*

MORGENSTEIN, George E
Pearl Harbor: the story of the secret war *(New York: Devin-Adair 1947), 425p.*

PARKINSON, Roger
Attack on Pearl Harbor *(London: Wayland 1973), 128p, bib.*

SAKAMAKI, Kazuo
I attacked Pearl Harbor *(New York: Assoca 1949), 5-133p.*

THEOBALD, Robert A
The final secret of Pearl Harbor *(New York: Devin-Adair 1954), xix, 204p.*

TREFOUSSE, Hans L (ed)
What happened to Pearl Harbor?: documents pertaining to the Japanese attack of December 7, 1941, and its background *(New York: Twayne 1958), 324p.*

US CONGRESS Joint Committee on the investigation of the Pearl Harbor attack
Pearl Harbor attack: hearings before the . . . *(Washington DC: Government Printing Office 1946), 39 vols.*

WOHLSTETTER, Roberta
Pearl Harbor: warning and decision *(Stanford, Calif: Stanford UP 1962), 426p.*

PELELIU

FALK, Stanley Lawrence
Bloodiest victory *(New York: Ballantine 1974), 159p.*

HOUGH, Frank O
The assault on Peleliu *(Washington DC: USMC 1950), 209p.*
The island war: the United States Marines Corps in the Pacific *(Philadelphia, Pa: Lippincott 1947), 413p.*

HUNT, George P
Coral comes high *(New York: Harper 1946), xiv, 15-127p.*

PERSONAL NARRATIVE

APELDOORN, Jan van (pseud)
Departure delayed *(London: Robertson & Mullens 1943), 220p.*

BAKER, Amy J
Hell's odyssey (coal boat cargo) *(London: Hutchinson 1942), 160p; US title:* Mediterranean odyssey.

BANKSON, Budd
I should live so long *(Philadelphia, Pa: Lippincott 1952), 7-287p.*

BARTEK, John F *and* PARDUE, Austin
Life out there: a story of faith and courage *(New York: Scribner 1943), xviii, 117p.*

BEATON, Cecil
Near East *(London: Batsford 1943), vii, 149p.*

BEATTIE, Edward W
Freely to pass *(New York: Crowell 1942), vi, 372p; UK title:* Passport to war.

BELL, Jack
Line of fire *(Coral Gables, Fla: Glade House 1948), 269p.*

BLOOM, Ursula
War isn't wonderful *(London: Hutchinson 1961), 222p.*

BODLEY, Ronald V C
Flight into Portugal *(London: Jarrolds 1941), xi, 13–224p.*

BOSMELET, Diana de
In golden spurs *(London: Muller 1945), 6–109p.*

BREWSTER, Ralph
Wrong passport *(London: Cohen & West 1954), xi, 274p.*

BROCK, Ray
Nor any victory *(New York: Reynal 1942), x, 351p.*

BROWN, Alfred J
Ground staff: a personal record *(London: Eyre & Spottiswoode 1943), 185p.*

BROWN, Joe E
Your kids and mine *(New York: Doubleday 1944), 5–192p.*

BROWN, John M
Many a watchful night *(London: Hamilton 1944), 219p.*

BYROM, James
The unfinished man *(London: Chatto & Windus 1957), 252p.*

CALLISON, Talmadge P
Hit the silk! *(New York: Comet 1954), 91p.*

CAREW, Tim
All this and a medal too *(London: Constable 1954), ix, 252p.*

CARPENTER, Deverton
Dear folks *(Boston, Mass: Humphries 1947), 5–244p.*

CARTLAND, Barbara H
The years of opportunity, 1939–1945 *(London: Hutchinson 1948), 276p.*

CASEY, Robert J
This is where I came in *(Indianapolis, Ind: Bobbs-Merrill 1945), 307p.*

CASH, Gwen
A million miles from Ottawa *(Toronto: Macmillan 1942), x, 152p.*

CISZEK, Walter J *and* FLAHERTY, D L
He leadeth me *(London: Hodder & Stoughton 1974), 216p.*

CLARKE, Dorothy M
No time to weep *(London: Hale 1942), 222p.*

CLARKE, Dudley W
Seven assignments *(London: Cape 1948), 264p.*
CODMAN, Charles R
Drive *(Boston: Mass: Little, Brown 1957), 335p.*
COHN, David L
This is the story *(Boston, Mass: Houghton Mifflin 1947), 563p.*
COLLIS, Robert *and* HOGERZIEL, Hans
Straight on *(London: Methuen 1947), 178p.*
CRAWFORD, William, *jun*
Gore and glory: a story of American heroism *(New York: McKay 1944), xiv, 17–192p.*
CURIE, Eve
Journey among warriors *(London: Heinemann 1943), viii, 501p.*
DAVIDSON, William
Cut off *(New York: Pyramid 1974), 220p.*
DAVIS, Harry (ed)
This is it! *(New York: Vanguard 1944), xi, 11–224p.*
DENNIS, Owen
The rest go on *(Bognor Regis, Sussex: Crowther 1942), 132p.*
DENNY, Harold N
Behind both lines *(New York: Viking 1942), xi, 209p.*
DICKEY, Charles W
Here we go again *(New York: Pageant 1951), 165p.*
DMITRI, Ivan (pseud)
Flight to everywhere *(New York: McGraw-Hill 1944), 9–240p.*
DOLLMAN, Eugen
Call me coward *(London: Kimber 1956), 201p.*
DORMER, Hugh
Diaries *(London: Cape 1947), 5–159p.*
DOWNING, Rupert
What kind of people *(London: Muller 1942), 128p.*
DUKE, Florimond *and* SWAART, C M
Name, rank and serial number *(Des Moines, Iowa: Meredith 1969), 162p.*
DYE, John T
Golden leaves *(Los Angeles, Calif: Ward Ritchie 1962), 227p.*
ECHLIN, Elisabeth G
Live unafraid *(London: Hodge 1944), 289p.*
EDGAR, *Mrs* Louise E
Out of bounds *(Philadelphia, Pa: Dorrance 1950), 227p.*
ELLSWORTH, Lyman R
Guys on ice *(New York: McKay 1952), 277p.*

ELOY, Victor
The fight in the forest *(London: Hale [1950]), 192p.*

FAUTEUX, Claire
Fantastic interlude *(London: Vantage 1962), 132p.*

FORGY, Howell M
. . . and pass the ammunition *(New York: Appleton 1944), x, 242p.*

FORTESCUE, *Lady* Winifred
Trampled lilies *(London: Blackwood 1941), viii, 236p.*

FOULK, Leonard M
Still my world *(San Francisco, Calif: Edwards 1945), viii, 11-70p.*

FOX, Monro L
Blind adventure *(Philadelphia, Pa: Lippincott 1946), 7-205p.*

GALLAGHER, O'Dowd
Retreat in the east *(London: Harrap 1942), 190p; US title:* Action in the East.

GALLANT, Thomas G
The friendly dead *(New York: Doubleday 1964), 189p.*

GEORGE, Willis de V
Surreptitious entry *(New York: Appleton 1946), 214p.*

GERDY, Robert S
From the letters of . . . 1942-1945: a personal record of World War II *(Philadelphia, Pa: Dorrance 1969), 355p.*

GERVASI, Frank
The war has seven faces *(New York: Doubleday 1942), xvi, 296p.*

GIBSON, Walter
Highland laddie *(London: W H Allen 1954), 189p.*

GILCHRIST, Derek C
Blue hell *(London: Heath 1943), 126p.*

GLEESON, James *and* WALDRON, Thomas J
Now it can be told *(London: Elek 1952), 188p.*

GLUCK, Gemma La G
My story *(New York: McKay 1961), 116p.*

GOLDSTEIN, Bernard
The stars bear witness *(London: Gollancz 1950), [5], 295p.*

GRAHAM, Garrett
Banzai Noel! *(New York: Vanguard 1944), 9-159p.*

GRAVES, Charles
Great days *(London: Hutchinson 1944), 272p.*
Off the record *(London: Hutchinson 1942), vi, 7-223p.*
Pride of the morning *(London: Hutchinson 1945), 182p.*

GREENWALL, Harry J
Three years of hell *(London: W H Allen 1943), 217p.*

GRUBER, R J
No room for heroes *(New York: Vantage 1972), 148p.*
GUERNSEY, Isabel R
Free trip to Berlin *(London: Macmillan 1943), ix, 230p.*
GUEST, John
Broken images: a journal *(London: Longmans 1949),* [7], *231p.*
GUNNISON, Royal A
So sorry, no peace *(New York: Viking 1944), ix, 272p.*
HADLEY, Peter
Third class to Dunkirk *(London: Hollis & Carter 1944), 150p.*
HALLEY, David
We missed the boat *(London: Hodge 1946), 236p.*
HASTINGS, Macdonald
Passed as censored *(London: Harrap 1942), 160p.*
HEALY, Thomas E A
Tourist under fire: the journal of a wartime traveler *(New York: Holt 1945), x, 301p.*
HICKEY, Raymond M
Scarlet dawn *(Montreal: Palm 1950), 277p.*
HODGKINSON, Colin
Best foot forward *(London: Odhams 1957), 255p.*
HOLDEN, Inez
It was different at the time *(London: Lane 1943), 95p.*
HOLMAN, Dennis
The man they couldn't kill *(London: Heinemann 1960), vii, 232p.*
HOWARD, William, *8th earl of Wicklow*
Fireside fusilier *(Dublin: Clonmore & Reynolds 1958), 145p.*
IRGANG, Frank J
Etched in purple *(Caldwell, Idaho: Caxton 1949), 241p.*
JACOB, Naomi E
Me - in war time *(London: Hutchinson 1940), 286p.*
Me - over there *(London: Hutchinson 1947), 224p.*
JAMES, Malcolm (pseud)
Born of the desert *(London: Collins 1945), 320p.*
JEANTY, Ninette H
Certified sane *(London: Sheppard 1948), 243p.*
JOHNSON, Franklyn A
One more hill *(New York: Funk 1949), 181p.*
JOHNSON, Robert S
Thunderbolt! *(New York: Rinehart 1958), 305p.*
JOHNSTON, Denis
Nine rivers from Jordan: the chronicle of a journey and a search *(London: Verschoyle 1953),* [8], *458p.*

KARST, Georg M (pseud)
Beasts of the earth *(New York: Albert Unger 1942), 185p.*
KAUFFMAN, Russell W
Fifty thousand human corks *(Philadelphia, Pa: Dorrance 1957), 163p.*
KELLY, Charles E
One man's war *(New York: Knopf 1944), vii, 181p.*
KERN, Erich
Dance of death *(London: Collins 1951), 256p.*
KINSELLA, Patrick
Letters from Patrick: letters of life and love from an R.A.F. pilot bombardier to the American actress Claire Luce *(Philadelphia, Pa: Chilton 1965), 182p.*
KLITGAARD, Kaj
Oil and deep water *(Chapel Hill, NC: North Carolina UP 1945), 182p.*
KNAPP, Stefan
The square sun *(London: Museum [1957]), 172p.*
KNEEBONE, Stanley D (comp)
Hazardous missions *(London: Hamilton 1963), 3-141p.*
KNOX, Walter K
Darken ship *(New York: Vantage 1966), 180p.*
KOSPOTH, B J
Red wins *(London: Macdonald 1946), 220p.*
KOWALIK, Ernest E
Alone and unarmed *(New York: Carlton 1968), 317p.*
LECKIE, Robert
A helmet for my pillow *(New York: Random House 1957), 311p.*
LEE, Robert E
To the war *(New York: Knopf 1968), 179p.*
LINKLATER, Eric
The art of adventure *(London: Macmillan 1947), vii, 292p.*
LODWICK, John
Bid the soldiers shoot *(London: Heinemann 1958), 296p.*
LONGHURST, Henry
I wouldn't have missed it *(London: Dent 1945), 207p.*
LUSSU, Joyce
Freedom has no frontier *(London: Joseph 1969), 158p.*
MACINNES, Colin
To the victors the spoils *(London: MacGibbon & Kee 1950), 350p.*
MACKENZIE, Colin
Sailors of fortune *(New York: Dutton 1944), 13-190p.*

MANISCALCO, Giuseppe
Miles and miles and miles *(Cape Town: Timmins 1968), 191p; UK title:* The longest walk.
MARK, Moshe
Sparks of glory *(New York: Shengold 1974), 154p.*
MASKELYNE, Jasper
Magic - top secret *(London: Paul 1949), 191p.*
MAUGERI, Franco
From the ashes of disgrace *(New York: Reynal & Hitchcock 1948), 376p.*
MICHIE, Allan A
Everyman to his post *(London: Allen & Unwin 1943), 105p.*
MILLIN, Sarah G
Fire out of heaven *(London: Faber 1947), 316p.*
Pit of the abyss *(London: Faber 1946), 304p.*
Reeling earth *(London: Faber 1945), 305p.*
Seven thunders *(London: Faber 1948), 335p.*
Sound of the trumpet *(London: Faber 1947), 260p.*
World blackout *(London: Faber 1944), 269p.*
MOATS, Alice L
A blind date with Mars *(New York: Doubleday 1943), 486p.*
No passport for Paris *(New York: Putnam 1945), 275p.*
MOORE, Thomas
The sky is my witness *(New York: Putnam 1943), 135p.*
MORIN, Relman
Circuit of conquest *(New York: Knopf 1943), 361p.*
MUEHL, John F
American sahib *(New York: Day 1946), vi, 242p.*
MULGAN, John
Report on experience *(New York: OUP 1947), 150p.*
MURPHY, Audie
To hell and back *(New York: Holt 1949), 274p.*
MURRAY, William
Atlantic rendezvous *(Lymington, Hants: Nautical 1970), xviii, 317p, bib.*
MUSTARDE, John C
The sun stood still *(London: Pilot 1944), 240p.*
MYERS, James E
Hell is a foxhole: an autobiography 1942-1946 *(New York: Vantage 1966), 112p.*
NEUMANN, Peter
Other men's graves *(London: Weidenfeld & Nicolson [1958]), 286p.*

NEWMAN, Bernard
One man's year *(London: Gollancz 1941), 277p.*

NICHOLSON, *Mrs* Phyllis
Cornish cream *(London: Murray 1942), 168p.*

OLIPHANT, *Sir* Lancelot
An ambassador in bonds *(London: Putnam 1946), 227p.*

O'REILLY, Tom
Purser's progress: the adventures of a sea-going office boy *(New York: Doubleday 1944), x, 209p.*

ORR, James E
I saw no tears *(London: Marshall, Morgan & Scott 1948), 128p.*

PACHALE, Alfred
At the mercy of godless hordes *(Lyndock, South Aust: Kies 1951), 320p.*

PEABODY, Polly
Occupied territory *(London: Cresset 1941), 292p.*

PEACOCK, Basil
Tinker's mufti: memories of a part-time soldier *(London: Seeley 1974), 214p.*

PERCIVAL, Winifred D
Not only music, signora! *(Altrincham, Chesh: Sherratt 1947), 207p.*

PLEASANTS, Eric
I killed to live *(London: Cassell 1957), viii, 9-223p.*

PUDNEY, John
The world still there *(London: Hollis & Carter 1945), 104p.*

QUINTERLEY, Esmond
My airman days *(London: Fortune 1948), 262p.*

REYBURN, Wallace
Some of it was fun *(Toronto: Nelson 1949), 199p.*

REYNOLDS, Quentin J
The curtain rises *(London: Cassell 1944), 300p.*

RHODES, Anthony
Sword of bone *(London: Faber 1942), 235p.*

RICHARDSON, Anthony
No place to lay my head *(London: Odhams 1958), 254p.*

ROBINSON, Georgette
Green avalanche: the story of an English girl's adventures as a combatant in World War 2 *(Sidcup, Kent: Pythagorean 1960),* [7], *225p.*

ROWDON, Maurice
Of sins and winter *(London: Chatto & Windus 1955),* [7], *182p.*

ROY, Jules
Return from hell *(London: Kimber 1954), x, 229p.*

SAVARY, Gladys S
Outside the walls *(New York: Vantage 1954), 206p.*

SCHIMANSKI, Stefan *and* TREECE, Henry (eds)
Leaves in the storm: a book of diaries *(London: Drummond 1947), 299p.*

SEVAREID, A E
Not so wild a dream *(New York: Knopf 1946), 516p.*

SHEEAN, Vincent
Between the thunder and the sun *(New York: Random House 1943), 428p.*

SHOMON, Joseph J
Crosses in the wind *(New York: Statford House 1947), 191p.*

SKATTEBOL, Lars
The last voyage of the Quien Sabe *(New York: Harper 1944), viii, 255p.*

SKIDMORE, Robert D
More lives than one *(Boston, Mass: Houghton Mifflin 1945), 265p.*

SMART, Charles A
The long watch *(New York: World 1968), 237p.*

SMEETON, Miles
A change of jungles *(London: Hart-Davis 1962), 192p.*

STANFORD, John K
Tail of an army *(London: Phoenix House 1966), v, 218p.*

STARR, Freya
East is West *(London: Murray 1945), 218p.*

STEINBECK, John
Once there was a war *(New York: Viking 1958), xxi, 233p.*

STEPHENS, Ian
Monsoon morning *(London: Benn 1966), xii, 291p.*

STERN, Michael
Into the jaws of death *(New York: McBride 1944), 7-237p.*

STEWART, George
These men my friends *(Caldwell, Idaho: Caxton 1954), 400p.*

STOWE, Leland
No other road to freedom *(New York: Knopf 1941), 432p.*

STRAUSS, Cyric A
A soldier looks back: the journals of . . . *(London: Falcon 1951), 257p.*

TAILLIEZ, Philippe
Acquarius *(Paris: France-Empire 1961), 366p.*

TAYLOR, Henry *jun.*
Men and power *(New York: Dodd 1946), 257p.*
TAYLOR, Henry J
Time runs out *(London: Collins 1942), viii, 333p.*
TERASAKI, Hidenari
Bridge to the sun *(Chapel Hill, NC: North Carolina UP 1957), 277p.*
THOMPSON, Reginald W
An echo of trumpets *(London: Allen & Unwin 1964), 222p.*
Men under fire *(London: Macdonald 1946), 160p.*
TREANOR, Thomas C
One damn thing after another: the adventures of an innocent man trapped between public relations and the Axis *(New York: Doubleday 1944), ix, 294p.*
TRUMBULL, Robert
The raft *(New York: Holt 1942), 205p.*
TUCHET-JESSON, Henry
And beacons burn again: letters from an English soldier *(New York: Appleton 1940), ix, 81p.*
VERNEY, John
A dinner of herbs *(London: Collins 1966), 224p.*
Going to the wars: a journey in various directions *(London: Collins 1955), 255p.*
WALKER, Patrick G
The lid lifts *(London: Gollancz 1945), vi, 7-96p.*
WARDROP, Jacob R
Wardrop of the Fifth: the diary of Sgt. J. R. Wardrop (Jake) of 5th Royal Tank Regiment, Nov. 1940–Jan. 1944 *(Bovington Camp, Dorset: RAC Tank Museum 1968), iv, 94p.*
WATERFIELD, Gordon
Morning will come *(London: Murray 1944), x, 194p.*
WAUGH, Alec
His second war *(London: Cassell 1944), 204p.*
WELKER, Robert H
A different drummer: the odyssey of a home-grown rebel *(Boston, Mass: Beacon* [*1958*]*),* [*7*]*, 404p.*
WEST, Adam
Just as they came *(London: Longmans Green 1946), 199p.*
WEST, Frank L
Lifeboat number seven *(London: Kimber 1960), 208p.*
WESTRATE, Edwin V
Forward observer *(New York: Dutton 1944), 11-179p.*

WEYMOUTH, Anthony (pseud)
A journal of the war years . . . and one year later *(Worcester: Littlebury 1948), 2 vols.*
WILLANS, Geoffrey
One eye on the clock *(London: Macmillan 1943), v, 177p.*
WILLIAMS, Annabelle R
Operation grease-paint *(Hollywood, Calif: House-Warren 1951), 240p.*
WINN, Godfrey H
Scrap book of victory: further extracts from a war-time scrapbook *(London: Hutchinson 1945), 124p.*
WOOD, Alan
Flying visits *(London: Dobson 1946), vii, 9–149p.*
YOUNG, Scotty
Descent into danger *(London: Wingate 1954), 240p.*
ZAMMIT, Romeo M
They will rise again *(Ilfracombe, Devon: Stockwell 1954), 76p.*

PETAIN

GRIFFITHS, Richard
Marshal Petain *(London: Constable 1970), xix, 379p, bib.*
HUDDLESTON, Sisley
Petain, patriot or traitor? *(London: Dakers 1951), 270p.*
MARTEL, Francis
Petain, Verdun to Vichy *(New York: Dutton 1943), 9–226p.*
[*see also* FRANCE, VICHY]

PHILIPPINES

ABAYA, Hernando J
Betrayal in the Philippines *(New York: Wyn 1946), 8–272p.*
BACLAGON, Oldarico S
Philippine campaigns *(Manila: Graphic 1952), 388p.*
BOGGS, Charles W
Marine aviation in the Philippines *(Washington DC: USMC 1951), 166p.*
BROUGHER, William E
South of Bataan, north to Mukden: prison diary *(Athens, Ga: Georgia UP 1971), 207p.*
BROWN, Robert M *and* PERMMENTER, Donald
I solemnly swear *(New York: Vantage 1957), 160p; UK title:* A G.I. named Brown.

BUENAFE, Manuel E
Wartime Philippines *(Manila: Philippine Education Foundation 1950), 248p.*

BUSTOS, Felixberti G
And now comes Hoxas: a story of the occupation and a leader *(Manila: Bustos 1945), 253p.*

DOMANTAY, Pat
My terrible days and survival in World War II *(New York: Vantage 1972), 78p.*

DOROMAL, Jose D
War in Panay: a documentary history of the resistance movement in Panay during World War II *(Manila: Advocate 1952), 313p.*

FALK, Stanley L
Liberation of the Philippines *(New York: Ballantine 1970), 160p, bib.*

FRIEND, T
Between two Empires: the ordeal of the Philippines, 1929–1946 *(New Haven, Conn: Yale UP 1965), 312p.*

GALANG, Ricardo C
Secret mission to the Philippines *(Manila: Philippine Islands Universal 1948), xiii, 234p.*

GIMENEZ, Pedro M
Under the shadows of the 'Kempi' *(Manila: Narvaez 1946), 337p.*

GO, Puan Seng
Refuge and strength *(New York: Prentice Hall 1970), 224p; UK title:* Exile.

HARKINS, Philip
Blackburn's headhunters *(London: Cassell 1956), ix, 326p.*

HARTENTOP, A V H
The Santo Tomas story *(New York: McGraw-Hill 1964), 446p.*

HAWKINS, Jack
Never say die *(Philadelphia, Pa: Dorrance 1961), 196p.*

HERNADEZ, Al
Bahala na, come what may: the story of mission ISRM (I shall return MacArthur) *(Berkeley, Calif: Howell-North 1961), 315p.*

HERNANDEZ, Juan B
Not the sword: a true story of the courageous people of the Philippines during the Japanese occupation in World War II *(New York: Greenwich 1960), 215p.*

HIND, Renton
Spirits unbroken: a chronicle of civilian internment in the Philippines *(San Francisco, Calif: Howell 1947), 291p.*

INGHAM, Travis
Rendezvous by submarine: the story of Charles Parsons and the guerrilla soldiers in the Philippines *(New York: Doubleday 1945), 255p.*

KEATS, John
They fought alone *(Philadelphia, Pa: Lippincott 1963), 400p.*

KLESTADT, Albert
The sea was kind *(London: Constable 1959), ix, 208p.*

LICHAUCO, Marcial P
'Dear mother Putnam': a diary of the war in the Philippines *(Manila: Lichauco 1949), 219p.*

LOCKWOOD, Charles A *and* ADAMSON, H C
Battles of the Philippine Sea *(New York: Crowell 1967), 229p.*

McGEE, John H
Rice and salt: a history of the defense and occupation of Mindanao during World War II *(San Antonio, Tex: Naylor 1962), 242p.*

MARQUEZ, Adalia
Blood on the rising sun: a factual story of the Japanese invasion of the Philippines *(New York: Tanko 1957), 253p.*

MELLNIK, Stephen M
Philippine diary 1939–1945 *(New York: Van Nostrand-Reinhold 1969), 316p.*

MONAGHAN, Forbes J
Under the red sun: a letter from Manila *(New York: Declan X. McMullen 1946), 279p.*

MORTON, Louis
The fall of the Philippines *(Washington DC: Department of Army 1953), 626p.*

OGAWA, Tetsuro
Terraced hell: a Japanese memoir of defeat and death in Northern Luzon, Philippines *(Rutland, Vt: Tuttle 1972), 222p.*

PANLILIO, Yay
The crucible: an autobiography *(New York: Macmillan 1950), xi, 348p.*

PHILLIPS, Claire *and* GOLDSMITH, Myron B
Manila espionage *(Portland, Ore: Binfords & Mort 1947), 226p.*

PORTER, Catherine L
Crisis in the Philippines *(New York: Knopf 1942), vi, 156p.*

RECTO, Claso M
Three years of enemy occupation: the issue of political collaboration in the Philippines *(Manila: People's 1946), 189p.*

ROMULO, Carlos P
I saw the fall of the Philippines *(New York: Doubleday 1942), viii, 323p.*

RUTHERFORD, Ward
Fall of the Philippines *(New York: Ballantine 1971), 160p, bib.*

SMITH, Robert R
The approach to the Philippines *(Washington DC: Department of Army 1953), 623p.*
Triumph in the Philippines *(Washington DC: Department of Army 1963), 756p.*

SNEED, Bessie
Captured by the Japanese: being the personal experiences of a miner's wife caught in the Philippines, at the outbreak of World War II *(Denver, Colorado: Bradford-Robinson 1946), 108p.*

STAHL, Alfred J
How we took it: vignettes of Japanese internment camps in the Philippines *(New York: Stahl 1945), 118p.*

STEINBERG, David J
Philippine collaboration in World War II *(Ann Harbor, Mich: Michigan UP 1967), 235p.*

STEWART, Sidney
Give us this day *(London: Staples 1956), 246p.*

UTINSKY, Margaret
Miss U *(San Antonio, Tex: Naylor 1948), xi, 172p.*

VALTIN, Jan
Children of yesterday *(New York: Readers 1946), 429p.*

VANCE, John R
Doomed garrison - the Philippines *(Ashland, Oregon: Vance 1974), 248p.*

VOLCKMANN, Russell W
We remained: three years behind the enemy lines in the Philippines *(New York: Norton 1954), 244p.*

WHITE, William L
They were expendable *(London: Hamilton 1942), 209p.*

WOLFERT, Ira
An American guerilla in the Philippines *(New York: Simon & Schuster 1945), 152p; UK title:* Guerilla.
[*see also* BATAAN]

PHILOSOPHY

BRITISH INSTITUTE OF PHILOSOPHY
The deeper causes of the war and its issues *(London: Allen & Unwin 1940), 7-206p.*

JOAD, Cyril E M
Journey through the war mind *(London: Faber 1940), 7-279p.*
What is at stake, and why not say so *(London: Gollancz 1940), 120p.*
MUELLER, Gustav E
Philosophy and the war *(Oklahoma, Okl: Harlow 1943), 65p.*
MURSELL, James L
Personal philosophy for war time *(Philadelphia, Pa: Lippincott 1942), 9-205p.*
PERRY, Ralph B
Our side right *(Cambridge, Mass: Harvard UP 1942), vi, 153p.*
SHEEN, Fulton J
Philosophies at war *(New York: Scribner 1943), 200p.*
STRACHEY, Evelyn J St L
A faith to fight for *(London: Gollancz 1941), 146p.*
WELLS, Herbert G
'42 to '44: a contemporary memoir upon human behaviour during the crisis of the world revolution *(London: Secker & Warburg 1944), 212p.*
WILLKIE, Wendell L
One world *(London: Cassell 1943), 1699p.*

PHOTOGRAPHIC INTELLIGENCE

BABINGTON SMITH, Constance
Evidence in camera: the story of photographic intelligence in World War II *(London: Chatto & Windus 1958), 256p; US title:* Air spy.
MILLINGTON, Geoffrey
The unseen eye *(London: Gibbs & Phillips 1961), 192p.*
RODGER, George
Far on the ringing plains: 75,000 miles with a photo reporter *(New York: Macmillan 1943), xiv, 295p; UK title:* Red moon rising.

PHOTOGRAPHY

ALLEY, Norman
I witness *(New York: Funk 1941), 370p.*
BONNEY, Therese
War comes to the people *(London: Pendock 1944), 103p.*
CAPA, Robert
Images of war *(London: Hamlyn [1964]), 175p.*
Slightly out of focus *(New York: Holt 1947), 243p.*

FROM beachhead to Berlin: a story in pictures of a great feat of arms *(London: Loescher 1945), 128p.*

HENSSER, Henry
A camera at war *(London: Jarrolds 1944), 92p.*

JOSSWICK, Jerry J
Combat cameraman *(Philadelphia, Pa: Chilton 1961), 200p.*

LEGG, Frank
The eyes of Damien Parer *(London: Angus & Robertson 1963), 54p.*

LOOK (periodical)
Movie lot to beachhead: the motion picture goes to war and prepares for the future *(New York: Doubleday 1945), 291p.*

SIMKINS, Peter
'Illustrated' book of World War II: the first record in full-colour photographs *(London: Sidgwick & Jackson 1972), 128p.*

PIGEONS

OSMAN, William H (ed)
Pigeons in World War 2 *(London: Racing Pigeon 1951), vi, 146p.*

PLOESTI

DUGAN, James *and* STEWART, Carroll
Ploesti: the great ground-air battle of 1 August 1943 *(New York: Random 1962), viii, 309p, bib.*

WOLFF, Leon
Low level mission *(New York: Doubleday 1957), 240p.*
[*see also* BOMBERS, RUMANIA, USAAF]

PLYMOUTH

SAVIGNON, Andre
With Plymouth through fire: a documentary narrative of 1940–1941 *(Penzance, Cornwall: Wordens of Cornwall 1968), 140p.*

POLAND

ALDOR, Francis
Germany's death space: the Polish tragedy *(London: Aldor 1940), 261p.*

ANDERS, Wladyslaw
An army in exile: the story of the Second Polish Corps *(New York: Macmillan 1949), xvi, 319p.*

APENSZIAK, Jakob *and* POLAKIEWICZ, Mojzesz
Armed resistance of the Jews in Poland *(New York: American Federation for Polish Jews 1944), 80p.*

BERENSTEIN, Taliana *and* RUTKOWSKI, Adam
Assistance to the Jews in Poland, 1939–1945 *(Warsaw: Polonia 1963), 82p.*

BETHELL, Nicholas
The war Hitler won, September, 1939 *(London: Allen Lane 1972), viii, 472p, bib.*

BIRENBAUM, Halina
Hope is the last to die: a personal documentation of Nazi terror *(New York: Twayne 1972), 246p.*

THE BLACK book of Polish Jewry: an account of the martyrdom of Polish Jewry under the Nazi occupation *(New York: Roy 1943), xvi, 343p.*

BOR-KOMOROWSKI, Tadeusz
The secret army *(London: Gollancz 1950), 407p.*

BRYAN, Julien H
Siege *(New York: Doubleday 1940), 9–64p.*

CARDWELL, Ann S
Poland, here is the record: an American's view *(Ann Harbor, Mich: Michigan Committee of Americans for Poland 1945), 64p.*

CIECHANOWSKI, Jan
Defeat in victory *(New York: Doubleday 1947), 397p.*

CSOKOR, Franz T
A civilian in the Polish war *(London: Secker & Warburg 1940), 156p.*

CYPRIAN, Tadeusz *and* SAWICKI, Jerzy
Nazi rule in Poland, 1939–1945 *(Warsaw: Polonia 1961), 262p.*

CZARNOMSKI, Francis B (ed)
They fight for Poland: the war in the first person *(London: Allen & Unwin 1941), 284p.*

THE DARK side of the moon *(London: Faber 1946), 232p.*

DRAGOMIR, U
It started in Poland *(London: Faber 1941), 249p.*

EVANS, John
The Nazi new order in Poland *(London: Gollancz 1941), 184p.*

GARLINSKI, Jozef
Poland, S.O.E. and the Allies *(London: Allen & Unwin 1969), 248p, bib.*

GAZEL, Stefan
To live and kill *(London: Jarrolds 1958), 215p.*

GENERAL SIKORSKI HISTORICAL INSTITUTE
Documents on Polish-Soviet relations, 1939-1945 *(London: Heinemann 1961), vol. I: 1939-1943; xi, 625p, bib.*
Documents on Polish-Soviet relations, 1939-1945 *(London: Heinemann 1967: vol. 2: 1943-1945; lvi, 868p.*

GERMAN crimes in Poland *(London: The Reader 1946), 276p.*

GERMAN invasion of Poland *(London: Hutchinson 1940), 128p.*

GERMAN occupation of Poland *(London: Greystone 1942), x, 240p.*

GERMAN new order in Poland *(London: Hutchinson 1942), xiv, 585p; US title:* Black book of Poland.

GINTER, Maria
Life in both hands *(London: Hodder & Stoughton 1964), 253p.*

GORESCKI, J
Stones for the rampart: the story of two lads in the Polish underground movement *(London: Polish Boy Scouts and Girl Guides Association 1945), 68p.*

GRAY, Martin
For those I loved *(Boston, Mass: Little, Brown 1972), xi, 351p.*

HADAR, Alizia R
The Princess Elnasari *(London: Heinemann 1963), [6], 217p.*

HALPERN, Ada
Liberation - Russian style *(London: Maxlove 1945), vii, 9-106p; US title:* Conducted tour.

HERBERT, J M (pseud)
G - for Genevieve *(New York: Roy 1944), 254p.*

HOLLINGWORTH, Clare
The three weeks' war in Poland *(London: Duckworth 1940), 180p.*

IRVING, David
Accident: the death of General Sikorski *(London: Kimber 1967), 231p.*

I SAW Poland suffer *(London: Drummond 1941), 127p.*

JAMAR, K
With the tanks of the 1st Polish Armoured Division *(Holland: Smith 1946), 332p.*

JANTA, Aleksander
I lied to live: a year as a German family slave *(New York: Roy 1944), viii, 312p.*

JEDRZEJEWICZ, Waclaw *and* RAMSEY, P C (eds)
Poland in the British Parliament, 1939-1945 *(New York: Jozef Pilsudski Institute 1959), 3 vols.*

KARSKI, Jan (pseud)
The story of a secret state *(Boston, Mass: Houghton Mifflin 1944), 391p.*

KENNEDY, Robert M
The German campaign in Poland, 1939 *(Washington DC: Department of the Army 1956), 141p.*
KOT, Stanislaw
Conversations with the Kremlin; and dispatches from Russia *(London: Oxford UP 1963), xxx, 285p.*
KRZESINSKI, Andrew J
Poland's rights to justice *(New York: Devin-Adair 1946), 120p.*
KUNCEWICZOWA, Maria
Keys: a journey through Europe at war *(London: Hutchinson 1946), 176p.*
KURCZ, F S
Black brigade *(London: Atlantis 1943), 233p.*
LANE, Arthur B
I saw Poland betrayed *(Indianapolis, Ind: Bobbs-Merrill 1948), 17-344p.*
LANGER, *Mrs* Rulka
The mermaid and the Messerschmitt *(New York: Roy 1942), 372p.*
LEDNICKI, Waclaw
Reminiscences: the adventures of a modern Gil Blas during the last war *(The Hague: Monton 1971), 278p.*
LIPSCHUTZ, Norman
Victory through darkness and despair *(New York: Vantage 1960), 123p.*
LISIEWICZ, M (ed)
Destiny can wait: a history of the Polish Air Force in the Second World War *(London: Heinemann 1949), xvi, 420p.*
LITYNSKI, Zygmunt
I was one of them *(London: Cape 1941), 272p.*
MACLAREN, Anna
Poland at arms *(London: Murray 1942), xii, 116p.*
MAJEWSKI, Stefan
The Eleventh in action *(Edinburgh: Scottish-Polish Society 1944), 55p.*
MAKS, Leon
Russia by the back door *(London: Sheed and Ward 1954), viii, 264p.*
MAZUR, Tadeusz *and others* (eds)
We have not forgotten, 1939-1945 *(Warsaw: Polonia 1960), 266p.*
MIKOLAJCZYK, Stanislaw
The rape of Poland: pattern of Soviet aggression *(New York: Whittlesey 1948), 309p.*

MOWRER, Lilian
Arrest and exile: the true story of an American woman in Poland and Siberia, 1940–41 *(New York: Morrow 1941), 274p.*

MY NAME is million: the experiences of an Englishwoman in Poland *(London: Faber 1940), 284p.*

THE NAZI 'Kultur' in Poland *(London: HMSO 1945), unp.*

NIRENSTEIN, Albert (ed)
A tower from the enemy: contributions to a history of Jewish resistance in Poland *(New York: Orion 1959), 372p.*

NORWID-NEUGEBAUER, Mieczuslaw
Defence of Poland (September 1939) *(London: Kolin 1942), 9–228p.*

ORME, Alexandra
From Christmas to Easter: a guide to a Russian occupation *(London: Hodge 1949), 343p; US title:* Comes the comrade!

PADOWICZ, *Mrs* Barbara
Flight to freedom *(New York: Duell 1942), 257p.*

PINKUS, Oscar
The house of ashes *(Cleveland, Ohio: World 1964), 243p.*

POLAND accuses: an indictment of the major German war criminals *(London: Council of Polish Political Parties 1946), 58p.*

POLAND. Ministry of Information
The German fifth column in Poland *(London: Hutchinson 1941), 157p.*

POLE, Aline
Escape *(London: Temple 1946), 158p.*

PRUSZYNSKI, Ksawery
Poland fights back: from Westerplatte to Monte Casino *(London: Hodder & Stoughton 1941), 215p.*
The Polish invasion *(London: Minerva 1941), 112p.*

RACZYNSKI, Edward, *count*
In Allied London *(London: Weidenfeld & Nicolson [1963]), xiv, 381p.*

RUDNICKI, K S
The last of the war horses *(London: Bachman & Turner 1974), 255p.*

SALTER, Cedric
Flight from Poland *(London: Faber 1940), 7–226p.*

SCAEVOLA (pseud)
A study in forgery *(London: Rolls 1945), 123p.*

SLEDZIFISKI, Waclaw
Governor Frank's dark harvest *(Newtown, Mon: Montgomery 1946), 250p.*

STRZETELSKI, Stanislaw
Where the storm broke: Poland from yesterday to tomorrow *(New York: Roy 1942), 11-257*

STYPULKOWSKI, Zbigniew F
Invitation to Moscow *(New York: McKay 1951), xvi, 359p.*

SZOSZKIES, Henryk J
No traveler returns *(New York: Doubleday 1945), xiii, 267p.*

TENENBAUM, Joseph L *and* TENENBAUM, Sheila
In search of a lost people: the old and the new Poland *(New York: Beechhurst 1948), viii, 312p.*
Underground: the story of a people *(New York: Philosophical Library 1952), 532p.*

THE UNSEEN and silent: adventures from the underground movement narrated by paratroops of the Polish Home Army *(London: Sheed & Ward 1954), 350p.*

WARFIELD, Hania *and* WARFIELD, Gailler
Call us to witness: a Polish chronicle *(New York: Ziff-Davis 1945), 434p.*

WASHINGTON, *Mrs* Pat
Eagles in exile *(London: Maxlove 1942), 128p.*

WEGIERSKI, Dominik
September 1939 *(London: Minerva 1940), 180p.*

WIERZYNSKI, Kazimierz
Forgotten battlefield *(New York: Roy 1944), 7-179p.*

ZAJACKOWSKA, Anna
Poland: the untold story *(London: Brown 1945), 54p.*

[*see also* CONCENTRATION CAMPS, EASTERN EUROPE, JEWS, RUSSIA, WARSAW]

POLITICS

BECKLES, Gordon
Birth of a Spitfire: the story of Beaverbrook's Ministry and its first £10,000,000 *(London: Collins 1941), 160p.*

BORSODY, Stephen
The triumph of tyranny: the Nazi and Soviet conquest of Central Europe *(London: Cape 1960), 285p.*

DAHLERUS, Johan B E
The last attempt *(London: Hutchinson 1948), 134p.*

DEBORIN, Grigorii A
The Second World War: a politico-military survey *(New York: Universal 1964), 560p.*

DONNISON, Frank S V
Civil affairs and military government: central organization and planning *(London: HMSO 1966), xvii, 400p.*
DULLES, Allen W
The secret surrender *(New York: Harper 1966), [9], 268p, bib.*
EBENSTEIN, William
The German record: a political portrait *(New York: Farrar 1945), 334p.*
EDINGER, Lewis J
German exile politics: the social democratic executive committee in the Nazi era *(Berkeley, Calif: California UP 1956), 329p.*
FEIS, Herbert
Churchill, Roosevelt, Stalin: the war they waged and the peace they sought *(Princeton, NJ: Princeton UP 1957), xi, 692p.*
FISCHER, Louis
The great challenge *(New York: Duell 1946), 346p.*
FODOR, Marcel W
The revolution is on *(Boston, Mass: Houghton Mifflin 1940), xv, 239p.*
GARRATT, Geoffrey T
Europe's dance of death *(London: Allen & Unwin 1940), 332p; US title:* What has happened to Europe?
GERMANY. Forschungsamt
Breach of security: the German secret intelligence file in events leading to the Second World War *(London: Kimber 1968), 216p.*
GOLLANCZ, Victor (ed)
Betrayal of the left *(London: Gollancz 1941), xxiii, 324p.*
HANKEY, Maurice, *1st baron Hankey*
Politics, trials and errors *(Oxford: Pen-in-hand 1950), 150p.*
HARVEY, Ray F *and others*
The politics of this war *(New York: Harper 1943), v, 328p.*
KAMENETSKY, Ihor
Secret Nazi plans for Eastern Europe: a study of Lebensraum policies *(New York: Bockman 1961), 263p.*
KECSKEMETI, Paul
Strategic surrender: the politics of victory and defeat *(Stanford, Calif: Stanford UP 1958), ix, 287p, bib.*
MITCHELL, *Sir* Harold P
Into peace *(London: Hutchinson 1945), 124p.*
NAYLOR, Guy H
The secret war *(London: Long 1940), 281p.*
NEWSOME, Noel F *and* BULLOCK, Alan (eds)
Europe liberated *(London: Staples 1945), 91p.*

PARKINSON, Roger
Peace for our time: Munich to Dunkirk – the inside story *(London: Hart-Davis 1971), xx, 412p.*

ROOSEVELT, Franklin Delano
Roosevelt's foreign policy, 1933–1941 *(New York: Funk & Wignall 1942), xv, 634p.*

STIPP, John L (ed)
Devil's diary: the record of Nazi conspiracy and aggression *(Yellow Springs, Ohio: Antioch 1955), 236p.*

WALTER, David O
The American government at war *(Chicago, Ill: Irwin 1942), x, 235p.*

WINTRINGHAM, Thomas H
The politics of victory *(London: Routledge 1941), xx, 139p.*

WOODWARD, *Sir* Ernest L
British foreign policy in the Second World War *(London: HMSO 1962), 592p.*

[*see also* DIPLOMATIC HISTORY, HISTORY: INDIVIDUAL COUNTRIES]

POST OFFICE

HALSTEAD, Ivor
Post haste: the story of the Post Office in peace and war *(London: Drummond 1944), vii, 156p.*

HAY, Ian (pseud)
The Post Office went to war *(London: HMSO 1946), 94p.*

POTSDAM

FEIS, Hubert
Between war and peace: the Potsdam Conference *(Princeton, NJ: Princeton UP 1960), viii, 367p, bib.*

KEPLICZ, Klemens
Potsdam: twenty years after *(Warsaw: Zachodnia Agencja, Prasowa 1965), 129p.*

US DEPARTMENT OF STATE
The Conference of Berlin, 1945 *(Washington DC: Government Printing Office 1960), 2 vols.*

PRESS

ASSOCIATED PRESS
Reporting to remember: unforgettable stories and pictures of World War II *(New York: Associated 1945), 71p.*

BAUME, Frederic E
I've lived another year: a journalist's diary of the year 1941 *(London: Harrap 1942), 212p.*

BROOKHOUSER, Frank
This was your war: an anthology of great writings from World War II *(New York: Doubleday 1960), 498p.*

CARROLL, Gordon (ed)
History in the writing, by the foreign correspondents of Time, Life and Fortune *(New York: Duell 1945), 401p.*

CUDAHY, John
Armies march: a personal report *(New York: Scribner 1941), xi, 304p.*

DAILY TELEGRAPH (newspaper)
The Daily Telegraph story of the war *(London: Hodder & Stoughton 1942–6), 5 vols.*

DRAWBELL, James W
The long year *(London: Wingate 1958), 242p.*

FLETCHER, Leonard
They never failed: the story of the provincial Press in wartime *(London: Newspaper Society 1946), 80p.*

GORDON, Matthew
News is a weapon *(New York: Knopf 1942), viii, 268p.*

GRAMLING, Oliver
Free men are fighting: the story of World War II *(New York: Farrar 1942), xvi, 488p.*

LANCUM, Frank H
'Press officer, please!' *(London: Lockwood 1946), 144p.*

LIFE MAGAZINE
Picture history of World War II *(New York: Times 1950), vii, 368p.*

MIDDLETON, Drew
Our share of night: a personal narrative of the war years *(New York: Viking 1946), 380p.*

MONKS, Noel
Eye-witness *(London: Muller 1956), 344p.*

THE NEW YORKER (magazine)
The New Yorker book of war pieces *(New York: Reynal & Hitchcock 1947), 562p.*

NEW YORK HERALD TRIBUNE (newspaper)
Front page history of the Second World War *(New York: New York Herald Tribune 1946), 112p.*

NEW YORK TIMES (newspaper)
Days of decision: wartime editorials from the New York Times *(New York: Doubleday 1941), xxiv, 278p.*
OESTREICHER, John C
The world is their beat *(London: Essential 1945), viii, 254p.*
PYLE, Ernest T
Ernie Pyle in England *(New York: McBride 1941), xiv, 228p.*
RIESS, Curt (ed)
They were there: the story of World War II and how it came about *(New York: Putnam 1944), xliii, 670p.*
STARS AND STRIPES (newspaper)
The story of World War II *(New York: McKay 1960), 504p.*
STEED, Henry W
The fifth arm *(London: Constable 1940), 162p.*
THE TIMES (newspaper)
Europe under the Nazi scourge: a picture and an indictment: a reprint of some recent articles in The Times on conditions in the countries of Europe which have fallen under Nazi oppression *(London: The Times 1940), viii, 146p.*
WILLIS, Jerome
It stopped at London: being the last days of the free people of Barcelona and the free people of Paris, and the great days of the people of London in the years, 1938–1941 *(London: Hurst & Blackett 1944), 144p.*
WINN, Godfrey H
The hour before the dawn *(London: Collins 1942), 192p.*
On going to the wars *(London: Collins 1941), 192p.*
Scrapbook of the war *(London: Hutchinson 1943), 94p.*
YANK (periodical)
Yank - the G.I. story of the war *(New York: Duell 1947), 319p.*
ZIEGLER, Richard
Faces behind the news *(London: Dobson 1946), 126p.*
[*see also* WAR CORRESPONDENTS]

PRISONER OF WAR CAMPS

AIDA, Yuji
Prisoner of the British: a Japanese soldier's experiences in Burma *(London: Cresset 1966), xiv, 202p.*
AMBRIERE, Francis
The long holiday *(New York: Ziff-Davis 1948), viii, 249p; UK title:* The exiled.
ARGALL, Phyllis
My life with the enemy *(New York: Macmillan 1944), viii, 290p.*

ASLANIS, Anastasios
The man of confidence *(New York: Vantage 1963), 236p.*
BARBER, Noel
Prisoner of war: the story of British prisoners held by the enemy *(London: Harrap 1944), 135p.*
BEATTIE, Edward W
Diary of a Kriegie *(New York: Crowell 1946), 312p.*
BENNETT, Lowell
Parachute to Berlin *(New York: Vanguard 1945), 252p.*
BENUZZI, Felice
No picnic on Mount Kenya *(London: Kimber 1952), 230p.*
BERG, Erik R
Behind barbed wires among war prisoners in Germany *(Minneapolis, Minn: Augustana 1944), 95p.*
BEST, Sigismund P
The Venlo incident *(London: Hutchinson* [*1950*]*), 260p.*
BILLANY, Don *and* DOWNIE, David
The cage *(London: Longmans 1949), 189p.*
BOYLE, Martin
Yanks don't cry *(New York: Geis 1963), 249p.*
BRADING, A C P
And so to Germany *(Ilfracombe, Devon: Stockwell 1966), 71p.*
BRINES, Russell
Until they eat stones *(Philadelphia, Pa: Lippincott 1944), 7-340p.*
BROOMHEAD, Edwin N
Barbed wire in the sunset *(London: Book Depot 1945), xii, 148p.*
BURNEY, Christopher
The dungeon democracy *(London: Heinemann 1945), 100p.*
Solitary confinement *(London: Clerke & Cockeran 1952), 152p.*
CAILLOU, Alan
The world is six feet square *(London: Davis 1954),* [*4*]*, 214p.*
CALNAN, Thomas D
Free as a running fox *(London: Macdonald 1970), 323p.*
CASTLE, John
The password is courage *(London: Souvenir 1954), 224p.*
CHIESL, Oliver M
Clipped wings *(London: Dayton Kimball 1948), 1 vol.*
CHURCHILL, Peter
The spirit in the cage *(London: Hodder & Stoughton* [*1954*]*), 251p.*
CLIFTON, George
The happy hunted *(London: Cassell 1952), 392p.*

COHEN, Bernard M *and* COOPER, Maurice Z
A follow-up study of World War II prisoners-of-war *(Washington DC: Government Printing Office 1954), 81p.*

CONNELL, Charles
The hidden catch *(London: Elek [1955]), 176p.*

COWARD, Roger V
Sailors in cages *(London: Macdonald 1967), 237p.*

CZAPSKI, Joseph
The inhuman land *(London: Chatto & Windus 1951), xvi, 301p.*

DALDRUP, Leo
The other side *(London: Hodder & Stoughton [1954]), viii, 9-256p.*

DOBRAN, Edward
P.O.W.: the story of an American prisoner of war during World War II *(New York: Exposition 1953), 123p.*

DOMVILLE, *Sir* Barry
From Admiral to cabin boy *(London: Boswell 1947), 163p.*

DOWARD, Jan S
The seventh escape *(Mountain View, Calif: Pacific 1968), 119p.*

DUNNING, George
Where bleed the many *(London: Elek 1955), 256p.*

EGGERS, Reinhold
Colditz: the German story *(London: Hale [1961]), 190p.*

FILI, William J
Of lice and men: a true story of depersonalization and survival of a P.O.W. *(New York: Dorrance 1973), 133p.*

FUCIK, Julius
Notes from the gallows *(London: New Central 1948), xiv, 112p.*

GALLEGOS, Adrian
From Capri into oblivion *(London: Hodder & Stoughton [1960]), 256p.*

GANT, Roland
How like a wilderness *(London: Gollancz 1946), 160p.*

GERSTEL, Jan
The war for you is over *(Chatswood, Aust: Adventure 1960), 299p.*

GOODMAN, Julien M
M.D. P.O.W. *(New York: Exposition 1972), 218p.*

GREEN, Julius M
From Colditz in code *(London: Hale 1971), 192p.*

GUERLAIN, Robert (pseud)
They who wait *(New York: Crowell 1943), xi, 206p; UK title:* Prisoner in Germany.

HAEDRICH, Marcel (pseud)
Barrack 3, room 12 *(New York: Reynal 1943), xiv, 229p.*

HARSH, George
Lonesome road *(New York: Norton 1971), 222p.*

INSTONE, Gordon
Freedom the spur *(London: Burke 1953), 256p.*

JANTA, Alexander
Bound with two chains *(New York: Roy 1945), 234p.*

JENNINGS, C O
An ocean without shores *(London: Hodder & Stoughton [1950]), 4, 223p.*

JOFFE, Constantin
We were free *(New York: Smith & Durrell 1943), 9-237p.*

KYDD, Sam
For you the war is over *(London: Bachman & Turner 1973), 315p.*

LEEMING, John F
Always tomorrow *(London: Harrap 1951), 188p; US title:* The natives are friendly.

LOMNITZ, Alfred
Never mind, Mr. Lom! or, The uses of adversity *(London: Macmillan 1941), ix, 191p.*

LUDDEN, Robert W
Barbed wire interlude: a souvenir of Kriegsgefangenlager der Luftwaffe Nr. 4, Deutschland 1944 *(Baltimore, Md: National Advertising 1945), 77p.*

LUMIERE, Cornel
Kura! *(Brisbane, Aust: Jacaranda 1966), 258p.*

MARSH, Eileen
Barbed wire *(London: Hutchinson 1945), 168p.*

MORETON, George
Doctor in chains *(London: Howard Baker 1970), [10], 251p.*

MORGAN, Guy
Only ghosts can live *(London: Lockwood 1945), 168p; US title:* P.O.W.

NABARRO, Derrick
Wait for the dawn *(London: Cassell 1952), [6], 207p.*

NEWBY, Eric
Love and war in the Apennines *(London: Hodder & Stoughton 1971), 221p.*

NEWCOMB, Alan H
Vacation with pay: being an account of my stay at the German rest

camp for tired Allied airmen at beautiful Barth-on-the-Baltic *(Haverhill, Mass: Destiny 1947), 198p.*

PABEL, Reinhold
Enemies are human *(Philadelphia, Pa: Winston 1955), 248p.*

PAUL, Daniel *and* ST JOHN, John
Surgeon at arms *(London: Heinemann 1958), [10], 227p.*

PHILPOT, Oliver
Stolen journey *(London: Hodder & Stoughton 1950), 412p.*

PIOTROWSKI, Marian
Adventures of a Polish prisoner *(London: Drummond 1943), 207p.*

PORTWAY, Christopher
Journey to Dana *(London: Kimber 1955), xii, 13–248p.*

PRYCE, Joseph E
Heels in line *(London: Barker 1958), vi, 7–223p.*

REINER, Ella L
Prisoners of fear *(London: Gollancz 1948), 208p.*

RILEY, Gerard
Fugitive in France *(London: Hutchinson 1942), 83p.*

ROMILLY, Giles *and* ALEXANDER, Michael
The privileged nightmare *(London: Weidenfeld & Nicolson 1954), vii, 246p.*

SABEY, Ian
Stalag scrapbook *(Melbourne, Aust: Cheshire 1947), 136p.*

SANDULESCU, Jacques
Doubas *(New York: McKay 1968), 217p.*

SEWELL, William G
Strange harmony *(London: Edinburgh House 1946), 192p.*

SHIBER, *Mrs* Etta
Paris-underground *(New York: Scribner 1943), vi, 392p.*

SIMMONS, Kenneth W
Kriegie *(New York: Nelson 1960), 256p.*

SMITH, Donald
And all the trumpets *(London: Bles 1954), [9], 245p.*

SPIER, Eugen
The protecting power *(London: Skeffington 1951), 252p.*

STONE, Brian
Prisoner from Alamein *(London: Witherby 1944), 189p.*

STONE, James F
A holiday in Hitlerland *(New York: Carlton 1970), 74p.*

STRONG, Tracy (ed)
We prisoners of war: sixteen British officers and soldiers speak from a German prison camp *(London: Associated 1942), 90p.*

TANTRI, K'tut
Revolt in paradise *(New York: Harper 1960), 308p.*
TAYLOR, Geoff
Return ticket *(London: Davies 1972), [5], 178p.*
THOMPSON, Douglas W
Captives to freedom *(London: Epworth 1955), 188p.*
TOLEDANO, Marc
The Franciscan of Bourges *(London: Harrap 1970), 174p.*
TOSCHI, Elios
Ninth time lucky *(London: Kimber 1955), 216p.*
VAN DER POST, Laurens
A bar of shadow *(London: Hogarth 1954), 58p.*
VIETOR, John A
Time out: American airmen at Stalag Luft I *(West Ridge, NH: Smith 1951), 9-192p.*
WARD, Edward
Give me air *(London: Lane 1946), 253p.*
WINDSOR, John
The mouth of the wolf *(London: Hodder & Stoughton [1967]), 224p.*
WOOD, Jerry E R (ed)
Detour: the story of Oflag IV C *(London: Falcon 1946), 308p.*
[*see also* ESCAPES, JAPANESE PRISON CAMPS, RUSSIAN PRISON CAMPS]

PROPAGANDA

AUCKLAND, Reginald G
Aerial propaganda over Great Britain *(Sandridge, Herts: Auckland [1963]), [3], 43p.*
BORNSTEIN, Joseph *and* MILTON, Paul R
Action against the enemy's mind *(Minneapolis, Minn: Bobbs-Merrill 1942), xxi, 294p.*
BRAMSTEAD, Ernest K
Goebbels and National Socialist propaganda, 1925-1945 *(East Lauring, Mich: Michigan State UP 1965), 488p.*
CARROLL, Wallace
Persuade or perish *(Boston, Mass: Houghton Mifflin 1948), 392p.*
CAUSTON, Bernard
Moral blitz: war propaganda and Christianity *(London: Secker & Warburg 1941), 128p.*
CHILDS, Harwood L *and* WHITTON, J B (eds)
Propaganda by short wave *(Princeton, NJ: New Jersey UP 1942), xii, 355p.*

FRAENKEL, Heinrich
Help us Germans to beat the Nazis! *(London: Gollancz 1941), 120p.*

FRYE, Alton
Nazi Germany and the American hemisphere, 1933–1941 *(New Haven, Conn: Yale UP 1967), ix, 229p, bib.*

GEORGE, Alexander L
Propaganda analysis: a study of inferences made from Nazi propaganda in World War II *(Westport, Conn: Greenwood 1959), 287p.*

GOMBRICH, Ernst H
Myth and reality in German war-time broadcasts *(London: Athlone 1970), [4], 28p.*

HAFFNER, Sebastian
Offensive against Germany *(London: Secker & Warburg 1941), 127p.*

HUNT, Robert (comp)
Swastika at war *(London: Cooper 1975), 160p.*

JUDD, Denis
Posters of World War Two *(London: Wayland 1972), vii, [327p.]*

LANGDON-DAVIES, John
The fifth column *(London: Murray 1940), 60p.*

LAVINE, Harold *and* WECKSLER, J A
War propaganda and the United States *(New Haven, Conn: Yale UP 1940), x, 363p.*

LERNER, Daniel (ed)
Propaganda in war and crisis: materials for American policy *(New York: Stewart 1951), 500p.*

LOCKHART, Robert B
Comes the reckoning *(London: Putnam 1947), viii, 384p.*

MANN, Thomas
Listen, Germany!: twenty-five radio messages to the German people over B.B.C. *(New York: Knopf 1943), 112p.*

MEO, Lucy D
Japan's radio war on Australia, 1941–1945 *(Melbourne, Aust: Melbourne UP 1968), xv, 300p, bib.*

MERTON, Robert K
Mass persuasion: the social psychology of a war bond drive *(New York: Harper 1946), 210p.*

QUALTER, Terence H
Propaganda and psychological warfare *(New York: Random House 1962), 172p.*

SAYERS, Michael *and* KAHN, A E
Sabotage!: the secret war against America *(New York: Harper 1942), 266p.*

SCIPIO (pseud)
100,000,000 allies - if we choose *(London: Gollancz 1940), 118p.*

SETH, Ronald
The truth-benders: psychological warfare in the Second World War *(London: Frewin 1969), 204p, bib.*

SINGTON, Derrick *and* WEIDENFELD, Arthur
The Goebbels experiment: a study of the Nazi propaganda machine *(London: Murray 1942), 260p.*

SMITH, Bruce L *and others*
Propaganda, communication and public opinion: a comprehensive reference guide *(Princeton, NJ: Princeton UP 1946), 435p.*

TAYLOR, Edmond
Strategy of terror; Europe's inner front *(Boston, Mass: Houghton Mifflin 1940), 278p.*

THOMPSON, Dorothy
Listen, Hans *(Boston, Mass: Houghton Mifflin 1942), x, 292p.*

THOULESS, Robert H
Straight thinking in wartime *(London: English UP 1942), 224p.*

WARBURG, James P
Unwritten treaty *(New York: Harcourt 1946), 186p.*

ZEMAN, Zbynek A B
Nazi propaganda *(London: Oxford UP 1964), xiii, 226p, bib.*

[*see also* PRESS, PSYCHOLOGY, RADIO]

PSYCHOLOGY

AHRENFELDT, Robert H
Psychiatry in the British Army in the Second World War *(London: Routledge 1958), xv, 312p, bib.*

BARUCH, *Mrs* Dorothy
You, your children, and war *(New York: Appleton 1942), ix, 234p.*

BENEDEK, Therese
Insight and personality adjustment: a study of the psychological effects of war *(New York: Ronald 1948), 305p.*

COOKE, Elliot D
All but me and thee: psychiatry at the foxhole level *(Washington DC: Infantry Journal Press 1946), 215p.*

DAUGHERTY, William E *and* JANOWITZ, Morris
A psychological warfare casebook *(Baltimore, Md: Johns Hopkins 1958), 880p.*
GRINKER, Roy R *and* SPIEGEL, J P
Men under stress *(Toronto: Blakiston 1945), xii, 484p.*
War neuroses *(Toronto: Blakiston 1945), ix, 145p.*
HILL, Reuben L
Families under stress: adjustment to the crises of war separation and reunion *(New York: Harper 1949), x, 443p.*
LINEBARGER, Paul M A
Psychological warfare *(Washington DC: Infantry Journal Press 1948), 259p.*
MAAS, Henry (ed)
Adventures in mental health: psychiatric social work with the armed forces in World War II *(New York: Columbia UP 1951), 334p.*
MARGOLIN, Leo J
Paper bullets: a brief story of psychological warfare in World War II *(New York: Froben 1946), 149p.*
PADOVER, Saul K
Psychologist in Germany *(London: Phoenix House 1946), 320p; US title:* Experiment in Germany.
REES, John R
The shaping of psychiatry by war *(London: Chapman & Hall 1945), 158p.*
ROETTER, Charles
Psychological warfare *(London: Batsford 1974), 199p.*
SAVA, George (pseud)
War without guns: the psychological front *(Toronto: Ryerson 1943), 156p.*
SOCIAL SCIENCE RESEARCH COUNCIL
Studies in social psychology in World War II *(Princeton, NJ: Princeton UP 1949–50), 4 vols.*
VAUGHAN, Elizabeth H
Community under stress: an internment camp culture *(Princeton, NJ: Princeton UP 1949), xiv, 160p.*

QUAKERS

HINSHAW, David
An experiment in friendship *(New York: Putnam 1947), 147p.*
KERSHNER, Howard E
Quaker service in modern war *(New York: Prentice-Hall 1950), 195p.*

WILSON, Roger C
Quaker relief: an account of the relief work of the Society of Friends, 1940–48 *(London: Allen & Unwin 1952), 373p.*
[*see also* AMBULANCES]

QUISLING

HAYES, Paul M
Quisling: the career and political ideas of Vidkun Quisling, 1887-1945 *(Newton Abbot, Devon: David & Charles 1971), 368p, bib.*
HEWINS, Ralph
Quisling, prophet without honour *(London: Allen 1965), 384p.*
KNUDSEN, Harold F
I was Quisling's secretary *(London: Britons 1967), 192p, bib.*
[*see also* NORWAY]

RADAR

CARNE, Daphne
The eyes of the few *(London: P R Macmillan 1960), xii, 13-238p.*
PRICE, Alfred
Instruments of darkness *(London: Kimber 1967), 254p.*
ROWE, Albert P
One story of radar *(Cambridge: Cambridge UP 1948), 207p.*
SAWARD, Dudley
The bomber's eye *(London: Cassell 1959), xiii, 264p.*
WATSON-WATT, *Sir* Robert A
The pulse of radar: the autobiography of Sir Robert Watson-Watt *(New York: Dial 1959), 438p.*
Three steps to victory: a personal account of radar's greatest pioneer *(London: Odhams 1957), 480p.*

RADIO

BRITISH BROADCASTING CORPORATION
War report: a record of dispatches broadcast by the B.B.C.'s war correspondents with the Allied Expeditionary Force, 6 June 1944–5 May 1945 *(London: Oxford UP 1946), 452p.*
COLUMBIA BROADCASTING SYSTEM
From D-Day through victory in Europe: the eye-witness story as told by war correspondents *(New York: CBC 1945), 314p.*
From Pearl Harbor into Tokyo: the story as told by war correspondents on the air *(New York: CBC 1945), 312p.*

DELMER, Sefton
Black boomerang *(London: Secker & Warburg 1962), 320p.*
Trail sinister *(London: Secker & Warburg 1961), 423p.*

EWING, William
Good evening: a collection of radio broadcasts, reporting the progress of the war *(Honolulu: Star Bulletin 1943), 80p.*

FRIEDMANN, Otto
Broadcasting for democracy *(London: Allen & Unwin 1942), 62p.*

HENSLOW, Miles
The miracle of radio: the story of radio's decisive contribution to victory *(London: Evans 1946), 127p.*

KALTENBORN, Hans von
Kaltenborn edits the news *(New York: Dutton 1942), 5-96p.*

KIRBY, Edward M *and* HARRIS, Jack W
Star-spangled radio *(Chicago, Ill: Ziff-Davis 1948), 278p.*

KRABBE, Henning (ed)
Voices from Britain: broadcast history, 1939-1945 *(London: Allen & Unwin 1947), 304p.*

KRIS, Ernst *and* SPEIER, Hans
German radio propaganda: report on home broadcasts during the war *(London: Oxford UP 1944), xiv, 529p.*

LEAN, Edward T
Voices in the darkness: the story of the European radio war *(London: Secker & Warburg 1943), 243p.*

LET'S face the facts: [a series of radio addresses by Dorothy Thompson and others] *(London: Lane 1941), 212p.*

NATIONAL BROADCASTING COMPANY
This is the story of the liberation of Europe from the fall of Rome to victory - as NBC newsmen relayed it by radio to American listeners *(New York: NBC 1945), 50p.*

OLDFIELD, Barney
Never a shot in anger *(New York: Duell 1956), 334p.*

PAUL, Oscar
Underground Europe calling *(London: Gollancz 1942), 160p.*

PRIESTLEY, John B
Postscripts *(London: Heinemann 1940), 100p.*

RIGBY, Charles A
War on the short waves *(London: Cole 1944), 68p.*

ROLO, Charles J
Radio goes to war: the fourth front *(New York: Putnam 1942), xviii, 293p.*

SWINTON, *Sir* Ernest D
War commentary: broadcasts delivered between October 1939 and March 1940 *(London: Hodder & Stoughton 1940), 126p.*
[*see also* PROPAGANDA, WAR CORRESPONDENTS]

RAILWAYS

BELL, Robert
History of the British railways during the war, 1939–45 *(London: Railway Gazette 1946), 291p.*
DARWIN, Bernard R M
War on the line: the story of the Southern Railway in wartime *(London: Southern Railway 1946), 215p.*
FARRINGTON, Selwyn K
Railroads at war *(New York: Curl 1944), xviii, 320p.*
NASH, George C
The LMS at war *(London: LMS Railway 1946), 87p.*
NOCK, O S
British railways at war 1939–1945 *(London: Allan 1971), 224p.*
SIMPSON, Evan J (pseud)
Time table for victory: British railways war history 1939–1945 *(London: British Railways 1948), 268p.*

RAMSGATE (KENT)

KEMPE, A B C
Midst bands and bombs, by the top hat Mayor of Ramsgate *(Maidstone, Kent: Kent Messenger 1946), 135p.*

RED CROSS

AYE, Lillian
Iran caboose *(Hollywood, Calif: House-Warven 1951), 190p.*
BARING, Norah
A friendly hearth *(London: Cape 1946), 128p.*
BERNADOTTE OF WISBORG, Folke, *greve*
Instead of arms *(Stockholm: Bonniers 1948), 227p.*
CAMPBELL, Alfred S
Guadalcanal round-trip: the story of an American Red Cross Field Director in the present war *(Lambertville, NJ: Campbell 1945), 112p.*
INSH, George P
The war-time history of the Scottish Branch, British Red Cross Society *(Glasgow: Jackson 1952), 207p.*

INTER arma caritas: the work of the International Committee of the Red Cross during the Second World War *(Geneva 1947), 135p.*

REPORT of the International Committee of the Red Cross on its activities during the Second World War, September 1, 1939–June 30, 1947 *(Geneva 1948), 3 vols.*

ISSERMAN, Ferdinand M
A Rabbi with the American Red Cross *(New York: Whittier Books 1958), 334p.*

JUNOD, Marcel
Warrior without weapons *(London: Cape 1951), 318p.*

KORSON, George G
At his side: the story of the American Red Cross overseas in World War II *(New York: Coward-McCann 1945), 322p.*

MALONEY, John W
Let there be mercy: the odyssey of a Red Cross man *(New York: Doubleday 1941), xiii, 337p.*

SAUNDERS, Hilary St G
The Red Cross and the white: a short history of the joint war organization of the British Red Cross Society and the Order of St. John of Jerusalem during the war, 1939–1945 *(London: Hollis & Carter 1949), 195p.*

SKIMMING, Sylvia
Sand in my shoes: the tale of a Red Cross welfare officer with the British Hospitals overseas in the Second World War *(Edinburgh: Oliver & Boyd 1948), 182p.*

REFERENCE BOOKS

BALLIN, Alexander (comp)
The German occupation of the USSR in World War II: a bibliography *(Washington DC: Department of State 1955), 76p.*

BAXTER, Arthur B
Men, martyrs and mountebanks: inner story of personalities and events behind the war *(London: Hutchinson 1940), 9–286p.*

CANG, Joel
Who's Who of the Allied Governments *(London: Allied 1941), 5–79p.*

DEWEERD, Harvey A
Great soldiers of World War II *(New York: Norton 1944), 8–316p.*

DEWILDE, John C *and others*
Handbook of the war *(Boston, Mass: Houghton Mifflin 1939), vi, 248p.*

THE GENERALS and the Admirals *(New York: Devin-Adair 1945), 2 vols.*

HOLBROOK, Stewart H
None more courageous: American war heroes of today *(New York: Macmillan 1942), x, 245p.*

REID, Alan
A concise encyclopaedia of the Second World War *(Reading, Bucks: Osprey 1974), 232p.*

ROHMER, Jurgen *and* HUMMELCHEN, G
Chronology of the war at sea, 1939–1945 *(London: Allan 1972–4), 2 vols.*

SPIER, Henry O (comp)
World War II in our magazines and books, September 1939 to September 1945: a bibliography *(New York: Stuyvesant 1945), 96p.*

STEEL, Johannes
Men behind the war: a Who's Who of our time *(New York: Sheridan 1942), xviii, 447p.*

STOKES, Donald H
Men behind victory *(London: Hutchinson 1944), 168p.*

THOMAS, Lowell J
These men shall never die *(Washington DC: War Department 1943), xii, 308p.*

TUNNEY, Christopher
A biographical dictionary of World War II *(London: Dent 1972), viii, 216p.*

TUOHY, Ferdinand
Twelve lances for liberty *(London: Nicholson & Watson 1940), 264p.*

WELLS, Linton
Salute to valor: heroes of the United States *(New York: Random House 1942), viii, 280p.*

ZIEGLER, Janet (comp)
World War II: books in English 1945–65 *(Stanford, Calif: Hoover Institute 1971), 223p.*

REFUGEES

BENTWICH, Norman
I understand the risks: the story of the refugees from Nazi oppressions who fought in the British Forces in the World War *(London: Gollancz 1950), 192p.*
They found refuge: an account of British Jewry's work for the victims of Nazi oppression *(London: Cresset 1956), xii, 227p.*

BILLINGSLEY, Chris
The Nazis called me traitor: the wartime memoirs of a teen-age refugee *(New York: Exposition 1966), 232p.*

BODER, David P
I did not interview the dead *(Urbana, Ill: Illinois UP 1949), 220p.*

BRITAIN'S new citizens: the story of the refugees from Germany and Austria, 1941–1951 *(London: Association of Jewish Refugees in Great Britain 1951), 75p.*

DEMBITZER, Salamon
Visas for America: a story of an escape *(Sydney: Villon 1952), 267p.*

FORD, Herbert
Flee the captor *(Nashville, Tenn: Southern 1966), 373p.*

FORREST, Alec J
But some there be *(London: Hale 1957), 252p.*

FRUMKIN, Grzegorz
Population changes in Europe since 1939 *(London: Allen & Unwin 1951), 191p.*

HARBINSON, Robert
Song of Erne *(London: Faber 1960), 244p.*

HAY, John (pseud)
Peaceful invasion *(London: Hodder & Stoughton 1946), 238p.*

HEIDE, Dirk van der (pseud)
My sister and I: the diary of a Dutch boy refugee *(London: Faber 1941), 95p.*

HIRSCHMANN, Ira A
Life line to a promised land *(New York: Vanguard 1946), 214p.*

HUXLEY-BLYTHE, Peter J
The East came West *(Caldwell, Ohio: Caxton 1964), 225p.*

JUDEX (pseud)
Anderson's prisoners *(London: Gollancz 1940), 124p.*

KIMCHE, Jon *and* KIMCHE, David
The secret roads: the illegal migration of a people, 1938–1948 *(London: Secker & Warburg 1954), 223p.*

LAMBERT, D
The sheltered days *(London: Deutsch 1965), 192p.*

LASKER, Bruno
Asia on the move: population pressure, migration, and re-settlement in Eastern Asia under the influence of want and war *(New York: Holt 1945), 207p.*

MARITSKY, Victor (pseud)
My pupils and I *(New York: Comet 1955), 78p.*

PROUDFOOT, Malcolm J
European refugees: a study in forced population movement *(Evanston, Ill: Northwestern UP 1956), 542p.*
STONE, Isador F
Underground to Palestine *(New York: Boni & Gaer 1946), 240p.*
TRAVERS, Pamela L
I go by sea, I go by land *(New York: Norton 1964), 233p.*
[*see also* DISPLACED PERSONS]

RELIEF WORK

BRIGGS, David G
Action amid ruins *(New York: American Field Service 1945), 174p.*
CHARITY abounding: the story of Papal relief work during the war *(London: Burns, Oates 1945), 51p.*
ELLIS, Jean M
Face powder and gunpowder *(Toronto: Saunders 1947), 229p.*
FERGUSON, Sheila *and* FITZGERALD, Hilde
Studies in the social services *(London: HMSO 1954), 367p.*
FORTESCUE, Winifred B
Beauty for ashes *(Edinburgh: Blackwood 1948), 318p.*
GREAT BRITAIN. Central Office of Information
Friends in need: the story of British War Relief Inc. of the United States of America, 1939–1945 *(London: HMSO 1947), 75p.*
LUTZ, Alma (comp)
With love, Jane: letters from American women on the war fronts *(New York: Day 1945), 199p.*
MACDONALD, Florence
For Greece a tear: the story of the Greek War Relief Fund of Canada *(Fredericton, NB: Brunswick 1954), 193p.*
SEYMOUR, Harold J
Design for giving: the story of the National War Fund Inc., 1943–1947 *(New York: Harper 1947), 182p.*

RELIGION

ADAMS, Hampton
Christian answers to war questions *(New York: Revell 1943), 5–96p.*
AMOURY, Daisy
Father Cyclone *(New York: Messner 1958), 253p.*

BARTH, Karl
A letter to Great Britain from Switzerland *(London: SPCK 1941), x, 53p; US title:* This Christian cause.

BASSETT, George
This also happened *(London: Epworth 1947), 125p.*

BELL, George K A
The Church and humanity, 1939–1946 *(London: Longmans, Green 1946), 252p.*

BRINK, Ebenezer C
And God was there *(Toronto: Ambassador 1944), 13–92p.*

BRUCKBERGER, Raymond L
One sky to share *(New York: Kennedy 1952), 248p.*

CALDWELL, Daniel T *and* BOWMAN, Benjamin
They answered the call *(Richmond, Va: John Knox 1952), 142p.*

CAMMAERTS, Emile
Flower of grass *(London: Cresset 1944), 160p.*

CARLSON, Alvin O
He is able: faith overcomes fear in a foxhole *(Grand Rapids, Mich: Zondervan 1945), 82p.*

CARMER, Carl L (ed)
The war against God *(New York: Holt 1943), xiii, 261p.*

CHURCH, Leslie F
Between ourselves: letters to my brethren *(London: Epworth 1944), 110p.*

CLARK, Cecil H D
God within the shadow: the divine hand in the First and Second Great Wars of the twentieth century *(London: Regency 1970), 171p, bib.*

CLAYPOOL, James V
God on a battlewagon *(Philadelphia, Pa: Winston 1944), xiv, 110p.*

COCHRANE, Arthur C
The Church and the war *(Toronto: Nelson 1940), xxix, 152p.*

DARK, Sidney
The Church: impotent or triumphant? *(London: Gollancz 1941), 120p.*

DAWSON, Christopher H
Judgment of the nations *(New York: Sheed & Ward 1942), 222p.*

DENNIS, Clyde H (ed)
These live on: the best of true stories unveiling the power and presence of God in World War II *(Chicago, Ill: Good 1945), 204p.*

ELDRIDGE, Retha H
Bombs and blessings *(Washington DC: Review & H 1946), 256p.*

ELLIOTT, Wallace H
Look through my window *(London: Muller 1942), 79p.*

FLORENCE, Frank T
Feet of clay: the true story of a P.W.'s search for God *(New York: Exposition 1958), 98p.*

GOLDMANN, Gereon K
The shadow of his wings *(Chicago, Ill: Franciscan Herald 1964), 285p.*

HAFER, Harold F
Evangelical and Reformed Churches and World War II *(Philadelphia, Pa: Heidelberg 1948), vii, 6–137p.*

HERSHBERGER, Guy F
The Mennonite Church in the Second World War *(Scottdale, Pa: Mennonite 1951), 308p.*

HICKOX, Percy M
Mine eyes have seen *(Boston, Mass: Mosher 1950), 109p.*

HINSLEY, Arthur, *cardinal*
Bond of peace and other war-time addresses *(London: Burns, Oates 1941), xii, 148p.*

HOPWOOD, Percy G S
Out of the blitz: the gates of hell shall not prevail *(New York: Revell 1942), 7-190p.*

HOUGH, Donald
Darling, I am home *(New York: Norton 1946), 176p.*

HOUSELANDER, Frances C
This war is the passion *(New York: Sheed & Ward 1941), x, 185p.*

INGRAM, Kenneth
The night is far spent *(London: Allen & Unwin 1941), 126p.*

JOERS, Lawrence E C
God is my captain *(Mountain View, Calif: Pacific 1945), 5–174p.*

JONES, William R
Let's try reality *(London: Allen & Unwin 1941), vi, 9–168p.*

KELLER, Adolf
Christian Europe today *(New York: Harper 1942), x, 310p.*

KERTZER, Morris N
With an H on my dog tag *(New York: Behrman House 1947), 197p.*

KNOX, John (ed)
Religion and the present crisis *(Chicago, Ill: Chicago UP 1942), xi, 165p.*

LEBER, Charles T
The Church must win!: the place, power and promise of the Christian Church in the conflict of our time *(New York: Revell 1944), 7-185p.*
Unconquerable: concerning the Christian mission in a world at war *(New York: Revell 1943), 5-160p.*

LEUSCHNER, Martin L *and others* (eds)
Religion in the ranks *(Cleveland, Ohio: Roger Williams 1946), 128p.*

LOGISTES (pseud)
Diplomacy and God *(New York: Longmans 1941), ix, 237p.*

MCKEE, Elmore M
Beyond the night *(New York: Scribner 1944), ix, 243p.*

MAAHS, Arnold M
Our eyes were opened *(Columbus, Ohio: Wartburg 1946), 110p.*

MARTIN, Hugh *and others*
Christian counter-attack: Europe's Churches against Nazism *(London: SCMP 1943), 11-125p.*

MOELLERING, Ralph L
Modern war and American Churches: a factual study of the Christian conscience on trial from 1939 to the cold war crisis of today *(New York: American 1947), 141p.*

MORRISON, Charles
My battle *(Boston, Mass: Meador 1942), 7-206p.*

MORRISON, Charles C
The Christian and the war *(Chicago, Ill: Willett 1942), v, 145p.*

MURRY, John M
The betrayal of Christ by the Churches *(London: Dakers 1940), 191p.*

NANCE, Ellwood C (ed)
The faith of our fighters *(St Louis, Miss: Bethany 1944), 7-304p.*

NELSON, Ralph W
Soldier, you're it *(New York: Association 1945), 132p.*

PERRIN, Henri
Priest workman in Germany *(London: Sheed & Ward 1947), vii, 230p.*

POLING, Daniel A
A preacher looks at war *(New York: Macmillan 1943), xvi, 101p.*

POTEAT, Edwin M
Four freedoms and God *(New York: Harper 1943), 155p.*

RITTENHOUSE, William H
God's P.O.W. *(New York: Greenwich 1957), 91p.*

ROTHERMEL, John E
Hiroshima and Nagasaki from God's point of view *(New York: Carlton 1970), 55p.*
SARGANT, Tom
These things shall be *(London: Heinemann 1941), 152p.*
SHOLTY, Alva H
Twice in two thousand years *(Dayton, Ohio: Ottobein 1946), 220p.*
SNYDER, Robert S
And when my task on earth is done: the day by day experiences of a Christian G.I. *(Kansas City, Kan: Graphic Laboratory 1950), 160p.*
SPELLMAN, Francis J, *cardinal*
Action this day: letters from the fighting fronts *(New York: Scribner 1943), xiii, 256p.*
No greater love: the story of our soldiers *(New York: Scribner 1945), 147p.*
The road to victory *(New York: Scribner 1942), xi, 131p.*
STEVEN, Walter T
In this sign *(Toronto: Ryerson 1948), xiii, 182p.*
VAN DUSEN, Henry P
They found the Church there: the Armed Forces discover Christian missions *(New York: Scribner 1945), 148p.*
WALLACE, Robert N A (ed)
God's workings in World War II, or Prophecies and their fulfillments, book no. 2 *(Placentia, Calif: Undenominational Church of the Lord 1947), 115p.*
YOUELL, George
Africa marches *(London: SPCK 1949), 144p.*
[*see also* CATHOLICISM]

REMAGEN BRIDGE

HECHLER, Kenneth
The bridge at Remagen *(New York: Ballantine 1957), 238p.*
ZARISH, Joseph M
The collapse of the Remagen Bridge *(New York: Vantage 1968), 137p.*
[*see also* WESTERN EUROPE 1944–5]

REPATRIATION

EPSTEIN, Julius
Operation keelhaul: the story of forced repatriation from 1944 to the present *(New York: Devin-Adair 1973), 255p.*

RESCUE SHIPS

SCHOFIELD, Brian B *and* MARTYN, L F
The rescue ships *(Edinburgh: Blackwood 1968), xx, 172p.*

RESISTANCE

ARMY TIMES (newspaper)
Heroes of the resistance *(New York: Dodd 1967), 123p.*
BAGNALL, Florence N
Let my people go! *(Salt Lake City, Utah: Publishers 1968), 253p.*
BATTAGLIA, Roberto
The story of the Italian resistance *(London: Odhams [1958]), 287p.*
BIRD, Michael J
The secret battalion *(New York: Holt 1964), 189p.*
BIRD, Will R
The two Jacks: the adventures of Major Jack L. Fairweather and Major Jack M. Veness *(London: Kimber 1955), 205p.*
BRADDON, Russell
Nancy Wake: the story of a very brave woman *(London: Cassell 1956), [II], 274p; US title:* The white mouse.
BRIGG, Emil
Stand up and fight *(London: Harrap 1972), 176p.*
BROME, Vincent
The way back: the story of Lieut. Commander Pat O'Leary, G.C., D.S.O., R.N. *(London: Cassell 1957), xi, 267p.*
CARSE, Robert
The unconquered: Europe fights back *(New York: McBride 1942), 9-225p.*
COLLIER, Richard
Ten thousand eyes *(London: Collins 1958), 320p.*
COWAN, Lore
Children of the resistance: the young ones who defied the Nazi terror *(London: Frewin 1968), 191p.*
DREUX, William B
No bridges blown *(Notre Dame, Ind: Notre Dame UP 1972), 322p.*
DUPUY, Trevor N
Asian and Axis resistance movements *(New York: Watts 1965), [8], 88p.*
European resistance movements *(New York: Watts 1965), [7], 88p.*

EHRLICH, Blake
Resistance: France, 1940–1945 *(Boston, Mass: Little, Brown 1965),* [7], *278p; UK title:* The French resistance, 1940–1945.

EUROPEAN resistance movements, 1939–1945: first international conference on the history of the resistance movements, Liege *(London: Pergamon 1960), xvii, 410p, bib.*

EUROPEAN resistance movements, 1939–1945: second international conference, Milan *(New York: Macmillan 1964), 663p.*

FOURCADE, Marie M
Noah's ark *(London: Allen & Unwin 1973), 3–377p.*

GRAML, Herbert *and others*
The German resistance to Hitler *(London: Batsford 1970), xxi, 281p.*

GUILLAIN DE BENOUVILLE, Pierre
Unknown warriors: a personal account of the French resistance *(New York: Simon & Schuster 1949), viii, 372p.*

HAWES, Stephen *and* WHITE, Ralph (eds)
Resistance in Europe 1939–1945 *(London: Lane 1975), 248p.*

HESLOP, Richard
'Xavier': the famous British agent's dramatic account of his work in the French resistance *(London: Hart-Davis 1970), 272p.*

INSTONE, Gordon
Freedom the spur *(London: Burke 1953), 256p.*

JONG, Louis de
The German fifth column in the Second World War *(London: Routledge 1956), xi, 308p.*

KRAUS, Rene
Europe in revolt *(New York: Macmillan 1942), x, 563p.*

MARSDEN, Alexandrina
Resistance nurse *(London: Odhams 1961), 208p.*

MICHEL, Henri
The shadow war: resistance in Europe, 1939–1945 *(London: Deutsch 1972), 416p, bib.*

MIKSCHE, F O
Secret forces: the technique of underground movements *(London: Faber 1950), 181p.*

MILLAR, George
Maquis *(London: Heinemann 1945), 286p; US title:* Waiting in the night.

NOVICK, Peter
The resistance versus Vichy: the purge of the collaborators in liberated France *(London: Chatto & Windus 1968), xv, 245p, bib.*

ORBAAN, Robert
Duel in the shadows: true accounts of anti-Nazi underground warfare during World War II *(New York: Doubleday 1965), 229p.*

PROSSER, David G
Journey underground *(New York: Dutton 1945), 347p.*

REMY (pseud)
The silent company *(London: Barker 1948), 406p.*

RESISTANCE in Europe 1939–1945: an introduction *(Salford, Lancs: Salford UP 1973), 36p, bib.*

RIESS, Curt
Underground Europe *(New York: Dial 1942), xiii, 17–325p.*

SANDERSON, James D
Behind enemy lines *(Princeton, NJ: Van Nostrand 1959), 322p.*

SCHOLL, I
Six against tyranny *(London: Murray 1955), 99p.*

SCOTT, Lionel
I dropped in *(London: Barrie & Rockliff 1959), 224p.*

SETH, Ronald
How the resistance worked *(London: Bles 1961), 157p; US title:* The noble saboteurs.
The undaunted: the story of resistance in Western Europe *(London: Muller [1956]), 327p, bib.*

SIXTH column: inside the Nazi occupied countries *(Chicago, Ill: Alliance 1942), xi, 313p.*

SOUTHON, Alfred
Alpine partisan *(London: Hammond 1957), 222p.*

TCHOK, Ivan M
The first to resist: the story of the first underground movement in this war *(London: New Europe 1945), 64p.*

THORNE, Charles B
St. George and the octopus *(London: Love 1945), 158p.*

TILMAN, Harold W
When men and mountains meet *(Cambridge: Cambridge UP 1946), 232p.*

WACHSMAN, Z H
Trail blazers for invasion *(New York: Ungar 1943), 284p.*

WALDHEIM-EMMERICK, *Mrs* Ragnhild S von
In the footsteps of Joan of Arc: true stories of heroines of the French resistance in World War II *(New York: Exposition 1959), 153p.*

WALTERS, Anne-Marie
Moondrop to Gascony *(London: Macmillan 1946), [4], 239p.*

WOODMAN, Dorothy
Europe rises: the story of resistance in occupied Europe *(London: Gollancz 1943), 154p.*
[*see also* INDIVIDUAL COUNTRIES, *e.g.* BELGIUM]

ROCKETS

BURCHARD, John E (ed)
Rockets, guns and targets: rockets, target information, erosion information and hypervelocity guns developed during World War II by the Office of Scientific Research and Development *(Boston, Mass: Little, Brown 1948), 482p.*
COLLIER, Basil
The battle of the V-weapons, 1944–45 *(London: Hodder & Stoughton 1964), 191p.*
DORNBERGER, Walter
V 2 *(London: Hurst & Blackett 1954), 264p.*
HUZEL, Dieter
Peenemunde to Canaveral *(New York: Prentice-Hall 1962), 247p.*
JOUBERT de la FERTE, *Sir* Philip B
Rocket *(London: Hutchinson 1957), 190p.*
KLEE, Ernst *and* MERK, Otto
The birth of the missile: the secrets of Peenemunde *(New York: Dutton 1965), 126p.*

ROME

ADLEMAN, Robert H *and* WALTON, George
Rome fell today *(Boston, Mass: Little, Brown 1968),* [*9*], *336p, bib.*
DAVIS, Melton S
Who defends Rome?: the forty-five days, July 25–September 8, 1943 *(London: Allen & Unwin 1972), xiv, 560p, bib.*
DE WYSS, M
Rome under the terror *(London: Hale 1946), 216p.*
JACKSON, William G F
The battle for Rome *(London: Batsford 1969), viii, 224p, bib.*
KATZ, Robert
Death in Rome *(London: Cape 1967), 334p.*
SCRIVENER, Jane (pseud)
Inside Rome with the Germans *(New York: Macmillan 1945), 204p.*

STERN, Michael
An American in Rome *(New York: Geis 1964), 336p.*
TOMPKINS, Peter
A spy in Rome *(New York: Simon & Schuster 1962), 347p.*
[*see also* ITALY]

ROMMEL

DOUGLAS-HOME, Charles
Rommel *(London: Weidenfeld & Nicolson 1973), 224p, bib.*
GREGORY, Frank H
Rommel *(London: Wayland 1974), 96p, bib.*
LEWIN, Ronald
Rommel as military commander *(London: Batsford 1968), x, 262p, bib.*
ROMMEL, Erwin J E
The Rommel papers *(London: Collins 1953), xxx, 545p.*
SPEIDEL, Hans
Invasion 1944: Rommel and the Normandy campaign *(Chicago, Ill: Regnery 1950), xiii, 176p.*
YOUNG, Desmond
Rommel *(London: Collins 1950), 316p.*
[*see also* AFRIKA KORPS]

ROOSEVELT

BEARD, Charles A
President Roosevelt and the coming of the war, 1941: a study in appearances and realities *(Hamden, Conn: Shoe String 1968), 614p.*
BURNS, James M
Roosevelt: the soldier of freedom, 1940–1945 *(New York: Harcourt 1970), xiv, 722p, bib.*
CROCKER, George N
Roosevelt's road to Russia *(Chicago, Ill: Regnery 1959), 312p.*
DIVINE, R A
Roosevelt and World War Two *(Baltimore: Johns Hopkins 1969), 107p.*
HASSETT, William
Off the record with F.D.R., 1942–1945 *(New Brunswick, NJ: Rutgers UP 1958), 366p.*
ROOSEVELT, Franklin D
America chooses!: in the words of President Roosevelt *(New York: Harrap 1941), 144p.*
Mr. Roosevelt speaks: four speeches *(London: Oxford UP 1941), 40p.*

Nothing to fear: selected addresses, 1932-1945 *(Boston, Mass: Houghton Mifflin 1946), xxi, 470p.*

Rendezvous with destiny: addresses and opinions *(New York: Dryden 1944), xiv, 367p.*

Roosevelt's foreign policy 1933-1941: unedited speeches and messages *(New York: Funk 1942), xv, 634p.*

War message: being the addresses of the President to the nation and Congress concerning the involvement of the United States in a war with the Empire of Japan and Axis powers *(Philadelphia, Pa: Ritten House 1942), 64p.*

Wartime correspondence between President Roosevelt and Pope Pius XII *(New York: Macmillan 1947), 127p.*

SHERWOOD, Robert E

Roosevelt and Hopkins: an intimate history *(New York: Harper 1948), xvii, 979p.*

ROYAL AIR FORCE

ALLEN, Hubert R

The legacy of Lord Trenchard *(London: Cassell 1972), xi, 228p, bib.*

AUSPEX (pseud)

Victory from the air *(London: Bles 1942), 234p.*

BALDWIN, Arthur W, *3rd earl Baldwin of Bewdley*

A flying start *(London: Davies 1967), [5], 218p.*

BALEY, Stephen (ed)

Two Septembers, 1939 and 1940: a diary of events *(London: Allen & Unwin 1941), 9-77p.*

BEAUMAN, Eric B (ed)

Winged words: our airmen speak for themselves *(London: Heinemann 1941), 261p; US title:* Airmen speak.

BEEDLE, James

43 Squadron Royal Flying Corps, Royal Air Force: the history of the Fighting Cocks, 1916-1966 *(London: Beaumont Aviation [1966]), 336p.*

BOLITHO, Hector

A penguin in the eyrie: an R.A.F. diary, 1939-1945 *(London: Hutchinson 1955), xii, 13-254p.*

BOWYER, Michael J F

2 Group R.A.F.: a complete history, 1936-1945 *(London: Faber 1974), 532p.*

BRICKHILL, Paul

Reach for the sky: the story of Douglas Bader, D.S.O., D.F.C. *(London: Collins 1954), 384p.*

CAPKA, Jo
Red sky at night: the story of Jo Capka, D.F.M. *(London: Blond 1958), 192p.*

CHANCE, John N
Yellow belly *(London: Hale 1959), 191p.*

CHARLTON, Lionel E O
Deeds that held the Empire: by air *(London: Murray 1940), 280p.*
The Royal Air Force from September 1939 to December 1940: a complete record *(London: Hutchinson 1941), viii, 9–320p.*

CHEESEMAN, E C
Brief glory: the story of A.T.A. *(Leicester: Harborough 1946), 248p.*

CLARKE, D H
What were they like to fly? *(London: Allen & Unwin 1964), 128p.*

DUKE, Neville
Test pilot *(London: Wingate 1953), 215p.*

EMBRY, *Sir* Basil E
Mission completed *(London: Methuen 1957), 350p.*

FENWICK-OWEN, Roderic
Desert air force *(London: Hutchinson 1948), 276p.*

FINN, Sidney
Lincolnshire air war, 1939–1945 *(Lincoln: Aero Litho [1973]), 115p, bib.*

FORBES, Alexander
Quest for a Northern air route *(London: Oxford UP 1953), 141p.*

GARNETT, David
War in the air, Sept. 1939–May 1941 *(London: Chatto & Windus 1941), ix, 199p.*

GREAT BRITAIN. Air Ministry
Bomber Command: the Air Ministry's account of the Bomber Command's offensive against the Axis *(New York: Doubleday 1941), 7–124p.*
The origins and development of operational research in the Royal Air Force *(London: HMSO 1963), xx, 218p.*

GRIBBLE, Leonard R
Battle stories of the R.A.F. *(London: Burke 1945), 96p.*
Epics of the fighting R.A.F. *(London: Harrap 1943), 192p.*

GRIFFITH, Hubert F
The R.A.F. in Russia *(London: Hammond 1943), 104p.*

HALSTEAD, Ivor
Wings of victory: a tribute to the R.A.F. *(London: Drummond 1941), viii, 9–221p.*

HELMORE, William
Air commentary *(London: Allen & Unwin 1942), 90p.*

HEROES OF THE R.A.F.: the best adventure stories from the 'R.A.F. Flying Review' *(London: Jenkins 1960), 142p.*

HUNT, Leslie
Twenty-one Squadron: the history of the Royal Auxiliary Air Force, 1935–1957 *(London: Garnstone 1972), 432p.*

JACKSON, Robert
Before the storm: the story of Royal Air Force Bomber Command, 1939–42 *(London: Barker 1972), 264p, bib.*

JONES, Ira
Tiger Squadron: the story of the 74th Squadron R.A.F. in two world wars *(London: Allen & Unwin 1954), 295p.*

JOUBERT de la FERTE, *Sir* Philip B
The forgotten ones: the story of the ground crews *(London: Hutchinson 1961), 255p.*

LANDAU, Rom
The wing: confessions of an R.A.F. officer *(London: Faber 1945), 331p.*

LEE, Arthur S G
Special duties: reminiscences of a Royal Air Force staff officer in the Balkans, Turkey and the Middle East *(London: Sampson Low 1946), 308p.*

LYALL, Gavin
The war in the air, 1939–1945: an anthology of personal experience *(London: Hutchinson 1968), xv, 422p, bib.*

MACMILLAN, Norman
The Royal Air Force in the World War *(London: Harrap 1942–50), 4 vols.*

MARSH, Garry
Sand in my spinach *(London: Barker 1958), 192p.*

M-M, S
Together we fly *(London: Bles 1942), 276p.*

MONKS, Noel
Squadrons up!: a first-hand story of the R.A.F. *(London: Gollancz 1941), ix, 260p.*

MUNSON, Kenneth G
ABC British aircraft of World War II *(London: Allen & Unwin 1961), 64p.*

NARRACOTT, Arthur H
How the R.A.F. works *(London: Muller 1941), 158p.*
War news had wings: a record of the R.A.F. in France *(London: Muller 1941), xviii, 19–224p.*

ORMES, Ian
Clipped wings *(London: Kimber 1973), 192p, bib.*

RAPIER, Brian J
White Rose base *(Lincoln: Aero Litho 1972), 103p.*

RAYMOND, R *and* LANGDON, David
Slipstream: a Royal Air Force anthology *(London: Eyre & Spottiswoode 1946), 260p.*

REMY (pseud) *and* LIVRY-LEVEE
The gates burst open *(London: Arco 1955), x, 11–192p.*

REVIE, Alastair
The lost command *(London: Bruce & Watson 1971), ix, 276p.*

RHYS, John L
England is my village *(London: Faber 1941), 200p.*

RICHARDS, Denis *and* SAUNDERS, Hilary St G
The Royal Air Force, 1939–1945 *(London: HMSO 1953–4), 3 vols.*

SARGENT, Eric
The Royal Air Force *(London: Sampson Low 1943), 2nd ed., xvi, 814p.*

SHERBROOKE-WALKER, Ronald
Khaki and blue *(London: St Catherine 1952), viii, 135p.*

SHORES, Christopher F
2nd TAF *(Reading, Berks: Osprey 1970), xi, 298p.*

SIMPSON, William
One of our pilots is safe *(London: Hamilton 1942), xii, 226p.*

THE SKY their battleground: true adventure stories from the 'R.A.F. Flying Review' *(London: Jenkins 1962), 143p.*

SLESSOR, *Sir* John
The Central Blue *(London: Cassell 1956), 724p.*

SPAIGHT, James M
The sky's the limit: a study of British air power *(London: Hodder & Stoughton 1940), 7–160p.*

SUTTON, Barry
The way of a pilot: a personal record *(London: Macmillan 1942), xiv, 117p.*

SUTTON, Harry T
Raiders approach!: the fighting tradition of the Royal Air Force Station Hornchurch and Sutton's Farm *(Aldershot, Hants: Gale & Polden 1956), 181p.*

TAYLOR, John W R *and* MOYES, P J R
Pictorial history of the R.A.F. *(London: Allan 1969), 3 vols.*

TEMPEST, Victor
Near the sun: the impressions of a medical officer of Bomber Command *(Brighton, Sussex: Crabtree 1946), 84p.*

VEALE, Sydney E (ed)
Warfare in the air; the R.A.F. at war since the Battle of Britain *(London: Pilot 1942), 48p.*

WALKER, Nigel
Strike to defend: a book about some of the men who served in R.A.F. Bomber Command during World War II *(London: Spearman 1963), 128p.*

WALLACE, Graham
R.A.F. Biggin Hill *(London: Putnam 1957), 256p.*

WISDOM, Thomas H
Wings over Olympus: the story of the Royal Air Force in Libya and Greece *(London: Allen & Unwin 1942), 229p.*

WYKEHAM, Peter
Fighter Command: a study of air defence, 1914–1960 *(London: Putnam 1960), 320p.*
[*see also* AIR WARFARE, BATTLE OF BRITAIN, BOMBERS, FIGHTERS]

ROYAL MARINES

HOLLIS, *Sir* Leslie
One Marine's tale *(London: Deutsch 1956), 188p.*

LOCKHART, *Sir* Robert H B
The Marines were there: the story of the Royal Marines in the Second World War *(London: Putnam 1950),* [7], *229p.*

ST JOHN, John
To the war with Waugh *(London: Whittingdon 1973), xi, 57p.*

THOMPSON, James A
Only the sun remembers *(London: Dakers 1950), x, 276p.*
[*see also* COMMANDOS]

ROYAL NAVY

ARMSTRONG, Warren
H.M. small ships *(London: Muller* [*1959*]*), ix, 199p.*

AUSTIN, John
The man who hit the Scharnhorst: the ordeal of Leading-Seaman Nick Carter *(London: Seeley 1973), 189p.*

BARTIMEUS (pseud)
East of Malta, West of Suez: the official Admiralty account of the Mediterranean Fleet, 1939-1943 *(Boston, Mass: Little, Brown 1944), x, 221p.*

BELOT, Raymond de
The struggle for the Mediterranean, 1939–1945 *(Princeton, NJ: Princeton UP 1951), xix, 287p, bib.*

BENYON-TINKER, W E
Dust upon the sea *(London: Hodder & Stoughton 1947), 216p.*

BULL, Peter
To sea in a sieve *(London: Davies 1956), 224p.*

BURN, Lambton
Down ramps: saga of the eighth armada *(London: Carroll & Nicholson 1948), x, 262p.*

CHATTERTON, Edward K *and* EDWARDS, Kenneth
The Royal Navy: from September 1939 to September 1945 *(London: Hutchinson 1942–7), 5 vols.*

CHERRY, Alex H
Yankee, R.N.: being the story of a Wall Street banker who volunteered for active duty in the R.N. before America came into the war *(London: Jarrolds 1951), 544p.*

CORBETT, Edmund (comp)
Waves of battles *(London: Arco 1959), vii, 280p.*

DAVIES, John
The stone frigate *(London: Macmillan 1947), 178p.*

DICKSON, Robert K
Naval broadcasts *(London: Allen & Unwin 1946), 91p.*

DIVINE, Arthur D
Behind the fleets *(London: Murray 1940), 148p.*

DONALD, William
Stand by for action: a sailor's story *(London: Kimber 1956), 200p.*

DREW, Nicholas
Amateur sailor *(London: Constable 1944), v, 291p.*

DUPUY, Trevor N
The naval war in the West: the raiders *(New York: Watts 1963), [4], 68p.*

EDWARDS, Kenneth
Seven sailors *(London: Collins 1945), 255p.*

FIEDLER, Arkady
Thank you, Captain, thank you! *(London: Maxlove 1945), 145p.*

FREEDOM'S Battle *(London: Hutchinson 1967), vol. I:* the war at sea, 1939–1945, an anthology of personal experience, *iii–xx, 416p; US title:* The war at sea: the British Navy in World War II.

GORDON, Oliver L
Fight it out *(London: Kimber 1957), 238p.*

GRAVES, Charles
Life line *(London: Heinemann 1941), vi, 238p.*

GREAT BRITAIN. Admiralty
Ships of the Royal Navy: statement of losses during the Second World War, 3rd September, 1939, to 2nd September, 1945; Amendment no. 1 *(London: HMSO 1947-50), 2 vols.*

GRENFELL, Russell
Main fleet to Singapore *(New York: Macmillan 1952), 238p.*

GRIFFITHS, Bernard
Macnamara's band *(London: Kimber 1960), 192p.*

HARDY, Alfred C
Everyman's history of the sea war *(London: Nicholson & Watson [1950-1]), 3 vols.*

HARLING, Robert
Amateur sailor *(London: Chatto & Windus 1952), 291p.*
The steep Atlantic stream *(London: Chatto & Windus 1946), 231p.*

HICKLING, Harold
Sailor at sea *(London: Kimber [1965]), 224p.*

HINSLEY, F H
Command of the sea: the naval side of British history from 1918 to the end of the Second World War *(London: Christophers 1950), xii, 13-104p.*

HOLMAN, Gordon
In danger's hour *(London: Hodder & Stoughton 1948), 224p.*

HUNT, Cecil
Gallant little Campeador *(London: Methuen 1941), vii, 72p.*

HURD, *Sir* Archibald S
Britannia has wings!: the Fleet in action - on, over and under the sea *(London: Hutchinson 1942), 112p.*

JAMES, *Sir* William M
The British Navies in the Second World War *(London: Longmans 1946), 255p.*
The Portsmouth letters *(London: Macmillan 1946), 285p.*

JOHNSTON, George H
The battle of the seaways: from the Athenia to the Bismarck *(London: Gollancz 1942), xii, 13-148p.*

JULLIAN, Marcel
H.M.S. Fidelity *(London: Souvenir 1957), 204p.*

KEMP, Peter K
Victory at sea, 1939-1945 *(London: Muller [1958]), 383p.*

KENNEDY, Ludovic H C
Sub-Lieutenant: a personal record of the war at sea *(London: Batsford 1942), 104p.*

KERR, James L *and* JAMES, David (eds)
Wavy navy, by some who served *(London: Harrap [1950]), 263p.*

KING, Cecil
Rule Britannia *(London: Studio 1941), xii, 13–280p.*

KING, William
The stick and the stars *(London: Hutchinson 1958), 192p.*

LANGMAID, Rowland
'The Med': the Royal Navy in the Mediterranean, 1939–45 *(London: Batchworth 1948), 130p.*

LENTON, Henry T *and* COLLEDGE, James J
Warship losses of World War II: British and Dominion Fleets *(London: Allan [1965]), 64p.*

LITTLE, Eric H
Liberty men, fall in *(Cape Town: Unie Volkspers 1945), 189p; later published as:* Action Pacific.

LODWICK, John
The filibusters: the story of the special boat service *(London: Methuen 1947), 188p.*

MACDONNELL, James C
Valiant occasions *(London: Constable 1952), 261p.*

MACINTYRE, Donald
The battle for the Mediterranean *(London: Batsford 1964), 216p, bib.*
Fighting ships and seamen *(London: Evans 1963), 192p.*
The naval war against Hitler *(London: Batsford 1971), 376p, bib.*
Wings of Neptune: the story of naval aviation *(London: Davies 1963), 269p.*

McLACHLAN, Donald
Room 39: naval intelligence in action, 1939–1945 *(London: Weidenfeld & Nicolson 1968), xvii, 438p.*

MITCHELL, Mairin
The Red Fleet and the Royal Navy *(London: Hodder & Stoughton 1942), 98p.*

NIXON, John
Front-line of freedom: eye-witness with the Royal Navy *(London: Hutchinson 1942), viii, 9–64p.*

OGDEN, Graeme
My sea lady: the story of H.M.S. 'Lady Madeleine' from February 1941 to February 1943 *(London: Hutchinson 1963), 203p.*

OUR Penelope, June 1941-June 1942 *(London: Harrap 1942), v, 119p.*

PHILIP, Hugh
Two rings and a red: a naval surgeon's log *(London: International 1945), 135p.*

PHILLIPS, G P
Dark seas remember *(London: Paul 1944), 148p.*

POOLMAN, Kenneth
The battle of Sixty North *(London: Cassell 1958), 191p.*

POPE, Dudley
Flag 4: the battle of coastal forces in the Mediterranean *(London: Kimber 1954), xvi, 17-300p.*

ROBERTSON, Terence
Walker, R.N.: the story of Captain Frederic John Walker, C.B., D.S.O. and three bars, R.N. *(London: Evans 1956), 216p.*

ROSKILL, Stephen W
The Navy at war, 1939-1945 *(London: Collins 1960), 480p; US title:* White ensign.
The war at sea, 1939-1945 *(London: HMSO 1954-61), 3 vols in 4 pts.*

SCOTT, Ian
My war at sea *(London: Jenkins 1943), vii, 11-190p.*

SHAW, Frank H
Epic naval fights *(London: Laurie 1955), 208p.*

SILVER phantom: H.M.S. Aurora *(London: Muller 1945), 7-93p.*

SIMPSON, George W G
Periscope view: a professional autobiography *(London: Macmillan 1972), 315p.*

SIRED, Ronald
Enemy engaged: a naval rating with the Mediterranean Fleet, 1942-44 *(London: Kimber 1957), 205p.*

SMITH, Bertie W
The Navy strikes *(London: Blackie 1942), 224p.*
The war at sea, 1941-1943 *(London: Blackie 1944), 192p.*

SMITH, Peter C
Task Force 57: the British Pacific Fleet, 1944-1945 *(London: Kimber 1969), 206p.*

STITT, George
Under Cunningham's command, 1940-1943 *(London: Allen & Unwin 1944), 269p.*

STUBBS, Bernard
The Navy at war *(London: Faber 1940), 280p.*

TAFFRAIL (pseud)
Western Mediterranean, 1942–45 *(London: Hodder & Stoughton 1948), 461p.*

TAYLOR, John E S R
The last passage *(London: Allen & Unwin 1946), 137p.*
Northern escort *(London: Allen & Unwin 1945), 127p.*

THURSFIELD, Henry G
Action stations!: the Royal Navy at war *(London: Black 1941), 78p*
Epic deeds of the Navy *(London: Hutchinson 1942), 268p.*

VIAN, *Sir* Philip
Action this day: a war memoir *(London: Muller 1960), 223p.*

WARRENDER, Simon George
Score of years *(Melbourne, Aust: Wren 1973), 255p.*

WEMYSS, David E G
Walker's groups in the Western Approaches *(Liverpool: Liverpool Daily Post & Echo 1948), 167p; later published as:* Relentless pursuit.

WHITMAN, J E A
Britain keeps the seas: some naval incidents during the first two years of the World war *(London: Oxford UP 1943), 128p.*

WIGBY, Frederick
Stoker, Royal Navy *(Edinburgh: Blackwood 1967),* [7], *202p.*

WILKINSON, Burke
By sea and by stealth *(London: Davies 1957), xiv, 224p.*

WINGATE, John
Last ditch: the English Channel, 1939–1943 *(London: Heinemann 1971),* [*10*], *176p.*

WINN, Godfrey H
Home from the sea: a chronicle in a prologue, three acts and an epilogue *(London: Hutchinson 1944), 131p.*

WINTON, John
The forgotten fleet *(London: Joseph 1969),* [2], *433p, bib.*

WOODROOFFE, Thomas
In good company *(London: Faber 1947), 229p.*

YOUNG, John
A dictionary of Royal Navy warships, 1939–45 *(London: Stephens 1974), 224p.*

[*see also* AIRCRAFT CARRIERS, BATTLESHIPS, CRUISERS, DESTROYERS, NAVAL WARFARE, SUBMARINES]

ROYAL OBSERVER CORPS

WHITTY, H R (comp)
Observer's tale: the story of Group 17 of the R.O.C. *(London: Roland 1950), 51p.*
WILTON, Eric
Centre crew: a memory of the Royal Observer Corps *(Bromley, Kent 1946), 84p.*

RUMANIA

CRETZIANU, Alexandre
The lost opportunity *(London: Cape 1957), 188p, bib.*
GRAEFENBERG, Rosie
Athene palace *(New York: McBride 1942), 11–357p.*
ILEANA, *princess of Rumania*
I live again *(London: Gollancz 1952), 374p.*
KORMOS, C
Rumania *(Cambridge: Cambridge UP 1944), vi, 122p.*
PAVEL, Pavel
Why Rumania failed *(London: Alliance 1944), 282p.*

RUNSTEDT

BLUMENTRITT, Guenther
Von Runstedt: the soldier and the man *(London: Odhams 1952), 288p.*

RUSSIA

ARMSTRONG, John A (ed)
Soviet partisans in World War II *(Madison, Wis: Wisconsin UP 1964), 792p.*
Ukranian nationalism *(New York: Columbia UP 1963), 361p.*
ARMY of heroes: true stories of Soviet fighting men *(London: Universal 1944), 171p.*
BETHELL, Nicholas
The last secret: forcible repatriation to Russia, 1944–7 *(London: Deutsch 1974), 240p.*
BROWN, James E
Russia fights *(New York: Scribner 1943), xi, 276p.*
CARROLL, Wallace
We're in this with Russia *(Boston, Mass: Houghton Mifflin 1942), viii, 264p.*

CARTER, Herbert D
Russia's secret weapon *(London: Muller 1944), 102p.*
CASSIDY, Henry C
Moscow date line, 1941-1943 *(London: Cassell 1943), 256p.*
CITRINE, *Sir* Walter M
In Russia now *(London: Hale 1942), 154p.*
COATES, William P *and* COATES, Z K
Why Russia will win: the Soviet military, naval and air power *(London: Eldon 1942), 104p.*
COLE, George D H
Europe, Russia and the future *(London: Gollancz 1941), 186p.*
DALLIN, Alexander
German rule in Russia, 1941-1945: a study of occupation policies *(London: Macmillan 1957), xx, 695p.*
The Kaminsky Brigade, 1941-1944: a case study of German military exploitation of Soviet disaffection *(Marshall Air Base, Ala: Air University 1952), 96p.*
Odessa, 1941-1944: a case study of Soviet territory under foreign rule *(Santa Monica, Calif: Rand 1957), 466p.*
Soviet espionage *(New Haven, Conn: Yale UP 1956), 558p.*
DALLIN, D J
Soviet Russia's foreign policy, 1939-1942 *(New Haven, Conn: Yale UP 1942), xx, 452p.*
DAVIES, Raymond A
Inside Russia today *(Winnipeg, Can: Contemporary 1945), 92p.*
Odyssey through hell *(New York: Fischer 1946), 235p.*
DAVIES, Raymond A *and* STEIGER, A J
Soviet Asia: democracy's first line of defense *(New York: Dial 1942), xiii, 15-384p.*
DEMIANOVA, Genia
Comrade Genia: the story of a victim of German brutality in Russia *(London: Nicholson & Watson 1941), xi, 13-128p.*
DRUM, Karl
Airpower and Russian partisan warfare *(New York: Arno 1968), 63p.*
EHRENBURG, Ilya G
Russia at war *(London: Hamilton 1943), xvii, 277p; US title:* The tempering of Russia.
EINSIEDEL, Heinrich, *Graf* von
The shadow of Stalingrad: being the diary of a temptation *(London: Wingate 1953), 254p; US title:* I joined the Russians
ELVIN, Harold
A cockney in Moscow *(London: Cresset 1958), 222p.*

EMMENS, Robert G
Guests of the Kremlin *(New York: Macmillan 1949), viii, 291p.*
FAINSOD, Merle
Smolensk under Soviet rule *(Cambridge, Mass: Harvard UP 1958), 484p.*
FISCHER, George
Soviet opposition to Stalin: a case study in World War 2 *(Cambridge, Mass: Harvard UP 1952), ix, 230p, bib.*
GOLLANCZ, Victor
Russia and ourselves *(London: Gollancz 1941), 131p.*
GRAEBNER, Walter
Round trip to Russia *(Philadelphia, Pa: Lippincott 1943), 9–216p.*
GROSSMAN, Vasilii S
The years of war, 1941–1945 *(Moscow: Foreign Languages 1946), 451p.*
GUILLAUME, Augustin L
Soviet arms and Soviet power, the secrets of Russia's might *(Washington DC: Infantry Journal Press 1949), 212p.*
HALDANE, Charlotte
Russian newsreel: an eye-witness account of the Soviet Union at war *(London: Secker & Warburg 1942), 207p.*
HOWELL, Edgar M
The Soviet partisan movement, 1941–1944 *(Washington DC: Department of Army 1956), 217p.*
HUGHES, William R (comp)
Those human Russians: a collection of incidents related by Germans *(London: Gollancz 1950), 128p.*
IGNATOV, Petr K
Partisans of the Kuban *(London: Hutchinson 1945), 212p.*
JORDAN, George R *and* STOKES, R L
From Major Jordan's diaries *(New York: Harcourt 1952), 284p.*
JORDAN, Philip F
Russian glory *(London: Cresset 1942), 181p.*
KALININ, Mikhail I
The Soviet President speaks: speeches, broadcast address and articles on the great patriotic war of the Soviet Union *(London: Hutchinson 1945), 79p.*
KAMENETSKY, Ihor
Hitler's occupation of Ukraine, 1941–1944: a study of totalitarian imperialism *(Milwaukee, Wis: Marquette UP 1956), 101p.*
KOURNAKOFF, Sergei N
Russia's fighting forces *(New York: Duell 1942), ix, 258p.*
What Russia did for victory *(New York: New Century 1945), 63p.*

KOVPAK, Sydir A
Our partisan course *(London: Hutchinson 1947), 126p.*
LAUTERBACH, Richard F
These are the Russians *(New York: Harper 1945), 368p.*
LESUEUR, Laurence R
Twelve months that changed the world *(New York: Knopf 1943), 345p.*
MACALPIN, Michael
Russia fights *(London: Lawrence & Wishart 1941), 72p.*
MCLANE, Charles B
Soviet policy and the Chinese communists, 1931-1946 *(New York: Columbia UP 1958), 310p.*
MAISKII, Ivan M
Who helped Hitler? *(London: Hutchinson 1964), 216p.*
MARKS, Stanley J
The bear that walks like a man: a diplomatic and military analysis of Soviet Russia *(Philadelphia, Pa: Dorrance 1943), 15-340p.*
MEN of the Stalin breed: true stories of the Soviet youth in the great patriotic war *(Moscow: Foreign Languages 1945), 186p.*
MIKHAILOV, Nikolia N
The Russian glory *(London: Hutchinson 1945), 142p; US title:* The Russian story
MOORE, Harriet L
Soviet Far Eastern policy, 1931-1945 *(London: Oxford UP 1945), 284p.*
MURPHY, John T
Russia on the march: a study of Soviet foreign policy *(London: Lane 1941), 128p.*
NEKRICH, A M
June 22, 1941: Soviet historians and the German invasion *(Columbia, SC: South Carolina UP 1968), 322p.*
NEW Soviet documents on Nazi atrocities *(London: Hutchinson 1943), 128p.*
PANETH, Philip
The epic of the Soviet cities *(London: Alliance 1943), vi, 7-127p.*
Meet our Russian allies *(London: Alliance 1943), 84p.*
PARRY, Albert
Russian cavalcade: a military record *(New York: Washburn 1944), 334p.*
PETROV, Vladimir
My retreat from Russia *(New Haven, Conn: Yale UP 1950), 357p.*
PILIAR, Iurii
It all really happened *(Moscow: Foreign Languages 1960), 187p.*

POLEVOI, Boris N
To the last breath *(London: Hutchinson 1945), 79p.*
PRUSZYNSKI, Ksawery
Russian year: the notebook of an amateur diplomat *(New York: Roy 1944), 189p.*
REITLINGER, Gerald
The house built on sand: the conflicts of German policy in Russia, 1939–1945 *(London: Weidenfeld & Nicolson [1960]), 495p, bib.*
REYNOLDS, Quentin J
Only the stars are neutral *(London: Cassell 1943), xi, 299p.*
SCHACHER, Gerhard
He wanted to sleep in the Kremlin *(New York: Reynal 1942), 261p.*
SEVASTOPOL, November 1941–July 1942 *(London: Hutchinson 1943), 9–76p.*
SIMONOV, Konstantin
No quarter *(New York: Fischer 1943), 231p.*
SLOAN, Patrick A
Russia in peace and war *(London: Pilot 1941), 72p.*
Russia resists *(London: Muller 1941), 117p.*
SNOW, Edgar
The pattern of Soviet power *(New York: Random House 1945), xii, 219p.*
SOVIET documents on Nazi atrocities *(London: Hutchinson 1942), 190p.*
SOVIET foreign policy during the patriotic war: documents and materials *(Hutchinson 1946), 2 vols.*
STEVENS, Edmund
Russia is no riddle *(New York: Greenburg 1945), 300p.*
STRIK-STRIKFELDT, Wilfried
Against Stalin and Hitler: a memoir of the Russian liberation movement, 1941–5 *(London: Macmillan 1970), 270p.*
STRONG, Anne L
The Soviets expected it *(New York: Dial 1941), viii, 9–279p.*
TOLSTOI, Aleksei N
My country: articles and stories of the great patriotic war of the Soviet Union *(London: Hutchinson 1944), 117p.*
VOITEKHOV, Boris I
The last days of Sevastopol *(London: Cassell 1943), 150p.*
WERTH, Alexander
Russia at war, 1941–1945 *(London: Barrie & Rockliff 1964), xxv, 1100p, bib.*
The year of Stalingrad: an historical record and a study of Russian mentality, methods and policies *(London: Hamilton 1946), 478p.*

WETTLIN, Margaret
Russian road: three years of war in Russia as lived through by an American woman *(London: Hutchinson 1945), 126p.*

WHITE, Margaret B
Russia at war: photographs *(London: Hutchinson 1942), 80p.*
Shooting the Russian war: photographs *(New York: Simon & Schuster 1942), xiv, 298p.*

WHITE, William L
Report on the Russians *(New York: Harcourt 1945), 309p.*

WINTERTON, Paul
Report on Russia *(London: Cresset 1945), 138p.*

ZACHAROFF, Lucien (ed)
The voice of fighting Russia *(Chicago, Ill: Alliance 1942), xix, 336p.*
We made a mistake - Hitler: Russia's surprising defence against Germany *(New York: Appleton 1941), 213p.*

[*see also* MOSCOW, STALINGRAD]

RUSSIAN AIR FORCE

LEE, Asher
The Soviet Air Force *(New York: Harper 1950), 9-207p.*

SCHWABEDISSEN, Walter
The Russian Air Force in the eyes of German commanders *(New York: Arno 1968), 434p.*

WAGNER, Ray (ed)
The Soviet Air Force in World War II: the official history *(New York: Doubleday 1973), 440p.*

RUSSIAN ARMY

BIALER, Seweryn
Stalin and his generals: Soviet military memoirs of World War II *(New York: Pegasus 1969), 644p, bib.*

HEISLER, J B
Russia's fighting men *(London: New Europe 1945), 95p.*

KERR, Walter B
The Russian Army: its men, its leaders and its battles *(London: Gollancz 1944), 140p.*

KORIAKOV, Mikhail
I'll never go back: a Red Army officer talks *(New York: Dutton 1948), 9-248p.*

KRUILOV, Ivan
Soviet staff officer *(London: Falcon 1951), vi, 298p.*

POLIAKOV, Aleksandr
Russians don't surrender *(New York: Dutton 1942), 5-191p.*
VIRSKY, Fred
My life in the Red Army *(New York: Macmillan 1949), 260p.*

RUSSIAN NAVY

GOLOVKO, Arsenic G
With the Red Fleet: the war memoirs of the late Admiral Arsenic G. Golovko *(London: Putnam 1965), 248p.*
ISAKOV, Ivan S
The Red Fleet in the Second World War *(London: Hutchinson 1947), 124p.*

RUSSIAN PRISONS

BECKER, Hans
The devil on my shoulder *(London: Jarrolds 1955), 216p.*
BEGIN, Menahem
White nights: the story of a prisoner in Russia *(London: Macdonald 1957), 240p.*
CISZEK, Walter J
With God in Russia *(New York: McGraw-Hill 1965), xvii, 302p.*
DANGERFIELD, Elma
Beyond the Urals *(London: British League for European Freedom 1946), 94p.*
EKART, Antoni
Vanished without trace: the story of seven years in Soviet Russia *(London: Parrish 1954), 320p.*
FEHLING, Helmut M
One great prison: the story behind Russia's unreleased P.O.W.'s *(Boston, Mass: Beacon 1951), xvi, 175p.*
FITTKAU, Gerhard
My thirty-third year: a priest's experience in a Russian work camp *(New York: Farrar 1958), 263p.*
GLIKSMAN, Jerzy
Tell the West: an account of his experiences as a slave laborer in the Union Of Socialist Republics *(New York: Gresham 1948), 358p.*
GOLLWITZER, Helmut
Unwilling journey: a diary from Russia *(London: SCMP 1953), 316p.*

GROSSMAN, Moishe
In the enchanted land: my seven years in Soviet Russia *(Tel Aviv, Israel: Rachel 1960–1), 383p.*

HADOW, Maria
Paying guests in Siberia *(London: Harvell 1959), 189p.*

KELLY, Frank
Private Kelly, by himself *(London: Evans 1954), 224p.*

KRASNOV, Nikolai N
The hidden Russia: my ten years as a slave laborer *(New York: Holt 1960), 341p.*

LARSEN, Otto M
Nightmare of the innocents *(London: Melrose 1955), 240p.*

LIAS, Godfrey
I survived *(London: Evans 1954), 224p.*

NORK, Karl
Hell in Siberia *(London: Hale 1957), 222p.*

WIGMANS, Johan H
Ten years in Russia and Siberia *(London: Darton 1964), 234p.*

WITTLIN, Tadeusz
A reluctant traveller in Russia *(London: Hodge 1952), 236p.*

YAMAMOTO, Tomomi
Four years in hell: I was a prisoner behind the Iron Curtain *(Tokyo: Asian 1952), 300p.*

ST NAZAIRE

MASON, David
The raid on St. Nazaire *(New York: Ballantine 1970), 160p, bib.*

PHILLIPS, Cecil E L
The greatest raid of all *(London: Heinemann 1958), xviii, 288p.*

RYDER, Robert E D
The attack on St. Nazaire, 28th March, 1942 *(London: Murray 1947), 118p.*
[*see also* COMMANDOS]

SALERNO

MASON, David
Salerno: foothold in Europe *(New York: Ballantine 1972), 160p, bib.*

POND, Hugh
Salerno *(London: Kimber 1961), 256p.*

WERSTEIN, Irving
The battle of Salerno *(New York: Crowell 1965), 152p.*
[*see also* ITALIAN CAMPAIGN]

SALVAGE

KEEBLE, Peter
Ordeal by water *(London: Longmans, Green 1957), xi, 216p.*
MASTERS, David
Epics of salvage: wartime feats of the Marine Salvage men in World War II *(London: Cassell 1953), 264p.*

SAN FRANCISCO

HAMILTON, James W *and* BOLCE, William J
Gateway to victory *(Stanford, Calif: Stanford UP 1946), 220p.*

SCANDINAVIA

PETROW, Richard
The bitter years: the invasion and occupation of Denmark and Norway Apr 1940–May 1945 *(New York: Morrow 1974), 403p, bib.*
[*see also* DENMARK, NORWAY]

SCAPA FLOW

BRIDGES, Antony
Scapa ferry *(London: Davies 1957), 231p.*
BROWN, Malcolm *and* MEEHAN, Patricia
Scapa Flow: the reminiscences of men and women who served in Scapa Flow in the two world wars *(London: Allen Lane 1968), 264p.*
KORGANOFF, Alexandre
The phantom of Scapa Flow *(London: Allan 1974), 235p.*

SCHELDT

THOMPSON, Reginald W
The eighty-five days: the story of the battle of the Scheldt *(London: Hutchinson 1957), 235p, bib.*
[*see also* HOLLAND, WESTERN EUROPE *1944–5*]

SCIENCE

BAR-ZOHAR, Michel
The hunt for German scientists *(London: Barker 1967), 207p.*

BAXTER, James P
Scientists against time *(Boston, Mass: Little, Brown 1946), xv, 473p.*

BROPHY, Leo P *and others*
The chemical warfare service: from laboratory to field *(Washington DC: Department of Army 1959), 496p.*
The chemical warfare service: organizing for war *(Washington DC: Department of Army 1959), 498p.*

BURCHARD, John E
Q.E.D.: M.I.T. in World War II *(New York: Wiley 1948), 354p.*

CHEMICAL CORPS ASSOCIATION WASHINGTON DC
Chemical warfare service in World War II: a record of accomplishments *(New York: Reinhold 1948), 222p.*

CLARK, Ronald W
The rise of the boffins *(London:Phoenix House 1962), 265p.*
Tizard *(Cambridge, Mass: MIT 1965), 458p.*

CROWTHER, James G *and* WHIDDINGTON, Richard
Science at war *(London: HMSO 1947), 185p.*

CUSHING, Emory C
History of entomology in World War II *(Washington DC: Smithsonian Institute 1957), 117p.*

DUGGAN, Stephen *and* DRURY, Betty
The rescue of science and learning: the story of the emergency committee in aid of displaced foreign scholars *(New York: Macmillan 1948), 214p.*

EGGLESTON, Wilfrid
Scientists at war *(London: Oxford UP 1951), x, 291p.*

GOUDSMIT, Samuel
ALSOS *(New York: Schuman 1947), 259p; UK title:* The failure of German science.

HARROD, Roy F
The Prof: a personal memoir of Lord Cherwell *(London: Macmillan 1959), 281p.*

HARTCUP, Guy
The challenge of war: scientific and engineering contributions to World War II *(Newton Abbot, Devon: David & Charles 1970), 295p.*

NOYES, William A (ed)
Chemistry: a history of the chemistry components of the National Defense Research Committee, 1940–1946 *(Boston, Mass: Little, Brown 1948), 524p.*

SIMON, Leslie E
German research in World War II: an analysis of the conduct of research *(London: Chapman & Hall 1947), 218p.*
German scientific establishments *(New York: Mapleton House 1947), 228p.*

STEWART, Irvin
Organizing scientific research for war: the administrative history of the Office of Scientific Research and Development *(Boston, Mass: Little, Brown 1948), 358p.*

THIESMEYER, Lincoln R *and* BURCHARD, John E
Combat scientists *(Boston, Mass: Little, Brown 1947), 412p.*

US Office of Scientific Research and Development
Applied physics *(Boston, Mass: Little, Brown 1948), 3 vols in 1.*

SECRET SERVICE

ACCOCE, Pierre *and* QUET, Pierre
The Lucy Ring *(London: W H Allen 1967), 224p.*

ASTIER de la VIGERIE, Emmanuel d'
Seven times seven days *(London: MacGibbon & Kee 1958), 221p.*

BAKER, Peter
My testament *(London: Calder 1955), 285p.*

BARTZ, Karl
The downfall of the German secret service *(London: Kimber 1956), 202p.*

BELL, Leslie
Sabotage!: the story of Lt. Col. J. Elder Wills *(London: Laurie 1957), 189p.*

BLEICHER, Hugo
Colonel Henri's story: the war memoirs of Hugo Bleicher, former German secret agent *(London: Kimber 1954), 200p.*

BORODIN, George
No crown of laurels *(London: Laurie [1950]), 224p.*

BRISSAUD, Andre
The Nazi secret service *(London: Bodley Head 1974), 320p, bib.*

BRYANS, John L
Blind victory (secret communications Halifax-Hassell) *(London: Skeffington 1951), 191p.*

BUSCH, Tristan (pseud)
Secret service unmasked *(London: Hutchinson 1950), 272p.*

BUTLER, Ewan
Amateur agent *(London: Harrap 1963), 240p.*

CARRÉ, Mathilde
I was 'The Cat': the truth about the most remarkable woman spy since Mata-Hari, by herself *(London: Souvenir 1960), 223p.*

CASKIE, Donald C
The tartan pimpernel *(London: Oldbourne 1957), 270p.*

CHAPMAN, Eddie
The Eddie Chapman story *(London: Wingate 1953), vi, 7–258p.*
The real Eddie Chapman story *(London: Library 33 1966), 253p.*

CHURCHILL, Peter
Duel of wits *(London: Hodder & Stoughton [1953]), 319p.*
Of their own choice *(London: Hodder & Stoughton [1952]), 218p.*

CLARKE, Dudley
Seven assignments *(London: Cape 1948), 262p.*

COLVIN, Ian
Flight 777 [Leslie Howard] *(London: Evans 1957), viii, 212p.*
The unknown courier *(London: Kimber 1953), 208p, bib.*

COOKRIDGE, E H (pseud)
Secrets of the British secret service: behind the scenes of the work of British counter espionage during the war *(London: Sampson Low 1948), 216p.*
They came from the sky: the stories of Lt.-Col. Francis Cammaerts, D.S.O., Legion of Honour, and Cpt. Harry Ree, D.S.O., O.B.E. *(London: Heinemann 1965), 264p.*

COOPER, Dick
The adventures of a secret agent *(London: Muller 1957), 256p.*

COWBURN, Benjamin
No cloak, no dagger *(London: Jarrolds 1960), 192p.*

DASCH, George J
Eight spies against America *(New York: McBride 1959), 241p.*

DAVIDSON-HOUSTON, James V
Armed pilgrimage *(London: Hale 1949), 313p.*

DELMER, Sefton
The counterfeit spy *(London: Hutchinson 1973), 256p.*

DENHAM, Elizabeth
I looked right *(London: Cassell 1956), 191p.*

DONEUX, Jacques
They arrived by moonlight *(London: Odhams [1957]), 230p.*

DOURLEIN, Pieter
Inside North Pole: a secret agent's story *(London: Kimber 1953), 206p.*

DOWNES, Donald
The scarlet thread: adventures in wartime espionage *(London: Verschoyle 1953), xiii, 207p.*

DUKE, Madelaine
Slipstream: the story of Anthony Duke *(London: Evans 1955), x, 11–243p.*

DUREN, Theo van
Orange above *(London: Staples 1956), 221p.*

DURRANI, Mahmood Khan
The sixth column: the heroic personal story of Mahmood Khan Durrani *(London: Cassell 1955), xi, 368p.*

EDLMANN, Edmund G
With my little eye *(London: Jarrolds 1961), 240p.*

ELISCU, William
Count five and die *(London: Souvenir 1958), 179p.*

EVANS, Jack
Confessions of a special agent *(London: Hale 1957), 192p; US title:* Face of death.

FARAGO, Ladislas
Burn after reading: the espionage history of World War II *(New York: Walker 1961), 391p.*

FARRAN, Roy A
Winged dagger: adventures on special service *(London: Collins 1948), 384p.*

FIRMIN, Stanley
They came to spy *(London: Hutchinson 1946), 156p.*

FOOTE, Alexander
Handbook for spies *(London: Museum 1949), 223p.*

FULLER, Jean O
Double webs *(New York: Putnam 1958), 256p; UK title:* Double agent?
Madeleine: the story of Noor Inayat Khan *(London: Gollancz 1952), 192p; later published as:* Born for sacrifice; *US title:* N.13, Bob.
The Starr affair *(London: Gollancz 1954), 222p.*

GARBY-CZERNIAWSKI, Roman
The big network *(London: Ronald [1961]), 248p.*

GEHLEN, Reinhard
The Gehlen memoirs: the first full edition of the memoirs of General Gehlen, 1942–1971 *(London: Collins 1972), 381p; US title:* The service.

GIMPEL, Erich
Spy for Germany *(London: Hale 1957), 238p.*

GISKES, H J
London calling North Pole *(London: Kimber 1953), 208p.*

GOLDSMITH, John
Accidental agent *(London: Cooper 1971), 192p.*

GRANOVSKY, Anatoli R
All pity choked: the memoirs of a Soviet secret agent *(London: Kimber 1955), 248p.*

HEARN, Cyril V
Desert assignment *(London: Hale 1963), 191p.*
Foreign correspondent *(London: Hale 1961), 191p.*

HEILBRUNN, O
The Soviet secret services *(London: Allen & Unwin 1956), 216p.*

HEPBURN, Sybil
Wingless victory *(London: Allen Wingate-Baker 1969), 190p.*

HOETTL, Wilhelm
Hitler's paper weapon *(London: Hart-Davis 1955), 187p.*
The secret front: the story of Nazi political espionage *(London: Weidenfeld & Nicolson 1953), 327p.*

HÖHNE, Heinz
Codeword: Direktor: the story of the Red Orchestra *(London: Secker & Warburg 1971), xxix, 310p, bib.*
Network *(London: Secker & Warburg 1972), xxxiii, 347p, bib.*

HOWARTH, Patrick (ed)
Special operations *(London: Routledge 1955), xiv, 239p.*

HYDE, Harford M
Cynthia: the spy who changed the course of the war *(New York: Farrar 1965), [9], 181p.*
The quiet Canadian: the secret service story of Sir William Stephenson *(London: Hamilton 1962), xii, 255p, bib; US title:* Room 3603.

ICARDI, Aldo
Aldo Icardi: American master spy: a true story *(Pittsburgh, Pa: Stalwart Enterprises 1954), 275p.*

JAMES, Meyrich E C
I was Monty's double *(London: Rider 1954), xv, 192p.*

JOHN, Otto
Twice through the lines: the autobiography of Otto John *(London: Macmillan 1972), 340p.*
KEMP, Peter
Alms for oblivion *(London: Cassell 1961), 188p.*
No colours or crest *(London: Cassell 1958), xiii, 305p.*
KIRSCHEN, Gilbert S
Six friends arrive tonight *(London: Nicholson & Watson 1949, 160p.*
KLEIN, Alexander
The counterfeit traitor *(London: Muller [1958]), 285p.*
LANGELAAN, George
Knights of the floating silk *(London: Hutchinson 1959), 320p.*
LAUGLIN, Austin
Boots and all: the inside story of the secret war *(Melbourne, Aust: Colorgravure 1951), 208p.*
LE CHENE, Evelyn
Watch for me by moonlight: a British agent with the French resistance *(London: Eyre Methuen 1973), 224p.*
LISTOWEL, Judith H, *countess of*
Crusader in a secret war *(London: Johnson 1952), 287p.*
LOCKHART, *Sir* Robert H B
Comes the reckoning *(London: Putnam 1947), 384p.*
LOVELL, Stanley P
Of spies and stratagems *(New York: Prentice-Hall 1963), 191p.*
LUSSEYRAN, Jacques
And there was light *(Boston, Mass: Little, Brown 1963), 312p.*
MACDONALD, Elizabeth P
Undercover girl *(New York: Macmillan 1947), 305p.*
MARSHALL, Bruce
The white rabbit: the story of Wing Commander F.F.E. Yeo-Thomas *(London: Evans 1952), ix, 262p.*
MARTELLI, George
Agent extraordinary: the story of Michel Hollard, D.S.O., Croix de Guerre *(London: Collins 1960), 286p.*
MINNEY, Rubeigh J
Carve her name with pride *(London: Newnes 1956), xii, 187p.*
MONTAGU, Ewen
The man who never was *(London: Evans 1953), 144p.*
MORGAN, William J
Spies and saboteurs *(London: Gollancz 1955), 183p.*
MOSLEY, Leonard
The cat and the mice *(London: Barker 1958), 160p, bib.*

MOSS, William S
A war of shadows *(New York: Macmillan 1952), 239p.*

PARKER, Geoffrye
The black scalpel *(London: Kimber 1968), 157p.*

PERRAULT, Gilles
The Red Orchestra *(London: Barker 1968), 496p, bib.*

PIELALKIEWICZ, Janusz
Secret agents, spies and saboteurs: secret missions of the Second World War *(Newton Abbot, Devon: David & Charles 1974), 528p.*

PINTO, Oreste
Friend or foe? *(London: Laurie [1953]), 188p.*
Spy-catcher *(London: Laurie [1952]), 175p.*
The spycatcher omnibus: the spy and counter-spy adventures of Lt. Col. Oreste Pinto *(London: Hodder & Stoughton 1962), 479p.*

PIQUET-WICKS, Eric
Four in the shadows: a true story of espionage in occupied France *(London: Jarrolds 1957), 207p.*

PIRIE, Anthony
Operator Bernhard: the greatest forgery of all time *(London: Cassell 1961), xix, 236p, bib.*

PITT, Roxanne
The courage of fear *(London: Jarrolds 1957), xi, 242p.*

POPOV, Dusko
Spy, counterspy *(London: Weidenfeld & Nicolson 1974), ix, 278p.*

RACHLIS, Eugene
They came to kill: the story of eight Nazi saboteurs in America *(New York: Random House 1961), 306p.*

RAKE, Denis
Rake's progress *(London: Frewin 1968), 271p.*

READER'S DIGEST (periodical)
Secrets and spies: behind-the-scenes stories of World War II *(Pleasantville, NY: Reader's Digest 1964), 576p.*

REMY (pseud)
Memoirs of a secret agent of Free France *(New York: McGraw-Hill 1948–50), 2 vols.*
Portrait of a spy *(London: Barker 1955), 224p.*
Ten steps to hope *(London: Barker 1960), 160p.*

RICHARDSON, Hal
One-man war: the Jock McLaren story *(Sydney: Angus & Robertson 1957),* [13], *189p.*

RIESS, Curt
Total espionage *(New York: Putnam 1941), xii, 318p.*

ROWAN, Richard W
Spy secrets *(New York: Buse 1946), 112p.*

SAELEN, Frithjof
None but the brave: the story of 'Shetlands' Larsen C.G.M., D.S.O., D.S.C., D.S.M. and bar *(London: Souvenir 1955),* [7], *232p.*

[SCHMIDT, Aage]
The dark city: being an account of the adventures of a secret agent in Berlin *(New York: Reinhart 1954), 255p.*

SCHWARZWALDER, John
We caught spies *(New York: Duell 1946), 296p.*

SCOTLAND, Alexander P
The London cage *(London: Evans 1957), 203p.*

SERGUEIEV, Lily
Secret service rendered *(London: Kimber 1968), 223p.*

SETH, Ronald
A spy has no friends *(London: Deutsch 1952), 206p.*
The true book about the secret service *(London: Muller 1958), 142p.*

SINEVIRSKII, Nikolai
Smersh *(New York: Holt 1950), 253p.*

SINGER, Kurt D
Duel for the Northland: the war of enemy agents in Scandinavia *(New York: McBride 1943), x, 212p.*
Spies and traitors of World War II *(New York: Grosset 1949), vi, 295p.*

SNOW, John H
The case of Tyler Kent *(New York: Domestic and Foreign Affairs and Citizens 1946), 59p.*

SOLTIKOW, Michael, *Graf*
The Cat: a true story of espionage *(London: MacGibbon & Kee 1957), 227p.*

STEAD, Philip J
Second Bureau *(London: Evans* [*1959*]*), viii, 9-212p, bib.*

TEARE, Thomas D G
Evader *(London: Hodder & Stoughton 1954), 256p.*

THOMAS, Jack
No banners: the story of Alfred and Henry Newton *(London: W H Allen 1955), 346p.*

TICKELL, Jerrard
Moon squadron *(London: Wingate 1956), 204p.*
Odette: the story of a British agent *(London: Chapman & Hall 1949), 286p.*

TOYNE, John
Win time for us *(New York: Longmans 1962), 241p.*
WALKER, David E
Adventure in diamonds *(London: Evans 1955), 186p.*
Lunch with a stranger *(London: Wingate 1957), 195p.*
WHEATLEY, Dennis
Stranger than fiction *(London: Hutchinson 1959), 364p.*
WHITE, John B
The big lie *(London: Evans 1955), 220p.*
WHITING, Charles
The war in the shadows *(New York: Ballantine 1973), 268p.*
WHITWELL, John
British agent *(London: Kimber 1966), 224p.*
WIGHTON, Charles
Pin-stripe saboteur: the story of 'Robin': British agent and French resistance leader *(London: Odhams 1959), 256p.*
WIGHTON, Charles *and* PEIS, Günter
They spied in England: based on the German secret service war diary of General von Lahousen *(London: Odhams 1958), 320p; US title:* Hitler's spies and saboteurs.
WILHELM, Maria
The man who watched the Rising Sun: the story of Admiral Ellis M. Zacharias *(New York: Watts 1967), 238p.*
WYNNE, Barry
Count five and die *(London: Souvenir 1958), 179p.*
The empty coffin: the story of Alain Romans *(London: Souvenir 1959), 196p.*
No drums . . . no trumpets: the story of Mary Liddell *(London: Barker [1961]), 278p.*
YOUNG, Gordon
The Cat with two faces *(London: Putnam 1957), 223p.*
In trust and treason: the strange story of Suzanne Warren *(London: Hulton 1959), 199p.*
[*see also* INTELLIGENCE, RESISTANCE]

SECRET WEAPONS

BERGIER, Jacques
Secret weapons - secret agents *(London: Hurst & Blackett 1956), 184p.*
FORD, Brian J
German secret weapons: blueprint for Mars *(New York: Ballantine 1969), 160p, bib.*

HOGG, Ian V
German secret weapons of World War II *(New York: Arco 1970), 80p.*
KEMP, Norman
The devices of war *(London: Laurie 1956), 232p.*
KIRK, John *and* YOUNG, Robert
Great weapons of World War II *(New York: Walker 1961), 347p.*
LUSAR, Rudolf
German secret weapons of the Second World War *(London: Spearman 1959), 264p.*
PAWLE, Gerald
The secret war, 1939–45 *(London: Harrap 1956), 297p.*
TERRELL, Edward
Admiralty brief: the story of inventions that contributed to victory in the battle of the Atlantic *(London: Harrap 1959), 240p.*

SHANGHAI

FARMER, Francis R
Shanghai harvest: a diary of three years in the China war *(London: Museum 1945), 294p.*
O'LEARY, Cedric P
A shamrock up a bamboo tree: the story of eight years behind the 8-ball in Shanghai, 1941–49 *(New York: Exposition 1956), 235p.*
WETTERN, Desmond
The lonely battle *(London: W H Allen 1960), 223p.*
[*see also* CHINA]

SHEFFIELD

ROBERTS, Eric S
Just as it came *(Sheffield: Northend 1945), 165p.*
SHEFFIELD at war *(Sheffield: Sheffield Telegraph 1948), 80p.*

SHIPBUILDING

FINNIE, Richard (ed)
Marinship: the history of a wartime shipyard *(San Francisco, Calif: Marinship 1947), 403p.*
SAWYER, Leonard Arthur *and* MITCHELL, W H
Victory ships and tankers *(Cambridge, Md: Cornell Maritime 1974), 230p.*

SICILY

BLUMENSON, Martin
Sicily: whose victory? *(New York: Ballantine 1968), 160p, bib.*

POND, Hugh
Sicily *(London: Kimber 1962), 224p.*

STEINHOFF, Johannes
The Straits of Messina: a diary of a fighter commander *(London: Deutsch 1971), 3-267p, bib.*
[*see also* ITALIAN CAMPAIGN]

SINGAPORE

ATTIWILL, Kenneth
The Singapore story *(London: Muller 1959), 253p, bib; US title:* Fortress.

BAILEY, Douglas
We built and destroyed *(London: Hurst & Blackett 1944), 132p.*

BARBER, Noel
Sinister twilight: the fall and rise again of Singapore *(London: Collins 1968), 319p, bib.*

BELL, Leslie
Destined meeting *(London: Odhams [1959]), 256p.*

BENNETT, Henry G
Why Singapore fell *(London: Angus & Robertson 1944), x, 262p.*

BURTON, Reginald
The road to three pagodas *(London: Macdonald 1963), 180p.*

CAFFREY, Kate
Out in the midday sun: Singapore, 1941–45 *(London: Deutsch 1974), 312p, bib.*

CORNELIUS, Mary D
Changi *(Ilfracombe, Devon: Stockwell [1953]), 80p.*

CRISP, Dorothy
Why we lost Singapore *(London: Crisp 1944), 178p.*

DONAHUE, Arthur G
Last flight from Singapore *(New York: Macmillan 1943), 168p.*

GILMOUR, Oswald W
Singapore to freedom *(Cheltenham, Glos: Burrow 1943), 128p.*
With freedom to Singapore *(London: Benn 1950), 227p.*

KIN, David G
Rage in Singapore: the cauldron of Asia boils over *(New York: Wisdom House 1942), 320p.*

KIRBY, Stanley W
Singapore: the chain of disaster *(London: Cassell 1971), xv, 270p, bib.*

LEASOR, James
Singapore: the battle that changed the world *(New York: Doubleday 1968), ix, 335p, bib.*

LOW, N I *and* CHENG, H M
This Singapore: our city of dreadful night *(Singapore: City Book Store 194–), 173p.*

MCCORMAC, Charles
'You'll die in Singapore' *(London: Hale 1954), 189p.*

OUTPOST (pseud)
Singapore nightmare: a story of the evacuation and an escape to Australia *(Bognor Regis, Sussex: Crowther 1943), 68p.*

OWEN, Frank
The fall of Singapore *(London: Joseph 1960), 216p.*

PLAYFAIR, Giles
Singapore goes off the air *(New York: Dutton 1943), 9–273p.*

ROSE, Angus J C
Who dies fighting *(London: Cape 1944), 160p.*

RUSSELL-ROBERTS, Denis
Spotlight on Singapore *(Douglas, IoM: Times 1965), 301p.*

SIMSON, Ivan
Singapore: too little, too late: some aspects of the Malayan disaster in 1942 *(London: Cooper 1970), 165p.*

SKIDMORE, Ian
Escape from the Rising Sun: the incredible voyage of the 'Sederhana Djohanis' *(London: Cooper 1973), 198p, bib.*

SMYTH, *Sir* John
Percival and the tragedy of Singapore *(London: Macdonald 1971), 298p.*

STRABOLGI, Joseph M K *10th baron*
Singapore and after: a study of the Pacific campaign *(London: Hutchinson 1942), 6–158p.*

SWINSON, Arthur
Defeat in Malaya: the fall of Singapore *(New York: Ballantine 1970), 160p, bib.*

TAYLOR, William
The Cambridgeshires at Singapore *(March, Cambs: Bevis 1971), ii–xiv, 115p.*

TSUJI, Masanobu
Singapore: the Japanese version *(Sydney: Smith 1960), xxv, 358p.*

WHARF, Michael (pseud)
Singapore is silent *(New York: Harcourt 1943), 312p.*
[*see also* MALAYSIA]

SKORZENY

FOLEY, Charles
Commando extraordinary *(London: Longmans, Green 1954), 251p.*
SKORZENY, Otto
Secret missions: war memoirs of the most dangerous man in Europe *(New York: Dutton 1950), 7-256p; UK title:* Skorzeny's special missions.

SLIM

CALVERT, Michael
Slim *(New York: Ballantine 1973), 160p, bib.*
EVANS, *Sir* Geoffrey
Slim as military commander *(London: Batsford 1969), 239p, bib.*
[*see also* BURMA]

SOCIOLOGY

MERRILL, Francis E
Social problems on the home front: a study of war-time influences *(New York: Harper 1948), x, 258p.*
TITMUSS, Richard M
Problems of social policy *(London: HMSO 1950), xi, 596p.*

SOLOMON ISLANDS

CAVE, Hugh B *and others*
Long were the nights: the saga of PT Squadron X in the Solomons *(New York: Dodd 1943), xi, 220p.*
DECK, Northcote
South from Guadalcanal *(Grand Rapids, Mich: Zondervan 1946), 124p.*
DONOVAN, Robert J
The war-time adventures of President John F. Kennedy *(London: Gibbs & Phillips 1962), 160p.*

FELDT, Eric A
Coastwatchers *(London: Oxford UP 1946), [9], 292p.*
GIRARDEAU, Marvin D
Dragon's peninsula *(New York: Vantage 1967), 141p.*
HORTON, Dick C
New Georgia: pattern for victory *(New York: Ballantine 1971), 160p, bib.*
US Marine Corps
Bourganville and the Northern Solomons *(Washington DC: USMC 1948), 166p.*
Marines in the Central Solomons *(Washington DC: USMC 1952), 186p.*
WOLFERT, Ira
The battle for the Solomons *(London: Jarrolds 1943), 96p.*
WRIGHT, Malcolm
If I die: coastwatching and guerilla warfare behind Japanese lines *(Melbourne, Aust: Lansdowne 1966), [8], 192p.*
[*see also* NEW GUINEA, PACIFIC, US MARINES]

SONGS

PAGE, Martin (ed)
Kiss me goodnight, Sergeant-Major: the songs and ballads of World War II *(London: Hart-Davis 1973), 192p.*
POSSELT, Erich (ed)
G.I. songs *(New York: Sheridan 1944), 253p.*
WARD-JACKSON, C H (comp)
The airman's song book *(London: Sylvan 1945), xiv, 190p.*

SOUTH AFRICA

BLAMEY, Arthur E
A company commander remembers: from El Yibo to El Alamein *(Durban, SA: Adams 1963), 201p.*
BROWN, James A
A gathering of eagles: the campaigns of the South African Air Force in Italian East Africa, June 1940–Nov. 1941 *(London: Purnell 1970), 342p.*
CAMPBELL, Alexander
Smuts and swastika *(London: Gollancz 1943), 168p.*
COWIN, John N (comp)
The story of the Ninth: a record of the 9th Field Company, South African Engineer Corps, July 1939–July 1943 *(Johannesburg: Gover, Dande 1948), 161p.*

DUFFUS, Louis
Beyond the laager *(London: Hurst & Blackett 1947), 168p.*

FIELDING, W L
With the 6th Division: an account of the activities of the 6th South African Armoured Division in World War II *(Pietermaritzburg: Shuter & Shorter 1946), 191p.*

JAMESON, K *and* ASHBURNER, D
South African W.A.A.F. *(Pietermaritzburg: Shuter & Shorter 1948), 68p.*

KLEIN, Harry
Springboks in armour: the South African armoured cars in World War II *(London: Macdonald [1965]), xv, 338p, bib.*

LONG, Basil K
In Smut's camp *(London: Oxford UP 1945), 162p.*

McCREATH, Stuart N
Theirs is the glory: the story of 12 Squadron South African Air Force during World War II *(Johannesburg: Marauder 1948), vi, 7-172p.*

ROBINSON, N I
Missing believed prisoner: the story of a South African prisoner of war *(Durban, SA: Robinson 1944), 74p.*

SCOTT, Douglas
My luck still held *(Cape Town: Unievolkspers Beperk 1946), 143p.*

SIMPSON, J S M
South Africa fights *(London: Hodder & Stoughton 1941), xv, 256p.*

SONNABEND, H
About myself and others *(Johannesburg: Eagle 1951), 228p.*

TUNGAY, Ronald W
The fighting Third *(Cape Town: Unievolkspers Beperk 1948), 410p.*

TURNER, Leonard C F *and others*
War in the Southern Oceans, 1939–45 *(Cape Town: Oxford UP 1961), xvi, 288p, bib.*

VOSS, Vivian
The story of No. 1 Squadron South African Air Force *(Cape Town: Meshantile Atlas 1952), 519p.*

WOOD, A M
Men of the Midlands: the story of Weenenklip River National Reserve Volunteers *(Pietermaritzburg: Natal Witness 1946), 63p.*

SOUTH EAST ASIA

ATTIWILL, Kenneth
The rising sunset *(London: Hale 1947), 206p.*

BOULLE, Pierre
My own River Kwai *(New York: Vanguard 1967), 214p.*
The source of the River Kwai *(London: Secker & Warburg 1967), 214p.*

BRADDON, Russell
The naked island *(London: Laurie 1952), [8], 266p.*

CAPLAN, Jack
From Gorbals to jungle *(Glasgow: MacLellan [1961]), 237p.*

GORDON, Ernest
Through the valley of the Kwai *(New York: Harper 1962), 257p; UK title:* Miracle on the River Kwai.

HARRISON, Kenneth
The brave Japanese *(London: Angus & Robertson 1967), 280p.*

HASTAIN, Ronald
White coolie *(London: Hodder & Stoughton 1947), 318p.*

MOUNTBATTEN, Louis, *1st earl Mountbatten of Burma*
Report to the Combined Chiefs of Staff by the Supreme Allied Commander, South-East Asia, 1943–1945 *(New York: Philosophical Library 1951), xi, 280p.*
[*see also* JAPANESE PRISON CAMPS, MALAYSIA, THAILAND]

SOUTHERN RHODESIA

MACDONALD, John F
The war history of Southern Rhodesia *(Salisbury, SR: Southern Rhodesia Government State Office 1947–50), 2 vols.*

SPAIN

DUFF, Charles
Key to victory: Spain *(London: Gollancz 1940), 120p.*

DUNDAS, Lawrence
Behind the Spanish mask *(London: Hale 1943), 111p.*

FEIS, Herbert
The Spanish story: Franco and the nations at war *(New York: Knopf 1948), x, 282p.*

HAYES, Carlton J H
Wartime mission in Spain, 1942–1945 *(London: Macmillan 1945), 313p.*

HOARE, Samuel J G, *1st viscount Templewood*
Ambassador on special mission *(London: Collins 1946), 320p; US title:* Complacent dictator.
PEERS, Edgar A
Spanish dilemma *(London: Methuen 1940), xiii, 129p.*

SPECIAL AIR SERVICES

COWLES, Virginia
The phantom major: the story of David Stirling and the S.A.S. Regiment *(London: Cassell 1957), 320p.*
FARRAN, Roy A
Operation Tombola *(London: Collins 1960), 256p.*
HARRISON, Derrick I
These men are dangerous: the Special Air Service at war *(London: Cassell 1957), xiii, 240p.*
MARRINAN, Patrick
Colonel Paddy *(Dungannon: Ulster [1968]), 207p.*
WARNER, Philip
The Special Air Service *(London: Kimber 1971), 285p.*

SPECIAL OPERATIONS EXECUTIVE

BUCKMASTER, Maurice J
Specially employed: the story of British aid to French patriots of the resistance *(London: Batchworth 1952), 200p.*
They fought alone: British agents in France *(London: Odhams 1958), 256p.*
COOKRIDGE, Edward H
Inside S.O.E.: the story of special operations in Western Europe, 1940–45 *(London: Barker [1966]), xvi, 640p, bib; later published as:* Set Europe ablaze.
FOOT, Michael R D
S.O.E. in France: an account of the work of the British Special Operations Executive in France, 1940–1944 *(London: HMSO 1966), xix, 550p.*
HAMILTON-HILL, Donald
SOE assignment *(London: Kimber 1973), [5], 186p.*
NICHOLAS, Elizabeth
Death be not proud *(London: Cresset 1958), 294p.*
SWEET-ESCOTT, Bickham
Baker Street irregular *(London: Methuen 1965), 278p.*
[*see also* SECRET SERVICES]

STALIN

DJILAS, Milovan
Conversations with Stalin *(London: Hart-Davis 1962), 211p.*

HYDE, Harford M
Stalin: the history of a dictator *(London: Hart-Davis 1971), 679p, bib.*

STALIN, Josef
Correspondence with Churchill, Attlee, Roosevelt and Truman, 1941-1945 *(New York: Dutton 1958), 2 vols in 1.*
On the great patriotic war of the Soviet Union *(London: Hutchinson 1945), 5-96p.*
Order of the day: speeches and important orders of the day *(Toronto: Progress 1944), 9-126p.*
War speeches, orders of the day and answers to foreign press correspondents during the great patriotic war, 3 July 1941 to 22 June 1945 *(London: Hutchinson 1946), 140p.*

ULAM, Adam B
Stalin the man and his era *(New York: Viking 1973), 760p.*

STALINGRAD

AGAPOV, Boris N
After the battle: Stalingrad sketches and notes of a guerilla fighter *(London: Hutchinson 1943), 78p.*

CHUIKOV, Vasilii I
The beginning of the road *(MacGibbon & Kee 1963), 388p; US title:* The battle for Stalingrad.

CRAIG, William
Enemy at the gates: the battle for Stalingrad *(London: Hodder & Stoughton 1973), xvii, 457p.*

DIBOLD, Hans
Doctor at Stalingrad: the passion of a captivity *(London: Hutchinson 1958), 191p.*

JUKES, Geoffrey
Stalingrad: the turning point *(New York: Ballantine 1968), 160p, bib.*

LAST letters from Stalingrad *(London: Methuen 1956), viii, 9-70p*

SAMMIS, Edward R
Last stand at Stalingrad: the battle that saved the world *(New York: Macmillan [1966]), 96p, bib.*

SCHROTER, Heinz
Stalingrad *(London: Joseph 1958), 263p.*

SETH, Ronald
Stalingrad: point of no return: the story of the battle, August 1942–February 1943 *(London: Gollancz 1959), x, 11–254p*

STALINGRAD: an eye-witness account *(London: Hutchinson 1943), 118p.*
[*see also* GERMAN ARMY, HITLER, RUSSIA]

STATISTICS

GREAT BRITAIN. Central Statistical Office
Statistical digest of the war *(London: HMSO 1951), xii, 248p.*

STORIES (general)

BRENT, Rafer (ed)
Great war stories: true adventures of fighting men in two world wars *(New York: Bartholomew House 1957), 188p.*

CONSIDINE, Bob (selector)
True war stories: a Crest anthology selected from True, the man's magazine *(Greenwich: Conn: Fawcett 1961), 239p.*

CONSTABLE, Trevor J
Hidden heroes: historic achievements of men of courage *(London: Barker 1971), [12], 195p.*

CUNNINGHAM, William H *and* STAUFFER, R M
They tell their story: 23 episodes in the global war *(New York: Harcourt 1943), vii, 280p.*

HIRSCH, Phil (ed)
Great untold stories of World War II *(New York: Pyramid 1963), 191p.*

HOARE, Robert J (comp)
True stories of capture and rescue *(London: Hamilton 1960), 143p.*

THE HUNDRED best true stories of World War II *(New York: Wise 1945), 896p.*

I WAS lucky to escape: twelve true stories of refugee and war-time escapes *(London: Drummond 1940), viii, 9–284p.*

LOOK (periodical)
My favorite war story *(New York: McGraw-Hill 1945), 155p.*

MARSHALL, Samuel L A
Battle at best *(New York: Morrow 1964), 257p.*

[RAMSEY, Guy (comp)]
Epic stories of the Second World War *(London: Odhams [1958]), 318p.*

RHOADS, Marian (ed)
All out for freedom: hero stories from the Second World War *(Boston, Mass: Ginn 1943), ix, 180p*

ROGERS, Stanley R H
Hazards of war *(London: Harrap 1944), 238p.*
More gallant deeds of the war *(London: Blackie 1942), 223p.*

THE SATURDAY EVENING POST (newspaper)
Battle: true stories of combat in World War II *(New York: Doubleday 1965), 310p.*

SCOGGIN, Margaret C
Battle stations: true stories of men in war *(New York: Knopf 1953), 306p.*

70 true stories of the Second World War *(London: Odhams [1953]), 288p.*

STERLING, Dorothy (ed)
I have seen war: 25 stories from World War II *(New York: Hill & Wang 1960), 273p.*

URQUART, Fred (ed)
Great true war adventures *(London: Arco [1956]), viii, 342p.*

WHYTE, A P L
Escape to fight again: stories of men and women who refused to accept defeat *(London: Harrap 1943), 258p.*

STRATEGY

ALPEROVITZ, Gar
Atomic diplomacy: Hiroshima and Potsdam; the use of the atomic bomb and the American confrontation with Soviet power *(New York: Simon & Schuster 1965), 317p, bib.*

ARNOLD, Ralph
A very quiet war *(London: Hart-Davis 1962), 176p,*

BALDWIN, Hanson W
Defence of the Western world *(London: Hutchinson 1941), ix, 11-304p; US title:* United we stand.
Strategy for victory *(New York: Norton 1942), 9-172p.*

BURNE, Alfred H
Strategy in World War II: a strategical examination of the land operations *(Harrisburg, Pa: Military Service 1947), 91p.*

BUTLER, J R M (ed)
Grand strategy *(London: HMSO 1956-72), 6 vols.*

CLINE, Ray S
Washington command post: the operations division *(Washington DC: Department of Army 1951), 413p.*

COLLIER, Basil
The Lion and the Eagle: British and Anglo-American strategy, 1900–1950 *(London: Macdonald 1972), x, 499p, bib.*

DALGLEISH, John
We planned the Second Front *(London: Gollancz 1945), 108p.*

FARAGO, Ladislas
Axis grand strategy: blue prints for the total war *(New York: Farrar 1942), ix, 614p.*

GREAT BRITAIN. Cabinet Office Historical Section
Orders of battle: United Kingdom and Colonial formations and units in the Second World War, 1939–1945 *(London: HMSO 1960), 2 vols.*

GREENFIELD, Kent R
American strategy in World War II: a reconsideration *(Baltimore, Md: Johns Hopkins 1963), 145p.*

HIGGINS, Trumbull
Soft underbelly: the Anglo-American controversy over the Italian campaign, 1939–1945 *(New York: Macmillan 1968), x, 275p, bib.*

HOWARD, Michael
The Mediterranean strategy in the Second World War: the Lees-Knowles lectures at Trinity College, Cambridge, 1966 *(London: Weidenfeld & Nicolson 1968), xii, 83p.*

JAVSICAS, Gabriel
Shortage of victory: cause and cure *(New York: Appleton 1943), xiv, 372p.*

KERNAN, William F
Defence will not win the war *(London: Heinemann 1942), 108p.*
We can win this war *(Boston, Mass: Little, Brown 1943), 176p.*

KINGSTON-MCCLOUGHRY, Edgar J
The direction of war, a critique of the political direction and high command in war *(London: Cape 1955), 261p.*

KIRALFY, Alexander
Victory in the Pacific: how we must defeat Japan *(New York: Day 1942), xiv, 283p.*

KREIPE, Werner *and others*
The fatal decision *(London: Joseph 1956), 261p.*

LEACH, Barry A
German strategy against Russia, 1939–1941 *(Oxford: Clarendon 1973), xv, 308p, bib.*

LIDDELL-HART, Basil H
Strategy: the indirect approach *(New York: Praeger 1954), 420p.*

MATLOFF, Maurice
Strategic plan for coalition warfare, 1941-2, 1943-4. *(Washington DC: Department of Army, 1953-9), 2 vols.*

MERGLEN, Albert
Surprise warfare: subversive, airborne and amphibious operations *(London: Allen & Unwin 1968), 3-212p.*

MORGAN, Henry G
Planning the defeat of Japan: a study of total war strategy *(Washington DC: Department of Army 1961), 197p.*

MORISON, Samuel E
American contributions to the strategy of World War 2 *(London: Oxford UP 1958), vii, 80p.*
Strategy and compromise *(Boston, Mass: Little, Brown 1958), 120p.*

MORTON, Louis
Strategy and command: the first two years *(Washington DC: Department of Army 1962), 761p.*

NECKER, Wilhelm
Nazi Germany can't win: an exposure of Germany's strategic arms and weaknesses *(London: Drummond 1940), xii, 364p.*

NICKERSON, Hoffman
Arms and policy, 1939-1944 *(New York: Putnam 1945), 356p.*

POGUE, Forrest C
The Supreme Command *(Washington DC: Department of Army 1946), 607p.*

ROMANUS, Charles F *and* SUNDERLAND, Riley
Stilwell's command problems *(Washington DC: Department of Army 1956), 518p.*

SARGEAUNT, Henry A *and* WEST, Geoffrey (pseuds)
Grand strategy *(London: Cape 1941), xi, 246p.*

SHIFRIN, Aleksander M (pseud)
Attack can win in '43 *(Boston, Mass: Little, Brown 1943), 216p.*

SLATER, Hugh
War into Europe: attack in depth *(London: Gollancz 1941), 166p.*

SMASH Hitler's international: the strategy of a political offensive against the Axis *(New York: Greystone 1941), 9-96p.*

SMITH, Percy McC
The Air Force plans for peace, 1943-1945 *(Baltimore, Md: Johns Hopkins 1970), xii, 132p.*

SMYTH, *Sir* John
Leadership in war, 1939-1945: the generals in victory and defeat *(Newton Abbot, Devon: David & Charles 1974), 247p, bib.*

STRATEGICUS (pseud)
War for world power *(London: Faber 1940), 304p.*

STRATEGY and tactics of the Soviet-German war *(London: Hutchinson 1942), vii, 9–148p.*
US Department of Army
Command decisions *(New York: Harcourt 1959), xiv, 477p.*
US Department of Defense
The entry of the Soviet Union into the war against Japan: military plans, 1941–45 *(Washington DC: 1955), 107p.*
VAN CREVELD, Martin L
Hitler's strategy, 1940–1941: the Balkan clue *(Cambridge: Cambridge UP 1973), 248p.*
WATSON, Mark S
Chief of Staff: prewar plans and preparations *(Washington DC: Department of Army 1950), 551p.*
WERNER, Max
The great offensive: the strategy of coalition warfare *(New York: Viking 1942), vi, 360p.*
The strategy and diplomacy of the Second World War *(London: Gollancz 1941), 288p; US title:* Battle for the world.
WHEELER-NICHOLSON, Malcolm
Are we winning the hard way? *(New York: Crowell 1943), xvii, 256p.*

SUBMARINES

ANSCOMB, Charles
Submariner *(London: Kimber 1957), 203p.*
BAX, Richard
Stand by to surface *(London: Cassell 1944), 208p.*
BEACH, Edward L
Submarine! *(New York: Holt 1952), 301p.*
BRYANT, Ben
One man band: the memoirs of a submarine C.O. *(London: Kimber 1958), 238p.*
CASEY, Robert J
Battle below: the war of the submarine *(Indianapolis, Ind: Bobbs-Merrill 1945), 380p.*
COPE, Harley F *and* KARIG, Walker
Battle submerged: submarine fighters of World War II *(New York: Norton 1951), xii, 244p.*
CROSS, Wilbur
Challengers of the deep: the story of submarines *(New York: Sloane 1959), 258p.*

DISSETTE, Edward *and* ADAMSON, H C
Guerilla submarines *(New York: Ballantine 1972), 238p.*
FARAGO, Ladislas
The Tenth Fleet *(New York: Obolensky 1962), 366p.*
FELL, William R
The sea our shield *(London: Cassell 1966), 232p.*
FRANK, Gerold *and* HORAN, James D
U.S.S. Seawolf: submarine raider of the Pacific *(New York: Putnam 1945), 197p.*
GALLAGHER, Thomas
'The X-craft raid' *(New York: Harcourt 1971), xv, 170p; UK title:* Against all odds: midget submarines against the 'Tirpitz'.
GIBSON, John F
Dark seas above *(Edinburgh: Blackwood 1947), viii, 286p.*
GREAT BRITAIN. Admiralty
His Majesty's submarines *(London: HMSO 1945), 64p.*
GRIDER, George W
War fish *(Boston, Mass: Little, Brown 1958), 282p.*
HART, Sydney
Discharged dead: a true story of Britain's submarines at war *(London: Odhams 1956), 208p.*
Submarine 'Upholder' *(London: Oldbourne 1960), 208p.*
HASHIMOTO, Moratsura
Sunk: the story of the Japanese submarine fleet, 1942–1945 *(London: Cassell 1954), 218p.*
HAWKINS, Maxwell
Torpedoes away, Sir!: our submarine Navy in the Pacific *(New York: Holt 1946), 268p.*
HOLMES, Wilfred J
Undersea victory: the influence of submarine operations on the war in the Pacific *(New York: Doubleday 1966), 505p.*
HORTON, Edward
The illustrated history of the submarine *(London: Sidgwick & Jackson 1974), 160p.*
ICENHOWER, Joseph B (ed)
Submarines in combat *(New York: Watts 1964), 180p.*
JEWELL, Norman L A
Secret mission submarine *(Chicago, Ill: Ziff-Davis 1945), 159p.*
KOLYSHKIN, Ivan A
Submarines in Arctic waters *(New York: Universal 1966), 253p.*
KUENNE, Robert E
The attack submarine: a study in strategy *(New Haven, Conn: Yale UP 1965), xi, 215p.*

LEWIS, David D
The fight for the sea: the past, present and future of submarine warfare in the Atlantic *(Cleveland, Ohio: World 1961), 350p.*

L'HERMINIER, Jean
Casabianca: the secret mission of a famous submarine *(London: Muller [1953]), xii, 243p.*

LIPSCOMBE, Frank W
The British submarine *(London: Black 1954), xiv, 269p.*

LOCKWOOD, Charles A
Hellcats of the sea *(New York: Greenberg 1955), 335p.*
Sink 'em all: submarine warfare in the Pacific *(New York: Dutton 1951), 7–416p.*

LOCKWOOD, Charles A *and* ADAMSON, Hans C
Through hell and deep water: the stirring story of the Navy's deadly submarine, the U.S.S. Harder *(New York: Greenberg 1956), 317p.*
Zoomies, subs and zeroes *(New York: Greenberg 1956), 301p.*

MACINTYRE, Donald
Fighting under the sea *(London: Evans 1965), 174p.*

MARS, Alastair
British submarines at war, 1939–1945 *(London: Kimber 1971), 256p, bib.*
'H.M.S. Thule' intercepts *(London: Elek [1956]), [9], 242p.*
'Unbroken': the story of a submarine *(London: Muller 1953), 224p.*

MASTERS, David
Up periscope *(London: Eyre & Spottiswoode 1942), 176p.*

PARRISH, Thomas D
Victory at sea: the submarine *(New York: Ridge 1959), 60p.*

ROBERTSON, Terence
The ship with two captains *(London: Evans 1957), 192p.*

ROSCOE, Theodore
United States submarine operations in World War II *(Annapolis, Md: US Naval Institute 1949), 577p; later published as:* Pig boats.

SHERIDAN, Martin
Overdue and presumed lost: the story of the U.S.S. Bullhead *(Francistown, NH: Jones 1947), 143p.*

SOPOCKO, Eryk K S
Orzel's patrol: the story of the British submarine *(London: Methuen 1942), xi, 146p.*

STERLING, Forest J
The wake of the Wahoo *(Philadelphia, Pa: Chilton 1960), 210p.*

TAYLOR, Theodore
Fire on the beaches *(New York: Norton 1958), 248p.*

THOMAS, David A
Submarine victory: the story of British submarines in World War II *(London: Kimber 1961), 224p.*

TRENOWDEN, Ian
The hunting submarine: the fighting life of H.M.S. Tally-Ho *(London: Kimber 1974), 224p.*

TRUMBULL, Robert
Silversides *(New York: Holt 1945), 217p.*

TURNER, John F
Periscope patrol: the saga of Malta submarines *(London: Harrap 1957), 218p.*

US OFFICE OF NAVAL OPERATIONS
United States submarine losses, World War II. Reissued with Appendix of Axis submarine losses *(Washington DC: 1963), 244p.*

WARREN, C E T *and* BENSON, James
'The Admiralty regrets . . .': the story of His Majesty's submarines 'Thetis' and 'Thunderbolt' *(London: Harrap 1958), 223p.*
Above us the waves: the story of midget submarines and human torpedoes *(London: Harrap 1953), 256p; US title:* Midget raiders.
Will not we fear: the story of His Majesty's submarine Seal *(London: Harrap 1961), 228p.*

WHITEHOUSE, Arch
Subs and submariners *(New York: Doubleday 1961), 416p, bib.*

YOUNG, Edward
One of our submarines *(London: Hart-Davis 1952), 320p; US title:* Undersea patrol.

SUMATRA

HARTLEY, Peter
Escape to captivity *(London: Dent 1952), ix, 210p.*

JEFFREY, Betty
White coolies *(Sydney: Angus & Robertson 1954),* [*11*], *204p.*

LEFFELAAR, Hendrik L
Through a harsh dawn *(South St Narre, Mass: Barre 1963), xiii, 258p.*

McDOUGALL, William H, *jun.*
By Eastern windows: the story of a battle of souls and minds in the prison camps of Sumatra *(New York: Scribner 1949), x, 349p.*
[*see also* JAPANESE PRISON CAMPS, JAVA]

SURVIVORS (sea)

BELL, *Mrs* Ethel
Adrift: the story of twenty days on a raft in the South Atlantic *(New York: Evangelical 1943), 125p.*

FOWLER, *Mrs* Elizabeth
Standing room only: the personal record of a woman's experience during ten days in a lifeboat with 34 men after their ship had been torpedoed by a German submarine *(New York: Dodd 1944), 195p.*

GIBSON, Walter
The boat *(London: W H Allen 1952), 96p.*

HAWKINS, Doris M
Atlantic torpedo!: the record of 27 days in an open boat following a U-boat sinking by the only woman survivor *(London: Gollancz 1943), 48p.*

MADDEN, Paul
Survivor *(Milwaukee, Wis: Bruce 1944), 68p.*

TURNER, John F
A girl called Johnnie: three weeks in an open boat *(London: Harrap 1963), 185p.*

SWEDEN

AUREN, Sven A G
Signature tune *(London: Hammond 1943), 226p.*

JOESTEN, Joachim
Stalwart Sweden *(New York: Doubleday 1943), vi, 215p.*

SWITZERLAND

HARTMANN, Frederick H
The Swiss Press and foreign affairs in World War II *(Gainsville, Fla: Florida UP 1960), 87p.*

HASLER, Alfred A
The lifeboat is full: Switzerland and the refugees, 1933–1945 *(New York: Funk & Wagnall 1969), 366p.*

KIMCHE, Jon
Spying for peace: General Guisan and Swiss neutrality *(London: Weidenfeld & Nicolson [1961]), xxii, 169p.*

ROSEN, Josef
Wartime food developments in Switzerland *(Stanford, Calif: Stanford UP 1947), 104p.*

TANKS

ANDERSON, Trezzvant W
Come out fighting: the epic tale of the 761st Tank Battalion, 1942–1945 *(Salzburg: Salzburger 1945), 135p.*

BECKLES, Gordon
Tanks advance! *(London: Cassell 1942), 9–128p.*

BRADFORD, George
Great tank battles of World War II: a combat diary of the Second World War *(New York: Arco 1970), unp.*

CASTAGNA, Edwin
The history of the 771st Tank Battalion *(Berkeley, Calif: 1946), 110p.*

CRISP, Robert
Brazen chariots: an account of tank warfare in the Western Desert, November-December, 1941 *(London: Muller 1959), 223p.*

FITZSIMMONS, Bernard (ed)
Tanks and weapons of World War II *(London: Phoebus 1973), 160p, bib.*

HALSTEAD, Ivor
The truth about our tanks *(London: Drummond 1943), 222p.*

HASSETT, Edward C (ed)
701st Tank Battalion: March 1943, Camp Campbell, Kentucky - June 1945, Gotha, Germany *(London: Nuremberg 1946), 239p.*

ICKS, Robert J
Famous tank battles *(New York: Doubleday 1972), ii–xvi, 365p, bib.*

MCLEAN, Donald B (ed)
Japanese tanks, tactics and antitank weapons *(Wickenburg, Ariz: Normount Technical 1973), 204p.*

MACKSEY, Kenneth J
Tank force: Allied armour in the Second World War *(New York: Ballantine 1970), 160p, bib.*

PERRETT, Bryan
The Churchill *(London: Allan 1974), 148p.*
The Matilda *(London: Allan 1973), 112p.*
The Valentine in North Africa, 1942–43 *(London: Allan 1972), 80p.*

POLIAKOV, Aleksandr
Westbound tanks *(London: Hutchinson 1943), 100p; US title:* White mammoths.

ROGERS, Hugh C B
Tanks in battle *(London: Seeley [1965]), 240p.*

RUBEL, George K
Daredevil tankers: the story of the 740th Tank Battalion, U.S. Army *(Ger: Gottingen 1945), 335p.*

US ARMY
717th Tank Battalion record *(San Angelo, Tex: Newsfoto 1946), 69p.*
[*see also* ARMOURED FORCES]

TARANTO

NEWTON, Don *and* HAMPSHIRE, Arthur C
Taranto *(London: Kimber 1959), 204p.*

SCHOFIELD, Brian B
The attack on Taranto *(London: Allan 1973), 94p, bib.*

TARAWA

HANNAH, Dick
Tarawa: the toughest battle in Marine Corps history *(New York: US Camera 1944), 13-126p.*

SHAW, Henry I
Tarawa: a legend is born *(New York: Ballantine 1968), 160p, bib.*

SHERROD, Robert L
Tarawa: the story of a battle *(New York: Duell 1944), vi, 183p.*

US MARINE CORPS
The battle for Tarawa *(Washington DC: USMC 1947), 86p.*

WERSTEIN, Irving
Tarawa: a battle report *(New York: Crowell 1965), 146p.*

WILSON, Earl J
Batio beachhead: U.S.Marines' own story of the battle for Tarawa *(New York: Putnam 1945), 160p.*
[*see also* PACIFIC, US MARINES]

TEDDER

OWEN, Roderic
Tedder *(London: Collins 1952), 320p.*

TEDDER, Arthur W, *1st baron Tedder*
With prejudice: the war memoirs of Marshal of the Royal Air Force, Lord Tedder *(London: Cassell 1966), [15], 718p, bib.*

TEHERAN

HAVAS, Laslo

The long jump *(London: Spearman [1967]), 256p; US title:* Hitler's plot to kill the big three.

IRAN. Ministry of Foreign Affairs

The Teheran conference: the three power declaration concerning Iran, December 1943 *(Iran 1945), 189p.*

WOJCIK, Andrzej J

The Teheran conference and Odra-Nisa boundary *(New York: Arlington 1959), 70p.*

THAILAND

ALLBURY, Alfred G

Bamboo and bushido *(London: Hale 1955), 192p.*

CARTER, Norman

G-string jesters *(London: Angus & Robertson 1966), viii, 195p.*

CHAYA, Prem (pseud)

The passing years: a record of five amazing years *(Bangkok: Chatra 1945), 95p.*

COAST, John

Railroad to death *(London: Commodore 1946), 316p.*

DURNFORD, John

Branch line to Burma *(London: Macdonald 1958), xiv, 17-207p.*

GILCHRIST, *Sir* Andrew

Bangkok top secret: being the experiences of a British officer in the Siam Country Section of Force 136 *(London: Hutchinson 1970), viii, 231p.*

KINVIG, Clifford

Death railway *(New York: Ballantine 1973), 160p, bib.*

PARKIN, Ray

Into the smother: a journal of the Burma-Siam railway *(London: Hogarth 1963), xv, 291.*

PAVILLARD, Stanley S

Bamboo doctor *(London: Macmillan 1960), ix, 206p.*

PEACOCK, Basil

Prisoners on the Kwai *(Edinburgh: Blackwood 1966), ii, 291p.*

RAWLINGS, Leo

And the dawn came up like thunder *(Harpenden, Herts: Rawlings, Chapman [1972]), xxxi, 160p.*

SMITH, Nicol *and* CLARK, Thomas B

Into Siam: underground kingdom *(Indianapolis, Ind: Bobbs-Merrill 1946), 315p.*

[*see also* JAPANESE PRISON CAMPS, SOUTHEAST ASIA]

TIBET

SINCLAIR, William B
Jump to the land of God: the adventures of a U.S. Air Force crew in Tibet *(Caldwell, Idaho: Caxton 1965), 313p.*

TITO

ARMSTRONG, Hamilton F
Tito and Goliath *(London: Gollancz 1951), 318p.*
CLISSOLD, Stephen
Whirlwind: an account of Marshal Tito's rise to power *(London: Philosophical Library 1949), 10–245p.*
DEDIJER, Vladimer
Tito speaks *(London: Weidenfeld & Nicolson 1953), 472p.*
With Tito through the war: partisan diary, 1941–1944 *(London: Hamilton 1951), 403p.*
PADEV, Michael
Marshal Tito *(London: Muller 1944), 7–129p.*
[*see also* YUGOSLAVIA]

TOBRUK

CARVER, Michael
Tobruk *(London: Batsford 1964), 3–271p.*
CUMPSTON, John S (comp)
The Rats remain: Tobruk siege 1941 *(Melbourne, Aust: Mayflower 1966), 256p.*
DEVINE, John B
The Rats of Tobruk *(London: Angus & Robertson 1943), xvi, 119p.*
FEARNSIDE, Geoffrey H
Sojourn in Tobruk *(Sydney: Smith 1944), 159p.*
HECKSTALL-SMITH, Anthony
Tobruk *(London: Blond 1959), 255p, bib.*
LANDSBOROUGH, Gordon
Tobruk commando *(London: Cassell 1956), viii, 216p.*
MURPHY, W E
The relief of Tobruk *(Wellington, NZ: Department of Internal Affairs 1961), 566p.*
ROSENTHAL, Eric
Fortress on sand: an account of the siege of Tobruk *(London: Hutchinson 1943), 112p.*

WILLISON, Arthur C
The relief of Tobruk: a tribute to the British soldier *(Parracombe, Devon: Willison 1951), 52p.*

YINDRICH, Jan
Fortress Tobruk *(London: Benn 1951), 214p.*
[*see also* AFRIKA KORPS, NORTH AFRICA]

TOKYO

CAIDIN, Martin
A torch to the enemy: the fire raid on Tokyo *(New York: Ballantine 1960), 160p.*

GLINES, Carroll V
Doolittle's Tokyo raiders *(Princeton, NJ: Van Nostrand, [1964]), xiv, 447p, bib.*

LAWSON, Ted W
Thirty seconds over Tokyo *(New York: Random House 1943), 221p.*

MERRILL, James M
Target Tokyo: the Halsey-Doolittle raid *(Chicago, Ill: Rand McNally 1964), 208p.*

TOLISCHUS, Otto
Tokyo record *(London: Hamilton 1943), 287p.*

WILDES, Harry E
Typhoon in Tokyo: the occupation and its aftermath *(London: Allen & Unwin 1954), vii, 357p.*
[*see also* JAPAN]

TRADE UNIONS

PRICE, John
British Trade Unions and the war *(London: Ministry of Information 1945), 55p.*

TRACEY, Herbert
Trade Unions fight – for what? *(London: Routledge 1940), 222p.*

TRANS-JORDAN

GLUBB, *Sir* John B
The story of the Arab Legion *(London: Hodder & Stoughton 1948), 371p.*

TRANSPORT

CHARLES, Roland W
Troopships of World War II *(Washington DC: Army Transportation 1947), 374p.*

CHELL, Randolph A
Troopship *(Aldershot, Hants: Gale & Polden 1948), 88p.*

CURNOCK, George C
Heroes of road and rail: a book of the Great War in Britain *(London: Road & Rail 1943), 98p.*

ELLIS, Chris
Military transport of World War II *(London: Blandford 1971), 177p.*

HUNGERFORD, Edward
Transport for war, 1942-1943 *(New York: Dutton 1943), 7-272p.*

JOHN, Evan (pseud)
Time table for victory: a brief and popular account of the railways and railway-owned dockyards of Great Britain and Northern Ireland during the six years' war, 1939-45 *(London: British Railways 1947), 268p.*

KNOX, Collie
Un-beaten track *(London: Cassell 1944), 199p.*

LA FARGE, Oliver
Eagle in the egg *(Boston, Mass: Houghton Mifflin 1949), xiii, 320p.*

ROSE, Joseph R
American wartime transportation *(New York: Crowell 1953), 290p.*

SAVAGE, Christopher I
Inland transport *(London: HMSO 1957), 678p.*

US OFFICE OF DEFENCE TRANSPORTATION
Civilian war transport: a record of control of domestic traffic operations, 1941–1946 *(Washington DC: Government Printing Office 1948), 361p.*

U.S.S. PONDERA (APA-191) *(San Diego, Calif: Frye & Smith 1946), 115p.*

WE FOUGHT the miles: the history of the South African railways at war, 1939-1945 *(Johannesburg: Railways & Harbours Board 1946), 120p.*

YOUNG, Patrick C
Transportation and total war *(London: Faber 1942), 144p.*

ZIEL, Ron
Steel rails to victory *(New York: Hawthorn 1970), 288p.*
[*see also* RAILWAYS]

TRAWLERS

FIRST LIEUTENANT (pseud)
Terriers of the Fleet: the fighting trawlers *(London: Hutchinson 1943), 96p.*
HAMPSHIRE, Arthur C
Lilliput fleet: the story of the Royal Naval Patrol Service *(London: Kimber 1957), xii, 13-204p.*
LUND, Paul *and* LUDLAM, Harry
Trawlers go to war: the story of 'Harry Tate's Navy' *(London: Foulsham 1971), 271p.*
WALMSLEY, Leo
Fishermen at war *(London: Collins 1941), 256p.*

TREASON

CORNELL, Julien
The trial of Ezra Pound: a documented account of the treason case by the defendant's lawyers *(New York: Day 1966), viii, 216p.*
SCHOFIELD, William G
Treason trail *(Chicago, Ill: Rand McNally 1964), 266p.*
WEST, Rebecca
The meaning of treason *(New York: Viking 1947), 307p; later published as:* The new meaning of treason.
[*see also* LORD HAW HAW, PETAIN, QUISLING]

TREATIES

GREAT BRITAIN. Foreign Office
Documents relating to the termination of the occupation regime in the Federal Republic of Germany, Bonn, 1952, Paris, 1954 *(London: HMSO 1955), vi, 171p.*
ROSSI, Angelo
The Russo-German Alliance, August 1939-June 1941 *(London: Chapman & Hall 1950), xiii, 218p.*
STATE treaty for the re-establishment of an independent and democratic Austria, May 1st, 1955 *(London: HMSO 1955), 32p.*

TRIESTE

SEDMAK, V *and* MEJAK, J
Trieste: the problem which agitates the world *(Belgrade: Jugoslavia 1953), 79p.*

TUNISIA

ALEXANDER, Harold R L G, *1st earl Alexander of Tunis*
The battle of Tunis *(Sheffield: Sheffield UP [1957]), 28p.*

AUSTIN, Alexander B
The birth of an Army *(London: Gollancz 1943), 160p.*

BENNETT, Lowell
Assignment to nowhere: the battle for Tunisia *(New York: Vanguard, 1943), viii, 11-316p.*

D'ARCY-DAWSON, John
Tunisian battle *(London: Macdonald 1943), xii, 13-215p.*

INGERSOLL, Ralph M
The battle is the pay-off *(London: Lane 1943), 192p.*

JORDAN, Philip F
Tunis diary *(London: Collins 1943), 256p.*

LARGE, William S
The diary of a Canadian fighter pilot: [the story of the Tunisian campaign, Dec 8, 1942-Jan 1 1943] *(Toronto: Saunders 1944), 9-64p.*

MACKSEY, Kenneth J
Crucible of power: the fight for Tunisia, 1942-1943 *(London: Hutchinson 1969), xiv, 325p, bib.*

RAME, David (pseud)
The road to Tunis *(London: Collins 1944), 256p.*

WISDOM, Thomas H
Triumph over Tunisia: being the story of the part of the R.A.F. in the African victory *(London: Allen & Unwin 1944), 9-202p.*

ZANUCK, Darryl F
Tunis expedition *(New York: Random House 1943), 9-159p.*
[*see also* MEDITERRANEAN, NORTH AFRICA]

TURKEY

PHILLIPS, Ernest
Hitler's last hope: a factual survey of the Middle East war-zone and Turkey's strategic position *(London: W H Allen 1942), 63p.*

U-BOATS

BRENNECKE, Hans J
Hunters and the hunted *(New York: Norton 1958), 320p.*

BUSCH, Harald
U-boats at war *(London: Putnam 1955), 288p.*

CHATTERTON, Edward K
Fighting the U-boats *(London: Hurst & Blackett 1942), 224p; later published as:* Beating the U-boats.
DRUMMOND, John D
H.M. U-boat: [how U-570 was captured from the air and became H.M.S. Graph] *(London: W H Allen 1958), 228p.*
DUPUY, Trevor N
The naval war in the West: the wolf packs *(New York: Watts 1963), [10], 62p.*
FRANK, Wolfgang
Enemy submarine: the story of Gunther Prien, captain of U47 *(London: Kimber 1954), 200p.*
The sea wolves: the story of the German U-boats at war *(London: Weidenfeld & Nicolson 1955), xii, 252p.*
GALLERY, Daniel V
Twenty million tons under the sea *(Chicago, Ill: Regnery 1956), 344p.*
We captured a U-boat *(London: Sidgwick & Jackson 1957), 268p.*
GASAWAY, Elizabeth B
Grey wolf, grey sea *(New York: Ballantine 1970), 10, 245p.*
GIBBS, Archie
U-boat prisoner: the life story of a Texas sailor *(Boston, Mass: Houghton Mifflin 1948), vi, 208p.*
GREAT BRITAIN. Central Office of Information
The battle of the Atlantic: the official account of the fight against the U-boats, 1939–1945 *(London: HMSO 1946), 108p.*
HOYT, Edwin P
The sea wolves: Germany's dreaded U-boats of World War II *(New York: Lancer 1972), 160p.*
LENTON, Henry T
Navies in the Second World War: German submarines 1–2 *(London: Macdonald 1966), 2 vols.*
LUND, Paul *and* LUDLAM, Harry
The night of the U-boats *(London: Foulsham 1973), 204p.*
MACINTYRE, Donald G F W
U-boat killer *(London: Weidenfeld & Nicolson 1956), 179p.*
MASON, David
U-boat – the secret menace *(New York: Ballantine 1968), 160p, bib.*
METZLER, Jost
The 'Laughing Cow': a U-boat captain's story *(London: Kimber 1955), 217p.*

NOLI, Jean
The Admiral's wolf pack *(New York: Doubleday 1974), 396p.*

ROBERTSON, Terence
The golden horseshoe *(London: Evans 1955), xiv, 15-210p; US title:* Night raider of the Atlantic.

ROSKILL, Stephen W
The secret capture U.110 *(London: Collins 1959), 3-161p.*

SCHAEFFER, Heinz
U-boat 977 *(London: Kimber 1952), 207p.*

SHOWELL, Jack P M
U-boats under the swastika: an introduction to German submarines *(London: Allan 1973), 167p, bib.*

THOMPSON, Lawrence R
The Navy hunts the CGR 3070 *(New York: Doubleday 1944), viii, 150p.*

WADDINGTON, Conrad H
O.R. in World War 2: operational research against the U-boat *(London: Elek 1973), xvii, 253p.*

WERNER, Herbert A
Iron coffins: a personal account of the German U-boat battles of World War II *(New York: Holt 1969), xvi, 329p.*
[*see also* GERMAN NAVY, NORTH ATLANTIC]

UNIFORMS

ADAIR, Robin
British Eighth Army, North Africa, 1940-43 *(London: Arms & Armour 1974), [i], 33p.*

ANGOLIA, John R
Daggers, bayonets and fighting knives of Hitler's Germany *(London: Scott 1971), 332p, bib.*

DAVIES, Howard P
British Parachute Forces, 1940-45 *(London: Arms & Armour 1974), [I], 33p.*
United States Infantry, Europe, 1942-45 *(London: Arms & Armour 1974), [I], 33p.*

DAVIS, Brian L
German Army uniforms and insignia, 1933-1945 *(London: Arms & Armour 1971), 224p, bib.*
Luftwaffe Air Crews, Battle of Britain, 1940 *(London: Arms & Armour 1974), [I], 33p.*

DILLEY, Roy
United States Army uniforms, 1939–1945 *(London: Almark 1972), 80p.*

ELLIS, Chris
German military combat dress, 1939–1945 *(London: Almark 1973), 88p.*

FOSTEN, D S V
Waffen SS: its uniforms, insignia and equipment, 1938–1945 *(London: Almark 1971), 112p.*

GORDON-DOUGLAS, Stewart R
German combat uniforms, 1939–1945 *(London: Almark 1970), 2nd ed. rev. and expanded, 48p.*

MOLLO, Andrew
Army uniforms of World War 2 *(London: Blandford 1973), 183p.*

Uniforms of the SS *(London: Historical Research Unit 1971–2), 4 vols pub.*

NEW notes on the Red Army, No. 2: uniforms and insignia *(London: HMSO 1944), 41p.*

SMET, J L de
Colour guide to German Army uniforms, 1933–1945 *(London: Arms & Armour 1973),* [7], *65p.*

WILKINSON, Frederick
Battle dress: a gallery of military style and ornament *(London: Guiness Signatures 1970),* [8], *256p, bib.*

UNITED NATIONS

ARNE, Sigrid
United Nations primer: the key to the conferences *(New York: Rinehart 1948), 266p.*

BENTWICH, Norman de M
From Geneva to San Francisco: an account of the international organization of the new order *(London: Gollancz 1946), 111p.*

BULWER-LYTTON, Victor, *2nd earl of Lytton*
First Assembly: the birth of the United Nations Organization *(London: Hutchinson 1946), 96p.*

GOODRICH, Leland M *and* HAMBRE, Edward
Charter of the United Nations: commentary and documents *(Boston, Mass: World Peace Foundation 1946), 413p.*

HOLBORN, Louise W (ed)
War and peace aims of the United Nations, September 1, 1939–December 31, 1942 *(Boston, Mass: World Peace Foundation 1943), xv, 730p.*
War and peace aims of the United Nations *(Boston, Mass: World Peace Foundation 1943–8), 2 vols.*

KLEMME, Marvin
The inside story of UNRAA, an experience in internationalism: a first-hand report on displaced people of Europe *(New York: Lifetime 1949), 307p.*

ROYAL INSTITUTE OF INTERNATIONAL AFFAIRS
United Nations documents, 1941–1945 *(London 1946), 271p.*

RUSSELL, Ruth B
A history of the United Nations Charter: the role of the United States, 1940–1945 *(Washington DC: Brookings Institute 1958), 1140p.*

SCHNAPPER, Morris B (ed)
United Nations agreements *(Washington DC: American Council on Public Affairs 1944), xxxiii, 376p.*

STRAIGHT, Michael W
Make this the last war: the future of the United Nations *(London: Allen & Unwin 1943), 276p.*

UNITED NATIONS
The surrender of Italy, Germany and Japan, World War II: instruments of surrender, public papers and addresses of the President and of the Supreme Commanders *(Washington DC: Government Printing Office 1946), 111p.*

THE UNITED Nations in the making: basic documents *(Boston, Mass: World Peace Foundation 1945), 136p.*

U.N.R.A.A.: The history of the United Nations Relief and Rehabilitation Administration *(London: Oxford UP 1950), 3 vols.*

UNITED STATES OF AMERICA

ABEND, Hallett
Pacific Charter: our destiny in Asia *(New York: Doubleday 1943), viii, 308p.*

ALTSCHUL, Frank
Let no wave engulf us *(New York: Duell 1941), 60p.*

AMERICA organizes to win the war; a handbook on the American war effort *(New York: Harcourt 1942), x, 395p.*

ANGELL, *Sir* Norman
America's dilemma: alone or allied? *(New York: Harper 1940), 226p.*

BACON, Francis L
The war and America *(New York: Macmillan 1942), 125p.*
BARBER, Noel
How strong is America? *(London: Harrap 1941), 144p.*
BENET, Stephen V *and others*
Zero hour: a summons to the free *(New York: Farrar 1940), 244p.*
BRAILSFORD, Henry N
America our Ally *(London: Gollancz 1940), 120p.*
From England to America: a message *(New York: McGraw-Hill 1940), x, 130p.*
BROWDER, Earl R
Second imperialistic war *(New York: International 1940), viii, 309p.*
Victory - and after *(New York: International 1942), 7-256p.*
BROWN, William B *and others*
America in a world at war *(New York: Silver 1942), vii, 328p.*
BUCHANAN, Albert R
The United States and World War II *(New York: Harper 1964), 2 vols, bib.*
BUCK, Pearl
American unity and Asia *(New York: Day 1942), 7-140p.*
CALLENDER, Harold
Preface to peace *(London: Allen & Unwin 1944), xi, 288p.*
CATTON, Bruce
War lords of Washington *(New York: Harcourt 1948), 313p.*
CHADWIN, Mark L
The hawks of World War II *(New York: Chapel Hill, NC: North Carolina UP 1968), 310p.*
CHAMBERLAIN, Thomas H
The Generals and the Admirals: some leaders of the United States Forces in World War II *(New York: Devin-Adair 1945), 1 vol.*
America's second crusade *(Chicago, Ill: Regnery 1950), viii, 372p.*
CHILDS, Marquis W
I write from Washington *(New York: Harper 1942), ix, 331p.*
This is your war *(Boston, Mass: Little, Brown 1942), 200p.*
COLE, Wayne S
America first: the battle against intervention, 1940-1941 *(Madison, Wis: Wisconsin UP 1953), 305p.*
COMPTON, James V
The swastika and the Eagle: Hitler, the United States and the origins of the Second World War *(London: Bodley Head 1968), xii, 297p, bib.*

CONN, Stetson *and others*
Guarding the United States and its outposts *(Washington DC: Department of Army 1964), 593p.*
COOK, Don
Fighting Americans of today *(New York: Dutton 1944), 7-191p.*
CORNELL UNIVERSITY
The impact of the war on America: six lectures *(Ithaca, NY: Cornell UP 1942), viii, 159p.*
CURRENT, Richard N
Secretary Stimson: a study in statecraft *(New Brunswick, NJ: Rutgers UP 1954), 272p.*
DAVIS, Forrest *and* LINDLEY, E K
How war came: an American white paper from the fall of France to Pearl Harbor *(New York: Simon & Schuster 1942), viii, 342p.*
DAVIS, Kenneth S
The American experience of war, 1939-1945 *(New York: Doubleday 1965), xii, 704p, bib.*
DAWSON, Raymond H
The decision to aid Russia, 1941: foreign policy and domestic politics *(Chapel Hill, NC: North Carolina UP 1959), 315p.*
DECEMBER 7: the first thirty hours, by the correspondents of Time, Life and Fortune *(New York: Knopf 1942), vi, 229p.*
DIARY of U.S. participation in World War II *(New York: International Business Machines 1950), 374p.*
DIVINE, Robert A
The reluctant belligerent American entry into World War II *(New York: Wiley [1965]), xiii, 172p, bib.*
DOCUMENTS on American foreign relations *(Boston, Mass: World Peace Foundation 1939-48), 8 vols.*
DRUMMOND, Donald F
The passing of American neutrality, 1937-1941 *(Ann Harbor, Mich: Michigan UP 1955), 409p.*
DRURY, Allen
A Senate journal, 1943-1945 *(New York: McGraw-Hill 1963), 503p.*
DULLES, Allen W *and* ARMSTRONG, H F
Can America stay neutral? *(New York: Harper 1939), 277p.*
EISINGER, Chester E (ed)
The 1940's: profile of a nation in crisis *(New York: Anchor 1969), xxxii, 526p.*
EYRE, James K
The Roosevelt-MacArthur conflict *(Chambersburg, Pa: Craft 1950), 234p.*

FEIS, Herbert

The road to Pearl Harbor: the coming of the war between the United States and Japan *(Princeton, NJ: Princeton UP 1950), xii, 356p.*

FLEMING, Denna F

While America slept: a contemporary analysis of world events from the fall of France to Pearl Harbor *(Nashville, Tenn: Abingdon Cokesbury 1944), 269p.*

FRIEDLANDER, Saul

Prelude to downfall: Hitler and the United States, 1939–1941 *(London: Chatto & Windus 1967), xi, 328p, bib.*

GIBBS, *Sir* Philip H

America speaks *(London: Heinemann 1942), 269p.*

GOODMAN, Jack (ed)

While you were gone: a report on war-time life in the United States *(New York: Simon & Schuster 1946), viii, 625p.*

GRAFTON, Samuel

American diary *(New York: Doubleday 1943), ix, 246p.*

HARRIS, Marc (pseud)

The United States in the Second World War *(New York: Barnes & Noble 1946), 167p.*

HART, Scott

Washington at war, 1941–1945 *(New York: Prentice-Hall 1970), 296p.*

HAY, Ian (pseud)

America comes across *(London: Hodder & Stoughton 1942), 191p.*

HINSHAW, David

Home front *(New York: Putnam 1943), xii, 352p.*

HITCHENS, Harold L (ed)

Dec. 7th 1941: America goes to war *(Chicago, Ill: Columbia Educational 1942), 127p.*

HODSON, James L

And yet I like America: being some account of a journey to the United States of America in the winter and spring of 1943–1944 and of meetings there and about what was said to me *(London: Gollancz 1945), 302p.*

HOEHLING, Adolf A

America's road to war 1939–1941 *(London: Abelard-Schuman 1970), xxi, 178p, bib.*

Home front, U.S.A. *(New York: Crowell 1965), 178p.*

The week before Pearl Harbor *(New York: Norton 1963), 189p, bib.*

HOOVER, Herbert C
Addresses upon the American road, World War II *(New York: Van Nostrand 1946), 442p.*

INGERSOLL, Ralph
America is worth fighting for *(Minneapolis, Minn: Bobbs-Merrill 1941), 7-152p.*

JOHNSON, Hugh S
Hell-bent for war *(Minneapolis, Minn: Bobbs-Merrill 1941), 5-115p.*

KENNEY, William
The crucial years, 1940–1945 *(New York: McFadden-Bartell 1962), 207p.*

LAFEBER, Walter (ed)
The origins of the Cold War, 1941-1947: a historical problem with interpretations and documents *(New York: Chichester Wiley 1971), xii, 172p, bib.*

LANGER, William L *and* GLEASON, S E
Challenge to isolation, 1937-1940 *(New York: Harper 1952), xv, 794p.*
Undeclared war, 1940–1941 *(New York: Harper 1953), 963p.*

LASKI, Harold J
The strategy of freedom: an open letter to American youth *(New York: Harper 1941), 144p.*

LAWRENCE, David
The diary of a Washington correspondent *(New York: Kinsey 1942), 356p.*

LAWSON, Don
The United States in World War II: crusade for world freedom *(New York: Abelard-Schuman 1963), 224p.*

LERNER, Max
Public journal: marginal notes on wartime America *(New York: Viking 1945), 414p.*

LEVER, Harry *and* YOUNG, Joseph
Wartime racketeers *(New York: Putnam 1945), 226p.*

LOMBARD, Helen C C
While they fought: behind the scenes in Washington, 1941-1946 *(New York: Scribner 1947), 322p.*

MARKHAM, Peter
America next *(New York: Minneapolis, Minn: Bobbs-Merrill 1940), 9–370p.*

MEAD, James M
Tell the folks back home *(New York: Appleton 1944), xii, 298p.*

MENEFEE, Selden C
Assignment U.S.A. *(New York: Reynal 1943), vii, 301p.*

MEYER, Agnes E
Journey through chaos *(New York: Harcourt 1944), xvii, 388p.*

MISSELWITZ, Henry F
The melting pot boils over: a report on America at war *(Boston, Mass: Christopher 1946), 242p.*

MOHAIR, Annie L *and* BENADETTE, Doris (eds)
American expression on the war and the peace *(New York: Am. Bk 1943), VIII, 326p.*

MORRIS, R B *and* WOODRESS, J
Global conflict: the United States in World War II; 1937–1946 *(St Louis, Miss: Webster 1962), 58p.*

POLENBERG, Richard (ed)
America at war: the homefront, 1941-1945 *(New York: Prentice-Hall 1968), 175p.*

WAR AND SOCIETY: the United States, 1941-1945 *(Philadelphia, Pa: Lippincott 1972), 289p.*

PORTER, Sylvia F
If war comes to the American home: how to prepare for the inevitable adjustment *(New York: McBride 1941), xv, 304p.*

PRATT, Fletcher
America and total war *(New York: Smith & Durrell 1941), 318p.*
War for the world: a chronicle of war fighting forces in World War II *(New Haven, Conn: Yale UP 1950), 364p.*

PRITT, Denis N
The State Department and the Cold War: commentary on its publication, 'Nazi-Soviet relations, 1939-1941' *(New York: International 1948), 96p.*

RESTON, James B
Prelude to victory *(London: Heinemann 1942), 160p.*

ROSE, Lisle A
After Yalta *(New York: Scribner 1973), 216p.*
Dubious victory: the United States and the end of World War II *(Ohio: Kent State UP 1973), 392p.*

ROSEBERY, Mercedes
This day's madness: a story of the American people against the background of the war effort *(New York: Macmillan 1944), xiii, 262p.*

RUSSETT, Bruce M
No clear and present danger: a skeptical view of the United States entry in World War II *(New York: Harper 1972), 111p.*
SARGENT, Porter E
Getting U.S. into war *(Boston, Mass: Sargent 1941), 640p.*
SARKISS, Harry J
The will to freedom *(New York: Revell 1941), 7-256p.*
SCANDRETT, Richard B
Divided they fall: a plea for unity *(New York: Harper 1941), xvi, 76p.*
SCHLAMM, William S
This second war of independence: a call to action *(New York: Dutton 1940), 11-260p.*
SCHOONMAKER, *Mrs* Nancy *and* REID, D F (eds)
We testify *(New York: Smith & Durrell 1941), xiv, 306p.*
SHELDON, Vivian A
Americans on guard *(New York: Johnson 1941), ix, 230p.*
SMITH, Denys H H
America and the Axis war *(London: Cape 1942), 363p.*
SOBEL, Robert
The origins of interventionism: the United States and the Russo-Finnish war *(New York: Bookman 1961), 204p.*
STEELE, Richard W
The first offensive, 1942: Roosevelt, Marshall and the making of American strategy *(Bloomington, Ind: Indiana UP 1973), 239p.*
STERNBERG, Fritz
Fivefold aid to Britain: to save her and keep us out of the war *(New York: Day 1941), 9-76p.*
STRAUSZ-HUPE, Robert
Axis America: Hitler plans our future *(New York: Putnam 1941), xvii, 274p.*
SWEENY, Charles
Moment of truth: a realistic examination of our war situation *(New York: Scribner 1943), 305p.*
THOMAS, Norman M
What is our destiny? *(New York: Doubleday 1944), ix, 192p.*
TOULMIN, Harry A
A diary of democracy: the Senate War Investigating Committee *(New York: Smith 1947), 277p.*
US BUREAU OF THE BUDGET
The U.S. at war: development and administration of war program by the Federal Government *(Washington DC: Government Printing Office, 1946), 555p.*

US Congress Senate Committee on Foreign Relations
A decade of American foreign policy; basic documents (1941-1949) *(Washington DC: Government Printing Office 1950), 1381p.*

US Department of State
Foreign relations of the United States: diplomatic papers: vols. for 1939-1944 *(Washington DC: Government Printing Office 1956-67).*

US War Department Bureau of Public Relations
The background to our war: lectures *(New York: Farrar 1942), xiv, 279p.*

Vinde, Victor
America at war *(London: Hutchinson 1944), 136p.*

Wallace, Henry A
Democracy reborn *(New York: Regnal 1944), vii, 280p.*

Waller, G M (ed)
Pearl Harbor: Roosevelt and the coming of the war *(Boston, Mass: Heath 1953), 112p.*

Walters, John
Will America fight? *(London: Hutchinson 1940), 128p.*

Warburg, James P
Our war and our peace *(New York: Farrar 1941), xxii, 227p.*

Welles, Sumner
The time for decision *(London: Hamilton 1944), vii, 431p.*

What America thinks: editorials and cartoons *(Chicago, Ill: What America Thinks Inc. 1941), 1495p.*

Wheeler-Nicholson, Malcolm
America can win *(New York: Macmillan 1941), viii, 246p.*

Whitney, William D
Who are the Americans? *(London: Eyre & Spottiswoode 1941), 191p.*

Wilcox, Francis O *and* Kalijarvi, Thorsten V
Recent American foreign policy: basic documents, 1941-1951 *(New York: Appleton 1952), 927p.*

Wood, Edward F L, *1st earl of Halifax*
The American speeches of the Earl of Halifax *(London: Oxford UP: 1947), 449p.*

Young, Roland A
Congressional politics in the Second World War *(New York: Columbia UP 1956), 281p.*

[*see also* DIPLOMATIC HISTORY, POLITICS, STRATEGY]

UNITED STATES ARMY (general)

ABBOTT, Harry P
The Nazi '88' made believers *(Dayton, Ohio: Otterbein 1946), 150p.*

ADLEMAN, Robert H *and* WALTON, G H
The devil's brigade *(Philadelphia, Pa: Chilton 1966), 259p.*

ALTIERI, James
The spearheaders *(Indianapolis, Ind: Bobbs-Merrill 1960), 318p.*

ARRINGTON, Grady P
An infantryman at the front *(New York: Vanguard 1959), 244p.*

BAER, Alfred E
'D-for Dog': the story of a Ranger Company *(Memphis, Tenn 1946), 119p.*

BEFORE I die *(Los Angeles, Calif: Circle-V 1942), ix, 415p.*

BOWMAN, Waldo *and others*
Bulldozers come first: the story of U.S. war construction in foreign lands *(New York: McGraw-Hill 1944), viii, 278p.*

BURHANS, Robert D
The First Special Service Force: a war history of the North Americans, 1942–1944 *(Washington DC: Infantry Journal Press 1947), 376p.*

COMBAT Divisions of World War II Army of the United States *(Washington DC: Army Times 1946), 96p.*

CRONIN, Francis D
Under the Southern Cross: the saga of the American Division *(Washington DC: Combat Forces 1951), 432p.*

DUPUY, Richard E
Soldier's album *(Boston, Mass: Houghton Mifflin 1946), 173p.*

FAIRCHILD, Byron *and* GROSSMAN, Jonathan
The Army and industrial manpower *(Washington DC: Department of Army 1959), 291p.*

FRY, James C
Combat soldier *(Washington DC: National 1968), 356p.*

GILES, Henry E
The G.I. journal of Sergeant Giles *(Boston, Mass: Houghton Mifflin 1965), 399p.*

GRAY, Jesse G
The warriors: reflections on men in battle *(New York: Harper 1967), xxiv, 242p.*

GREENFIELD, Kent R *and others*
The organization of ground combat troops *(Washington DC: Department of Army 1947), 540p.*

GUSTAFSON, Walter
My time in the Army: the diary of a World War II soldier *(Chicago, Ill: Adams 1968), 182p.*

HAMMOND, Ralph C
My aching back *(New York: Hobson 1946), 169p.*

HORNSBY, Henry H
The trey of sevens *(Dallas, Tex: Mathis, Van Nort 1946), 126p.*

JONES, Ken
Destroyer Squadron 23: combat exploits of Arleigh Burke's gallant force *(Philadelphia, Pa: Chilton 1959), 283p.*

LEE, Raymond E
The London journal of General Raymond E. Lee, 1940-1941 *(Boston, Mass: Little, Brown 1971), xxi, 489p.*

LEIGH, Randolph
48 million tons to Eisenhower: the role of the SOS in the defeat of Germany *(Washington DC: Infantry Journal Press 1945), 179p.*

LOCKWOOD, Theodore
Mountaineers *(Denver, Colorado: Artcraft 1950), 65p.*

MACDONALD, Charles B
Company commander *(Washington DC: Infantry Journal Press 1947), 278p.*

MARTIN, Ralph G
The GI war, 1941-1945 *(Boston, Mass: Little, Brown 1967), 402p.*

MAUDLIN, William H
Up front *(New York: World 1945), 228p.*

MILLETT, John D
The organization and role of the Army Service Corps *(Washington DC: Department of Army 1954), 494p.*

ORDER of battle of the United States Army ground forces in World War II: Pacific theater of operations: administrative and logistical commands, armies, corps and divisions *(Washington DC: Department of Army 1959), 697p.*

OUR Army at war: the story of American campaigns in World War II told in official War Department photographs *(New York: Harper 1944), unp.*

PALMER, Robert R *and others*
The Army ground forces: the procurement and training of ground combat troops *(Washington DC: Department of Army 1948), 696p.*

QUEEN of battles: pictorial history of the Army ground forces *(New York: Wise 1949), 386p.*

RANDALL, Howard M
Dirt and doughfeet: combat experiences of a rifle-platoon leader *(New York: Exposition 1955), 113p.*

THOMPSON, Clary (ed)
Unsung heroes!: your service forces in action: a photographic record of ASF operations of World War II *(New York: Wise 1949), 385p.*

TUMEY, Ben
A G.I.'s view of World War II: the diary of a combat Private *(New York: Exposition 1959), 64p.*

US OFFICE OF WAR INFORMATION
The American Army in Europe *(Washington DC: Government Printing Office 1945), 117p.*

VALTIN, Jan (pseud)
Children of yesterday *(New York: Readers' 1946), 429p.*

WATSON, Elvey
The Carib Regiment of World War II *(New York: Vantage 1964), 149p.*

WATT, Donald C
World War II outside Europe *(Milton Keynes, Bucks: Open UP 1973), 77p.*

WEBER, Wayne M
My war with the U.S. Army *(New York: Pageant 1957), 148p.*

WHITTINGHAM, Richard
Martial justice: the last man's execution in the United States *(Chicago, Ill: Regnery 1971), 281p.*

WILLIAMS, Mary H (comp)
Chronology, 1941-1945 *(Washington DC: Department of Army 1960), 660p.*

(Third Army)

ALLEN, Robert S
Lucky forward: the history of Patton's Third U.S. Army *(New York: Vanguard 1947), 424p.*

A SOUVENIR booklet for the officers, enlisted men and civilians who made history with the Third U.S. Army in the European Theater of operations *(Bad Tolz, Ger: 1945), 1 vol.*
[*see also* PATTON]

(Sixth Army)

KRUEGER, Walter
From down under to Nippon: the story of the Sixth Army in World War II *(Washington DC: Combat Forces 1953), 393p.*

THE SIXTH Army in action: a photo history, January 1943–June 1945 *(Kyoto, Japan 1945), 68p.*

(Ninth Army)

CONQUER: the story of the Ninth Army, 1944–1945 *(Washington DC: Infantry Journal Press 1947), 404p.*

(Corps)

THE PHANTOM Corps [III Corps] *(Camp Polk, La 1945), 53p.*

DYER, George
XII Corps: spearhead of Patton's Third Army *(Baton Rouge, La: Military Press of Louisiana 1947), 560p.*

HISTORY of the XVI Corps from its activation to the end of the war in Europe *(Washington DC: Infantry Journal 1947), 111p.*

(Divisions)

HURKULA, John
The fighting First Division *(New York: Greenwich 1958), 201p.*

KAHN, Ely J *and* MCLEMORE, Henry
Fighting Division *(Washington DC: Infantry Journal 1945), 218p.*

LOOMIS, William
The fighting FIRSTS *(New York: Vantage 1958), 343p.*

HISTORY of the 3rd Infantry Division in World War II *(Washington DC: Infantry Journal 1947), 574p.*

THE FIFTH Infantry Division in the European Theater of operations *(Atlanta, Ga: Love n.d.), unp.*

THE SIXTH Infantry Division in World War II, 1939–1945 *(Washington DC: Infantry Journal Press 1947), 179p.*

LOVE, Edmund G
The hourglass: a history of the 7th Infantry Division in World War II *(Washington DC: Infantry Journal Press 1950), 496p.*

WHITE, Nathan W
From Fedala to Berchtesgaden: a history of the Seventh U.S. Infantry in World War II *(Essex, Mass 1947), 320p.*

MITTELMAN, Joseph B
Eight stars to victory: a history of the veteran Ninth U.S. Infantry Division *(Washington DC: The 9th Infantry Association 1948), 406p.*

THE FINAL thrust: the Ninth Infantry Division in Germany, September 1944 to May 1945: a history *(Munich 1945), 73p.*

30TH SIGNAL Company, Thirteenth Infantry Division *(Hof, Ger: Kleemeier 1945), 206p.*

HEIDENHEIMER, Arnold J
Vanguard to victory: history of the 18th Infantry *(Aschaffenburg, Ger: 18th Infantry 1954), 64p.*

KAROLEVITZ, Robert F (ed)
The 25th Division and World War II *(Baton Rouge, La: Army & Navy 1946), 202p.*

LOVE, Edmund G
The 27th Infantry in World War II *(Washington DC: Infantry Journal Press 1949), 677p.*

COLBAUGH, Jack
The bloody patch: a true story of daring: 28th Infantry Division *(New York: Vantage 1973), xxxvii, 131p.*

EWING, Joseph H
29, Let's go!: a history of the 29th Infantry Division in World War II *(Washington DC: Infantry Journal Press 1948), 315p.*

HEWITT, Robert L
Work horse of the Western front: the story of the 30th Infantry Division *(Washington DC: Infantry Journal Press 1946), 356p.*

HISTORY of the 31st Infantry Division in training and combat, 1940–1945 *(Baton Rouge, La: Army & Navy 1946), 188p.*

THE GOLDEN cross: a history of the 33rd Infantry Division in World War II *(Washington DC: Infantry Journal Press 1948), 404p.*

HOUGEN, John H
The story of the famous 34th Infantry Division *(Arlington 1949), 1 vol.*

HUSTON, James A
The biography of a battalion; 3rd Battalion, 134 Infantry 35th Division: being the life and times of an Infantry Battalion in Europe in World War II *(Gering, Neb: Courier 1950), 306p.*

PRESENTING the 35th Infantry Division in World War II, 1941–1945 *(Atlanta, Ga: Love 1946), 244p.*

FRANKEL, Stanley A
The 37th Infantry Division in World War II *(Washington DC: Infantry Journal 1949), 348p.*

HOGE, Peyton (ed)
38th Infantry Division: 'Avengers of Bataan', Luzon campaign: battle pictures *(Atlanta, Ga: Love 1947), 1 vol.*

40TH Infantry Division: the years of World War II, 7 December 1941–7 April 1946 *(Baton Rouge, La: Army & Navy 1947), 180p.*

DALY, Hugh C
42nd 'Rainbow' Infantry Divisions: a combat history of World War II *(Baton Rouge, La: Army & Navy 1946), 105p.*

DALY, Hugh C (*cont*)
COMBAT history of the 324th Infantry Regiment, 44th Infantry Division *(Baton Rouge, La: Army & Navy 1946), 132p.*
ROBINSON, Don
News of the 45th *(Norman, Okl: Oklahoma UP 1944), 158p.*
THE FIGHTING Forty-Fifth: the combat report of an Infantry Division *(Baton Rouge, La: Army & Navy 1946), 200p.*
DAVIS, Albert H *and others*
The 56th Fighter Group in World War II *(Washington DC: Infantry Journal 1948), 222p.*
PHOTOGRAPHIC cavalcade: pictorial history of the 75th Infantry Division, 1944–1945 *(Baton Rouge, La: Army & Navy 1946), 1 vol.*
HUTNIK, Joseph J *and* KOBRICK, Leonard (eds)
We ripened fast: the unofficial history of the Seventy-Sixth Infantry Division *(Frankfurt-am-Main 1946), 248p.*
THE 305TH Field Artillery Battalion, 77th Infantry Division *(Hakodate, Japan: Yuji Itagaki 1946), 72p.*
LIGHTNING: the history of the 78th Infantry Division *(Washington DC: Infantry Journal Press 1947), 301p.*
PEARSON, Ralph E
Enroute to the Redoubt: a soldier's report as a Regiment goes to war, to the members of the 80th Infantry Division, and particularly those of the 318th Infantry: a chronological account of some of the activities of the 318th in Europe *(Fort Bragg, NC 1957–9), 5 vols.*
THE 81ST Infantry wildcat Division in World War II *(Washington DC: Infantry Journal Press 1948), 324p.*
THE THUNDERBOLT across Europe: a history of the 83rd Infantry Division, 1942–1945 *(Munich: Bruckmann 1946), 119p.*
MATSON, Clifford H *and* STEIN, Elliot K
We were the line: a history of Company G, 335th Infantry, 84th Infantry Division *(Fort Wayne 1946), 219p.*
SCHULTZ, Paul L
85th Infantry Division in World War II *(Washington DC: Infantry Journal Press 1949), 240p.*
BRIGGS, Richard A
Black hawks over the Danube: the history of the 86th Infantry Division in World War II *(Louisville, Kty: 1954), 127p.*
THE 89TH Infantry Division, 1942–1945 *(Washington DC: Infantry Journal Press 1947), 270p.*
ROBBINS, Robert A
The 91st Infantry Division in World War II *(Washington DC: Infantry Journal Press 1947), 423p.*

STROOTMAN, Ralph E
History of the 363rd Infantry: one Regiment of the 91st Division in World War II *(Washington DC: Infantry Journal Press 1947), 354p.*

BYRNES, Laurence G (ed)
History of the 94th Infantry Division in World War II *(Washington DC: Infantry Journal Press 1948), 527p.*

FUERMAN, George M *and* CRANZ, F E
Ninety Fifth Infantry Division history, 1918–1946 *(Atlanta, Ga: Love 1947), 1 vol.*

LAVER, Walter E
Battle babies: the story of the 99th Infantry Division in World War II *(Baton Rouge, La: Military Press of Louisiana 1951), 351p.*

MICK, Allan H (ed)
With the 102nd Infantry Division through Germany *(Washington DC: Infantry Journal Press 1947), 541p.*

MUELLER, Ralph *and* TURK, Jerry
Report after action: the story of the 103rd Infantry Division *(Innsbruck 1945), 165p.*

HOEGH, Leo A *and* DOYLE, Howard J
Timberwolf tracks: the history of the 104th Infantry Division, 1942–1945 *(Washington DC: Infantry Journal Press 1946), 444p.*

DUPUY, Richard E
St. Vith; lion in the way: the 106th Infantry Division in World War Two *(Washington DC: Infantry Journal Press 1949), 262p.*

HASSON, Joseph S (comp)
With the 114th in the E.T.O.: a combat history, France, Germany, Austria *(Baton Rouge, La: Army & Navy 1945), 192p.*

THE 129TH Infantry in World War II *(Washington DC: Infantry Journal Press 1947), 250p.*

(Regiments)

JOHNSON, Gerden F
History of the Twelfth Infantry Regiment in World War II *(Boston, Mass 1948), 443p.*

MACGREGOR, Harold
History of the 28th Infantry Regiment *(Washington DC: Infantry Journal Press 1947), 104p.*

BUSH, Byron O (ed)
We lead the way: the Twenty-ninth Infantry Regiment in World War II, 1941–1946 *(Frankfurt-am-Main 1946), 125p.*

BINKOSKI, Joseph *and* PLANT, Arthur
The 115th Infantry Regiment in World War II *(Washington DC: Infantry Journal Press 1948), 370p.*

MCCREEDY, William W
Sunburst saga: a story of the 160th Infantry Regiment *(Louisville, Kty: Bishops 1947), 214p.*

MUNSELL, Warren P
The story of a Regiment: a history of the 179th Regimental Combat Team *(New York 1946), 152p.*

HIGGINS, John F (ed)
Trespass against them: a history of the 271st Infantry Regiment, 15 May 1943–25 May 1945 *(Naumburg, East Ger: Saale 1945), 91p.*

WEST, Charles O *and others* (eds)
Second to none!: the story of the 305th Infantry in World War II *(Washington DC: Infantry Journal Press 1949), 243p.*

EDWARDS, L R *and* LEBLANC, A O
Combat diary: 357 Infantry *(Tirschenreuth, Bavaria: Bruck A Nickl 1945), 105p.*

VON ROEDOR, George (comp)
Regimental history of the 357th Infantry *(Weiden, Bavaria: F Nickl 1945), 74p.*

HISTORY of the 376th Infantry Regiment between the years of 1921–1945 *(Wuppertal-Barmen, Ger 1945), 202p.*

IRWIN, John G
History of the 389th Infantry Regiment in World War II *(New York: Hobson Book 1946), 224p.*

FINKELSTEIN, Samuel M
Regiment of the century: the story of the 397th Infantry Regiment *(Stuttgart, Ger 1945), 314p.*

BOSTON, Bernard (ed)
History of the 398th Infantry Regiment in World War II *(Washington DC: Infantry Journal Press 1947), 204p.*

EAST, William *and* GLEASON, William F
The 409th Infantry in World War II *(Washington DC: Infantry Journal Press 1947), 167p.*

HISTORY of the 413th Infantry Regiment *(Los Angeles, Calif: Lewis 1946), 171p.*

(Cavalry)

HAYNES, George L
The Eleventh Cavalry from the Roer to the Elbe, 1944–1945 *(Erlangen, Ger 1945), 95p.*

FARRELL, Harry G
Recon diary: combat history of the 79th Cavalry Reconnaissance Troop *(San Jose, Calif), 172p.*

WINGFOOT, Rhineland and Central Europe campaigns: official history, 101st Cavalry Group, mechanized *(Weinheim, Ger: Diesvach 1945), 112p.*

THE 106TH Cavalry Group in Europe, 1944–1945 *(Augsburg, Ger: Himmer 1945), 254p.*

(Combat Teams)

STRAUSS, Jack M *and* FRIEDBERG, G
We saw it through: history of the 331st Combat Team, today, tomorrow, forever *(Munich: Buchmann 1945), 239p.*

SHIREY, Orville C
Americans: the story of the 442nd Combat Team *(Washington DC: Infantry Journal Press 1947), 151p.*

(Corps of Engineers)

COLL, Blanche D *and others*
The Corps of Engineers: troops and equipment *(Washington DC: Department of Army 1958), 622p.*

SECOND ENGINEER Combat Battalion, October 1943–May 1945: World War II, European Theater of Operations *(Omaha, Neb 1945), 196p.*

HISTORY of the Second Engineer Special Brigade, USA, World War II *(Harrisburg, Pa: Telegraph 1946), 269p.*

HISTORY of the IX Engineer Command, from its beginning to V-E Day *(Wiesbaden, Ger 1945), 213p.*

WE the 48th *(Heidelberg, Ger: Brausdruck 1945), 352p.*

RISTIG, James F (ed)
History of the 155th Engineer Combat Battalion from activation April 15, 1943 to deactivation April 1946 *(Portland, Ore 1946), I vol.*

DUGGAN, Thomas V
History of the 234th Engineer Combat Battalion *(Long Island City: Duggan 1947), 117p.*

RYAN, Allen L
Rough and ready unit history: 276 Engineer Combat Battalion *(Fort Belvoir, Va: Engineers School 1946), 206p.*

BELL, Frank F
The 373rd Engineer General Service Regiment in World War II *(Dallas, Tex [1947]), 281p.*

816TH Engineer Aviation Battalion passes in review *(Munich: Bruckmann 1945), 176p.*

THUS we served: the deeds and accomplishments from activation to demobilization [834th Engineer Aviation Battalion] *(Nuremberg, Ger 1945), 1 vol.*

DEVEIKIS, Casey
The Eager Beaver Regiment: the Regimental history of the 1303 Engineers *(Chicago, Ill 1952), 407p.*

AMORY, Robert (ed)
Surf and sand: the saga of the 53rd Engineer boat and shore Regiment and 1461st Engineer Maintenance Company, 1942–1945 *(Andover, Hants 1947), 408p.*

PADDOCK, Robert H (ed)
The 1876th Engineers in World War II *(Madison, Wis 1947), 147p.*

(Ordnance)

THE ODYSSEY of Company G, a unit of the 611th Ordnance Base Armament Maintenance Battalion: history from November 16, 1942 to August 17, 1945 *(Frankfurt-am-Main: Heinrich 1945), 96p.*

HOWSEMAN, Robert S (ed)
612th Ordnance Base Armament Maintenance: a brief history *(Le Mans, France: Information and Education Center 1945), 1 vol.*

(Quartermaster Corps)

THE QUARTERMASTER Corps *(Washington DC: Department of Army 1953–5), 2 vols.*

STAUFFER, Alvin P
The Quartermaster Corps: operations in the war against Japan *(Washington DC: Department of Army 1956), 358p.*

(Railways)

THE SOLDIER-RAILROADERS' story of the 716th Railway Operating Battalion *(Stuttgart, Ger 1945), 120p.*

THE 727TH Railway Operating Battalion in World War II *(New York: Simmons-Boardman 1948), 102p.*

(Signal Corps)

TERRET, Dulany
The Signal Corps: the emergency to December 1941 *(Washington DC: Department of Army 1956), 383p.*

THOMPSON, George R *and others*
The Signal Corps: the test (December 1941 to July 1943), *(Washington DC: Department of Army 1957), 621p.*

HISTORY of the 43rd Signal Heavy Construction Battalion from activation to V-J Day, 7 February 1944 to 2 September 1945 *(Frankfurt-am-Main: Heinrich 1945), 114p.*

33 MONTHS with the One Hundredth Signal Company, 100th Infantry Division *(Stuttgart, Ger 1945), 100p.*

116TH Signal Radio Intelligence Company: history from date of activation, 18 May, 1942 until V-J Day, 2 September 1945 *(Munich: Oldenbourg 1945), 128p.*

(Tank Destroyers)

JOSOWITZ, Edward L (comp)
An informal history of the 601st Tank Destroyer Battalion *(Salzburg 1945), 95p.*

McGRANN, Roy T
The 610th Tank Destroyer Battalion, April 10 1942–December 7, 1945 *(Elizabeth, Pa 1946), 146p.*

VICTORY TD; the history of the 628th Tank Destroyer Battalion in training and combat *(Göttingen, Ger: 'Muster-Schmidt' 1945), 201p.*

(Transportation Corps)

BYKOFSKY, Joseph *and* LARSON, Harold
The Transportation Corps: operation overseas *(Washington DC: Department of Army 1957), 671p.*

WARDLOW, Chester
The Transportation Corps: movements, training and supply *(Washington DC: Department of Army 1956), 564p.*

(Miscellaneous)

BROWER, David R
Remount blue: the combat story of the 3rd Battalion, 86th Mountain Infantry *(Berkeley, Calif 1948), 112p.*

GILLIES, Frederick W
The story of a squadron: an illustrated overseas war-diary-album, 1942–1945; 154th (Observation, Reconnaissance) Weather Reconnaissance Squadron *(Medford, Mass 1946), 137p.*

SCHEUFLER, Karl W (ed)
Carthaginians, Romans and Americans, overseas with the 355th Anti-Aircraft Searchlight Battalion *(Cincinnati, Ind: Gibson & Perin 1946), 276p.*

HISTORY of the Second Chemical Mortar Battalion *(Salzburg 1946), 63p.*

ANGIER, John C
MOS 1542: a dramatic true story of combat in World War Two *(New York: Greenwich 1959), 59p.*

UNITED STATES ARMY AIR FORCE

ADLEMAN, Robert H *and* WALTON, George
The champagne campaign *(Boston, Mass: Little, Brown 1969), iii-xiv, 248p, bib.*

BECK, Henry C
The 397th Bomb Group (M): a pictorial history *(Cleveland, Ohio: Howard 1946), 122p.*

BIRDZELL, Bill C
Sky train, adventures of a troop carrier squadron, February 10, 1943-August 10, 1944 [67th Troop Carrier Squadron] *(Sydney: Angus & Robertson 1945), 217p.*

BOMBS AWAY!; your Air Force in action: a photographic epic of A.A.F. operations of World War II . . . from the dark day of Pearl Harbor to final victory in 1945 *(New York: Wise 1947), 386p.*

BOVE, Arthur P
First over Germany: a story of the 306th Bombardment Group *(San Angelo, Tex: Newsfoto 1946), 148p.*

CARLISLE, Norman V *and others*
Air Forces reader: Army and Navy Air Forces *(Minneapolis, Minn: Bobbs-Merrill 1944), 15-406p.*

CASTENS, Edward H (ed)
The story of the 446th Bomb Group *(San Angelo, Tex: Newsfoto 194-), 1 vol.*

COLEMAN, John M
The development of tactical services in the Army Air Force *(New York: Columbia UP 1950), 298p.*

CRAVEN, Wesley F *and* CATE, James L (ed)
The Army Air Forces in World War II *(Chicago, Ill: Chicago UP 1948-58), 7 vols.*

DOLL, Thomas E
Flying leathernecks in World War II *(Fallbrook, Calif: Aero 1971), 95p.*

FORBES, Alexander
Quest for a Northern air route *(Cambridge, Mass: Harvard UP 1953), xvii, 141p, bib.*

FRANCILLON, Rene J
American fighters of World War II *(Chalfont St Giles, Bucks: Hylton Lacy 1968), vol. I, 64p.*

FRANCIS, Devon E
Flak bait: the story of the men who flew the Martin Marauders *(New York: Duell 1948), xvii, 331p.*

FREEMAN, Roger A
The mighty Eighth: units, men and machines: a history of the U.S. 8th Army Air Force *(London: Macdonald 1970), [5], 311p.*

GENOVESE, Joseph G
We flew without guns *(Philadelphia, Pa: Winston 1945), 304p.*

GLINES, Carroll V *and* MOSELEY, W F
Grand old lady: story of the DC-3 *(Cleveland, Ohio: Pennington 1959), 250p; later published as:* Proud old lady.

GURNEY, Gene
Five down and glory: a history of the American Air ace *(New York: Putnam 1958), 302p.*
Journey of the giants *(New York: Coward-McCann 1961), 280p; later published as:* The B-29 story.

HAIRE, T B
The history of a bombing outfit, the 386th Bomb Group *(St Truiden, Ger 1945), 72p.*

HARDISON, Priscilla *and* WORMSER, Anne
Susy-Q *(Boston, Mass: Houghton Mifflin 1943), viii, 170p.*

HARVELL, Ursel P
Liberators over Europe: 44th Bomb Group *(San Angelo, Tex: Newsfoto 194–), 1 vol.*

HERRING, Robert R (ed)
From Dobodura to Okinawa: history of the 308th Bombardment Wing *(San Angelo, Tex: Newsfoto 194–), 1 vol.*

HINTON, Harold B
Air victory: the men and the machines *(New York: Harper 1948), xix, 428p.*

HUTTON, Bud *and* ROONEY, A A
Air gunner *(New York: Farrar 1944), xiii, 236p.*

LIND, Ragnar G (ed)
The falcon: combat history of the 79th Fighter Group, USAAF 1942–1945 *(Munich 1946), 286p.*

LIPPINCOTT, Benjamin *and others*
From Fiji through the Philippines with the Thirteenth Air Force *(San Angelo, Tex: Newsfoto 1948), 193p.*

LUKAS, Richard C
Eagles East: the Army Air Force and the Soviet Union, 1941–1945 *(Florida: Florida State UP 1970), 256p.*

MCCRARY, John R
First of the many: a journal of action with the men of the Eighth Air Force *(New York: Simon & Schuster 1944), xvi, 241p.*

MCKEE, Philip
Warriors with wings *(New York: Crowell 1947), 266p.*

MANUEL, Gordon
Seventy thousand to one *(New York: Random House 1946), 156p.*

MARX, Joseph L
Seven hours to zero *(New York: Putnam 1967), 256p.*

MAURER, Maurer (ed)
Air Force combat units of World War II *(Washington DC: Government Printing Office 1961), 506p.*

MORRISON, Wilbur H
Hell birds: the story of the B-29's in combat *(New York: Duell 1960), 181p.*

MORROW, James E (ed)
61st Service Squadron *(Ottumwa, Iowa: Messenger 1946), 120p.*

THE NINTH Air Force Service Command in the European Theater of Operations: a pictorial review *(Philadelphia, Pa: AA Forces Aid Society 1945), 96p.*

PEASLEE, Budd J
Heritage of valor: the 8th Air Force in World War II *(Philadelphia, Pa: Lippincott 1963), 288p.*

PURCELL, John F
Flights to glory *(New York: Vanguard 1944), 11–184p.*

REDDING, John M *and* LEYSHON, H I
Skyways to Berlin: with the American flyers in England *(Indianapolis, Ind: Bobbs-Merrill 1943), 15–209p.*

REINBURG, J H
Combat serial escapades: a pilot's log book *(New York: Carlton 1966), 165p.*

RICKENBACKER, Edward V
Seven came through *(New York: Doubleday 1943), x, 118p.*

RUST, Kenn C *and others*
The 9th Air Force in World War II *(Fallbrook, Calif: Aero 1967), 245p.*

SHERIDAN, Jack W
They never had it so good: the personal unofficial story of the 350th Bombardment Squadron H, 100th Bombardment Group H USAAF, 1942–1945 *(San Francisco: Stark-Rath 1946), 165p.*

SHORES, Louis
Highways in the sky: the story of AACS *(New York: Barnes & Noble 1947), 269p.*

SINTON, Russell L (comp)
The menace from Moresby: a pictorial history of the 5th Air Force in World War II *(San Angelo, Tex: Newsfoto 195–), 1 vol.*

SMITH, Edwin S
History of the Army Air Forces 34th Bombardment Group *(San Angelo, Tex: Newsfoto 1947), 2nd ed., 1 vol.*

SNYDER, Earl A
General Leemy's circus: a navigator's story of the 20th Air Force in World War II *(New York: Exposition 1955), 175p.*

STEELE, Theodore M
A pictorial record of the combat duty of patrol bombing Squadron One Hundred Nine in the Western Pacific, 20 April 1945–15 August 1945 *(New York: General Offset 1946), unp.*

STILES, Bert
Serenade to the big bird *(New York: Norton 1952), 216p.*

STRAUBEL, James H
Air Force diary: 111 stories from the official service journal of the USAAF *(New York: Simon & Schuster 1947), 492p.*

SWEETMAN, John
Schweinfurt - disaster in the skies *(New York: Ballantine 1971), 160p, bib.*

THOMAS, Rowan T
Born in battle: round the world adventures of the 513th Bombardment Squadron *(Philadelphia, Pa: Winston 1944), xii, 367p.*

USAAF
Army Air Forces in the war against Japan, 1941-1942 *(Washington DC: Government Printing Office 1945), 171p.*

Combat Air Forces of World War II, Army of United States *(Washington DC: Army Times 1945), 95p.*

Mediterranean theater of operations: defeat *(Washington DC: HQs AAF 1946), 80p.*

100th Bombardment Group; contrails, my war record: a history of World War II as recorded at USAAF Station No. 139 Thorpe Abbots, near Diss, county of Norfolk, England *(New York: Callahan 1947), 284p.*

The crusaders: a history of the 42nd Bombardment Group M *(Baton Rouge, La: Army & Navy Pictorial 1946), 204p.*

The diary of the 8th Photo Squadron, New Guinea *(New York: Ad 1945), 217p.*

Official guide to the Army Air Forces; AAF: a directory, almanac and chronicle of achievement *(New York: Simon & Schuster 1944), vii, 380p.*

Target; Germany: the Army Air Forces' official story of the VIII Bomber Commands' first year over Europe *(New York: Simon & Schuster 1943), vi, 121p.*

Team B, 326th Air Service Group: a pictorial history of the unsung heroes who kept 'em flying in World War II *(Los Angeles, Calif: Wetzel 1946), 137p.*

20th Fighter Bomber Wing, Weathersfield, England *(London: Montgomery Enterprises 1953), 95p.*

Warpath of the Air Apaches *(San Angelo, Tex: Newsfoto 1946), 277p.*

WILBER, Edwin L *and* SCHOENHOLTZ, E R

Silver wings: true action stories of the U.S. Air Force *(New York: Appleton 1948), 281p.*

WILSON, Robert E

Earthquakers: overseas history of the 12th Bomb Group *(Tacoma, Wash: Wilson 1947), 147p.*

[*see also* AIR WARFARE, BOMBERS, FIGHTERS]

UNITED STATES MARINES

AURTHUR, Robert A *and* COHIMIA, Kenneth

The Third Marine Division *(Washington DC: Infantry Journal Press 1948), 385p.*

AYLING, Keith

Semper Fidelis: the U.S. Marines in action *(Boston, Mass: Houghton Mifflin 1943), 194p.*

BOSWELL, Rolfe

Medals for Marines *(New York: Crowell 1945), 211p.*

BOYINGTON, Gregory

Baabaablacksheep *(New York: Putnam 1958), 384p.*

BROWN, David T

Marine from Virginia: letters, 1941-1945 *(Chapel Hill, NC: North Carolina UP 1947), 105p.*

CASS, Bevan G (ed)

History of the Sixth Marine Division *(Washington DC: Infantry Journal Press 1948), 262p.*

CHAPIN, John C

The Fourth Marine Division in World War II *(Washington DC: USMC 1945), 89p.*

CONDIT, Kenneth W *and others*
Marine Corps ground training in World War II *(Washington DC: USMC 1956), 353p.*

CONNER, Howard M
The spearhead: the World War II history of the 5th Marine Division *(Washington DC: Infantry Journal Press 1950), 325p.*

CRANE, Aimee (ed)
Marines at war *(New York: Scribner 1943), 7-128p.*

DAVIS, Russell G
A Marine at war *(Boston, Mass: Little, Brown 1961), 258p.*

DE CHANT, John A
Devilbirds: the story of the United States Marine Corps aviation in World War II *(New York: Harper 1947), 265p.*

FOSS, Joe
Joe Foss, flying Marine: the story of his flying circus *(New York: Dutton 1943), 5-160p.*

HERSEY, John R
Into the valley: a skirmish of the Marines *(London: Hodder & Stoughton 1943), 96p.*

HUBLER, Richard G *and* DE CHANT, John A
Flying leathernecks *(New York: Doubleday 1944), xii, 225p.*

JOHNSTON, Richard W
Follow me!: the story of the Second Marines Division of World War II *(New York: Random House 1948), 305p.*

LECKIE, Robert
Strong men armed: the U.S. Marines against Japan *(New York: Random House 1962), 563p.*

MCMILLAN, George
The old breed: a history of the First Marines Division in World War II *(Washington DC: Infantry Journal Press 1949), 483p.*

MCMILLAN, George *and others*
Uncommon valor, Marine Divisions in action *(Washington DC: Infantry Journal Press 1946), 256p.*

METCALF, Clyde H (ed)
Marine Corps reader *(New York: Putnam 1944), xiv, 600p.*

MONKS, John R
A ribbon and a star: the Third Marines at Bouganville *(New York: Holt 1945), 242p.*

O'SHEEL, Patrick *and* COOK, Gene (eds)
Semper Fidelis, the U.S. Marines in the Pacific, 1942-1945 *(New York: Sloane 1947: 360p.*

PRATT, Fletcher
Marines' war: an account of the struggle for the Pacific from both American and Japanese sources *(New York: Sloane 1948), 456p.*

SCHMID, Albert A
Al Schmid, Marine *(New York: Norton 1944), 9-142p.*

SHERROD, Robert L
The history of Marine Corps aviation in World War II *(Washington DC: Combat 1952), xiv, 496p.*

SMITH, Stanley (ed)
The United States Marine Corps in World War II: the 1 volume history from Wake to Tsingtao *(New York: Random House 1969), xxi, 965p.*

TOWER, Hansel H
Fighting the devil with the Marines *(Philadelphia, Pa: Dorrance 1945), 13-172p.*

US Marine Corps
History of the U.S. Marine Corps operations in World War II *(Washington DC: USMC 1958-), 1 vol.*
Hit the beach!: your Marine Corps in action: a photographic epic of Marine Corps operations of World War II *(New York: Wise 1948), 386p.*
The Ninth Marines: a brief history of the Ninth Marine Regiment, 1942-1945 *(Washington DC: Infantry Journal Press 1946), 375p.*

WILLARD, Warren W
The leathernecks come through *(New York: Revell 1944), 7-224p.*
[*see also* BATAAN, CORRIGEDOR, IWO JIMA, NEW GUINEA, OKINAWA, PACIFIC, PAPUA, PHILIPPINES, SOLOMON ISLANDS, TARAWA, WAKE ISLAND]

UNITED STATES NAVY

ADAMSON, Hans C *and* KOSCO, G F
Halsey's typhoons: a firsthand account of how two typhoons, more powerful than the Japanese, dealt death and destruction to Admiral Halsey's Third Fleet *(New York: Crown 1967), 206p.*

BALDWIN, Hanson W
The American Navy: what we should know about it *(London: Allen & Unwin 1942), 219p; US title:* What the citizen should know about the Navy.

BALISON, Howard J
Newport News ships: their history in two World Wars *(Newport News, Va: Mariners Museum 1954), 372p.*

BATTLE stations!; your Navy in action: a photographic epic of the Naval operations of World War II *(New York: Wise 1946), 402p.*

BENNETT, Edwin G
Coming through: the story of the Thirty-first Special Naval Construction Battalion *(Tokyo: Dai Nippon 1946), 64p.*

BERRY, Robert B
The gunners get the glory: story of the Navy's armed guard *(Indianapolis, Ind: Bobbs-Merrill 1943), 13-293p.*

BLASSINGAME, Wyatt
The Navy's fliers in World War II *(Philadelphia, Pa: Westminster 1967), 258p.*

BUCHANAN, A R (ed)
The Navy's air war: a mission completed *(New York: Harper 1946), 432p.*

CANT, Gilbert
America's Navy in World War II *(New York: Day 1945), 279p.*
The war at sea; with photographs and diagrams *(New York: Day 1942), xii, 340p.*

CARSE, Robert
There go the ships *(New York: Morrow 1942), 11-156p.*

CASEY, Robert J
Torpedo junction: with the Pacific fleet from Pearl Harbor to Midway *(Minneapolis, Minn: Bobbs-Merrill 1942), 13-423p.*

CASTILLO, Edmund L
The Seabees of World War II *(New York: Random 1963), 190p.*

CAVE, Hugh B
We build, we fight: the story of the Seabees *(New York: Harper 1944), 122p.*

CHILDS, John F
Navy gun crew *(New York: Crowell 1943), 111p.*

CRUMP, Irving
Our tanker fleet *(New York: Dodd 1952), 244p.*

CUSTER, Joe J
Through the perilous night: the Astoria's last battle *(New York: Macmillan 1944), x, 243p.*

DICKINSON, Clarence E
Flying guns: cockpit record of a naval pilot from Pearl Harbor through Midway *(New York: Scribner 1942), vii, 196p.*

DI PHILLIP, John
Gunner's diary *(Boston, Mass: Meador 1946), 111p.*

FETRIDGE, William H (ed)
Navy reader *(Indianapolis, Ind: Bobbs-Merrill 1943), 21–443p.*
Second Navy reader *(Indianapolis, Ind: Bobbs-Merrill 1944), 17–383p.*

GALLERY, Daniel V
Clear the decks! *(New York: Morrow 1951), 242p.*

HOPKINS, Harold
Nice to have you aboard *(London: Allen & Unwin 1964), 3–217p.*

JAMES, Joe
Teacher wore a parachute *(South Brunswick, NJ: Barnes [1966]), 171p.*

KARIG, Walter *and others*
Battle report: prepared from official sources *(New York: Rinehart 1942–1952), 6 vols.*

LOTT, Arnold S
Brave ship, brave men *(Indianapolis, Ind: Bobbs-Merrill 1965), 272p.*

MCDONALD, Jack
Navy retread *(New York: Vantage 1969), 318p.*

MARSDEN, Lawrence A
Attack transport: the story of the U.S.S. Doyen *(London: Oxford UP 1946), ix, 200p.*

MELLOR, William B
Sank same *(New York: Howell, Soskin 1944), 11–224p.*

MILLER, Max
Always the Mediterranean *(New York: Dutton 1952), 256p.*

MINARIK, William H
Sailors, subs and senoritas *(Boston, Mass: Branden 1968), 349p.*

MORISON, Samuel E
History of United States Naval operations in World War II *(Boston, Mass: Little, Brown 1947–62), 15 vols.*
The two-ocean war: a short history of the U.S. Navy in the Second World War *(Boston, Mass: Little, Brown 1963), 611p.*

PERRY, George S *and* LEIGHTON, I
Where away: a modern odyssey *(New York: McGraw-Hill 1944), viii, 249p.*

PRATT, Fletcher
The Navy has wings *(New York: Harper 1943), xiii, 224p.*
The Navy's war *(New York: Harper 1944), xiv, 295p.*

ST GEORGE, Thomas R
Proceed without delay *(New York: Crowell 1945), 181p.*

SAILOR, Robert W
Valor in the Navy *(Ithaca, NY: Cayuga 1944), 68p.*

SHALETT, Sidney
Old Nameless: the epic of a U.S. battle-wagon *(New York: Appleton 1943), x, 177p.*

SILVERSTONE, Paul H
U.S. warships of World War II *(New York: Doubleday 1965), 442p.*

SMITH, Stanley E (ed)
The United States Navy in World War II: the one-volume history from Pearl Harbor to Tokyo Bay *(New York: Morrow 1966), xxiii, 1049p.*

TANTUM, William H *and* HOFFSCHMIDT, E J (eds)
Navy uniforms, insignia and warships of World War II *(Old Greenwich, Conn: WE 1968), 268p.*

TAYLOR, Theodore
The magnificent Mitscher *(New York: Norton 1954), 364p.*

THOMAS, Charles W
Ice is where you find it *(Indianapolis, Ind: Bobbs-Merrill 1951), 378p.*

TOLLEY, Kemp
The cruise of the Lanikai: incitement to war *(Annapolis, Md: Naval Institute 1973), 345p.*

TURNER, John F
Battle stations: the U.S. Navy's war *(New York: Putnam 1960), 192p.*

US NAVY (Construction Battalions)

4th Construction Battalion
Lil'short runner presents the Fourth U.S. Naval Construction Battalion Penguin, 1944–45 *(Baton Rouge, La: Army & Navy Pictorial 1945), 171p.*

8th Construction Battalion
Pieces of eights *(Allentown, Pa: 194–), I vol.*

18th Construction Battalion
The Odyssey, Eighteenth Naval Construction Battalion *(San Francisco, Calif 1946), 94p.*

21st Construction Battalion
The Blackjack, 1944–1945: a story about and published by the 21st U.S. Naval Construction Battalion *(Baton Rouge: La: Army & Navy Pictorial 1946), 244p.*

34th Construction Battalion
The Thirty-fourth U.S. Naval Construction Battalion *(Arlington, Va: Marx 1946), 81p.*

34th Construction Battalion Special
Battalion review, Special 34th Battalion, U.S.N., 1944–45 *(Baton Rouge, La: Army & Navy Pictorial 1946), 100p.*
42nd Construction Battalion
Year book, 1944–45 *(Milwaukee, Wis 194–), 155p.*
43rd Construction Battalion
The log, 1942–1946 *(Baton Rouge, La: Army & Navy Pictorial 1946), 153p.*
50th Construction Battalion
The Fiftieth Seabees *(San Francisco, Calif: 1945), 108p.*
55th Construction Battalion
The 55 Seabees, 1942–1945 *(Baton Rouge, La: Army & Navy Pictorial 1945), 169p.*
57th Construction Battalion
Sopac saga: 57th Seabees, 1942–1945 *(Arlington, Va: Marx 1946), 182p.*
58th Construction Battalion
History of the 58th Seabees *(Brooklyn, NY: Foxcroft Commercial 1950), 252p.*
62nd Construction Battalion
'We did': the story of the 62nd NCB, December 7, 1942 to September 15, 1945 *(Baton Rouge, La: Army & Navy Pictorial 1946), 191p.*
82nd Construction Battalion
Eighty-second U.S. Naval Construction Battalion, 1943–1945 *(Greensburg, Pa: Henry 1946), 178p.*
96th Construction Battalion
96th Seabiography *(Baton Rouge, La: Army & Navy Pictorial 1946), 150p.*
102nd Construction Battalion
102 Construction Battalion 'Second to none' *(Baton Rouge, La: Army & Navy Pictorial 1946), 186p.*
107th Construction Battalion
The log, 1943–1945, a story of a Seabee Battalion conceived in war, dedicated to peace *(Baton Rouge, La: Army & Navy Pictorial 1946), 208p.*
116th Construction Battalion
Work and weapons: the story of the One Hundredth Sixteenth Naval Construction Battalion *(Portland, Ore 1946), 111p.*
121st Construction Battalion
Battalion history, May 10, 1943–August 15, 1945 *(Baton Rouge, La: Army & Navy Pictorial 1946), 91p.*

130th Construction Battalion
One Hundredth and Thirtieth U.S. Naval Construction Battalion *(Baton Rouge, La: Army & Navy Pictorial 1945), 209p.*
136th Construction Battalion
Photo-memories of a Seabee Battalion *(Yokosuha, Japan 1945), 1 vol.*
143rd Construction Battalion
143rd Naval Construction Battalion, advance base construction depot: a battalion biography *(New York 1946), 254p.*
Construction Battalion Maintenance Unit 635
CBMU 635 *(Baton Rouge, La: Army & Navy Pictorial 1946), 143p.*
Construction Battalion Detachment No. 1050
This is CBD 1050 *(Baton Rouge, La: Army & Navy Pictorial 1946), 138p.*

CHRONOLOGY of the Navy's war in the Pacific, World War II *(Washington DC: Government Printing Office 1947), 116p.*

UNITED STATES Naval chronology, World War II *(Washington DC: Government Printing Office 1955), 214p.*

VETTER, Ernest G
Death was our escort *(New York: Prentice-Hall 1944), vii, 323p.*

WOLFERT, Ira
Torpedo 8: the story of Swede Larsen's bomber squadron *(Boston, Mass: Houghton Mifflin 1943), xi, 127p.*
[*see also* AIRCRAFT CARRIERS, BATTLESHIPS, CRUISERS, DESTROYERS, MIDWAY ISLAND, PACIFIC, PEARL HARBOR, SUBMARINES]

VAAGSO RAID

DEVINS, Joseph H
The Vaagso raid *(London: Hale 1967), 222p.*
[*see also* COMMANDOS]

VATICAN [see CATHOLICISM]

VICHY

ARON, Robert
The Vichy regime, 1940–44 *(London: Pitman 1958), 536p.*

FARMER, P
Vichy, political dilemma *(London: Oxford UP 1955), 384p.*

HYTIER, Adrienne D
Two years of French foreign policy: Vichy, 1940–1942 *(New York: Loring 1959), 402p.*

JONES, Emrys
The shame of Vichy *(London: Hutchinson 1941), 96p.*

LANGER, William L
Our Vichy gamble *(New York: Knopf 1947), 412p.*

MARCHAL, Leon
Vichy, two years of deception *(New York: Macmillan 1943), vi, 251p.*

PAXTON, Robert O
Vichy France: old guard and new order, 1940–1944 *(London: Barrie & Jenkins 1972), x, 399, xxip.*

TISSIER, Pierre
The government of Vichy *(London: Harrap 1942), 350p.*
[*see also* FRANCE, PETAIN]

VICTORIA CROSS

HARE-SCOTT, K B
For valour: biographical sketches of some of World War II's winners of the Victoria Cross *(London: Garnett 1949), xi, 178p.*

JAMESON, Sir William S
Submariners V.C. *(London: Davies 1962), 208p.*

PHILLIPS, Cecil E L
Victoria Cross battles of the Second World War *(London: Heinemann 1973), xii, 292p.*

TURNER, John F
V.C.'s of the air *(London: Harrap 1960), 187p.*
V.C.'s of the Army, 1939–1951 *(London: Harrap 1962), 222p.*
V.C.'s of the Royal Navy *(London: Harrap 1956), 192p.*

VIRGINIA

ALBERMARLE COUNTY HISTORICAL SOCIETY
Pursuits of war: the people of Charlottesville and Albermarle County in the Second World War *(Charlottesville, Va: University of Virginia Library 1948), xxiv, 429p.*

CHERNOFF, Howard L
Anybody here from West Virginia? *(Charlottesville, Va: Charleston 1945), 105p.*

LUTZ, Earle
Richmond in World War II *(Richmond, Va: Dietz 1951), 623p.*

MARSH, Charles F *and others* (eds)
The Hampton Roads communities in World War II *(Chapel Hill, NC: North Carolina UP 1951), 337p.*
SCHLEGEL, Marvin W
Conscripted city: Norfolk in World War II *(Norfolk, Va: Norfolk War History Committee 1951), 396p.*
WHEELER, William R (ed)
The road to victory: a history of Hampton Roads port of embarkation in World War II *(New Haven, Conn: Yale UP 1946), 2 vols.*

V2 [see ROCKETS]

WAKE ISLAND

BAYLER, Walter L J
Last man off Wake Island: a first person narrative *(Indianapolis, Ind: Bobbs-Merrill 1943), 11-367p.*
CUNNINGHAM, Winfield S
Wake Island command *(Boston, Mass: Little, Brown 1961), 258p.*
DEVEREUX, James P S
The story of Wake Island *(Philadelphia, Pa: Lippincott 1947), 252p.*
US MARINE CORPS
Defense at Wake *(Washington DC: USMC 1947), 75p.*
WERSTEIN, Irving
Wake: the story of a battle *(New York: Crowell 1964), 145p.*
[*see also* US MARINES, US NAVY]

WAR CORRESPONDENTS

CASEY, Robert J
I can't forget: personal experiences of a war correspondent *(Minneapolis, Minn: Bobbs-Merrill 1941), 13-398p.*
CHAPLIN, William W
Seventy thousand miles of war: being one man's odyssey on many fronts *(New York: Appleton 1943), 14-287p.*
GRAY, Bernard
War reporter *(London: Hale 1942), 183p.*

HODSON, James L

The sea and the land: being some account of journeys, meetings, and what was said to me in Britain, France, Italy, Germany and Holland between March 1943 and May 1945 *(London: Gollancz 1945), 369p.*

Through the dark night: some account of a war correspondent's journeys, meetings, and what was said to him, in France, Britain and Flanders during 1939–1940 *(London: Gollancz 1941), 352p.*

Towards the morning: being some account of my journeys and what was said and written to me in Britain and Eire in the first quarter of 1941 *(London: Gollancz 1941), 216p.*

War in the sun: being some account of a war correspondent's journeys *(London: Gollancz 1942), 392p.*

The way things are: war diary *(London: Gollancz 1948), 329p.*

INGERSOLL, Ralph M

Covering all fronts: a personal account of the war on a 30,000 mile front *(London: Lane 1942), 304p; US title:* Action on all fronts.

JACOB, Alaric

A traveller's war: a journey to the wars in Africa, India and Russia *(London: Collins 1944), 448p.*

LEGG, Frank

War correspondent *(London: Angus & Robertson 1965), 266p.*

LUCAS, Jim G

Combat correspondent *(New York: Reynal 1944), xi, 210p.*

MILLER, Lee G

The story of Ernie Pyle *(New York: Viking 1950), 439p.*

PYLE, Ernest T

Brave men *(New York: Holt 1944), 474p.*

Last chapter *(New York: Holt 1946), 150p.*

RASMUSSEN, Albert H

Return to the sea *(London: Constable 1956), 207p.*

REYNOLDS, Quentin J

Don't think it hasn't been fun *(London: Cassell 1941), 282p.*

SNYDER, Louis L

Masterpieces of war reporting: the great moments of World War II *(New York: Messner 1962), 555p.*

WHAT we saw in Germany: with the Red Army to Berlin by thirteen leading Soviet war correspondents *(London: Soviet News 1945), 63p.*

WOODWARD, David

Front line and front page *(London: Eyre & Spottiswoode 1943), 232p.*

[*see also* PRESS]

WAR CRIMES

ABRAHAMS, Gerald
The day of reckoning *(London: W H Allen 1943), 64p.*

APPLEMAN, John A
Military tribunals and international crimes *(Indianapolis, Ind: Bobbs-Merrill 1954), 421p.*

BAR-ZOHAR, Michael
The avengers *(London: Barker 1968), 287p.*

CAREW, Tim
Hostages to fortune *(London: Hamilton 1971), xi, 175p, bib.*

CREEL, George
War criminals and punishment *(New York: McBride 1944), 7–303p.*

DICKS, Henry V
Licensed mass murder: a socio-psychological study of some SS killers *(London: Chatto-Heinemann Educational for Sussex UP 1972), 283p.*

EHRENBURG, Ilya G
We come as judges *(London: Soviet War News 1945), 63p.*

FISHMAN, Jack
The seven men of Spandau *(London: W H Allen 1954), 224p.*

KATZ, Robert
Black Sabbath: a journey through a crime against humanity *(London: Barker 1969), xvii, 398p, bib.*

KEENAN, Joseph B *and* BROWN, Brendan F
Crimes against international law *(Washington DC: Public Affairs 1950), 226p.*

KENWORTHY, Aubrey S
The tiger of Malaya: the story of General Tomoyuk; Yamashita and 'Death March' General Maraharu Homma *(New York: Exposition 1953), 112p.*

KRUUSE, Jens
Madness at Oradour, 10 June 1944 – & after *(London: Secker & Warburg, 1969), [5], 179p*

LACHS, Manfred
War crimes: an attempt to define the issues *(London: Stevens 1945), 108p.*

LESSER, Jonas
Germany: the symbol and the deed *(New York: Yoseloff 1965), 601p.*

LEVY, Alan
Wanted: Nazi criminals at large *(New York: Berkley 1962), 175p.*

MARTYRDOM of the Serbs: persecutions of the Serbian Orthodox Church and massacre of the Serbian people *(Libertyville, Ill: Serbian St Sava Monastery 1943), xii, 301p.*

MAUGHAM, Frederic H M
U.N.O. and war crimes *(London: Murray 1951), 143p.*

MITSCHERLICH, Alexander *and* MIELKE, Fred
Doctors of infamy: the story of the Nazi medical crimes *(New York: Schuman 1949), xxxix, 172p.*

MYERSON, Moses H
Germany's war crimes and punishment: the problem of individual and collective criminality *(New York: Macmillan 1945), x, 272p.*

NEW Soviet documents on Nazi atrocities *(London: Hutchinson 1943), 128p.*

PIOTROWSKI, Stanislaw
Hans Franck's diary *(New York: A Vanous 1961), 320p.*

RUSSELL, Edward F L, *2nd baron Russell of Liverpool*
Knights of bushido: a short history of Japanese war crimes *(London: Cassell 1958), 335p.*
The scourge of the swastika: a short history of Nazi war crimes *(London: Cassell 1954), xii, 260p.*

SOVIET Government statements on Nazi atrocities *(London: Hutchinson 1946), 320p.*

STROOP, Jurgen
The report of Jurgen Stroop, concerning the uprising in the Ghetto of Warsaw and the liquidation of the Jewish residential area *(Warsaw: Jewish Historical Institute 1958), 123p.*

TENENBAUM, Joseph L
Underground: the story of a people *(New York: Philosophical Library 1952), ix, 532p.*

VEALE, Frederick J P
Crimes discreetly veiled *(London: Cooper 1958), 240p.*

WEIL, Joe (ed)
The bloody record of Nazi atrocities *(New York: Arco 1944), 47p.*

WIESENTHAL, Simon
The sunflower *(London: W H Allen 1970), 190p.*

WYNNE, Milton J
Why I hate the Nazis *(New York: ACA Gallery 1945), 78p.*
[*see also* JEWS, KATYN WOOD, POLAND, RESISTANCE]

WARSAW

BERG, Mary
Warsaw ghetto: a diary *(New York: Fischer 1945), 253p.*

BIELECKI, Tadeusz *and* SZYMANSKI, Leszek
Warsaw aflame, the 1939–1945 years *(Los Angeles, Calif: Polamerica 1973), 188p.*

BRUCE, George
The Warsaw uprising, 1 August–2 October 1944 *(London: Hart-Davis 1972), 224p, bib.*

BRYAN, Julien H
Warsaw: 1939 siege; 1959 Warsaw revisited *(New York: International Film Foundation 1960), 177p.*

CELT, Marck
By parachute to Warsaw *(London: Crisp 1945), 88p.*

CIENCHANOWSKI, Jan M
The Warsaw rising of 1944 *(Cambridge: Cambridge UP 1974), xi, 332p, bib.*

DESCHOVER, Gunther
Warsaw rising *(New York: Ballantine 1972), 160p, bib.*

FRIEDMAN, Philip (ed)
Martyrs and fighters: the epic of the Warsaw ghetto *(New York: Praeger 1954), 325p; UK title:* The epic of the Warsaw ghetto.

GOLDSTEIN, Bernard
The stars bear witness *(New York: Viking 1949), 295p; later published as:* Five years in the Warsaw ghetto.

GOLDSTEIN, Chaim I
The bunker *(Philadelphia, Pa: Jewish 1970), 262p.*

KAPLAN, Chaim A
Scroll of agony: the Warsaw diary of Chaim Aron Kaplan *(New York: Macmillan 1965), xvi, 329p.*

KORBONSKI, Stefan
Fighting Warsaw: the story of the Polish underground State, 1939–1945 *(London: Allen & Unwin 1956), viii, 496p.*

KORWIN, Marta
The mark of warriors: the siege of Warsaw, Sept. 1939 *(New York: Libra 1964), 191p.*

ORSKA, Irena
Silent is the Vistula: the story of the Warsaw uprising *(New York: Longmans 1946), 275p.*

POLONIUS, Alexander (pseud)
I saw the siege of Warsaw *(London: Hodge 1941), vii, 364p.*

RINGELBLUM, Emmanuel
Notes from the Warsaw ghetto *(New York: McGraw-Hill 1958), 369p.*

RUDNICKI, Adolf (ed)
Lest we forget *(Warsaw: Polonia Foreign Languages 1955), 170p.*
TUSHNET, Leonard
To die with honour: the uprising of the Jews in the Warsaw ghetto *(London: Citadel 1965), 128p.*
UMADEVI (pseud)
All for freedom: the Warsaw epic *(Bombay: Padma 1946), 217p.*
WDOWINSKI, David
And we are not saved *(New York: Philosophical Library 1963), xi, 124p.*
WERSTEIN, Irving
The uprising of the Warsaw ghetto, November 1940–May 1943 *(New York: Norton 1968), 157p.*
ZAGORSKI, Waclaw
Seventy days *(London: Muller [1958]), 267p.*
ZIEMAN, Joseph
The cigarette sellers of Three Crosses Square *(London: Valentine, Mitchell 1970), 162p.*
ZYLBERBERG, Michael
A Warsaw diary, 1939–1945 *(London: Valentine, Mitchell 1969), 220p.*
[*see also* JEWS, POLAND]

WAR TRIALS

BONHOEFFER, Emmi
The Auschwitz trials: letters from an eye-witness *(Richmond, Va: John Knox 1967), 61p.*
BRAND, George (ed)
The trial of Heinrich Gerike, Georg Hessling, Werner Noth, Hermann Muller, Gustav Claus, Richard Demmerich, Fritz Flint, Valentina Bilien (The Velpke Baby Home Trial) *(London: Hodge 1950), liv, 356p.*
CAMERON, John (ed)
The 'Peleus' trial: trial of Kapitanleutnant Eck and four others *(London: Hodge 1948), 247p.*
FALKENHORST, Nikolaus von
The trial of Nikolaus von Falkenhorst, formerly Generaloberst in the German Army *(London: Hodge 1949), 278p.*
HANAYAMA, Shinsho
The way of deliverance: three years with the condemned Japanese war criminals *(New York: Scribner 1950), xv, 297p.*

HARUZO, Sumida *and others*
The trial of Sumida Haruzo and twenty others (The 'Double Tenth' trial) *(London: Hodge 1951), xxxii, 324p.*

KILLINGER, Erich *and others*
The trial of Erich Killinger, Heinz Junge, Otto Boehringer, Heinrich Eberhardt, Gustav Baure-Schlichtegroll: the Dulag Luft trial *(London: Hodge 1952), xviii, 255p.*

KINTER, Earl W
The Hadamar trial: trial of Alfons Klein and six others *(London: Hodge 1949), 250p.*

KRAMER, Josef
The trial of Josef Kramer and forty-four others: the Belsen trial *(London: Hodge 1949), 749p.*

LUNAU, Heinz
The Germans on trial *(New York: Storm 1948), 180p.*

MCDONALD, Bruce J S
The trial of Kurt Meyer *(Toronto: Clarke, Irwin 1954), 216p.*

MALLAL, Bashir A (ed)
The Double Tenth trial *(Singapore: Malayan Law Journal 1947), 652p.*

NAUMANN, Bernd
Auschwitz: a report on the proceedings against Robert Karl Ludwig Mulka and others before the court at Frankfurt *(London: Pall Mall [1967]), xxx, 433p.*

NEUMANN, Inge S
European war crimes trials: a bibliography *(New York: Carnegie Endowment for International Peace 1952), 113p.*

PAGET, Reginald T
Manstein: his campaigns and his trial *(London: Collins 1951), xv, 239p.*

PHILLIPS, Raymond (ed)
The Belsen trial *(London: Hodge 1949), 810p.*

REEL, Adolf F
The case of General Yamashita *(Chicago, Ill: Chicago UP 1949), vi, 324p.*

ROY, Jules
The trial of Marshal Petain *(New York: Harper 1968), xxiii, 264p.*

SLEEMAN, C (ed)
The trial of Cozawa Sadaichi *(London: Hodge 1948), 243p.*

ZEUSS, Wolfgang
The trial of Wolfgang Zeuss and others: the Natzweiler trial *(London: Hodge 1949), 233p.*

WAVELL

CONNELL, John
Wavell, scholar and soldier: to June 1941 *(London: Collins 1964), 574p, bib.*
Wavell, Supreme Commander, 1941-1943 *(London: Collins 1969), 317p, bib.*

WAVELL, Archibald P, *1st earl*
Speaking generally: broadcasts, orders and addresses in time of war, 1939–43 *(London: Macmillan 1946), 166p.*

WOOLLCOMBE, Robert
The campaigns of Wavell, 1939-1943 *(London: Cassell 1959), x, 228p, bib.*

WEAPONS

BARNES, Gladeon M
Weapons of World War II *(New York: Van Nostrand 1947), 317p.*

KIRK, John *and* YOUNG, Robert
Great weapons of World War II *(New York: Walker 1961), 347p.*

McLEAN Donald B (ed)
Illustrated arsenal of the Third Reich *(Wickenburg, Ariz: Normount Technical 1973), 490p.*

STEPHENS, Frederick J
Edged weapons of the Third Reich, 1933-1945 *(London: Almark 1972), 128p, bib.*

WEREWOLF

WHITING, Charles
Werewolf: the story of the Nazi resistance movement, 1944-1945 *(London: Cooper 1972), xiii, 209p, bib; US title:* Hitler's werewolves.

WESTERN EUROPE 1939-40

BARTLETT, Sir Basil H
My first war: an Army officer's journal for May 1940, through Belgium to Dunkirk *(London: Chatto & Windus 1940), 131p.*

BUCKLEY, Christopher
Norway; The Commandos; Dieppe *(London: HMSO 1952), 276p.*

BUTLER, Ewan *and* BRADFORD, J S
Keep the memory green: the first of the many, France 1939–40 *(London: Hutchinson [1950]), 180p.*

CATLING, Skene
Vanguard to victory: an account of the first months of the British Expeditionary Force in France *(London: Methuen 1940), 250p.*
DEWEY, Albert P
As they were *(New York: Beechhurst 1946), 283p.*
DIARY of a staff officer *(London: Methuen 1941), vii, 79p.*
DOORMAN, P L G
Military operations in the Netherlands from 10th–17th May, 1940 *(London: Allen & Unwin 1944), 99p.*
ELLIS, F L
The war in France and Flanders, 1939-1940 *(London: HMSO 1953), xix, 425p.*
EON, Joseph M
The battle of Flanders *(London: Continental 1943), 9-47p.*
From the battle of Flanders to the battle of Africa, the battle of France *(London: Continental 1944), 7-61p.*
GARDNER, Charles
A.A.S.F. (Advanced Air Striking Force) in France *(London: Hutchinson 1940), 255p; US title:* First blood for the R.A.F.
GIBBS, Anthony
Gibbs and a phoney war *(London: Dawnay 1967), 169p.*
GUN BUSTER (pseud)
Return via Dunkirk *(London: Hodder & Stoughton 1940), 256p.*
HABE, Hans
A thousand shall fall *(London: Harrap 1942), 320p.*
HUNT, Leslie C
Prisoner's progress: an illustrated diary of the march into captivity of the last of the British Army in France, June 1940 *(London: Hutchinson 1942), 24p.*
LA FALAISE, Henry de B, *marquis de*
Through hell to Dunkirk *(Harrisburg, Pa: Military Service 1943), 166p.*
MACDONALD, *Mrs* Yvonne
Red tape notwithstanding: a story of the Mechanised Transport Corps in France from Nov. 1939-June 1940 *(London: Hutchinson 1941), 256p.*
MICHIE, Allan A
Retreat to victory *(London: Allen & Unwin 1942), xiii, 492p.*
MRAZEK, James E
The fall of Eben Emael: prelude to Dunkirk *(Washington: Luce 1970), 192p, bib.*
REOCH, Ernest
The St. Valery story *(Edinburgh: Reoch [1965]), 227p.*

STRABOLGI, Joseph M K, *10th baron*
Campaign in the Low Countries: the first full-length account of the epic struggle in Holland and Belgium *(London: Hutchinson 1940), xi, 259p.*
TAYLOR, Telford
The march of conquest: the German victories in Western Europe, 1940 *(New York: Simon & Schuster 1958), 460p.*
US Military Academy, West Point
The campaign in the West, 1940 *(New York: West Point 1945), 69p.*
VILFROY, Daniel
The war in the West: the battle of France, May-June 1940 *(Harrisburg, Pa: Military Service 1942), 163p.*
WHITMAN, J E A
Gallant deeds of the war: stories of the B.E.F., on the Western Front and of the R.A.F., in the battles of France and Britain *(Toronto: Oxford UP 1942), vii, 120p.*
WINTRINGHAM, Thomas H
Deadlock war *(London: Faber 1940), 7-279p.*
[*see also* BELGIUM, FRANCE, HOLLAND, NORWAY]

WESTERN EUROPE 1944-5

ALLIED FORCES, SUPREME HQS, Psychological Warfare Division
The psychological warfare division, Supreme Headquarters, Allied Expeditionary Force: an account of its operations in the Western Europe Campaign, 1944–1945 *(Bad Homburg, Ger 1945), xxxv, 243p.*
ATWELL, Lester
Private *(New York: Simon & Schuster 1958), 444p.*
BAGNALL, Stephen
The attack *(London: Hamilton 1947), 200p.*
BAKER, Peter
Confession of faith *(London: Falcon 1946), 233p.*
BERLIN, Sven
I am Lazarus *(London: Gallery 1961), xi, 209p.*
BERNSTEIN, Walter S
Keep your head down *(New York: Viking 1945), 243p.*
BLUMENSON, Martin
The duel for France, 1944 *(Boston, Mass: Houghton Mifflin 1963), 432p.*
The U.S. Army in World War II: break out and pursuit *(Washington DC: Department of Army 1961), 748p.*

BOESCH, Paul
The road to Huertgen: forest in hell *(Houston, Tex: Gulf 1962), 254p.*

BRIGGS, Richard A
The battle of the Ruhr pocket: a combat narrative *(West Point, Kty: Tioga 1957), 84p.*

BRYANT, *Sir* Arthur
Triumph in the West, 1943–1946: based on the diaries and autobiographical notes of Field Marshal the Viscount Alanbrooke *(London: Collins 1959), 576p, bib.*

CARPENTER, Iris
No woman's world *(Boston, Mass: Houghton Mifflin 1946), 338p.*

CHAPLIN, William W
Fifty-two days: a NBC reporter's story of the battle that freed France *(Indianapolis, Ind: Bobbs-Merrill 1944), 11–215p.*

COLE, Hugh M
The Lorraine campaign *(Washington DC: Department of Army 1950), 657p.*

CONGDON, Don (ed)
Combat: European theatre; World War II *(New York: Dell 1958), 380p.*

CROSTHWAIT, A E L
Bridging Normandy to Berlin *(Hanover, Ger: British Army of the Rhine 1945), 192p.*

D'ARCY-DAWSON, John
European victory *(London: Macdonald 1946), 299p.*

DE POLO, Taber (ed)
Bridging Europe *(Munich: Bruckmann 1945), 193p.*

DONNISON, Frank S V
Civil affairs and military government, North-West Europe 1944–1946 *(London: HMSO 1961), xviii, 518p.*

EISENHOWER, Dwight D
Report by the Supreme Commander to the Combined Chiefs of Staff on the operations in Europe of the Allied Expeditionary Force, 6 June 1944 to 8 May 1945 *(Washington DC: Government Printing Office 1946), 123p.*

ELLIS, Lionel F *and others*
Victory in the West *(London: HMSO 1962–8), 2 vols.*

ELLISON, V C
Europe revisited: the East Riding Yeomanry in the liberation of Europe and the defeat of Germany *(Hull, Humberside: Brown 1946), 112p.*

ELSTOB, Peter
The battle of the Reichswald *(New York: Ballantine 1970), 160p, bib.*
ESSAME, Hubert *and* BELFIELD, Eversley
The North-West Europe campaign, 1944–1945 *(Aldershot, Hants: Gale & Polden 1962), xv, 111p, bib.*
GUNGAND, *Sir* Francis de
Operation victory *(London: Hodder & Stoughton 1947), 488p.*
HARKINS, Paul D
When the Third cracked Europe: the story of Patton's incredible army *(Washington DC: Army Times 1969), 95p.*
HUGILL, J A C
The hazard mesh *(London: Hurst & Blackett 1946), 128p.*
HUNTER, Kenneth E
The war against Germany: Europe and adjacent areas *(Washington DC: Department of Army 1951), 448p.*
JOHNS, Glover S
The clay pigeons of St. Lô *(Harrisburg, Pa: Military Service 1958), 257p.*
LIEBLING, Abbott J
The road back to Paris *(London: Joseph 1944), 260p.*
LYON, Allan
Toward an unknown station *(New York: Macmillan 1948), 286p.*
MACDONALD, Charles B
The battle of Huertgen Forest *(Philadelphia, Pa: Lippincott 1963), 215p.*
The mighty endeavour: American Armed Forces in the European theater in World War II *(London: Oxford UP 1969), 564p.*
The Siegfried Line campaign *(Washington DC: Department of Army 1963), 670p.*
Three battles: Arnaville, Altuzzo and Schmidt *(Washington DC: Department of Army 1952), 443p.*
McGOVERN, James
Crossbow and overcast *(New York: Morrow 1964), 279p.*
McKEE, Alexander
The race for the Rhine bridges, 1940, 1944, 1945 *(London: Souvenir 1971), 488p.*
MACKSEY, Kenneth
The shadow of Vimy Ridge *(London: Kimber 1965), 264p.*
MACMILLAN, Richard
Miracle before Berlin *(London: Jarrolds 1946), 160p.*
MAJDALANY, Frederick
The fall of fortress Europe *(New York: Doubleday 1968), 442p.*

MARTIN, Ralph G *and* HARRITY, Richard
World War II: a photographic record of the war in Europe from D-Day to V-E-Day *(Greenwich, Conn: Gold Medal 1962), unp.*

MICHIE, Allan A
Honour for all *(London: Allen & Unwin 1946), 218p.*

MILLIS, Walter
The last phase: Allied victory in Western Europe *(Boston, Mass: Houghton Mifflin 1946), 130p.*

MONTGOMERY, Bernard L, *1st viscount Montgomery of Alamein*
Normandy to the Baltic *(London: Hutchinson 1947), xiii, 224p.*

ON the way: combat experiences of the 693rd Field Artillery Battalion in the European theater of operations: Normandy, Northern France, Rhineland, Central Europe *(Salzburg, Aus: Muller 1945), 89p.*

PEARLE, Donald R
Journal of a war: North-West Europe 1944–1945 *(London: Macmillan 1965), 188p.*

SHULMAN, Milton
Defeat in the West *(London: Secker & Warburg 1948), 336p.*

STRATEGICUS (pseud)
The victory campaign, May 1944–August 1945 *(London: Faber 1947), 282p.*

THOMPSON, Reginald W
The battle for the Rhineland *(London: Hutchinson 1958), xiv, 242p.*

US MILITARY ACADEMY, WEST POINT
The war in Western Europe *(New York: West Point 1952), 2 pts.*

US WAR DEPARTMENT
Small unit actions, France: 2nd Ranger Battalion at Pointe de How; Saipan: 27th Division on Tanapay Plain; Italy; 351st Infantry at Santa Maria Infanta; France: 4th Armored Division at Singling *(Washington DC: 1946), 212p.*

WERSTEIN, Irving
The battle of Aachen *(New York: Crowell 1962), 146p.*

WHITING, Charles
The battle of the Ruhr pocket *(New York: Ballantine 1971),* [*1*], *160p, bib.*
The end of the war; Europe: A. 15–My 23, 1945 *(New York: Stein & Day 1973), 178p.*
Finale at Flensburg: the story of Field-Marshal Montgomery's battle for the Baltic *(London: Cooper 1973), 174p, bib.*

WINGFIELD, Rex M
The only way out: an infantryman's autobiography of the North-West Europe campaign, August 1944–February 1945 *(London: Hutchinson 1955), 190p.*
WOOD, Alan
Falaise road *(London: W H Allen 1944), 64p.*
[*see also* BELGIUM, FRANCE, GERMANY, HOLLAND, NORMANDY]

WINGATE

MOSLEY, Leonard
Gideon goes to war *(London: Barker 1955), 256p.*
TULLOCH, Derek
Wingate in peace and war *(London: Macdonald 1972), [4], 300p.*
[*see also* BURMA, CHINDITS]

WOMEN

ALSOP, Gulielma F *and* MCBRIDE, M F
Arms and the girl: a guide to personal adjustment in war work and war marriage *(New York: Vanguard 1943), xiii, 302p.*
ANTHONY, Susan B
Out of the kitchen - into the war: woman's winning role in the nation's drama *(Brattlesboro, Vt: Daye 1943), 246p.*
AYLING, Keith
Calling all women *(New York: Harper 1942), ix, 208p.*
BAKER, *Mrs* Laura
Wanted: women in industry *(New York: Dutton 1943), 9–215p.*
BANNING, *Mrs* Margaret
Women for defense *(New York: Duell 1942), vii, 243p.*
BENSON, Theodora
Sweethearts and wives: their part in war *(London: Faber 1942), 114p.*
BIDDLE, Margaret
Women of England *(Boston, Mass: Houghton Mifflin 1941), ix, 99p.*
BIRDWELL, Russell
Women in battledress *(New York: Fine Editions 1942), 198p.*
BOLES, Antoinette
Women in khaki *(New York: Vantage 1953), 240p.*
BURSTEIN, Herbert
Women in war: a complete guide to service in the Armed Forces and war industries *(New York: Service 1943), 166p.*

BURTON, Elaine F
And your verdict? *(London: Muller 1943), 78p.*
What of the women: a study of women in wartime *(London: Muller 1941), xiv, 15–224p.*

DANENBERG, Elsie
Blood, sweat and lipstick *(New York: Greenberg 1945), 298p.*

GILES, Nell
Punch in, Susie!: a woman's war factory diary *(New York: Harper 1943), xiv, 143p.*

GOLDSMITH, Margaret L
Women at war *(London: Drummond 1943), 224p.*

HARLAND, Elizabeth M
Farmer's girl *(London: Cassell 1942), 224p.*

HASLETT, Caroline
Munitions girl: a handbook for the women of the industrial army *(London: English UP 1942), viii, 9–92p.*

HAWES, Elizabeth
Why women cry; or, Wenches for the wrenches *(New York: Reynal 1943), xviii, 221p.*

HODGINS, J H *and others*
Women at war *(Toronto: Maclean 1944), 190p.*

KATIN, Zelma *and* KATIN, Louis
Clippie: the autobiography of a war-time conductress *(London: Gifford 1945), 124p.*

LANDIS, Carole
Four Jills in a jeep *(New York: Random House 1944), viii, 180p.*

PRIESTLEY, John B
British women go to war *(London: Collins 1943), vi, 7–59p.*

ROSS, Mary S
American women in uniform *(New York: Garden City 1943), 6–71p.*

SCOTT, Peggy
They made invasion possible *(London: Hutchinson 1944), 148p.*

SETTLE, Mary L
All the brave promises: memories of Aircraft woman 2nd class 2146391 *(New York: Dial 1966), 176p.*

STAFFORD, Ann
An army without banners *(London: Collins 1942), 192p.*

TREADWELL, Mattie E
The Women's Army Corps *(Washington DC: Department of Army 1954), 841p.*

VON MIKLOS, Josephine
I took a war job *(New York: Simon & Schuster 1943), viii, 223p.*

WILDING, Frances
Land girl at large *(London: Elek 1972), 141p.*
WOOD, Ethel M
Mainly for men *(London: Gollancz 1943), 128p.*
WOOD, Winifred
We were WASPS *(Coral Gables, Fla: Glade House 1946), 195p.*
WRIGHT, Esther T
A pilot's wife's tale: the diary of a camp follower *(London: Lane 1942), 189p.*
[*see also* AUXILIARY TERRITORIAL SERVICE, HOSPITALS, NURSES, WRNS]

WOMEN'S ROYAL NAVAL SERVICE

DRUMMOND, John D
Blue for a girl: the story of the W.R.N.S. *(London: W H Allen 1960), 207p.*
SCOTT, Peggy
British women in war *(London: Hutchinson 1940), 324p.*

WYOMING

LARSON, Taft A
Wyoming's war years, 1941-1945 *(Laramie, Wyo: Wyoming UP 1954), 400p.*

YALTA

CLEMENS, Diane S
Yalta *(New York: Oxford UP 1970), xii, 356p, bib.*
FENNO, Richard F
The Yalta Conference *(Boston, Mass: Heath 1955), 112p.*
KUTER, Laurence S
An airman at Yalta *(New York: Duell 1955), 180p.*
SNELL, John L (ed)
The meaning of Yalta: Big Three diplomacy and the new balance of power *(Louisiana: Louisiana State UP 1966), 239p.*
STETTINIUS, Edward R, *jun.*
Roosevelt and the Russians: the Yalta Conference *(London: Cape 1950), 320p.*
WITTMER, Felix
Yalta betrayed: data on the decline and fall of Franklin Delano Roosevelt *(Caldwell, Idaho: Caxton 1953), 136p.*

YMCA

Bosanquet, Mary
Journey into a picture *(London: Hodder & Stoughton 1947), 196p.*
Taylor, Leslie
So passed my year *(Sydney: Hylton 1944), 96p.*

YWCA

Creedy, Brooks S
Women behind the lines: YWCA program with war production workers, 1940–1947 *(New York: Woman's 1949), 227p.*
Gerken, Mable R
Ladies in pants: a home front diary *(New York: Exposition 1949), 96p.*

YUGOSLAVIA

Brown, Alec
Mihailovich and Yugoslav resistance *(London: Lane 1943), vi, 90p.*
Caffin, James
Partisan *(Auckland, NZ: Collins 1945), 186p.*
Calder-Marshall, Arthur
Watershed *(London: Contact 1947), 216p.*
Colakovic, Rodoljut
Winning freedom *(London: Lincolns-Prager 1962), 432p.*
Davidson, Basil
Partisan picture *(New York: Universal 1945), 351p.*
Deakin, Frederick W D
The embattled mountain *(London: Oxford UP 1972), xx, 284p.*
Epic of Yugoslavia, 1941–1944 *(London: United Committee of South-Slavs in London 1945), 96p.*
Eton, Peter *and* Leasor, James
Conspiracy of silence *(London: Angus & Robertson 1960), 239p; US title:* Wall of silence.
Fotitch, Constantin
The war we lost: Jugoslavia's tragedy and the failure of the West *(New York: Viking 1948), 344p.*
General Mihailovich, the world's verdict *(Gloucester: Bellows 1947), 223p.*
Hecimovic, Joseph
In Tito's death marches and extermination camps *(New York: Carlton 1962), 209p.*

HUOT, Louis
Guns for Tito *(New York: Fischer 1945), 273p.*
INKS, James M
Eight bailed out *(New York: Norton 1954), 222p.*
ITALIAN crimes in Yugoslavia *(London: Yugoslavia Information Office 1945), 82p.*
JONES, W
Twelve months with Tito's partisans *(Bedford: Bedford 1946), 128p.*
JOVICHIC, Lenka A
Within closed frontiers: a woman in wartime Jugoslavia *(Edinburgh: Chambers 1956), 253p.*
JUKIC, Ilija
The fall of Yugoslavia *(New York: Harcourt 1974), 315p.*
LAWRENCE, Christie N
Irregular adventure *(London: Faber 1947), 276p.*
MACLEAN, *Sir* Fitzroy
The battle of Neretva *(London: Panther 1970), 144p.*
Eastern approaches *(London: Cape 1949), 543p; US title:* Escape to adventure.
MARKHAM, Reuben H
Tito's imperial communism *(Chapel Hill, NC: North Carolina UP 1947), 292p.*
MARTIN, David
Ally betrayed: the uncensored story of Tito and Mihailovich *(New York: Prentice-Hall 1946), 372p.*
MELVILLE, Cecil F
Balkan racket: the inside story of the political gangster plot which destroyed Yugoslavia and drove Britain out of the Balkans *(London: Jarrolds 1941), 111p.*
MIKES, George
We were there to escape: the true story of a Jugoslav officer *(London: Nicholson & Watson 1945), 251p.*
MITCHELL, Ruth
Ruth Mitchell, Chetnik, tells the facts about the fighting Serbs, Mihailovich and Yugoslavia *(Arlington, Va: Serbian National Defense Council 1943), 68p.*
The Serbs choose war *(New York: Doubleday 1943), vi, 265p.*
MORACA, Pero *and* KUCAN, Viktor
The war and revolution of the peoples of Yugoslavia, 1941–1945 *(New York: Vanous 1964), 206p.*
NEIL, Roy S
Once only *(London: Cape 1947), 285p.*

PADEV, Michael
Marshal Tito *(London: Muller 1944), 7–129p.*

PAVLOWITCH, K St
The struggle of the Serbs *(London: Standard Art 1943), xii, 88p.*

PENIAKOFF, Vladimir ('Popski')
Private army *(London: Cape 1950), 512p.*

PETROVIC, Svetislar S
Free Jugoslavia calling *(New York: Greystone 1941), xvii, 21–356p.*

PRCELA, John *and* GUIDESCU, Stanko (eds)
Operation slaughterhouse: eyewitness accounts of post-war massacres in Yugoslavia *(Philadelphia, Pa: Dorrance 1970), 557p.*

RADLOVIC, I M
Tito's republic *(London: Coldharbour 1948), 241p.*

RAYNER, Louisa
Women in a village: an English woman's experiences and impressions of life in Yugoslavia under German occupation *(London: Heinemann 1957), viii, 147p.*

RISTIC, Dragisha N
Yugoslavia's revolution of 1941 *(Pennsylvania, Pa: State UP 1966), 175p, bib.*

ROBERTS, Walter R
Tito, Mihailovic and the Allies, 1941–1945 *(New Brunswick, NJ: Rutgers UP 1973), 406p.*

ROGERS, Lindsay
Guerilla surgeon *(London: Collins 1957), 254p.*

ROOTHAM, Jasper
Miss fire: the chronicle of a British mission to Mihailovich, 1943–1944 *(London: Chatto & Windus 1946), 224p.*

SAVA, George (pseud)
The Chetniks *(London: Faber 1942), 260p.*

STRUTTON, Bill
Island of terrible friends *(London: Hodder & Stoughton 1961), 192p.*

SUDJIC, Milivoj J
Yugoslavia in arms *(London: Drummond 1942), 128p.*

THAYER, Charles
Hands across the caviar *(London: Joseph 1953), 222p.*

YOVITCHITCH, Lena A
Within closed frontiers: a woman in wartime Jugoslavia *(London: Chambers 1956), 253p.*

YUGOSLAVIA WAR REPARATIONS COMMISSION
Human and material sacrifices of Yugoslavia in her war efforts, 1941-1945 *(Belgrade 1946), 53p.*
[*see also* RESISTANCE]

ZHUKOV

CHANEY, Otto P
Zhukov *(Norman, Okl: Oklahoma UP 1971), xxiii, 512p, bib.*
ZHUKOV, Georgii K
The memoirs of Marshal Zhukov *(London: Cape 1971), 3-703p.*

AUTHOR INDEX

Author Index

Author Index

Author Index

SUBJECT INDEX

Subject Index